Citizens and saints

Citizens
and saints

Politics and anti-politics
in early British socialism

Gregory Claeys

Associate Professor of History,
Washington University, St Louis

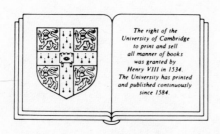

The right of the
University of Cambridge
to print and sell
all manner of books
was granted by
Henry VIII in 1534.
The University has printed
and published continuously
since 1584.

Cambridge University Press

Cambridge
New York   Port Chester
Melbourne   Sydney

Published by the Press Syndicate of the University of Cambridge
The Pitt Building, Trumpington Street, Cambridge CB2 1RP
40 West 20th Street, New York, NY 10011, USA
10 Stamford Road, Oakleigh, Melbourne 3166, Australia

© Cambridge University Press 1989

First published 1989

Printed in Great Britain at
Redwood Burn Limited, Trowbridge, Wiltshire

British Library cataloguing in publication data

Claeys, Gregory
Citizens and saints: politics and anti-politics in early
British socialism.
1. Great Britain. Socialism, 1815–1860
I. Title
335′.00941

Library of Congress cataloguing in publication data

Claeys, Gregory.
Citizens and saints: politics and anti-politics in early
British socialism/Gregory Claeys.
    p.   cm.
Bibliography.
Includes index.
ISBN 0–521–36490–6
1. Socialism – Great Britain – History – 19th century ▓▓▓ Owen,
Robert, 1771–18▓▓ 3. Political science – Great Britain –
History – 19th century.   4. Great Britain – Politics and
government – 19th century.   I. Title.
HX242.C57   1989
335′.1–dc19   88–37165 CIP

ISBN 0 521 36490 6

For
Christine

Contents

Acknowledgements

This book was first presented as a doctoral dissertation to the Faculty of History of the University of Cambridge in 1982. It underwent a long period of revision at the University of Hanover, West Germany, and finally sees the light of day in St Louis, Missouri. During this gestation many friends, acquaintances and colleagues have offered comments on aspects of the text or its arguments. My greatest debt is to my supervisor, Gareth Stedman Jones, who was unfailingly inspiring, supportive and incisive, and who has remained a good friend. I have also learned much from John Dunn's approach to the history of socialism and political thought generally, and am grateful for his kindness and encouragement from the outset of my research. Istvan Hont has always combined warm friendship, critical acumen and technological capacity, a pleasing trinity of virtues. The thesis was examined by J. F. C. Harrison, whose unparalleled knowledge of Owenism was very discerningly applied and who has remained a sympathetic supporter, and Iorwerth Prothero, who helpfully pointed to a variety of alternative readings of the evidence. Initial and later encouragement was lent by Duncan Forbes, Bhikhu Parekh, Richard Tuck and Jim Tully. For comments on conference papers and on various segments of the text itself, many thanks go to Bert Altena, Andrew Cunningham, Vic Gatrell, John Halstead, Iain Hampsher-Monk, Frits van Holthoon, Jochen Hoock, Joanna Innes, Donald Kelley, Prue Kerr, Reinhart Koselleck, Marcel van der Linden, Bernd-Peter Lange, John Pocock, Sidney Pollard, Karl Rohe, John Saville, M. W. H. Schreuder, John Seed, Terry Shinn, Judith Shklar, Keith Snell, Keith Tribe, A. V. N. van Worden, Norbert Waszek, Richard Whitely, Raymond Williams, Donald Winch, Eileen Yeo, and a variety of anonymous interrogators and referees. Help in acquiring materials is gratefully acknowledged to Angela Whitelegge, Dee Berkeley, Jan Fairholme, Mary Graham, Gwen Revell, David Goodway, Roy Garratt, Mieke Ijzermans, and Rudolph Ellenbogen. Many librarians had their patience sorely tried and went well beyond the call of duty in fetching and searching for materials. I am particularly thankful to the staff of the British Library, Great Russell Street and the Newspaper Library, Colindale; the Goldsmiths' Library and the Cambridge University Library, who were most long suffering with my requests. In addition I would like to thank the following libraries and archives for their help: the National Library of Scotland; Edinburgh University Library; Glasgow University Library; the Mitchell Library, Glasgow; the London School of Economics Library; Dr Williams' Library; the Library of University College, London; the Bishopsgate Institute Library; the India Office Library; the Public Records Office, Kew; the Library of the Feltrinelli Foundation, Milan; the Library of the International Institute of Social History, Amsterdam; the State Library, Moscow; the Library of Congress; the New York Public Library; Columbia University Library; The Widener Library of Harvard University; the Kress Library of Harvard Business School; Washington University Library; the libraries of the University of California, Berkeley; and the University of Michigan, Ann Arbor; Vanderbilt University Library; the Library of the Workingmen's Institute, New Harmony; the Center for Research Libraries, Chicago; the Bodleian Library, Oxford; Nuffield College Library; the Libraries of Jesus and King's Colleges, Cambridge; the Co-operative Union Library, Manchester; Manchester Public Library; the Birmingham Central Reference Library; the City of Liverpool Library; Leeds University Library; Sheffield Public Library; Newcastle upon Tyne Central Library; Newport Public Library; the Library of the University of Wales, Aberystwyth; the Labour Party Library; Douglas Public Library; Cork City Library; Cork County Library; the National Library of Ireland; the Library of Trinity College, Dublin; Bedfordshire County Record Office and the Landesbibliothek, Hanover. Financial assistance was partially provided by Jesus College, Cambridge, to the Master and Fellows of which, and particularly Jim Roseblade and Peter Glazebrook, I am especially grateful for their generosity and warm hospitality; the Cambridge Historical Society; the Provost of King's College, Cambridge; and Managers of the King's College Research Centre (with special thanks to G. E. R. Lloyd); the University of Hanover; and the Department of History, Washington University. Special assistance with materials was provided by Saroj Datta and Alan Hertz. Gerd Birkner was generous in securing research assistance in Hanover. Trudi Tate proved to be a very valuable copy editor. Various journals have published early drafts of segments of the book, and I am grateful for permission to reprint material from the *International Review of Social History*, the *Journal of the History of Ideas*, and *History of Political Thought*. Last, and most, I want to thank my wife, Christine Lattek, to whom this book is dedicated, for the love, understanding and patience which made writing it a much greater pleasure.

Abbreviations

AACAN	Association of All Classes of All Nations
AC	*Age of Civilization*
AEC	*Archivum Europae Centro-Orientalis*
AH	*Actualités de l'Histoire*
AHR	*American Historical Review*
APSR	*American Political Science Review*
AWC	*Advocate of the Working Classes*
BAPCK	British Association for the Promotion of Co-operative Knowledge
BCG	*Birmingham Co-operative Gazette*
BD	*Black Dwarf*
BFHS	*Bulletin of the Friends' Historical Society*
BH	*Brazen Head*
BJPS	*British Journal of Political Science*
BJRL	*Bulletin of the John Rylands Library*
BNR	*Bronterre's National Reformer*
BP	*Brighton Patriot*
BRP	*Barker's Review of Politics*
BS	*British Statesman*
BSSLH	*Bulletin of the Society for the Study of Labour History*
BT	*Brazen Trumpet*
CC	*Chartist Circular*
ChP	*Chartist Pilot*
CL	*Cap of Liberty*
CM	*Communist Miscellany*
CMPM	*Carpenter's Monthly Political Magazine*
CN	*Co-operative News*
ComS	*Common Sense*
CP	*Cause of the People*
CPG	*Cleave's Penny Gazette*
CPL	*Carpenter's Political Letters and Pamphlets*

CPR	Carlile's Political Register
CS	Christian Socialist
CSE	Christian Social Economist
CWPG	Cleave's Weekly Police Gazette
CWPR	Cobbett's Weekly Political Register
DeR	Defoe's Review
DJWN	Douglas Jerrold's Weekly Newspaper
DLA	Democrat and Labour Advocate
DN	Daily News
DPMC	Destructive, and Poor Man's Conservative
DR	Democratic Review
DU	Daily Union
ECC	English Chartist Circular
ECCA	Educational Circular and Communist Apostle
EconHR	Economic History Review
ECS	Eighteenth Century Studies
EHR	English Historical Review
EMD	Edinburgh Monthly Democrat
EP	English Patriot and Irish Repealer
ER	English Republic
ES	Evening Star
FE	Free Enquirer
FH	Family Herald
FM	Freethinker's Magazine
FP	Fleet Papers
GNCTU	Grand National Consolidated Trades' Union
GS	Glasgow Sentinel
HC	Herald of Co-operation
HEI	History of European Ideas
HF	Herald of the Future
HJ	Historical Journal
HM	Halfpenny Magazine
HO	Home Office Papers
HowJ	Howitt's Journal
HPT	History of Political Thought
HRI	Herald of the Rights of Industry
HT	History Today
HTA	Herald to the Trades' Advocate
HTD	Hetherington's Twopenny Dispatch
IHB	Indiana History Bulletin
IRSH	International Review of Social History
IW	Independent Whig
JA	Journal of Association

JBS	*Journal of British Studies*
JHI	*Journal of the History of Ideas*
JI	*Jersey Independent*
JMH	*Journal of Modern History*
LA	*London American*
LabH	*Labor History*
LBMR	*Louis Blanc's Monthly Review*
LCM	*London Co-operative Magazine*
LCMM	*London Chartist Monthly Magazine*
LD	*London Dispatch*
LDem	*London Democrat*
LH	*Literature and History*
LL	*Labour League*
LMR	*Livesey's Moral Reformer*
LN	*London News*
LSR	*London Social Reformer*
LWLN	*Lloyd's Weekly London Newspaper*
LWMA	London Working Men's Association
MCI	*Midland Counties Illuminator*
MCJ	*McDouall's Chartist Journal*
MECW	Karl Marx and Frederick Engels, *Collected Works* (Lawrence and Wishart, 1975–)
MH	*Manchester Herald*
MHist	*Midland History*
MHQ	*Mennonite Historical Quarterly*
ML	*Monthly Liberator*
MM	*Monthly Messenger*
MO	*Manchester Observer*
MoR	*Monthly Repository*
MP	*Midland Progressionist*
MR	*Model Republic*
MRBH	*Midland Representative and Birmingham Herald*
MS	*Morning Star*
MSA	*Manchester and Salford Advertiser*
MT	*Mirror of Truth*
MTy	*Marxism Today*
MUK	*Magazine of Useful Knowledge*
MW	*Moral World*
NAG	*National Association Gazette*
NHG	*New Harmony Gazette*
NI	*National Instructor*
NL	*Northern Liberator*
NMW	*New Moral World*

NP	*Notes to the People*
NS	*Northern Star*
NT	*Northern Tribune*
NU	*National Union*
NUWC	National Union of the Working Classes
NV	*National Vindicator*
NVS	Robert Owen, *A New View of Society and Other Writings,* ed. John Butt (Dent, 1972)
NWC	*Newcastle Weekly Chronicle*
NWR	*Niles' Weekly Register*
OAHQ	*Ohio Archaeological and Historical Quarterly*
OF	*Odd Fellow*
OFP	*Operatives' Free Press*
OGTU	*Official Gazette of the Trades' Unions*
OrR	*Oracle of Reason*
P&P	*Past and Present*
PA	*Public Administration*
PAPS	*Proceedings of the American Philosophical Society*
PCA	*Promethean, or Communitarian Apostle*
PE	*Potters' Examiner*
PenS	*Penny Satirist*
PEUP	*Political Economist and Universal Philanthropist*
PIHS	*Publications of the Indiana Historical Society*
PJ	*Phrenological Journal*
PlS	*Plain Speaker*
PM	*People's Magazine*
PMA	*Poor Man's Advocate*
PMG	*Poor Man's Guardian*
PMGRF	*Poor Man's Guardian and Repealer's Friend*
PN	*People's Newspaper*
PolEx	*Political Examiner*
PolP	*Politics for the People*
PP	*People's Paper*
PPe	*Power of the Pence*
PPN	*Price-Priestley Newsletter*
PPP	*Penny Papers for the People*
PQ	*Philological Quarterly*
PR	*People's Review*
PS	*Political Soldier*
PSQ	*Political Science Quarterly*
PT	*Political Theory*
PWRM	*Pioneer, and Weekly Record of Movements*
QR	*Quarterly Review*

RO	Register for the First Society of Adherents to Divine Revelation at Orbiston
ROJ	Robert Owen's Journal
ROMG	Robert Owen's Millennial Gazette
RoR	Romanic Review
ROWL	Robert Owen's Weekly Letters
RP	Review of Politics
RPI	Reynolds's Political Instructor
RR	Reformist's Register
RSPT	Royal Society, Philosophical Transactions
RWN	Reynolds's Weekly Newspaper
SA	Spirit of the Age
SAPTJ	Some Account of the Progress of the Truth as It is in Jesus
ScT	Scottish Tradition
SE	Star in the East
SEC	Studies in Eighteenth Century Culture
SF	Standard of Freedom
SFP	Sheffield Free Press
SHP	Studies in History and Politics
SMM	Stephens's Monthly Magazine
Soc. Res.	Social Research
SP	Social Pioneer
SPR	Sherwin's Political Register
SR	Social Reformer
SS	Southern Star
ST	Spirit of the Times
StF	Star of Freedom
StS	Stepping Stone
STUG	Scottish Trades' Union Gazette
THAS	Transactions of the Hunter Archaeological Society
THLC	Transactions of the Historical and Literary Committee of the American Philosophical Society
THSLC	Transactions of the Historical Society of Lancashire and Cheshire
TMW	Trades' Weekly Messenger
TRHS	Transactions of the Royal Historical Society
TS	True Scotsman
UCSRR	Universal Community Society of Rational Religionists
USF	Uxbridge Spirit of Freedom
VASFE	Vocational Aspect of Secondary and Further Education
VP	Voice of the People
WA	Weekly Advisor
WB	Working Bee

WBG	*Wooler's British Gazette*
WFP	*Weekly Free Press*
WH	*White Hat*
WMF	*Working Man's Friend and Political Magazine*
WMFFI	*Working Man's Friend and Family Instructor*
WP	*Ware Patriot*
WPQ	*Western Political Quarterly*
WS	*Western Star*
WT	*Weekly Tribune*
WTS	*Weekly True Sun*
WV	*Western Vindicator*

Introduction:
socialism and political thought

Two conceptions of government and politics dominate modern political thought. The first of these, the theory of republican, representative
democracy, is often associated with the American revolution and its
efforts to improve upon the British parliamentary model by establishing a commercial republic. This involved reconciling the goal of active
civic participation associated with ancient Greek and Roman republicanism with the greater size, political lethargy, selfishness and luxury
of modern commercial societies. Popular participation was now rendered sufficiently sporadic and indirect, and no longer inclusive of
universal military service, such that public service was no onerous
burden for the majority. This was intended in part to inhibit the
tumultuousness to which republics were prone. Consequently the
health of the body politic was no longer expected to depend primarily
upon the robustness of public virtue. Individuals were instead
assumed to be concerned predominantly with their occupations and
the duties of private life. A relaxation of civic vigilance in commercial
republics was thought possible partially because the sphere of executive government was to be reduced considerably while that of civil
society was expanded correspondingly, and the mutual satisfaction of
economic interests through freedom of commerce assigned some responsibility for providing social stability.[1] Associated with this notion
of democracy, therefore, is the theory of what is usually termed 'negative liberty', where liberty is understood principally as the restraint of
state power in order to guarantee individual freedom from political
persecution, corruption and governmental economic interference.

The second revolution to define modern political thought began
some forty years later and brought forth socialist democratic theory. Its
origins have been considerably less well studied. But it is generally
accepted that most early socialists condemned as inadequate the insti-

[1] See Albert O. Hirschman, *The Passions and the Interests* (Princeton, Princeton University
Press, 1977).

1

tutions and policies associated with commercial democracies. This book attempts to explain how and why this critique of liberal representative democracy emerged amongst the followers of the British reformer Robert Owen. Both the politics and what will here be termed the 'anti-politics' of early British socialism derived from the belief that representative institutions and popular sovereignty were incapable of resolving the complex and deeply divisive problems of a market-oriented and industrialising society, and that indeed they mirrored its more insidious vices. 'Democracy' itself was credited with great value, but its potential was not identified with existing forms of government. Moreover, socialism was sceptical of the ability of majority rule alone in parliamentary institutions to confer justice and social welfare while existing inequalities of wealth persisted. Accordingly it proclaimed itself from the outset to be the continuation and culmination of liberal democracy as well as its logical and spiritual successor. But socialists themselves were deeply divided on these issues. By about 1850, the spectrum of socialist political thought was bounded on the one hand by various forms of republican and more traditionally democratic socialism. At the other extreme was a more millenarian, anti-political ideal which assumed that most sources of social conflict would vanish once economic justice and a new social order had been introduced, and thought that many of the mechanisms usually associated with 'politics' and the coercive state might therefore be dispensed with. The republican and anti-political ideals, however, were not pure types, and assumptions from each were intermixed, as we will see, in a variety of ways. Nonetheless no early socialists expected that the future representation of partisan interests could be as sharply expressed as under the existing system of private property and immense class distinctions.

The distance between socialism and liberalism was especially conspicuous in the early nineteenth century. By 1900 practical compromises in continental as well as British politics created various forms of social democracy and social or 'new' liberalism. But for much of the nineteenth century, socialism accepted little of either the theory or the policies of liberalism (and vice-versa). Politically it was dismissive of the lesser virtues condoned by the loss of participation in representative democracy, and in some respects it harkened back to a more classical notion of participation – as had Rousseau, for example, in the eighteenth century – in its refusal to restrict decision-making to a narrow elite and its frequent insistence upon small-scale societies. Deeply dismayed at the effects of industrialisation, moreover, socialism juxtaposed to increasing degradation a vision wherein not only the means of labour but also culture and the means of self-cultivation were accessible to all. From its origins it was thus associated with the ideal

now termed 'positive liberty', where liberty is defined chiefly as freedom from want, but also as the freedom to attain a more harmonious
and cultured personality than any system of great inequality has ever
offered the majority. However, both of these demands have been
clearly recognised to entail widespread assistance by both the state and
intermediary organisations in order to furnish the means of subsistence as well as opportunities for self-development. The determination
of the sphere of legitimate state activity, in turn, has remained the
central point of contention between modern socialism and liberalism.

For socialists and liberals alike, two events in this period chiefly
shaped thinking about the prospects of democratic institutions. The
subversion of the ancien régime in France was at first a moment of
enormous optimism and even millenarian enthusiasm for sympathetic
onlookers. But it would too soon cast a pall upon radicalism for many
reformers, to whom the emergence of tyranny and dictatorship from a
democratic revolution had seemed preposterous. The spectre of the
guillotine and the Napoleonic drive for imperial expansion convinced
many that popular sovereignty could not be instituted prematurely.
Some consequently urged a return to a pre-industrial, paternalist order
in which landowners strictly fulfilled their responsibility for the poor,
thus eliminating the need for wider political participation. Even those
who conceded the eventual desirability of a much wider franchise
acknowledged the problem of the degradation and necessary better-
ment of working class 'character', and correspondingly the duties of an
elite or 'clerisy' who could champion the cause of gradual political
reform until full popular participation was feasible.[2] Such concerns
were never crucial to Painite, Cobbettite and other forms of plebeian
radicalism in this period, though they too stressed the need for education and 'improvement'. But this approach was clearly mirrored in
socialism, which emerged in Britain in the wake of Napoleon's defeat
and was also unable to shake the imagery of the Terror and revolutionary conquest. Like most early socialists – Wilhelm Weitling and
his followers are one exception – the Owenites would therefore declare
violence abhorrent. But many socialists also concluded that the fate of
the revolution indicated the instability of mass reform activity given
the low level of education and political consciousness of the majority.
Thus was also inaugurated a debate within socialism – many of whose
adherents were skilled artisans at a considerable social distance from
the mass of unskilled labourers – about the exigency of leadership by
an advanced minority, or the prospect of the gradual, educational and

[2] On this theme see Ben Knights, *The Idea of the Clerisy in the Nineteenth Century* (Cambridge, Cambridge University Press, 1978), and Stefan Collini, 'The Idea of "Character" in Victorian Political Thought', *TRHS*, 5th series, 35 (1985), 29–50.

experimental extension of democracy to the working classes rather than the concession of universal suffrage all at once.

But popular ignorance alone did not make many socialists sceptical of the immediate advantages of increased representation. To some extent the outcome of the revolution was presumed to be inherent in republicanism itself as it had been traditionally understood. British socialism repudiated in particular what it deemed to be the overly martial, narrowly patriotic character model widely associated with ancient Greece and Rome, and sought to delineate a more benevolent and non-competitive character appropriate to the future polity. This course never involved the complete disavowal of republican and radical political thinking. But while it revived a more Platonic form of republicanism in its view of property and the family and also retained other republican interests, socialism discarded the notion that there should be any connection between the right of the franchise and the ownership of private property. Instead such ownership was perceived as itself a fateful source of social and political corruption, blinding the possessors to the suffering of the dispossessed, and with the increasing inequality of wealth gradually threatening the entire society with cataclysm. With this doctrine socialism thus broke sharply from the central assumptions of mainstream republicanism. To the extent that it also held traditional modes of representation in contempt, and commended unpolitical or anti-political forms of rule, it departed even further from democratic republicanism. Yet other socialists, as we will see, also sought to stretch the principle of participation into areas to which the concept had never been applied. Far less suspicious of popular sovereignty, they stressed instead that genuine democracy could not be confined merely to the parliamentary arena, but had to encompass other forms of organisation, notably the economic. The flaw of the French revolution, then, and the cause of all other forms of tyranny, was not that popular fervour had been unleashed but that majority rule was not sufficiently widespread.

The growing controversy about democracy was also modified by a second process. After 1815 industrialisation gave rise to what became widely known as the 'social' problem, industrial poverty and degradation. More directly inspired by the advent of the factory system than other early socialist school, Owenism increasingly conceded the value of the new techniques of production as well as the new needs which these engendered. As one of the greatest cotton spinners, Owen himself was well acquainted with the evils of both excessive *laissez-faire* and the overconcentration of factory labour. But a refusal to revert to subsistence agriculture meant that manufacturing also posed a particular political challenge. Correspondingly, it was first in Britain that socialists were forced to consider what the collective, though not necessarily centralised, management of production and exchange would entail, and to understand this, at least in part, as involving an extension of the democratic ideal generally.

The problem of socialist politics

The political ideas and practices of the Owenites have never been defined as central to their experience and have therefore never been carefully studied. To many of their contemporaries, Owen and the Owenites were mere eccentrics, disguising immoral aims behind their overly liberal views on marriage, verging on sectarian enthusiasm and heresy in their religious beliefs, bent on berating the public with the notion that the self-formation of character was some kind of social Original Sin, and dedicated to forming experimental communities of a few thousand farmers, operatives and artisans at a time when many seemed willing to abandon the land for the joys, or at least the employment prospects, of urban life. Given the continuing pressures of industrial society, these communities have retained an abiding interest for later generations. But historians have acknowledged that Owenite interests were by no means confined to communitarianism, and that, for example, socialists made substantial contributions to the movements for factory and poor law reform, labour exchange experiments and trades' unionism. The social history of these aspects of Owenism has been well served by J. F. C. Harrison's pioneering work, though many more detailed local as well as biographical studies are still badly needed.[3] Other areas of Owenism have also undergone recent exploration. Important research has clearly demonstrated how highly female equality was regarded in the movement.[4] Owenism's relation to the history of radical and socialist economic thought has also been reconstructed recently in my companion volume to the present study.[5] But its attitude towards politics and its treatment of organisation and administrative problems have never been examined in depth. Even standard accounts of early British socialism hardly touch upon the subject.[6]

[3] J. F. C. Harrison, *Robert Owen and the Owenites in Britain and America* (Routledge and Kegan Paul, 1969).

[4] Barbara Taylor, *Eve and the New Jerusalem. Socialism and Feminism in the Nineteenth Century* (Virago, 1982).

[5] See *Machinery, Money and the Millennium. From Moral Economy to Socialism, 1815–1860* (Princeton, Princeton University Press, 1987).

[6] G. D. H. Cole, *A History of Socialist Thought* (Macmillan, 1962), 1, p. 131, devotes scarcely a line to the subject. Max Beer, *A History of British Socialism* (G. Bell, 1929), 2, p. 45, is similarly uninformative, as is H. L. Beales, *The Early English Socialists* (Hamish Hamilton, 1933).

There are three primary reasons for this omission. The first proceeds from previous studies of Robert Owen himself. Owen's ideas on organisation and leadership have often been categorised as at best 'unpolitical', at worst conservative or even 'despotic'. His followers are credited with having had some contact with radicalism, but otherwise are frequently castigated for sharing a fundamental lack of interest in politics. However, this has not usually been seen as indicative of an interesting or difficult problem in the history of socialism. Several useful recent studies, notably by Keith Taylor and Barbara Goodwin, have begun to treat these wider questions more carefully, and with an eye to the evolution of socialism in the late nineteenth and twentieth centuries. But these have proceeded primarily by considering all of the early socialist schools at a more introductory level rather than by examining any in great depth, and have not attempted to trace the relation of many seventeenth- and eighteenth-century lines of thought to socialism.[7]

In fact a renewed interest in early socialism from a modern perspective has also coincided with the reinterpretation of the seventeenth- and eighteenth-century republicanism and radicalism. This line of inquiry has undoubtedly proven highly beneficial to our understanding of the transformation of political thought in this period, and can help to illuminate much of the language and programme of nineteenth century radicalism. Recent studies, however, have traced variations upon 'civic humanism' up to the French revolution without for the most part crossing the great divide into the nineteenth century or demonstrating any other than a negative interest in the history of socialism. J. G. A. Pocock, who has chiefly inspired this reconceptualisation of radicalism, has indicated in passing that Marx and Engels probably built upon some cardinal assumptions of late eighteenth century republicanism, particularly in relation to specialisation and the division of labour and the construction of their theory of alienation. But it remains unclear how their views may have been affected by developments during the first half of the nineteenth century, or the presence of other intellectual traditions. The eighteenth century thus has remained largely closed off to historians of socialism, the nineteenth to chroniclers of republicanism. Unless these periods are

---

[7] Keith Taylor, *The Political Ideas of the Utopian Socialists* (Cass, 1982), pp. 69–99 in particular, and Barbara Goodwin and Keith Taylor, *The Politics of Utopia* (Hutchinson, 1982); Barbara Goodwin, *Social Science and Utopia* (Brighton, Harvester Press, 1978). A helpful overview of the subject is given in Richard Adamiak's, 'State and Society in Early Socialist Thought', *Survey*, 26 (1982), 1–28. There are also useful comments in William Stafford's *Socialism, Radicalism, and Nostalgia. Social Criticism in Britain, 1775–1830* (Cambridge, Cambridge University Press, 1987), pp. 31–98.

bridged adequately, however, their political thought and consequently the shaping of modern political debate can never be properly understood.

This points to the third reason why Owenite political thought has been hitherto neglected. Most of those concerned to explore modern socialist politics have begun their investigations, after a brief glance at the 'precursors', with the works of Marx and Engels themselves. These are sufficiently rich, perplexing and entertaining to engage large numbers of scholars and to furnish considerable scope for interpretative disagreement. The *prima facie* case for looking more intently at early socialism is not therefore immediately evident. A large literature about 'socialist politics' has thus grown up around the assumption that nothing very worthwhile or historically meaningful was written on the subject before Marx and Engels began their own explorations. Once we begin to realise, however, that early socialism in fact formed a vital link in the process of the development of one strand of late eighteenth-century radicalism towards Marxism, and that modern socialism too still stands with one foot in an earlier epoch – and these are points which must yet be proven – it becomes clear that adequately detailed studies which also rise above their narrative to ascertain the larger relevance of the subject to the socialist tradition and to the history of political thinking generally are badly needed.

There are considerable risks, however, in being overly attentive to the begging demands of either predecessors or successors. A teleological search for the roots of later ideas induces anachronistic distortions in interpretation, and here often the assumption that early socialism remained imprisoned within earlier patterns of thought, and failed to develop as it ought to have done. Similar judgements might result from the view that eighteenth-century republicanism or its most direct nineteenth-century descendants were a more satisfactory form of radicalism. My own assumptions, of course, are not unbiassed, and in exploring the variety of political positions examined here, some have appeared to me to be more plausible and reasonable than others. In particular, it is difficult not to conclude that the anti-political and perfectionist elements in early socialism evidence a mentality which has been the source of enormous difficulties for socialist governments and organisations. Nonetheless this is merely a reflection upon the potentially wider relevance of such a study and an acknowledgement of an important element of continuity, rather than a point which can be argued carefully here.

Within the historiography of socialism generally several dominant interpretative premises have also inhibited more detailed studies of early socialism. Since the late nineteenth century, the almost universally accepted historiographic division of socialism into two chief phases – 'utopian', or early socialism, comprising Owenism, Fourierism, Saint-Simonism and other schools, and 'scientific' or Marxian socialism – has played a crucial role here. This classification – clearly a matter of the victors imposing terms upon the vanquished – originated with the *Communist Manifesto* (1848), and was sealed by Engels' reflections in *Anti-Dühring*, published separately in English as *Socialism, Utopian and Scientific* (1892). But despite the important differences between them, such a strict separation between earlier and later forms of socialism is no longer tenable in light of modern scholarship. Given Owen's adherence to a stadial conception of history derived from the Scottish writers and similar in many respects to some of Marx and Engels' later views, for example, it is manifestly an exaggeration to argue that the Owenites, in common with all other early socialist schools, believed that socialism was 'the expression of absolute truth, reason and justice', and had 'only to be discovered to conquer the world by virtue of its own power'. Nor do the articulation of the materialist conception of history, the choice of the industrial proletariat as the agency of historical change and of class struggle as its 'motor', and the predominance given to the theory of surplus value imply that Marxism lacks fundamental elements of continuity, even in these areas, with its predecessors.[8] It can certainly be argued, moreover, that many of the most essential apparent differences between early and later socialism – for example a focus upon communities rather than socialism at the level of the nation-state, or upon an economic basis of subsistence agriculture rather than increasing industrialisation – were in fact divergent trends within existing varieties of early socialism. From this viewpoint the latter became progressively more 'modern' (not always a beneficial development by any means) by the mid-1840s. It is no longer heretical to contend that, despite their considerable intellectual achievements, Marx and Engels stood much closer to their own times and to their own teachers than is usually assumed. Neither

---

[8] Frederick Engels, *Socialism, Utopian and Scientific* (New York, International Publishers, 1972), pp. 43, 53. John Plamenatz, *Man and Society* (Longmans, 1963), 2, pp. 83–93, also challenges the continuing utility of this distinction. See also Kurt Bayertz, 'From Utopia to Science? The Development of Socialist Theory Between Utopia and Science', in Everett Mendelsohn and Helga Nowotny, eds., *Nineteen Eighty-Four* (Dordrecht, D. Reidel, 1984), pp. 93–110 and Vincent Geoghegan, *Utopianism and Marxism* (Methuen, 1987).

the cause nor the study of modern socialism suffers by such a concession.

For with respect to many of the most important questions of social and political thought, Marx and Engels were relative latecomers to a debate which was some thirty years old before they began to consider seriously its central issues. The point is not merely that they built upon previous discussions, but that in so doing they incorporated into their own thought many hidden assumptions and even covert first principles which occasionally emerged to the discursive surface, but as often as not remained half-disclosed if not well buried. It was, in fact, Marx and Engels' ability to by-pass many of the existing (and sometimes central) issues of socialist debate (about the malleability or even the existence of 'human nature' and the characteristics of the future communist society, for example) which in part allowed them to formulate their own intellectual strategy so quickly and succinctly in the mid-1840s. Among the issues Marx and Engels chose to ignore, however, but whose resolution was equally tacit in their own assumptions, were some whose implications for their own programme were threatening at the least. These underlying conceptions cannot be excavated through internalist investigations of the Marxist canon alone. Recourse, instead, must be had to the works of the early socialists, though to reason from these in order to generalise at length and in detail about Marxist and later forms of socialism would require a thorough investigation of other pre-Marxian schools as well, which is clearly beyond the compass of this book.[9]

Doubtless the most important such political ideal held by Marx and Engels and many of their socialist predecessors concerned the abolition of organised coercion in the future communist society, or in Engels' famous phrase, the 'withering away of the state'. Though its precise meaning is far from clear, this notion more than any other symbolised the aspirations of those for whom 'anti-politics', the restraint of all forms of conflict, even perhaps at the cost of not tolerating legitimate differences of opinion, represented a vital step towards a more harmonious and humane future. A century of experimentation has induced considerable scepticism about the practicability of this conception in its most extreme formulations. But its crucial relevance

[9] For more detailed studies of the political ideas of other early socialist schools, see George Iggers, *The Cult of Authority: The Political Philosophy of the Saint-Simonians* (The Hague, Martinus Nijhoff, 1958), Gita Ionescu's introduction to *The Political Thought of Saint-Simon* (Oxford, Oxford University Press, 1976), Christopher Johnson, *Utopian Communism in France. Cabet and the Icarians* (Ithaca, Cornell University Press, 1974), Jonathan Beecher, *Charles Fourier. The Visionary and His World* (Berkeley, University of California Press, 1986), especially pp. 241–58.

to the socialist ideal historically remains undoubted.[10] For the norma-
tive goals of Marxism have never included only the provision of economic justice for all, but have also assumed a condition of political
stability and political justice. The ending of undue coercion, war and
social conflict generally, and the peaceful co-existence of a world of
nations in mutual respect for one another's rights, have always been
part of the vision shared by most schools of socialism. The belief in its
probability of success has usually been based upon the assumption of
technologically and commercially based opulence, with 'politics' becoming 'administration' (in Saint-Simon's famous phrase) in proportion to the correct application and guidance of industry. But socialists
have also generally presumed that human behaviour would be vastly
improved in a more humane and just future polity. Many, too, have
associated such an ideal with earlier societies, as Marx did with ancient
Indian communism and the Russian village community, and Engels
the North American natives.

Moreover, Marxism, like Owenism from the outset, also viewed
liberal, constitutional parliamentarism very ambivalently. As a means
of achieving justice and equality, limited political reform was dismissed as no substitute for thorough social change, with the persistence of the juxtaposition of 'social' to 'political' reform within late
socialism being the clearest indication of this line of criticism. As ends
in themselves, too, parliamentary institutions were also often rejected,
or at least regarded with considerable mistrust. The accusation that the
parliamentary process merely reflected the competitive model of capitalist society generally was an element of this suspicion, as was the
simple fear that too close an acquaintance with such procedures would
corrupt those imbued with higher or broader ideals. Associated with
this, throughout the history of socialism, has been a decided reluctance
to adopt what has often been condemned as a 'bourgeois' – the word
has a harsher, less neutral connotation in English than for instance
in French – vocabulary of civil and political rights and liberties.
Discussions of 'rights' among socialists, accordingly, have usually

[10] See generally William MacBride, 'Noncoercive Society: Some Doubts, Leninist and
Contemporary', in J. R. Pennock and J. W. Chapman, eds., *Coercion* (New York,
Atherton, 1982), pp. 3–26, Martin Krygier, 'Saint-Simon, Marx and the Non-
Governed Society', in Eugene Kamenka and Martin Krygier, eds., *Bureaucracy* (New
York, St. Martin's Press, 1979), pp. 34–60, and Daniel Tarschys, *Beyond the State: The
Future Polity in Classical and Soviet Marxism* (Stockholm, Läromedelsförlagen, 1971),
pp. 1–45. A recent account which suggests that Lenin shared many of these assumptions is A. J. Polan, *Lenin and the End of Politics* (Methuen, 1984). Here again, however,
the model of the commune, which mixed seemingly 'utopian' with more traditionally
democratic assumptions, loomed large. See further Neil Harding, *Lenin's Political
Thought* (2 vols., Macmillan, 1983). That the abolition of the state remains a viable
socialist goal is suggested in Andrew Levine's recent *The End of the State* (Verso Books,
1987).

focussed upon economic claims, ignoring the notion of any original or subsequent binding contract between rulers and ruled, and frequently invoking concomitant social duties. This attitude also reflects a more general, depoliticising tendency in socialism, whereby, for example, parliamentary institutions are also categorised primarily in terms of economic interests of the various parties composing them, while the goal of all political and administrative institutions is often reduced to the creation and maintenance of economic justice.[11]

A parliamentary model of competing parties representing divergent interests similarly has been rejected by most later forms of socialism as embodying assumptions valid only for a society characterised by class antagonisms. The notion of a legitimate clash of, and the need to represent, interests based upon non-economic disagreements, has proven awkward and extraordinarily difficult to theorise. These as well as many other reasons have made it easier for the model of a single party, without identifiable factions dividing it, to prevail in socialist theory since the early years of the Russian revolution and throughout most actually existing socialist societies, though this is by no means an inevitable development from any form of socialism. But there have been of course many ideas as to how even a single party should best be constituted, and socialists have remained deeply divided, for example, on the issue of whether, or when, the guidance of an elite in possession of 'scientific' knowledge is required.

A conflict between demanding greater popular participation and desiring less 'politics' is evident here, whose origins clearly lie in early socialism. Recent interpretations of Marx and Engels' political thought have emphasised their democratic and anti-authoritarian leanings.[12] This does not necessarily place them closer to classical liberalism, however. Like many early socialists, they in fact conceived of 'democracy' in relation to forms and locations other than the solely parliamentary, such as workers' councils involving rotation, frequent election, and other forms of accountability. Both the encouragement of large-scale popular participation and the avoidance of the creation of a permanent, alien political caste or bureaucratic elite were underlying aims here. 'Politics', in this sense, was hardly to be abolished, but rather, as participation, to be diffused throughout other institutions and relations in civil society, with greater egalitarianism characterising the family, and collective control the economy. Socialism from this perspective continues to understand itself as the most political move-

---

[11] The large debate on the treatment of rights within socialism is examined in Tom Campbell, *The Left and Rights* (Routledge and Kegan Paul, 1983).

[12] See Richard Hunt, *The Political Ideas of Marx and Engels*, Vol. 2, *Classical Marxism, 1850–1895* (Macmillan, 1984).

ment of modern times, even if this rarely stated as such. Yet such a conception of socialism cannot exist without considerable tension with the anti-political strains within it.

There also remain other ambiguities in Marx and Engels' political thought which can be illuminated by the careful exposition of the political ideas of early socialism. The socialist state, like any other, can be more federal, or more centralised. Ethnic, cultural and national identities can be subordinated to the traditions of the more powerful, moulded to the vision of the more 'rational', or given the facilities to flourish. Similarly, the diversity of individual personality can be seen as a goal of socialism, and the value of the self-formation of the personality recognised. Or the preference for a single character model can be imposed. Moreover, during the process of transition to the new world, men and women can be categorised as passively trapped within the assumptions and 'circumstances' (to use the Owenite term) of the past, and thus as requiring firm guidance into the future. Or they can be seen as capable through their own efforts of assuming (if gradually) the greater political responsibilities incumbent upon them in a more democratic society. Nor was this a problem for mainstream socialism alone. For example, John Stuart Mill, who eventually converted to a variety of co-operative socialism, took Owen's theory of the formation of character very seriously, and struggled to explain how human freedom could be reconciled with such views in order to create an 'active' civic personality.[13]

As we will see, Owenism also had certain political emphases which later forms of socialism largely did not. Most notable were its principled opposition to the use of violent revolution and temporary dictatorship as a means of social transformation, its repudiation of the idea that class hatred and conflict have any positive value, and its concentration (never exclusive) upon the small community as the ideal form of social organisation. In addition, Marxist political thought emerged with a range of central intellectual concerns which had been regarded as merely peripheral, or were simply not addressed significantly and at length in early socialism. These include the attempt to classify typologies of state power, and to explain the class basis and historical emergence of various states, which was never of great interest to early British socialism.

Nonetheless, if the characteristics both forms of socialism have in common allow us to define a shared political discourse, then the relevance of examining the origins of this discourse should by now be

---

[13] A good account of Marx's struggles on this question is Hal Draper, *Marx's Theory of Revolution* (New York, Monthly Review Press, 1977), 1, pp. 194–236, and 2, pp. 147–68. See Mill's *System of Logic* (Longmans, Green and Co., 1906), pp. 562–71.

clear. For the combination of perfectionism and ambiguity about both the parliamentary process and 'liberal' forms of democracy has created serious problems in many socialist societies. If liberal and conservative interpreters alike have tended far too easily to see socialism's claim to wish to extend democracy beyond parliamentary boundaries as merely masking ultimately authoritarian intentions, for which little evidence exists, socialists themselves have far too often ignored the threats to liberty which are not merely incidental to the revolutionary process, but actually embedded in the anti-political assumptions of socialist theory. And in so doing they have also often neglected those elements in their own tradition which stress the need to extend popular participation and representation even at the cost of less social order, greater disagreement about economic goals, and a slower process of political deliberation.

To make such a concession hardly involves embracing the Cold War assumption that all forms of socialism necessarily eventuated in 'totalitarian democracy'.[14] Nor need we accept the hypothesis that socialism-as-totalitarianism is rooted in some form of heretical, messianic millenarianism which has never remained far beneath the surface of Christian orthodoxy.[15] We simply need to recognise, as John Dunn has recently observed, that an anti-political bias has rendered socialism unable to theorise clearly either systems of power or structures of political organisation.[16] Socialist political thought thus cannot be refined further without reconstructing and re-examining its own severance from nineteenth-century liberal concerns with the rule of law, constitutional balances, political accountability, and the like. Otherwise socialist societies will remain markedly less stable as well as considerably less tolerant than they should be. Too strong a sense of private life will continue to be seen as detracting from devotion to the public good. Conflicts of opinion will still be perceived as threats to the

---

[14] See especially J. Talmon, *The Origins of Totalitarian Democracy* (New York, Praeger, 1960). The most careful rebuttal of this argument with respect to Marx is Richard Hunt's *The Political Ideas of Marx and Engels*, Vol. 1: *Marxism and Totalitarian Democracy, 1818–1850* (Macmillan, 1974).

[15] Cf. Norman Cohn, *The Pursuit of the Millennium* (2nd edn., New York, Harper Books, 1961), originally subtitled 'Revolutionary Messianism in Medieval and Reformation Europe and Its Bearing on Modern Totalitarian Movements', but then retitled 'A History of Popular Religion and Social Movements in Europe from the Eleventh to the Sixteenth Century'. A similar hypothesis is explored in Eric Voegelin, *The New Science of Politics* (Chicago, University of Chicago Press, 1966), pp. 107–90. More balanced is Judith Shklar's, 'The Political Theory of Utopia: From Melancholy to Nostalgia', in Frank Manuel, ed., *Utopias and Utopian Thought* (Boston, Beacon Press, 1967), pp. 101–15.

[16] John Dunn, *The Politics of Socialism* (Cambridge, Cambridge University Press, 1984), p. 21. A useful recent discussion of these issues is Christopher Pierson's *Marxist Theory and Democratic Politics* (Cambridge, Polity Press, 1987).

social order rather than as legitimate differences of perspective. The outcome of elections will remain too often preordained, instead of reflecting beneficial and critical shifts in public opinion. Transferrals of power will still frequently be attended with the risk of conflict, while longevity of rule will rest not upon popular acclamation but upon less defensible principles of order.

These solutions to social and political conflict in socialist societies are by no means inevitable. But it is no accident that one of the forms of rule which has proven most acceptable to many existing nominally socialist societies – gerontocracy – was first popularised by Robert Owen. For much of the treatment of power and conflict which remains at the core of modern socialist theory was first articulated in the early stages of the socialist movement. Not all socialists have shared these anti-political assumptions. But they have been profoundly important for over a century, and remain so today. Early socialist political thought has remained unexplored often because it has been dismissed as 'unpolitical'. But this, precisely, is part of its significance for the history of socialism, for 'anti-politics' is as much a theory of politics as any other. And the legacy of anti-political socialism is far from exhausted, just as the potential for 'political socialism', as it will here be termed, or the wider extension of democratic practices and accountability beyond the parliamentary arena, is far from tapped.

Owenism and political thought

The 'problem' of politics within socialist theory, if we may now call it that, might thus be stated in the following way: how did socialism, itself partly the offspring of the popular radical reform movement, depart so far at some points from the radical interpretation of the parliamentary ideal that its own commitment to this ideal often failed to be evident even to some socialists, and seemed utterly non-existent to many radical critics? Even the casual observer acknowledges that the socialist dismissal of liberal and radical politics together does not result solely from the identification of both with liberal political economy, important though this was, but also proceeded from many other criticisms of radical political thought and action. To comprehend this problem requires a careful investigation of the linkages of socialism to the previous radical and republican tradition, and a reconstruction of its sense of breaking from the central assumptions of these predecessors, both of which are attempted here for the first time. That there was a branch of Owenism far closer to traditional radicalism than is often assumed, and one which was concerned more clearly with the extension and fulfilment of democratic ideals than with their perfectionist transcendence, will be detailed at length here. Owenism was in fact closer to republicanism than most other early socialist schools were. But its very proximity to contemporary radicalism, and the continuous efforts made over some forty years to redefine the objects of radicalism in terms of newly-created 'social' ideals, in turn produced an approach to politics markedly different from traditional republicanism. From this exchange was born what will here be termed 'social radicalism', which sought to join political means to social ends as well as to link the moral and economic analysis of socialism to republicanism. From it, too, ensued the closely related creation of political socialism, a more traditionally democratic form of socialism which was profoundly suspicious of most attempts to supersede politics or to introduce principles of order markedly different from those sought by republicans. However, these new entities often differed only in emphasis, sense of priority, and degree of devotion to a socialist programme. For many radicals came to acknowledge the force of socialism's criticisms without accepting many of its proposals.

It is equally important, however, to show how a less republican and more utopian attitude towards politics within socialism (here identified primarily with Owen himself) emerged and took shape. This involves a close examination of two other streams in late eighteenth-century political thought which have played too small a role in previous discussions of republicanism and have never been adequately connected to the origins of socialism: the natural law tradition, and radical puritanism, particularly in its Quaker variant. For British socialism was primarily derived from the confluence of these three streams of thought, and the spectrum of political positions which it ultimately came to adopt can only be understood in terms of the relative weighting given to each of these components by any one writer.

Nor does the examination of early socialist views of politics illuminate only the histories of socialism and radicalism. It is also relevant to understanding the evolution of modern political thought generally. Though the lament that political philosophy is dead is now less frequently heard, a residual sense of its still largely indeterminate illness lingers on. It is now often conceded that the anti-political impulse in social and political thought after 1750 was much more extensive than was once believed, and was built upon a widely circulated and powerfully articulated distinction between state and society.[17] This contrast

---

[17] See Sheldon Wolin, *Politics and Vision* (Boston, Little, Brown, 1969), pp. 286–434; W. G. Runciman, *Social Science and Political Theory* (Cambridge, Cambridge University Press, 1965), pp. 22–42; Isaiah Berlin, 'Does Political Theory Still Exist?', in Peter Laslett and W. G. Runciman, eds., *Politics, Philosophy and Society*, 2nd series (Oxford, Basil Blackwell, 1962), pp. 1–33; Giovanni Sartori, 'What is Politics?', *PT*, 1 (1973), 5–26.

was stated in a variety of ways. The great radical and liberal utopias from Paine to Cobden were constructed upon the premise that the state would shrink as commercial society furnished the means of subsistence for all and the aristocracy declined in social and political power (though Paine also proposed to expand the welfare functions of the state). With the emergence of the new science of political economy in the last decades of the eighteenth century, the notion of a relatively independent, self-balancing economic mechanism requiring a minimum of state interference was gradually given wider currency. For Spencer and the British Comteans, 'social science' and 'sociology' – the knowledge of the laws of society – displaced older notions of the science of government. As Burrow, Collini and Winch's illuminating study of the science of politics in Victorian England has shown, such moves did not deal a death blow to the notion of an independent science of politics.[18] But they certainly displaced it for a number of decades, and only in the 1880s was the science of government revived fully on all fronts due to the growing popularity of the idea of the modern interventionist state. Early socialism shared in and contributed to all of these moments. The Owenites were the first to popularise the notion of 'social science' in Britain, and clearly intended the concept to replace the older sciences of government as well as the practice of 'politics' generally. They accepted something of the framework of argument dictated by political economy, though not of course its devotion to *laissez-faire*. And in their turn, they helped both to revive and to reformulate the notion of the 'paternal', active state. Here, too, they shared some ground with other Victorian critics of commercial and industrial society to whom both *laissez-faire* and any democratic or socialist alternative were equally repugnant, but who agreed that the duties of the state might well include the provision of subsistence, education and opportunities for work, if not industrial planning and social regimentation. Though the writings of Southey, Coleridge, Carlyle and Ruskin, for example, are not explored here, their relations to some aspects of the socialist project are obvious.[19]

[18] John Burrow, Stefan Collini, Donald Winch, *That Noble Science of Politics* (Cambridge, Cambridge University Press, 1983). See also Collini's 'Political Theory and the "Science of Society" in Victorian Britain', *HJ*, 23 (1980), 203–31. On Paine see my *Thomas Paine: Social and Political Thought* (Unwin Hyman, 1989).

[19] Older works on these writers include Crane Brinton, *The Political Ideas of the English Romantics* (Ann Arbor, University of Michigan Press, 1966), Benjamin Evans Lippincott, *Victorian Critics of Democracy* (Minneapolis, University of Minnesota Press, 1938). A more recent analysis is Jonathan Mendilow, *The Romantic Tradition in British Political Thought* (Croom Helm, 1986).

Labour history and the language of politics

Tracing and evaluating the emergence of a new language of politics in socialism poses a variety of formidable methodological problems. My scope here is confined to the political ideas and activities of the British Owenite socialists until the late 1850s. The rest of the contemporary socialist movement has had to be ignored, though some reference is made to American Owenism. Even so, the literature of British Owenism alone spans many dozens of periodicals, hundreds of pamphlets, and no small number of books, spread across some fifty years. This renders an analysis of the nuances and subtle shifts in the languages in which political ideas were expressed a difficult venture. Much of the most impressive methodological writing in political thought in recent years, and especially the work of John Dunn, John Pocock and Quentin Skinner, has insisted upon the need for a wider scope in order to clarify the intentions of authors and reconstruct their fundamental assumptions by analysing language as well as context.[20] This implies that longer periods and more extensive literatures must be studied: Pocock's *Machiavellian Moment* covers some five centuries, and Skinner's *Foundations of Modern Political Thought* is no less ambitious. Though intentions are usually easier to recover when dealing with single well-known texts by identifiable authors, the analysis of substantial language shifts requires that we cast our net more widely and interrogate minor and lesser texts with equal intensity. These concerns in fact demand much wider reading than a simple concentration upon 'great books' leaping epochs between 'great authors'. This, indeed, represents a major improvement over less historical readings of political theory. For we can only define accurately the parameters of a given political language or the holding of certain linguistic conventions by examining a maximum number of variations upon a single linguistic theme. Subtle shifts in political thinking are rarely evident in major political texts, but may first be obvious in unknown or forgotten authors. Texts may become controversial not because they are typical of their period, but because they break from established conventions. Certain individuals – in this case Owen – were always more 'influential' in the sense that their ideas were conveyed more widely, though they were not of course necessarily accepted by those who read or heard about them, much less understood by them in the same way.

[20] Quentin Skinner, *The Foundations of Modern Political Thought* (Cambridge, Cambridge University Press, 1978), 1, p. xi; J. G. A. Pocock, 'The History of Political Thought: A Methodological Enquiry', in Peter Laslett and W. G. Runciman, eds., *Philosophy, Politics and Society*, 2nd series (Oxford, Basil Blackwell, 1962), p. 183; John Dunn, 'The Identity of the History of Ideas', in Peter Laslett, W. G. Runciman and Quentin Skinner, eds., *Philosophy, Politics and Society*, 4th series (Oxford, Basil Blackwell, 1972), p. 160.

But the emergence of a political language is defined not merely by the diffusion of one set of views, but by the novelty of the usage, the variation of expression used, the subtle shift of innuendo and inflection, and the extent to which some variations were adopted and others rejected.

The sheer range and dispersion of the primary sources studied here, and the need to display and analyse their variety, render impossible a concentration upon the intentions of more than a few individual authors, or a narrow reconstruction of the intrinsic textual linkages and extrinsic connections of the use of language by any one author. In addition, biographical information about early socialist writers is frequently sparse or non-existent, making discussions of the social context from which particular ideas emerged difficult at best. Historians of the labour movement in particular, who have often had the greatest interest in Owenism, will probably find this irksome, and will demand that what seems too much like an abstract exercise in intellectual history be brought closer to the ground. But the problem is, at least for the time being, partially insurmountable.

This does not mean that we cannot discuss the emergence of a 'language of socialism' over a period of some forty years. But such a discourse appears considerably more disembodied than it would if we were to concentrate on Owen alone, for example, or upon a single decade of socialist development, or a select group of socialists, perhaps in a single trade or location. It entails, moreover, a degree of caution in our assumptions about the relations between language and historical reality. The method required for such a task is essentially a social history of language. It recognises that the social, political and economic context for the emergence and alteration of various concepts remains an important focus of investigation. But it nonetheless construes language itself as embodying traditions, 'discourses', or interwoven sets of assumptions which exist in a mutually dependent unity or 'paradigm', and which retain a vital degree of autonomy from their context, which does not therefore determine their expression. Moreover, language itself not only does not merely passively reflect experience, but has a peculiarly creative role in human activity insofar as it helps to define, constitute, limit or permit a certain range of behaviour. We cannot do what we do not think is possible, nor think what we lack the words to express. This autonomy must be particularly carefully acknowledged if we assume that shifting historical conditions demanded a new understanding and vocabulary to match, as is the case with much of the material under discussion here. Traditional modes of thinking can remain powerfully entrenched and wonderfully resistant to what may seem, retrospectively, to be an obvious shift in real circumstances. Historical consciousness, too, in the sense of loyalty to the traditional for (apparently) its own sake, and for the psychological and emotional support it may lend, is not to be under-estimated. But we must also be wary about mistaking the mere presence of words for the continuity of concepts and meaning, since, as we will see, one of the ways in which the vocabulary of socialism was popularised was by attaching new meanings to key terms in radical discourse. A pioneering effort of this type of analysis has been made recently by Gareth Stedman Jones, to whom my indebtedness in this regard is considerable.[21]

Outline

The general argument of this book is that Owenite political thought comprised a spectrum of positions which extended from the more utopian, quasi-millenarian perfectionism of Owen himself to the more traditional democratic conceptions of some of his followers. The ground between these extremes can be defined by reference to the particular influence of various types of puritan, natural law and repub-lican arguments, whose relative importance to socialism is explored in chapter 1. Following this a detailed exposition is offered of Owen's political thought, with particular emphasis being given to the meaning and application of the two most important terms usually applied to his political ideas, 'paternalism' and 'democracy'. Though virtually all Owenites saw themselves as extending democratic ideals, much of the significance of Owenism for the history of political thought lies in its confrontation with more traditional forms of radicalism, and particu-larly with the working class parliamentary reform movement. This critique assailed the radicals for having an inadequate understanding of the economy and for blaming economic distress on the expenditure of a corrupt government when deeper, underlying causes inherent in commercial and later industrial society were at fault. It denied that the exercise of popular sovereignty in parliament was alone sufficient to solve economic problems, also arguing that 'true democracy' could be achieved only in small communities or in other organisations such as co-operatives and trades' unions. The theory and practice of communi-tarian government are explored in chapter 3, which reviews the non-economic bases for assuming that most coercion would disappear in the future, investigates the role ideology was expected to play in this process, and looks briefly at how politics were actually conducted in some of the early communities. The following chapter studies the

[21] See Gareth Stedman Jones, 'Rethinking Chartism', in *Languages of Class* (Cambridge, Cambridge University Press, 1983), pp. 90–178.

economic arguments used against radicalism, concentrating upon the Owenites' conception of machinery, their use of the American model as evidence of the inadequacies of republicanism, and their notions of planning.

The next three chapters provide a chronological treatment of the relations between socialism and radicalism up to the mid-1850s. Chapter 5 surveys the first attempts to wed the two approaches to reform and the emergence of a new type of 'social radicalism' in the early 1830s. After examining such organisations as the British Association for the Promotion of Co-operative Knowledge and the National Union of the Working Classes, the chapter probes the quasi-syndicalist discussions which took place under the influence of Owenism during the Grand National Consolidated Trades' Union period in 1833–34. The following chapter explores relations between socialism and Chartism, the most important working class movement of the early nineteenth century. The centrality of Owenism to the creation of 'moral force' Chartism is discussed, and aspects of Owenism's contribution to the 'social' component of Chartism illuminated. Both disagreements and attempts at unity are considered, and relations between the two movements are shown to have been considerably more extensive and significant than was previously assumed. After the failure of Owenite communitarianism in 1845 and the severe setback suffered by the Chartists in 1848, leaders of both movements made serious attempts to reconcile their differences, and these are analysed carefully for the first time in chapter 7. A final chapter treats the condition of British socialism in the mid-1850s, concentrating as well on the role of Owenism in the evolution of the political ideas of the young Engels, the impact of both continental socialism and republicanism on British radicalism in the 1850s, and debates about the advantages of centralised and interventionist versus *laissez-faire* regimes at mid-century.

PART I

The roots of political and anti-political socialism

I

Republicanism, puritanism and natural jurisprudence

> Happy, indeed, would it be for mankind if the delegates of all civilised nations were to assemble in congress and submit their various institutions and customs to a strict comparison and scrutiny, and then synthetically form a scheme of universal polity. This could not be a Utopia, according to the general misapplication of that term, but a system deduced from experience upon the clearest principles of science.
>
> (John Minter Morgan, *Hampden in the Nineteenth Century: or, Colloquies on the Errors and Improvement of Society*, 1834, vol. 1, p. iii)

Three modes of thinking about government underlay Owenite attempts to design the ideal polity: republicanism, in both its eighteenth century country and ancient forms; radical puritanism, especially in the shape of Quakerism; and natural jurisprudence, upon which much late eighteenth-century moral philosophy and political economy was based. Though their components can be separately analysed, the divergencies between these traditions (at least as contemporaries understood them) should not be exaggerated. In the revived radical political discourse of the late eighteenth century, many reformers saw these approaches to politics as mutually reinforcing rather than conflicting responses to similar problems. Republicanism stressed the need for popular sovereignty, participation and public virtue in order to avoid 'corruption' resulting in the tyranny of one or of the few. Quakerism indicated the possibility of a purer and more stringent form of social morality. Natural law, as the reformers read it, centred upon rights as the basis of political legitimacy, tended to be concerned with the preservation of individual liberty against the encroachments of state power, and focussed correspondingly more upon individuals in their civil than in their political capacities.

These traditions were not accorded equal importance by all socialists. Republicanism, for example, was to be taken up by Owenism in two rather different ways. Owen's plan was first publicised during the post-war radical revival. With Painism and the foundation of the London Corresponding Society in the 1790s, a new strand of working class radicalism emerged which demanded universal manhood suffrage more fervently than most eighteenth-century radical Whigs had done. In search of plebeian support, and also impelled by its own egalitarianism and demand for economic justice, Owenism would carry forward this concern for participation. The movement, indeed, would be virtually torn apart in the 1840s by the issue. However, socialism did not focus primarily upon participation in the parliamentary process, but upon the creation of new institutions, particularly communities and economic organisations, which were neglected by existing theories of democracy. In this sense socialists claimed that they sought to extend participation beyond the scope defined by radicalism. But Owenism also specifically rejected many of those compromises of late eighteenth-century republicanism with both commercial society and the need for popular government in large states which defined, particularly in the American model, the emergence of modern radicalism. In several respects it instead harkened back to the more virtuous ideals of ancient republicanism. This was particularly the case in its treatment of the central question of the specialisation of functions and division of labour, and the relation of these to problems of individual independence and autonomy. A secondary goal associated with republicanism, moreover, was equality. Here socialism took up a more Aristotelian emphasis upon the equality of citizens. Moreover, it also invoked a Platonic strand in republicanism (dormant though reawakened by More and others), by which a community of goods and the notion of the collective education of children could be legitimised.

The desire to restore society to a condition of original purity was an important reason for the Owenite adoption of natural law ideas and its development of a theory of 'natural society'. Early socialism was much indebted to jurisprudential discussions of the state of nature and of the regulation of conflict in primitive societies, and it compared these with favourable contemporary accounts of such societies. Natural jurisprudence also furnished much of the theory of sociability which underlay the moral philosophy of Owenism. But after decades of the vindication of the necessary selfishness of commercial society by Defoe, Mandeville and others, the more enthusiastic and optimistic interpretation of the ideal of sociability associated with Shaftesbury was largely defunct by the beginning of the nineteenth century. Its revival with the birth of socialism had much to do with that atmosphere of millennial expectation which had been fuelled by the American and French revolutions, but which many socialists believed would centrally assist in the necessary passage from the old immoral to the new moral world and the subsequent transcendence of most forms of social conflict. In addition, natural law also lent some support to the notion of a society of institutionalised benevolence by reinforcing a Christian conception of the paternalist or patriarchal duties owed by property-owners, and governments acting in their name, towards the less fortunate. This was to assist in the formation of the idea of the interventionist state.

Owenism blended these approaches to social order in a mixture of political ideas which defied contemporary attempts at classification. As we will see, neither the use of republican arguments nor the discussion of sociability and of 'natural' authority and politics in themselves pointed towards either radicalism or conservativism. Far more egalitarian than any other important reform movement of its time, Owenism nonetheless employed a language of paternal care for the poor which could have been taken directly from eighteenth-century toryism (a milieu, as we will see, in which Owen has thus often been situated). Quick to condemn the tumultuous proceedings of popular radicalism, Owenism nonetheless promised a greater degree of popular participation in different types of decision-making than Paine, Cobbett or O'Connor even dreamed of. This combination of political ideals, often seen as contradictory, would eventually define a conception of politics which largely transcended all traditional categories of political inquiry, and continues to defy easy classification.

This chapter outlines the major theoretical sources for the two conceptions of socialist political thought with which this book is concerned. A brief survey is provided of republicanism and radicalism in their mainstream as well as puritan and millenarian forms. Particular attention is then given to the jurisprudential theory of natural society, which as an ideal could be construed as overlapping with certain republican assumptions. From these traditions two substantially different conceptions of politics emerged within socialism. One of these remained more traditionally constitutional and political, while attempting to extend the scope of democratic participation. The other, more utopian, anti-political and indebted to religiously inspired perfectionism, sought to transcend 'government' as it was understood generally. Particular attention is given here to two models of 'natural society' which were seminal for anti-political Owenism: Quakerism, and the patriarchalism of the North American Indians. The relation of socialism to the central republican problem of the specialisation of functions and the division of labour is then reconsidered. One of the most important departures of socialism from republicanism, it is argued, took place over this question, debates about which are also central to understanding the differing forms which socialist doctrines assumed. To an important degree these depended upon the particular mixture of republican, Puritan and jurisprudential elements in individual socialist writers. For some Owenites, this combination resulted in a very different conception of independence from that at the centre of either earlier republicanism or contemporary radicalism. A clarification of this issue is thus central to understanding the exit routes of republicanism into nineteenth-century political thought. Finally, the development of the language of socialism is briefly explored with a view to ascertaining how a new discourse on politics and anti-politics was created out of the contemporary debate about the development of commercial society.

The republican heritage

The specific character of republicanism, its reception in seventeenth- and eighteenth-century England, and, more tentatively, its exit modes into the nineteenth century, have been carefully scrutinised in recent years. This has involved a reappraisal of the revival of classical republicanism after about 1500 as well as of the sources of plebeian radicalism at the end of the eighteenth century. The evolution of radicalism into Chartism in the 1830s and 1840s has also been re-examined. For the period prior to 1800, a central focus has been upon the development of an Anglo-American variant upon Aristotelian republicanism. Extending the work of Zera Fink, Caroline Robbins and others, J. G. A. Pocock in particular has traced the language of civic humanism from Machiavelli through the end of the eighteenth century in a series of influential books.[1] In this view, now widely shared even if its eighteenth-century impact and implications for later forms of radicalism remain contested, classical republicanism in Britain was revived during the English revolution by James Harrington in particular, and popularised in the eighteenth century by John Toland, Henry Neville and other later 'neo-Harringtonians'.[2]

[1] Zera Fink, *The Classical Republicans: An Essay in the Recovery of a Pattern of Thought in Seventeenth Century England* (Evanston, Northwestern University Press, 1945); Caroline Robbins, *The Eighteenth Century Commonwealthsmen* (Cambridge, MA, Harvard University Press, 1959); J. G. A. Pocock, *Politics, Language and Time. Essays on Political Thought and History* (New York, Atherton, 1971), *The Machiavellian Moment: Florentine Political Thought and the Atlantic Republican Tradition* (Princeton, Princeton University Press, 1975), *The Political Works of James Harrington* (Cambridge, Cambridge University Press, 1977), *Virtue, Commerce and History: Essays on Political Thought and History Chiefly in the Eighteenth Century* (Cambridge, Cambridge University Press, 1985).

[2] There are useful reviews of Pocock's work in J. H. Hexter, *On Historians* (Cambridge, MA, Harvard University Press, 1979), pp. 255–303, and Iain Hampsher-Monk, 'Political Languages in Time: the Work of J. G. A. Pocock', *BJPS*, 14 (1984), 89–116. See also Pocock's 'The *Machiavellian Moment* Revisited: A Study in History and Ideology', *JMH*, 53 (1981), 49–72.

Republicanism remained more a language and way of thinking about politics than a specific political programme, however. Most republicans did not seek the abolition of the monarchy, however, but wished to see a balance of the three main powers (monarchy, aristocracy, populace) reflected in political institutions which gave precedence to popular sovereignty and restrained the emergence of monarchical or oligarchical tyranny.[3] Few republicans prior to 1780 ever envisioned a very wide franchise, in fact. Instead, political power was thought to reside naturally with the landed gentry and the most talented members of the aristocracy, who were believed to have the greatest stake in ruling for the common good. Their possession of landed property, it was assumed, helped to guarantee political independence and avoid the corruption of electors by the Crown. Monarchical usurpation was also to be prevented by prohibiting a standing army liable to misuse by conniving princes, and the provision of a citizens' militia. Agrarian laws and other limits on the accumulation of landed property were deemed useful for the maintenance of a relative equality of landed wealth, though this was rarely insisted upon after 1700.[4] The possession by the landowning elite of 'virtue', defined in terms of public spirit and the love of country, was therefore held to be essential to national survival. 'Corruption', or the decline of virtue, was assumed to insinuate itself through a surfeit of luxury, a lack of concern about the common weal, or the increasing dependence of electors upon the Crown or the government upon fundholders who benefited from the national debt. Eternal vigilance was thus the price to be paid for the maintenance of virtue.

By the mid-eighteenth century the possibility of virtuous republicanism faced renewed challenge from the rapid diffusion of commerce.[5] Identified in the 1690s with the 'Old', 'True' or 'Real' Whigs, republicanism split in the following century into a 'Country' group which had both radical Whig and Tory adherents, and a 'Court' party. The latter was represented by the 'New Whig' ascendancy after 1714, which Country critics argued was tied too closely to the interests of commerce, the city, the funding system and national debt, the corrupt system of parliamentary and state patronage, and the increasing power of the executive.[6] But to the Country ideal of a society of agrarian

---

[3] For example, Henry Neville, 'Plato Redivivus: or, A Dialogue Concerning Government', in Caroline Robbins, ed., *Two English Republican Tracts* (Cambridge, Cambridge University Press, 1969), p. 92.

[4] For example, John Trenchard and Thomas Gordon, *The English Libertarian Heritage*, ed. David L. Jacobson (Indianapolis, Bobbs-Merrill, 1965), pp. 91–2.

[5] See especially Pocock, *Virtue, Commerce and History*, pp. 215–310, for a recent overview of this development.

[6] On the beginnings of the split from the Whig side see Mark Goldie, 'The Origins of True Whiggism', *HPT*, 1 (1980), 195–234.

freeholders exercising financial and personal independence in the name of public virtue, the defenders of commerce juxtaposed the new, jurisprudentially inspired vision of a more diversified nation of relatively interdependent individuals chiefly pursuing their own interests, and construing political liberty less as participation than in terms of the preservation of essential civil rights. By the early decades of the eighteenth century, moreover, notions of classical political virtue were further eroded by the new ideology of 'politeness', which vindicated commercial society through the claim that the refined manners of the moderns were more civilised, less vicious and therefore more universally applicable than any classical modes of behaviour.

The revival of the parliamentary reform movement in the last third of the eighteenth century saw republican arguments concerning the national debt, parliamentary corruption, executive power and a standing army taken up with renewed vigour. In the process, moreover, varieties of radicalism emerged which were real departures from and innovations upon all earlier forms of republicanism. John Brewer has shown, for example, that an important contribution of the Wilkesite radicals in the 1760s was to widen the Country vocabulary in order to render it more useful to urban concerns, in particular by extending the notion of independence, cutting its direct association with landed property, and generalising it to all forms of ownership.[7] Many reformers in the 1770s and 1780s still preferred some form of tax-paying or property qualification for the franchise. But by the 1790s, and especially with the emergence of the London Corresponding Society and the publication of Paine's *Rights of Man*, the call for universal male suffrage first revived by Major John Cartwright in 1776 was widely diffused.

Republicanism also underwent other changes at this time. After the American revolution, radicals generally conceded that representative democracy allowed republican government to be extended to territories of any size, and the classical theory of universal, direct participation was now set aside by nearly all republicans. Another effect of the American revolution was to bring more widely into usage the positive connotations of the term 'democracy', associating it with popular sovereignty generally (a meaning which in Montesquieu, for example, had inhered in the term 'republic') rather than with the

[7] John Brewer, 'English Radicalism in the Age of George III', in J. G. A. Pocock, ed., *Three British Revolutions: 1641, 1688, 1776* (Princeton, Princeton University Press, 1980), p. 345. See also H. T. Dickinson, *Liberty and Property: Political Ideology in Eighteenth Century Britain* (Methuen, 1977), as well as Simon Maccoby, *English Radicalism 1762–1785* (George Allen and Unwin, 1955) and *English Radicalism 1786–1832* (George Allen and Unwin, 1955).

requirement of the common assembly of all citizens.[8] More than anything else, it was the representative model of democracy which ended
the appeal of the classical conception of the republic. For Paine, the
most important radical writer in the last third of the century, representation was preferable to simple democracy in all cases, even in small
states.[9] Given this development, as we will later see, socialism can be
understood as an attempt to revive the more classical conception. In
Paine and others, increasing circulation was also given to Lockean
conceptions of natural and civil rights, which John Dunn and others
have shown were far less influential in the first two-thirds of the
century than was previously thought.[10] Nonetheless there were also
tensions evident among republicans about the degree to which
government should be seen as a necessary evil or a positive good, with
the more Lockean writers following the former course, and the more
Aristotelian, the latter.

Economic crisis in the 1790s and increasing impoverishment also
provoked a reconsideration of the economic aspects of the parliamentary reformers' programme. Various attempts to revive more Platonic forms of republicanism, which emphasised community of goods
rather than merely a relative, Harringtonian equality of landed property, also emerged after 1750, first in the writings of Robert Wallace and
William Ogilvie,[11] and later in the land nationalisation schemes of
Thomas Spence and the strongly anti-commercial utopianism of William Godwin. With Godwin, in particular, the 1790s also witnessed the
revival of a type of Nonconformist enthusiasm which coalesced in a
variety of ways with republicanism but at the same time sought the
supersession of many of its political features. This confrontation and
relationship will be of central importance to this chapter as well as to
the general argument of the book. For these fusions of millennialism
and republicanism were in many respects the most immediate predecessors to the rise of socialism, and as such merit close scrutiny here.

---

[8] See R. R. Palmer, 'Notes on the Use of the Word "Democracy" 1789–1799', *PSQ*, 68
   (1953), 203–26, and Gaetano Salvemini, 'The Concepts of Democracy and Liberty in
   the Eighteenth Century', in Conyers Read, ed., *The Constitution Reconsidered* (New
   York, Columbia University Press, 1958), pp. 105–19.
[9] Thomas Paine, *The Complete Writings of Thomas Paine*, ed. Philip Foner (New York,
   Citadel Press, 1945), 1, p. 371.
[10] See John Dunn, 'The Politics of Locke in England and America in the Eighteenth
   Century', in *Political Obligations in Their Historical Context* (Cambridge, Cambridge
   University Press, 1980), pp. 53–77, J. G. A. Pocock, 'The Myth of John Locke and the
   Obsession with Liberalism', in *John Locke* (Los Angeles, William Andrews Clark
   Library, 1980), pp. 1–24, and on the late eighteenth century revival of Lockean ideas,
   Isaac Kramnick, 'Republican Revisionism Revisited', *APSR*, 87 (1982), 629–64.
[11] William Ogilvie, *An Essay on the Right of Property in Land* (1781), Robert Wallace, *Various
   Prospects of Mankind, Nature and Providence* (1761).

Millennial republicanism and puritan radicalism

The emergence of millennial republicanism has been associated in particular with the prominent Rational Dissenters Richard Price and Joseph Priestley – most recently studied by Jack Fruchtman – though there are some grounds for including Paine as well as Godwin in this category.[12] Puritan notions of religious independence had coincided with the language of republican virtue and self-sufficiency in a variety of writers of the Commonwealth period, of whom Winstanley was the most notable. But the degree of religious enthusiasm required to proclaim the imminent arrival of the millennium was not reunited with a fervent devotion to the cause of political virtue in the eighteenth century until two essential 'signs' – the American and French revolutions – revealed the apparent political inclinations of the Deity. (Thereafter, of course, millennialists were by no means always republicans: witness Joanna Southcott.[13]) Late seventeenth-century republicans, reacting to the excesses of the civil wars, had in fact specifically abandoned the Puritan vision of a future paradise, substituting instead 'a universalist religion of nature', as Margaret Jacob has described it.[14] We will see below that important elements of the Leveller and Digger emphasis upon equality and greater democracy were in fact preserved in some of the more radical sects, especially the Quakers, whose conception of politics was to prove profoundly important for the origins of socialism. Most Dissenters, however, were sympathetic to the main body of the Whigs throughout the first two-thirds of the eighteenth century, in London aligning themselves with the government much of the time up to the 1770s, though remaining more oppositional in the provinces.[15]

This outlook was by no means eliminated by the influence of Price and Priestley, who were probably far more radical than their own congregations as well as other Dissenters.[16] Their propensity to interpret the American and French revolutions in terms of Providential

---

[12] See Jack Fruchtman, Jr, *The Apocalyptic Politics of Richard Price and Joseph Priestley, A Study in Late Eighteenth Century English Republican Millennialism* (Philadelphia, American Philosophical Society, 1983), and 'The Revolutionary Millennialism of Thomas Paine', *SEC*, 13 (1984), 65–77. See also generally J. F. C. Harrison, *The Second Coming: Popular Millennarianism 1780–1850* (Routledge and Kegan Paul, 1979).

[13] James K. Hopkins, *A Woman to Deliver Her People. Joanna Southcott and English Millennarianism in an Era of Revolution* (Austin, University of Texas Press, 1982), pp. 181–2.

[14] Margaret Jacob, *The Radical Enlightenment: Pantheists, Freemasons and Republicans* (George Allen and Unwin, 1981), p. 69.

[15] See James E. Bradley, 'Whigs and Nonconformists. Slumbering Radicalism in English Politics, 1739–1789', *ECS*, 9 (1975), 1–27, and generally Michael Watts, *The Dissenters* (Oxford, Clarendon Press, 1978), pp. 464–90.

[16] See John Seed, 'Gentlemen Dissenters: the Social and Political Meanings of Rational Dissent in the 1770s and 1780s', *HJ*, 28 (1985), 299–325.

development, however, and their insistence that some form of millennium was a probable result of these events, was important to the later development of socialism for several reasons. Both Price and Priestley expected a cessation of war, for example, to be one of the most immediate consequences of the millennium, and they associated this with the victory of radical/righteous principles. Price, for example, anticipated the day 'when the nations of the earth, happy under just governments, and no longer in danger from the passions of kings, will find out better ways of settling their disputes, and beat (as Isaiah prophecies) *their swords into ploughshares, and their spears into pruning hooks*'.[17] Both in addition identified the course of Providential history with the progress of true morality. For Price, again, Providence was 'an invisible and mighty power which rules over the operations of natural causes, and presides over all events. This power is a *righteous* power, and it must be friendly to the *righteous*; and, therefore, will direct events for the advantage of the country where they reside'.[18] Political development and Christian virtue here thus exactly coincided.

Yet despite Price and Priestley's concurrence in electing God a True Whig, there were fundamental differences between them on other issues which exemplified wider disagreements within eighteenth-century Dissenting radicalism. This is especially the case with respect to their views on commerce.[19] Priestley expressed some republican reservations about the harmful effects of luxury upon public virtue, but accepted the conveniences of the modern system of commerce, even to the extent of stressing the manifest advantages of the division of labour.[20] Priestley insisted that interdependence was preferable to the republican ideal of self-sufficiency and independence, and that 'a state of more perfect society admits of a proper distribution and division of the objects of human attention'. In such a state, men were 'connected with and subservient to one another; so that, while one man confines himself to one single object, another may give the same undivided

---

[17] Richard Price, *A Discourse on the Love of Our Country* (3rd edn., 1790), pp. 29–30. Fruchtman nonetheless exaggerates Price's millenarianism by quoting him as saying 'we shall enjoy the transporting joy of soon becoming members of a perfect community' and leaving out the next three words: 'in the heavens'. See his otherwise useful 'Politics and the Apocalypse: the Republic and the Millennium in Late Eighteenth Century English Political Thought', *SEC*, 10 (1981), 161.

[18] Richard Price, *A Sermon Delivered at a Congregation of Protestant Dissenters at Hackney* (1779), p. 24. See Joseph Priestley, *An Essay on the First Principles of Government* (2nd edn., 1771), pp. 2–3.

[19] See my 'Virtuous Commerce and Free Theology: Political Economy and the Dissenting Academies in Britain, 1740–1800', in Istvan Hont and Keith Tribe, eds., *Trade, Politics and Letters: the Art of Political Economy in British University Culture, 1750–1910* (Routledge, forthcoming).

[20] Joseph Priestley, 'Lectures on History and General Policy', in *The Theological and Miscellaneous Works of Joseph Priestley*, Vol. 24 (1803), p. 239.

attention to another object. Thus the powers of all have their full effect; and hence arise improvements in all the conveniences of life, and in every branch of knowledge.' The full implications of this view we will see shortly.[21]

This concession of the virtues of specialisation probably coincided with the views of a large majority of Dissenters, who were involved in technical and commercial development in a degree vastly disproportionate to their numbers. But others, of whom Price was probably the best known at the time of the outbreak of the French revolution, urged that some restraints be placed upon commerce, and especially that the flow of population from country to town be reversed and the national debt ended.[22] Country attitudes were clearly fundamental to Price's opposition to large cities, which he associated with both the moral and physical decline of the population. '*Moderate* towns, being seats of refinement, emulation, and arts, may be public advantages', he reflected, 'but *great* towns, long before they grow to half the bulk of London, become checks on population of too hurtful a nature, nurseries of debauchery and voluptuousness; and, in many respects, greater evils than can be compensated by any advantages.' Such ideas would also be crucial, as we will see, to the origins of communitarian socialism.[23]

Despite this emphasis upon simplicity, in which both republican and Puritan roots were interwoven, Price still found little to admire in simple republicanism of the ancient type.[24] The precedent of ancient Rome, for example, was repudiated for reasons linked to Price's Christian ethics as well as, to a lesser degree, his millennial expectations. Despite its glorious history, the Roman republic had continuously threatened the liberties of the rest of the world. National selfishness was also embodied in the modern theory of patriotism, where the love of one's country, as Price described it in his famous sermon on the 1688 revolution, was only 'a love of domination; a desire of conquest, and a thirst for grandeur and glory, by extending territory, and enslaving surrounding countries'. What was required instead was the application of that 'UNIVERSAL BENEVOLENCE' commended by Christianity, and the realisation that, even if, as Price believed 'we can do little for the interest of mankind at large', nonetheless

[21] Joseph Priestley, *An Essay on the First Principles of Government*, p. 3.

[22] Whether Price can be termed a republican has been questioned, though his support for the monarchy does not necessarily imply he was not. See however D. O. Thomas, 'Neither Republican nor Democrat', *PPN*, 1 (1977), 52, 57.

[23] Richard Price, 'Observations on the Expectations of Lives, the Increase of Mankind, the Influence of Great Towns on Population, and Particularly the State of London, with Respect to Healthfulness and Numbers of Inhabitants', *RSPT*, 59 (1769), 118–19.

[24] Richard Price, *The Evidence for a Future State of Improvement in the State of Mankind* (1787), pp. 30–1.

a narrower interest ought always to give way to a more extensive interest. In pursuing particularly the interest of our country, we ought to carry our views beyond it. We should love it ardently, but not exclusively. We ought to seek its good . . . but at the same time we ought to consider ourselves as citizens of the world, and take care to maintain a just regard to the rights of other countries.[25]

Such a view can be characterised as midway between republican patriotism and the more all-encompassing cosmopolitanism which emerged in early British socialism.

This sense of conflict between the ethical demands of Christianity and a republican conception of public virtue exhibits some of the most important roots of the new approach to politics made by socialism. Prior to Owen a similar contradiction was investigated at length in William Godwin's *Enquiry Concerning Political Justice* (1793), with whose doctrines Owen was certainly familiar, since Godwin was amongst his more important early confidants.[26] Godwin's political thought represents an essential link in the development of a strand of Rational Dissent into socialism for one key reason: he extended these contradictions between Christian ethics and republicanism to their logical limits. Now not only monarchy and aristocracy, but also democracy and republicanism were virtually swept away by the rigorous demands of universal benevolence and puritan independence of belief. From the standpoint of human perfectibility, democracy, too, might be superseded by a superior form of polity. Godwin's moral critique of the republican tradition was a devastating attack upon radical ideals of public virtue and political independence. It was also an overt rejection of the model and practice of parliamentary reform as these had evolved in the last thirty years.

Godwin's critique of republicanism centred upon two points. With regard to the problem of how best to secure the public good, firstly, 'true virtue' or 'benevolence' was described as being vastly superior to any more limited notion of duty, and specifically to love of one's country, or lesser forms of attachment to locality, family, friends, benefactors and the like. Both private and public affections could not be allowed to intrude upon higher forms of duty. Secondly, in relation to the problem of the best form of government, Godwin accepted the delegation and representation of power in certain circumstances, but opposed the creation of permanent representative assemblies. These,

---

[25] Richard Price, *Additional Observations on the Nature and Value of Civil Liberty and the War with America* (1777), p. 24; Price, *A Discourse on the Love of Our Country*, pp. 5, 10.

[26] This was first uncovered by Frederick Rosen, and is discussed in his 'Progress and Democracy: William Godwin's Contribution to Political Philosophy', unpublished Ph.D. dissertation, University of London (1965), pp. 214, 287–90. Godwin and Owen met some 30 times in 1813, 8 times in 1814, 7 times in 1816, 5 times in 1817, 3 times in 1818, and less frequently thereafter.

he felt, tended to create a fictitious unanimity instead of allowing individuals to form their own private judgement on all issues of importance. Most importantly for the development of Owen's views, Godwin also rejected the requirement of voting after all discussions, seeing this 'flagrant insult upon all reason and justice' as destructive of the intellectual improvement which debate could alone aim at, and as a reduction of the complexity of deliberation to simplistic alternatives. Given the tumult inherent in all such proceedings, he saw no merit in any form of political association. The secret ballot, too, merely invited us 'to draw a veil of concealment' over the performance of our duty, making us ashamed of our integrity. If the ballot had to be used, only open voting was acceptable. It is important that Godwin did not advise unanimity in such proceedings, as had the Sandemanian Baptists among whom he had been raised, and as did the Quakers, whose influence upon Owenism we will shortly examine. But, unlike most republicans, he saw no need for two houses of assembly, or for any separation between executive and legislative powers. For he was convinced that in an ideal society the opposition of interests and sentiments would never take such permanent forms. With the progress of social improvement, moreover, executive powers would 'comparatively speaking, become everything, and legislative nothing'. Here we are beginning to approach, from the viewpoint of the perfectibility of reason, the notion that in the future 'politics' would give way to 'administration'.[27]

Godwin's aim was the creation of a small-scale, parish-based society in which, while intellectual independence was to be cultivated to the highest degree, moral *dependence*, 'a censure to be exercised by every individual over the actions of another, a promptness to enquire into and judge over them', was a justifiable means of ensuring sociable conduct. In restraining the behaviour of others, only 'the calling in of force as the corrective of error' was deemed unacceptable. In a decentralised society – the Dissenting sects were clearly Godwin's chief inspiration here – reason alone was capable of governing, while in large nations there was 'no eye penetrating enough to detect every mischief in its commencement'. In addition – and here classical republicanism was more important in Godwin's thought – the division of labour was to be extremely limited, with all probably participating in agriculture for some portion of the time. None of the chief trades and professions was sufficiently virtuous to receive Godwin's blessing, and the soldier least so of all. Only a personality which was relatively undifferentiated, in fact, could scale the greater heights of virtue,

[27] See my 'William Godwin's Critique of Democracy and Republicanism and Its Sources', *HEI*, 7 (1986), 253–69.

though Godwin would later withdraw from such an extreme formulation.[28]

Godwin's criticism of the dependency involved in many occupations without doubt partially extended the republican critique of the standing army. Yet we are also here as clearly enmeshed in a rather different, Nonconformist discourse, bounded by a very dissimilar set of assumptions about both society and the individual. Evaluating this component in Godwin's thought is not easy, however. Godwin never disguised the impact of Greece and Rome upon his youthful development, or his theoretical conversion to republicanism (while remaining 'in practice a Whig') in 1779–80. He was more circumspect, however, about the Dissenting components in his intellectual make up, and these are correspondingly harder for us to isolate. Nor, of course, is 'Dissent' any less complex a concatenation of beliefs, opinions and tendencies than republicanism, though in the historiography of late eighteenth-century political thought it has received far less attention and has been the subject of greater simplification. Nonetheless there is no doubt that the core of Godwin's system was the preservation of 'private judgement', construed particularly as intellectual independence, and that this was a secular statement of the central interests of the Dissenters, whose social and economic survival depended upon toleration, and whose self-proclaimed intellectual authority rested upon their own exercise of freedom of thought. That the social model of mutually observant moral censors also owed much to sects like the Sandemanians is easily conceded.

Yet in another respect Godwin's critique of modern republicanism can be read in terms of a revival of ancient republicanism, albeit in a form in which all aspects of politics were to be first tested against the Dissenting demand for resolute sincerity and intellectual independence. Despite Price's exhortations to 'promote agriculture – drive the inhabitants of towns back into the country', no other Dissenters entertained the kind of reversion to primitive institutions which *Political Justice* counselled (at least in the first edition), or opposed specialisation to such a degree, or were as fervently committed to the ideal of intellectual independence.[29] What generated these positions in Godwin's thought was indeed the blending of republican fervour with Dissenting enthusiasm. But what is central for us in this confluence of ideals is the displacement of what were seen as more limited republican aims – especially patriotism – by the apparently more universal

---

[28] *Ibid.*; William Godwin, *Enquiry Concerning Political Justice* (1793; rpt. of 1798 edn.), ed. Isaac Kramnick (Harmondsworth, Penguin Books, 1976), pp. 745, 644.
[29] Richard Price, *Observations on Reversionary Payments* (2nd edn., 1772), pp. 364–5.

moral system of Christianity. Here, once again, we are at the frontiers of socialism. But the longing for a simpler society, and one which corresponded in some respects to millennial ideals, was not inspired by republican and radical ideology alone. Rather, it coalesced with several strands of thought which at the end of the eighteenth century also enjoyed a revival of sorts, and which we can here link under the notion of 'natural society'.

Natural society

The influence of natural law writers on early socialism has never been examined, though Owen and others clearly indicated that they were acquainted with such sources.[30] Any understanding of this debt hinges upon an examination of the use of the word 'society' by the Owenites. Some elements of a semantic history of this type are given below. This section will review the development of jurisprudential accounts of original or primitive societies, touching as well upon the concern among seventeenth- and eighteenth-century natural law theorists with human sociability, which was often bound up with attempts to refute the Hobbist or 'selfish' theory of morals. As with republicanism, we will find that jurisprudential arguments overlapped and fused with millenarian assumptions in the formation of socialist thought.

The conceptions of society and sociability discussed in eighteenth-century natural jurisprudence chiefly originated in Stoic notions of the law of nature as the source and standard of morals. Here the *jus gentium* of Rome came to be understood in terms of a fundamental code valid for all mankind, which was thus superior to positive legislation. In Christian thought the laws of nature were transmuted into the laws of God, with the ideas of Paradise and the Fall of Man being easily transposed upon early accounts of an egalitarian Golden Age or natural state. There were a number of variations upon this process. In the Augustinian conception of society which held sway until Aquinas' revival of Aristotelianism in the thirteenth century, the notion of the natural sociability of mankind was partially supplanted by a dualist juxtaposition of the City of God, an ideal unity of Christian believers, to the *civitas diabolis*, where self-love predominated and in which such institutions as the state were requisite means of regulating sin. Here the state was conceived as being almost exclusively concerned with police, and true justice was never attainable.[31] Augustine

---

[30] For example, *NHG*, 1, no. 50 (6 September 1826), 398, where Owen discusses 'the writers on natural law' on 'right of occupancy'.

[31] St. Augustine, *The City of God* (Dent, 1942), pt 3, pp. 4, 36, 38, 46.

did accept that social life was to some extent inevitable, but denied Aristotle's notion that political activity was in the same sense 'natural'.[32] This Manichean dualism (though not necessarily in its Augustinian form) and its pejorative conception of political activity persisted as an undercurrent throughout the history of Christian political thought, and retained considerable significance for the origins of modern anarchism and socialism alike. To some extent, in fact, this distinction underlies most later millennial conceptions of the abolition or supersession of 'politics'.

The idea of an original, primitive society remained central in the modern and early modern natural law tradition, playing a particularly important role in its theory of property. From about the sixteenth century onwards, an increasing concern with the sources of political legitimacy led to a number of attempts to trace the origins of political society from an imagined state of nature. In Mariana's influential *De Rege et Regis Institutione* (1599), typically, the state of nature was understood as having been without social organisation, positive law, ambition, warfare or private property. Nonetheless increasing wants, as well as the desire of preventing the stronger from preying on the weaker (for this was a postlapsarian rather than pre-Adamic theory), led to the foundations of political society through the choice of leaders.[33]

Most natural law writers did not see pre-political society as a condition of great conflict, but insisted instead on the bonds which brought individuals to co-operate peaceably. A number of influential seventeenth-century accounts stressed that the basis of natural society was what Grotius (in reference to Seneca) termed 'an impelling desire for society peculiar to the nature of man', which prevented human actions from being governed by the pursuit of self-interest alone. For Samuel Pufendorf, a leading authority for eighteenth-century British moral philosophers, the natural state of mankind, *pace* Hobbes, 'was one of peace rather than war', in which a simple system of kinship without common masters or social institutions had prevailed. Society or 'community' (the terms are here synonymous), rather than the state of nature, was the natural condition of mankind, and was characterised by the rule of reason rather than passion and by widespread

---

[32] See Herbert Deane, *The Political and Social Ideas of St. Augustine* (New York, Columbia University Press, 1963), pp. 116–53, and R. A. Markus, *Saeculum. History and Society in the Theology of St. Augustine* (Cambridge, Cambridge University Press, 1970), pp. 95–7. One of the best modern accounts of this split is Dolf Sternberger, *Drei Wurzeln der Politik* (Frankfurt, Insel Verlag, 1978), pp. 309–41.

[33] Quentin Skinner, *The Foundations of Modern Political Thought* (Cambridge, Cambridge University Press, 1978), 2, pp. 155–9; John Laures, *The Political Economy of Juan de Mariana* (New York, Fordham University Press, 1928), pp. 27–30.

tranquillity, security, opulence and knowledge. For Pufendorf, more-over, the principle of *socialitas* or natural sociability was elevated to become the first principle of natural law. The obligation to create a social life was therefore not only equally binding upon all men. Socia-bility also underlay the ability to enjoy the good things of life, thus rendering the satisfaction of one's own needs and happiness depen-dent upon that of others.[34] This point was to be central to the moral philosophy of Owenism. In another important characterisation of early society, John Locke's *Second Treatise of Government* (1690), the state of nature was portrayed as a condition of perfect freedom and equality where men were governed by the law of nature, reason. But as a result of various inconveniences, a social compact was formed which surrendered natural freedom in favour of an elective monarchy. This government sufficed through a period which Locke termed the 'Golden Age', until vanity, ambition and corruption degraded the true offices of government and invited the institution of absolute monarchy.[35]

From the early sixteenth century onwards, theories of natural so-ciety were also more widely circulated and lent a more optimistic form by the utopian writers, some of whom also sought to revive Platonic republicanism. More's *Utopia* (1516), whose starting point was the need to provide for the poor, projected a republican society whose chief magistrates were elected annually (the Prince, for life). Here the inhabitants engaged both in agriculture and some trade, rotation of the population between city and country being regarded as normal, and every family was governed by its eldest member, the younger always serving the older and the latter supervising the behaviour of the younger. This process was facilitated by the institution of common meals and the generally public nature of Utopian life.[36] Possessing only simple laws known to all, the Utopians also abolished lawyers, and a general restriction of this profession, as well as those of judges and physicians, occurred in many seventeenth-century utopias as well, for example in the utopian fragment in Burton's *Anatomy of Melancholy*

---

[34] Hugo Grotius, *De Jure Belli ac Pacis* (1625; rpt. Oxford, Clarendon Press, 1925), p. 11; Samuel Pufendorf, *De Jure Naturae et Gentium* (1672; rpt. Oxford, Clarendon Press, 1934), pp. 169, 207–8, 333; S. Pufendorf, *The Whole Duty of Man According to the Law of Nature* (5th edn., 1725), pp. 98, 192.

[35] John Locke, *Two Treatises of Government*, ed. Peter Laslett (2nd edn., Cambridge, Cambridge University Press, 1970), pp. 287, 356–60. See also Hans Aarsleff, 'The State of Nature and the Nature of Man in Locke', in John W. Yolton, ed., *John Locke: Problems and Perspectives* (Cambridge, Cambridge University Press, 1969), pp. 99–136.

[36] Thomas More, 'Utopia', in Henry Morley, ed., *Ideal Commonwealths* (1888), pp. 61–2, 90, 94–8, 103–8.

(1621), and in Francis Godwin's *Man in the Moone* (1638).[37] The restriction or elimination of 'unsociable' and 'unproductive' professions would also be central to socialism.

An emphasis upon the natural duty of sociability and man's social nature remained central to eighteenth-century natural jurisprudence, passing early in the century into the moral philosophy of the Scottish enlightenment, from Gershom Carmichael through Francis Hutcheson, holder of the first chair of moral philosophy at the University of Glasgow. Most jurisprudential writers of this period (for example Vattel) stressed that the passage from natural to civil society had resulted from a voluntary, mutual compact which had been aimed at advancing and perfecting mankind.[38] Concerned to refute Hobbes, many British natural law writers also gave special attention to the importance of benevolence to morality, and its roots in natural sociability. For Shaftesbury, probably the most important theorist of 'benevolence', the 'Sense of Fellowship' was as natural as any other appetite, as was its expression as an affection for the good of the species as a whole, though others doubted that the love of all could be sustained for very long.[39] For Richard Cumberland, whose views also circulated widely in the eighteenth century, the whole of the laws of nature could be 'reduced to that one, of Benevolence towards all Rationals', with the 'greatest happiness of our Mind' consisting in 'the Exercise and inward sense of Universal Benevolence'.[40] From such views of sociability emerged the common sense theory upon which much Scottish moral philosophy was based.

For our purposes the most important eighteenth-century discussion of sociability was in Bolingbroke. Here we encounter a clear distinction between 'natural society' and 'political society', with authority in the former being represented by paternal rule over families, whose needs led them gradually to unite and eventually to elect a monarch. Bolingbroke denied both Hobbes' account of a violent state of nature and Locke's conception of a state of perfect freedom and equality as overly individualistic, stressing instead the naturalness of paternal govern-

---

[37] *Ibid.*, p. 135; Robert Burton, 'An Utopia of Mine Own', in Glenn Negley and J. Max Patrick, eds., *The Quest for Utopia* (College Park, McGrath Publishing Co., 1971), p. 354; Francis Godwin, 'The Man in the Moone', ed. Grant McColley, in *Smith College Studies in Modern Languages* (Northampton, 1937–38), p. 41.

[38] Emmerich de Vattel, *The Law of Nations or the Principles of Natural Law* (1758; rpt. Washington DC, Carnegie Institute, 1916), 3, p. 6.

[39] Anthony Ashley Cooper, Third Earl of Shaftesbury, *Characteristics of Men, Manners, Opinions, Times* (1711), 1, pp. 110–11, 2, p. 78. On the origins of the common sense philosophy see D. D. Raphael, *The Moral Sense* (Oxford, Oxford University Press, 1947), S. A. Grave, *The Scottish Philosophy of Common Sense* (Oxford, Clarendon Press, 1960) and N. Waszek, *Man's Social Nature* (Bern, Peter Lang, 1986).

[40] Richard Cumberland, *A Treatise of the Laws of Nature* (1727), pp. 1, 5.

ment and its relative equality, and comparing these with the condition
of contemporary American Indians. Bolingbroke thus portrayed the
original social condition of mankind as in several respects vastly superior to the 'artificial' or 'political' society which later followed, and
which had been 'little less than a state of perpetual anarchy', war and
misery by comparison. In Bolingbroke, usually regarded as a tory, we
thus find an important justification for the naturalness of paternal
government which, while opposed to Filmer's absolutist patriarchalism, served as a precedent for later vindications of this type.[41] In this
regard we must again stress the extent to which socialism from its
origins would insist upon the paternal duties of governments towards
the poor. So, too, it invoked the memory of a society, regarded as only
recently lost, in which landowners and masters, without being identified with any particular party, took such responsibilities seriously and
did not abandon their servants and labourers to the vaguaries of the
market.[42] The imagery of 'natural society' could in this sense be
adapted to conservative as well as radical uses, or to both combined, as
it would later in 'tory radicalism', with which Owen can be connected
to some degree.

The idea of sociability was thus often linked to a half-remembered
past as well as a general ideal of moral capacity. In the language of
'sensibility', 'sentiment' and 'feeling', it was also to predominate in
eighteenth-century literature and poetry, and in romanticism often to
praise the advantages of country life and the rural virtues over commerce and the cities. By the mid-eighteenth century, 'benevolence' –
the practice of which was regarded as certain evidence of sociability –
was conceived of as a sense as well as in terms of the exercise of the
rational faculty. Nor were such concerns unique to British moral philosophy. It was at about this time on the continent that the emergence
of the term 'socialist' took place, first in Latin and then in Italian, to
denote that current of jurisprudence stemming from Pufendorf and
Cumberland and grounding natural law upon the social instincts.[43]
The first known English use of the term would not be for some eighty

---

[41] Henry St. John, Viscount Bolingbroke, *Works* (5 vols., 1754), 5, pp. 105–58, here 137.
     On Bolingbroke see in particular Isaac Kramnick, *Bolingbroke and His Circle* (Cam-
     bridge, MA, Harvard University Press, 1968). See generally Gordon J. Schochet,
     Patriarchalism in Political Thought (Oxford, Basil Blackwell, 1975), and on eighteenth
     century Toryism, Linda Colley, *In Defiance of Oligarchy. The Tory Party 1714–60* (Cam-
     bridge, Cambridge University Press, 1982), especially pp. 85–117.
[42] This is not thus to argue that 'paternalism' could have been solely a tory attitude. See
     Linda Colley, 'Eighteenth Century English Radicalism Before Wilkes', *TRHS*, 31
     (1981), 1–19.
[43] Hans Müller, *Ursprung und Geschichte des Wortes Sozialismus und seiner Verwandten*
     (Hannover, Verlag J. H. W. Dietz, 1967), pp. 25–46.

years, but of its derivation from similar sources, as we will see, there can be little doubt.

Through Bolingbroke and other authors, aided by the influence of Rousseau in England, as well as by Burke's *Vindication of Natural Society* (1756, evidently a satire on Bolingbroke), the notion of an idyllic, prepolitical state of nature thus became an important element in the landscape of eighteenth-century British social and political thought. Nonetheless its popularity had receded considerably by the end of the century. Many writers turned against earlier uses of the conception, with Hume, Bentham and others denying the historical possibility of any social contract, and much Scottish conjectural history following the jurisprudential account in asserting that progress from the more primitive stages was natural and necessary, the result especially of population growth rather than a deliberate decision to form a political society.[44] One effect of the Scottish search for the various lineages from barbarism to politeness was a greater emphasis upon the crudity and violence of the primitive state.[45] Some Scottish writers, it is true, did acknowledge the priority of 'a certain delight in their kind, congenial with all nature' (as James Dunbar put it) over the mere satisfaction of wants in the foundation and continuation of society.[46] Still others honoured the pride, independence and courage of many early peoples, as did Gilbert Stuart's account of the equality of the Germanic tribes and their successes in defeating the Romans.[47] But most Scots followed Hume in extolling the superiority of modern refinement over the primitive as well as ancient virtues, and found in the diffusion of politeness throughout commercial society an adequate substitute for the civic virtues of classical republicanism.[48]

Yet the arrival of commercial society hardly met with universal applause. In at least a few prominent cases, the product of the millennial upsurge of the sixteenth and seventeenth centuries, a deliberate return to a condition of primitive purity was sought, often conceived of in terms of apostolic simplicity. Such an attempt was made by the

[44] On this transformation see especially Istvan Hont, 'From Pufendorf to Adam Smith: Sociability, Commercial Society and the Four Stages Theory', in Anthony Pagden, ed., *The Languages of Political Theory in Early-Modern Europe* (Cambridge, Cambridge University Press, 1987, pp. 253–76). On the impact of Rousseau's 'primitivism' see Richard Sewall, 'Rousseau's Second Discourse in England from 1755 to 1762', *PQ*, 17 (1938), 97–114, and H. V. S. Ogden, 'The State of Nature and the Decline of Lockean Political Theory in England, 1760–1800', *AHR*, 46 (1940–41), 21–44.
[45] For example, Hugh Murray, *Enquiries Historical and Moral, Respecting the Character of Nations and the Progress of Society* (Edinburgh, 1808), p. 169.
[46] James Dunbar, *Essay on the History of Mankind in Rude and Cultivated Ages* (2nd edn., 1781), pp. 6–7.
[47] Gilbert Stuart, *A View of Society in Europe, in Its Progress from Rudeness to Refinement* (2nd edn., Edinburgh, 1792), p. 2.
[48] David Hume, *Essays, Moral, Political and Literary* (Grant Richards, 1903), pp. 275–89.

sixteenth century Anabaptists, who helped to revive and strengthen an Augustinian dualism (as had a variety of heretics before them), sharpening the distinction between the true church of Christ and the *civitas diaboli* to such a degree that they renounced as anti-Christian not only arms and the taking of life, but all participation in government, insofar as these were amongst its functions.[49] One of the most direct spiritual descendants of the Anabaptists in England were the Quakers, who even in their later quietism helped to carry forward crucial elements of the religious radicalism of the English Revolution. In mid seventeenth-century England, reversion to apostolic community was also sought by the Digger Gerrard Winstanley, whose views approximated those of the Quakers in many respects. For Winstanley, the coming of the millennium would bring universal justice in the form of a true magistracy, the ending of war and the abolition of soldiers, priests, lawyers, and of buying and selling. Here government was not to be abolished, but rather replaced by a magistracy of true righteousness, whose will would be diffused through the force of universal love. Controversies were to be settled through neighbourhood boards of arbitration instead of by professional lawyers. Important officers were to be elected annually, and something like a principle of natural or traditional authority would be reinstated. Every man above the age of sixty was therefore to be granted 'respect as a man of honour by all others that are younger', and all citizens would become exempt from labour after the age of forty, with officials being chosen from those aged between 40 and 80.[50] These proposals were similar in several important respects to those later put forward by Owen.

Two natural polities: Quakerism and the North American Indians

For those socialists who wished to model the future upon some conception of natural society, and above all for Owen himself, the problem of how authority was to be exercised could be resolved in several ways. The complete relinquishment of all authority was never to be seriously proposed. Antinomian tendencies, in fact, clearly had to be resisted, as it was well known that a number of Nonconformist sects had sunk under the burden of extreme individualism. Nor was theocracy, or its usual puritan form of the rule of the Saints, an acceptable alternative for an essentially secular movement, though

[49] See for example Hans Hillerbrand, 'The Anabaptist View of the State', *MHQ*, 32 (1958), 83–110, George Hurston Williams, *The Radical Reformation* (Philadelphia, Westminster Press, 1962), p. 355.

[50] *The Works of Gerrard Winstanley*, ed. George Sabine (New York, Russell & Russell, 1965), pp. 391, 467, 472, 512, 538–41, 638.

Owen would search widely for the best men of all sects and classes to help introduce the new world. By the early decades of the nineteenth century two precedents or variants upon the idea of natural society were more widely applauded. The first of these was drawn from the experience of Puritanism in the English Revolution and subsequently, and especially the most radical modes of sectarian government, the only important surviving example of which was the Quakers. The second was rooted in natural law, and was inspired to some degree by the government of some North American Indians. Each of these examples provided some insight into the possibility of creating a non-coercive society, though neither, as we will see, corresponded exactly with the aims of socialism.

That the Quakers should have excited Owen's admiration is not surprising. After an early, more confrontational period which lasted several decades into the Restoration, the Society of Friends had prospered greatly by their honest dealing and tendency to trade with one another, until in some quarters they became associated with a somewhat un-Christian devotion to wealth (Cobbett, who with relative equanimity was intolerant of most minorities, was fond of likening them to the Jews). By the early nineteenth century the Quakers' affluence and growing political quietism led some of their admirers to believe that, as John Bone (a convert from radicalism to Owen's views) put it, they could 'no longer be trusted' to hold to their original ideals, and to serve as a beacon of pure, moral radicalism. Nonetheless their opposition to violence, their refusal to swear oaths, their egalitarian 'Thou', their simple manners and clothes, their wearing of hats even in the presence of magistrates, the rejection of the payment of tythes and, by the late eighteenth century, their fervent opposition to slavery, ensured the Quakers a secure reputation as the most principled and morally rigorous of all the Dissenters. As a consequence they were also sometimes found enlisted among the moderns in the conflict between ancient virtue and Augustan politeness. The Scottish historian James Dunbar, for example, noted that the Pennsylvania Quakers' freeing of their slaves demonstrated 'a degree of pure and disinterested virtue in that people, beyond the example of the most virtuous communities of antient times'. Republican Dissenters like James Burgh also found much to admire in their industry and frugality.[51] Robert Owen, despite conflicts with his rather conservative Quaker partner at New Lanark,

[51] *AC*, no. 4 (4 April 1818), 62; James Dunbar, *Essays on the History of Mankind*, p. 411; James Burgh, *Political Disquisitions* 3 (1774), p. 201. On the origins of Quakerism see Hugh Barbour, *The Quakers in Puritan England* (New Haven, Yale University Press, 1964), and on its development, Rufus M. Jones, *The Later Periods of Quakerism* (Macmillan, 1921), and Frederick B. Tolles, *Quakers and the Atlantic Culture* (Macmillan, 1960).

William Allen, stated on a variety of occasions his profound admiration for Quaker charity and customs, and claimed that: 'No sect has ever done so much in attempting to introduce and maintain ... superior qualities and virtues in single families trained on the old notions'. He may even have contemplated formally joining them at some point prior to 1790, and without doubt respected their behaviour more than that of any other Dissenters, though departing from their theology when he became a deist sometime before 1800. The Quakers themselves reciprocated by their considerable, though unofficial, support for his plans, especially in the early years.[52]

As a consequence of his admiration of the Quakers, Owen was to attempt to adapt elements of Quaker internal government to socialist uses. In 1833, for example, he proposed that the aspiring general trades' association, the Grand National Consolidated Trades' Union, renounce 'all the paraphernalia and folly of law' by introducing tribunals of three persons 'selected for their superior knowledge and experience in the new principles', explicitly citing the Quakers as a precedent. This was apparently based more upon his observations of how Quaker organisation worked than upon any theoretical platform. As Barry Reay has recently reiterated, the Quakers in fact did not have a coherent political philosophy based upon theology or a specific set of texts. Unlike the Anabaptists, whose dualism was more extreme and foreshadowed modern anarchism, they certainly did not reject the state entirely. Nor did they believe that no disciple of Christ could participate in the state, accepting instead the possibility of Christian magistracy. They did conceive, however, that 'there would be no *Sect* in *Christendom*, nor in the world', as their early leader George Fox put it, once all had 'come to the truth in the Inward of Parts, to the Spirit of God within'. Once all were 'partakers of the divine nature', in the late seventeenth-century Quaker Robert Barclay's words, all became, as Saints, unified within Christ, 'born again, not of corruptible seed, but of incorruptibility, by the word of God'. Several aspects of Quaker self-government were attractive to socialists, though none apparently considered accepting the whole model. Obviously admirable was the general demeanor of equality, based upon the notion that the light of God shone equally in all hearts, which gave the Friends the reputation of being the most 'republican' of the Dissenting sects, and extended

---

[52] *NMW*, 11, no. 52 (24 June 1843), 430. For an instance of Quaker support for Owen, see the *Sun*, no. 9651 (30 July 1823), 2. On Owen's views of the Quakers see my 'From "Politeness" to Rational Character: the Critique of Culture in Owenite Socialism, 1800–1850', in: Lex Heerma van Voss and Frits van Holthoon, eds., *Working Class and Popular Culture* (Amsterdam, Stichting Beheer IISG, 1988), pp. 19–32.

even to relations between Quaker employers and employed.[53] In addition, the system of mutual moral observation, intended (as Thomas Clarkson, the chief interpreter of Quaker views in the early nineteenth century, put it) 'to be administered with tenderness and patience', was obviously central to any attempt to render 'government' informal.[54] In their own internal disciplinary proceedings, moreover, the Friends purportedly recognised no distinction between poor and rich, righteousness being their only concern. Decisions on censure were not taken by a majority, this having been rejected by George Fox, but instead by 'the apparent will of the virtuous, who might be present': the aim being, as Fox put it, to have 'no strife, no contention'. The heaviest penalty meetings could apply was expulsion from the sect, but prior to this offending parties were visited by 'overseers' (two or more men or women) appointed to observe the congregation and admonish any delinquencies therein. Even when 'disowned', moreover, ex-Quakers could appeal to quarterly and annual meetings of the sect.[55]

The conduct of Friends' meetings was also of some interest to outsiders. After discussing a particular issue, a decision was taken by general consensus. No voting or counting of opinions was permitted, no protest was entered into the record, no majority or minority recognised, much less the leadership of partisan groups (though there were factional splits on occasion). Minor opposition often resulted in the postponement of measures until consensus emerged, the general aim being the settlement of all issues in a spirit of brotherly love, as 'Friends'. Even the annual, national meetings had no visible head, 'Christ only being their president', as William Penn expressed it. Nor did the Elders of the Church, whose duty it was to oversee ministers, have other than hortatory powers, all issues of discipline relative to the Church government being settled by the yearly meeting or even the Church as a whole. Serious differences between individual Quakers were not supposed to be resolved by lawsuits, but were rather given over to arbitration 'by persons of exemplary character within the So-

---

[53] Owen, *Address of Robert Owen, at the National Equitable Labour Exchange* (1833); Barry Reay, *The Quakers and the English Revolution* (Temple Smith, 1985), pp. 40–1; George Fox, *An Epistle to All Professors* (1673), p. 11; Robert Barclay, *A Catechism and Confession of Faith* (13th edn., 1803), pp. 112–14. The origins of the Quaker view of politics has been explored in W. A. Cole, 'The Quakers and Politics, 1652–1660' (Unpublished Ph.D. dissertation, University of Cambridge, 1955). On Quaker business relations see Arthur Raistrick, *Quakers in Science and Industry* (New York, Philosophical Library, 1950), pp. 335–6.

[54] Thomas Clarkson, *A Portraiture of Quakerism* (3 vols., 1806), 1, p. 181.

[55] *Ibid.*, pp. 183, 190–5; Joseph Randall, *A Brief Account of the Quakers* (Dublin, 1786), pp. 20–1. An astute if hostile account of Quaker political practices is given in John Bunzel, *Anti-Politics in America* (New York, Alfred Knopf, 1967), pp. 130–89.

ciety'. Since none of their ministers were permanent, the Quakers could thus claim with some pride that they had dispensed with the professions of soldier (having adopted pacifism in 1661), priest, lawyer and fixed magistrate.[56] A similar ideal was to form a major component in the Owenite theory of independence after about 1820.

Beside the usual Quaker practice of government, Owen was familiar with two variations upon it, the first found in the writings of the late seventeenth century Friend John Bellers, and the second in the practices of the Shaking Quakers or Shakers. Bellers' *Proposals for Raising a College of Industry* (1696) inspired Owen chiefly insofar as it proposed to solve the problem of poverty through communitarian organisation and the application of a labour standard of value. But Bellers also recommended a partial system of government by age, with all labourers becoming overseers at the age of sixty, if not sooner, through merit.[57] And in this regard we should recall that gerontocracy was the net result of Quaker practice generally, and was probably more pronounced here than in other Dissenting sects, where Elders also wielded great influence. By the early Victorian period, in fact, this had become a cause of frequent complaint about the annual Quaker meeting.[58]

This was not, however, a problem in the North American Shaker communities, one of which Owen visited on his first trip to the United States in 1824. He was quite disappointed, however, with the passive type of character resulting from it. For while the Shakers too opposed the use of elections within the Church, their organisation was considerably more rigid and hierarchical. A ministry of four leaders held absolute power in each community, governed in turn by the leading Elder at the Mount Lebanon community, who retained complete power over the entire society, which had about 5000 members in the early nineteenth century. Like the main body of Quakers, the Shakers also insisted upon harmony, unity and the prevalence of the spirit of Christ in their meetings and throughout their society, seeking divine approbation for their decisions (though in practice often choosing

---

[56] George Fox, *The Journal of George Fox* (Dent, 1948), p. 169; Thomas Clarkson, *A Portraiture of Quakerism*, pp. 241–2, 270–5, 79–88; William Penn, *The Peace of Europe, the Fruits of Solitude, and Other Writings* (Dent, n.d.), p. 201. The well-known republican Algernon Sidney was a close friend of Penn's (the latter acted as his election agent at one point) and identified with the Quakers to some extent. See Blair Worden, 'The Commonwealth Kidney of Algernon Sidney', *JBS*, 24 (1985), 25–6. The origins of Quaker opposition to voting seem to have been with the Seekers. See Rufus M. Jones, *Mysticism and Democracy in the English Commonwealth* (Cambridge, MA, Harvard University Press, 1932), p. 56.

[57] John Bellers, 'Proposals for Raising a College of Industry', in A. Ruth Fry, ed., *John Bellers 1654–1725* (Cassell, 1935), p. 46.

[58] Elizabeth Isichei, *Victorian Quakers* (Oxford, Oxford University Press, 1970), p. 81.

leaders by common consent). But more than among the Friends, it was a government of saints which underlay Shaker practice. Orders and advice were extended from the more to the less perfect through a hierarchy of ministers (who did not live or eat with the others), Elders, and deacons or trustees, the basic 'family' unit being a group of six actual families presided over by two Elders and two Eldresses.[59]

A second practical model of a form of natural society was provided by the North American Indians. That Owen should have been interested in their government is again unsurprising. They were commonly discussed in eighteenth century philosophical or conjectural history as a typical example of social life in the hunting and gathering stages of development.[60] Following Locke, moral philosophers such as William Paley also contended that the point at which civil government had originated resembled the stage reached by the Indians.[61] James Burgh agreed that the Indians exemplified the most natural and simple form of government, where all assembled to deliberate, though he argued that this was compatible only with small dominions, with representation necessary in large states.[62] In this sense the Indians were, to a degree, living proof of many of the virtues of the ancient republicans.

There were also important connections between the Indian and the Quaker (and in America, the Moravian) ideals of character. The most important Quaker experiment in government, in Pennsylvania, had brought Friends and Indians together over a long period of time, and the Quakers – who emphasised the need to lead a 'natural' life – were pleased that the Indians seemed to accept quickly their central doctrine of the 'Inner Light', which seemed to correspond to their own primitive spirituality.[63] Many Indian traits were also considered admirable because of their correspondence to radical puritan ideals. The Delaware and Iroquois, for example, were praised for lacking any conception of rank, all being 'equally noble and free', for uniting their tribes 'neither by force nor compact, yet they consider themselves as one

---

[59] Henri Desroche, *The American Shakers. From Neo-Christianity to Presocialism* (Amherst, University of Massachusetts Press, 1971), pp. 211–19; Edward Denning Andrews, *The People Called Shakers* (New York, Dover Books, 1963), pp. 99, 55, 237, 254–7.

[60] For example, John Dalrymple, *An Essay Towards a General History of Feudal Property in Great Britain* (1758), pp. 90–3.

[61] William Paley, *Principles of Moral and Political Philosophy* (7th edn., 1790), 2, p. 116. One of the main arguments against Locke's view that the Indians should be seen as paradigmatic for social developments was by Josiah Tucker. See *Josiah Tucker. A Selection from His Political and Economic Writings*, ed. R. Schulyer (New York, Columbia University Press, 1931), pp. 497–509.

[62] James Burgh, *Political Disquisitions*, 1, p. 5.

[63] See Rayner Kelsey, 'American Indians and the Inner Light', *BFHS*, 8 (1918), 54–6, and Frederick Tolles, 'Nonviolent Contact: the Quakers and the Indians', *PAPS*, 107 (1964), 93–101.

nation, of which they have an exalted ideal', and for governing themselves without a 'regular political constitution . . . magistracy, law or
restraint. This they call liberty, and there is nothing which they value
more'. Chiefs, instead, who were only the most respected amongst
equals, were both empowered and obliged to keep good order and
settle all disputes, but had no right 'to command, compel, or punish
any one . . . The chief must endeavour to rule over his people merely by
calm reasoning and friendly exhortations'.[64] Another well-known contemporary account stressed that these tribes were 'remarkable for the
particular stress which they pay to old age', no other nation in the
world being comparable in this respect.[65] For those seeking such paral-
lels, these were prototypical puritans as well as republicans.

Owen no doubt was exposed in his youth to the ideal of the noble
savage and the specific virtues of primitive peoples.[66] Almost certainly
he would have associated the Stoic notion of the rule of the wise in the
Golden Age (Seneca was amongst his favourite authors) with actual
tribal organisation.[67] Even if, by the time of his own American experiments, he had ceased to equate innocence with virtue, there remained
some lingering respect for a variety of Indian achievements. Soon after
arriving on his first visit to America, Owen met a group of Chocktaw
and Chicksaw chiefs in Washington. He assured them that his own
race 'had learned to admire many points of their character', and that, as
his son William Owen related, 'he thought the Indians were superior
to the whites in many respects, in sincerity, friendship, and honest
dealings, tho' the whites certainly possessed many advantages over
them'. Ideally, therefore, 'all persons might be trained to whatever is
good both in the Indian and the European characters, and to be
without all that is bad in them'.[68] During this visit Robert Dale Owen
recorded in his diary of the Indians he had seen that 'I believe the evils
of the savage and of the civilised state are nearly balanced – They have
many excellent qualities, which we most irrationally neglect to culti-

---

[64] George Henry Loskiel, *History of the Mission of the United Brethren among the Indians in
North America* (1794), pp. 14–17, 130–2. The best modern analysis of, and indeed
defence of, these practices, is Pierre Clastres, *Society Against the State* (New York,
Urizen Books, 1977). There are also useful discussions in William MacLeod, *The
Origins and History of Politics* (John Wiley, 1931), pp. 23–40, and Stanley Diamond, 'The
Rule of Law and the Order of Custom', *Soc. Res.*, 51 (1984), 387–418.

[65] John Heckewelder, 'An Account of the History, Manners, and Customs, of the Indian
Nations, Who Once Inhabited Pennsylvania and the Neighbouring States', *THLC*
(Philadelphia, 1819), pp. 89, 152–5.

[66] Still useful on this matter is Hoxie N. Fairchild, *The Noble Savage. A Study in Romantic
Naturalism* (New York, Columbia University Press, 1928).

[67] Seneca, *Letters from a Stoic* (Harmondsworth, Penguin Books, 1969), pp. 162–3.

[68] 'The Diaries of Donald Macdonald 1824–1826', *PIHS*, 14 (1942), 217; Joel Hiatt, ed.,
Diary of William Owen, from Nov. 10, 1824, to April 20, 1825 (Clifton, Augustus M.
Kelley, 1973), p. 43.

vate, but they fail to attain much of which we are in possession', which was clearly his father's view.[69] The latter planned in fact to include both Indians and blacks in his communities, and actually brought an Indian back with him to London from this particular trip, whom, reported William Hazlitt, 'he carries about in great triumph and complacency'. Precisely how Owen felt that this would help garner support for his views is unclear.[70] But he had earlier praised 'the superior American native tribes' for their 'hardy, penetrating, elevated and sincere character, which was at a loss to comprehend how a rational being could desire to possess more than his nature could enjoy'. A decade later, too, he explained that the distribution of wealth had been 'the most justly effected by the North American Indians, before their characters were deteriorated by the white men and their superstitions'.[71]

Owen did not fail to find much to admire in the ancients, as well, claiming on one occasion that the highest virtue and happiness 'appears to have been the best known and practised by the Greeks, who exercised their physical and mental powers more equally than any other nation of antiquity whose records we possess', an example followed by 'the Romans, during the best days of their republic'. But it is clear that two other models linked to 'natural society', one connected more specifically to primitive Christianity in its revived, Quaker form, the other to primitive society generally, served primarily to inspire him respecting the moral character of the future.[72] However, the full implications of the use of these various ideals can only be clarified if we consider the socialist engagement with the problem of specialisation and the division of labour, where the reconceptualisation of the problem of the ideal, unified personality drew upon republican and Christian as well as primitivist sources.

Independence, specialisation and rational character

Although seventeenth century republican discussions of specialisation typically centred (in Harrington, for example) upon the

[69] Josephine M. Elliott, ed., *To Holland and New Harmony and Back. Robert Dale Owen's Travel Journal 1825–1826* (Indianapolis, Indiana State Historical Society, 1969), pp. 251–2.
[70] Owen to William Allen, 21 April 1825, National Library of Wales MS. 14352C; William Hazlitt, *The Spirit of the Age* (1825; rpt. Oxford, Oxford University Press, 1966), p. 15. According to Lloyd Jones, Owen also sought to get some Indians to settle with him in his ill-fated Mexican colonisation scheme (*Robert Owen*, p. 238).
[71] Owen, *NVS*, p. 71; Owen, *The Book of the New Moral World*, pt 5 (1844), p. 25.
[72] Owen, *The Book of the New Moral World*, pt 1 (1836), pp. 54–5. Other writers (such as Lafitau, writing in 1724) also linked the ancient Greeks and Romans with the Indians. See Peter Stein, *Legal Evolution* (Cambridge, Cambridge University Press, 1980), pp. 17–18.

dangers inherent in separating citizen from soldier, eighteenth century analyses ranged more widely.[73] Especially with Fletcher of Saltoun, the Scottish debate began as a restatement of republican themes in relation to the militia issue. But as the advent of commercial society was more generally discussed, it became evident that the greater specialisation which the widening of the market introduced posed an even larger threat to public spiritedness.[74] At stake, therefore, was no longer merely the question of a professional army becoming an engine of monarchical tyranny, but the existence of public virtue itself in a society where most energies were channelled into the acquisition of wealth. A love of country and devotion to the public good were universally recognised as the necessary 'spirit' underlying any popular form of government, the simple republic and mixed monarchy alike. But now civic virtue generally seemed threatened by the extensive specialisation of function, the luxury trade, and the passion for money-getting. Yet if vanquished, there was some compensation for its loss. Hume and the leading defenders of commerce considered that the polished manners which resulted from urban intercourse in a commercial society had supplanted much of the need for public virtue, at least insofar as they curtailed the sources of partisan antagonism. They also claimed that the refined intercourse of the moderns in fact surpassed the more uncouth, barbaric and aggressive demeanour of the ancients. The more republican of the Scots, most notably Adam Ferguson, issued a strong protest on behalf of the ancients.[75] But the prospect of actually relinquishing any major advantages derived from commercial society, of diminishing trade and returning to agrarian virtue, was only seriously considered by the most 'utopian' or Platonic of the Scottish republican writers, William Ogilvie and Robert Wallace.[76]

Pocock has found in these seemingly futile attempts to uphold the integrity of the classical conception of the autonomous, unspecialised citizen the sources of what was to become a central strand in nineteenth and twentieth century socialist political thought. Ferguson, John Millar and others plainly contended that an increasing division of labour entailed the degradation of the personality, the narrowness of the task corresponding to the mental horizons of the worker. The progress of commercial society was thus paradoxical, since increasing wealth generated by a further specialisation of functions accompanied

---

[73] J. G. A. Pocock, *The Machiavellian Moment*, pp. 499–503.
[74] Andrew Fletcher of Saltoun, 'A Discourse of Government with Relation to Militias', in David Daiches, ed., *Andrew Fletcher of Saltoun. Selected Political Writings and Speeches* (Edinburgh, Scottish Academic Press, 1979), pp. 1–26.
[75] Adam Ferguson, *An Essay on the History of Civil Society* (1767), ed. Duncan Forbes (Edinburgh, Edinburgh University Press, 1966), pp. 210–32.
[76] For example, Robert Wallace, *Various Prospects*, pp. 68–9.

the decline of individual character generated from the same source. This trend of thought strongly approximates the central allegation of the later Marxist theory of alienation, itself first shaped in a commentary on Adam Smith's treatment of the division of labour.[77] The supersession of alienation became one of the central claims of the Marxist revolutionary enterprise, and the theme of overcoming a narrow division of labour has remained important to many later varieties of socialism. But in the first half of the nineteenth century these goals were first given a socialist context by the Owenites.[78]

Once this relationship between republicanism and Marxism has been indicated, its implications for any history of early socialist political thought are clear. For the republican critique of specialisation evidently was an important source for other early socialist objections to specialisation, and not merely those of Marxism. Early socialism is thus an unexplored link in the stages of transmission of this aspect of republicanism into the nineteenth century, though this does not, as we will see, imply that it retained all or even most of its republican attributes in the process. Clarifying its treatment of this theme, misunderstood in the only serious attempt to analyse it, is thus central to rewriting the early history of modern radicalism.[79] Moreover, since Marx and Engels were obviously more indebted to their socialist predecessors than has usually been conceded, it is also of considerable relevance to the genesis of Marxism itself, and to its later nineteenth- and even twentieth-century history insofar as earlier views on these questions were carried forward, as the theory of 'all-rounded development' revealed by Marx and Engels in 1844–46 certainly was.[80]

Before we can categorise Owenism's relation to the republican treatment of specialisation, it might be useful to consider briefly how the division of labour was vindicated by various eighteenth-century writers. Here we encounter something of a paradox, for this was chiefly undertaken by the same natural law writers to whom, with respect to the theory of sociability, the Owenites were otherwise strongly indebted. Did the socialists simply ignore this element of natural jurisprudence? This would have been difficult, since in many natural law texts the virtues of specialisation were closely connected with the notion of sociability through the idea of Providential order.

[77] J. G. A. Pocock, ed., *The Political Writings of James Harrington*, p. 152; Pocock, *The Machiavellian Moment*, p. 502; Pocock, *Politics, Language and Time*, p. 103.

[78] On the treatment of specialisation within socialism generally, see Tom Bottomore, 'Socialism and the Division of Labour', in Bhikhu Parekh, ed., *The Concept of Socialism* (New York, Holmes and Meier, 1975), pp. 154–61.

[79] Maxine Berg, *The Machinery Question and the Making of Political Economy 1815–1848* (Cambridge, Cambridge University Press, 1980), pp. 291–314.

[80] On Marx and specialisation see Ali Rattansi, *Marx and the Division of Labour* (Macmillan, 1982).

Grotius, Pufendorf, Locke and Paine at a later point assumed both that the transition from the state of nature to civil society was natural, and that God had implanted greater needs than the state of nature was able to satisfy (thus requiring specialisation) precisely in order to compel the creation of a more perfect form of society than the state of nature permitted. By this means, the desire for sociability was satisfied on a higher level. The division of labour and the interdependence it entailed accordingly served as one of the mainsprings of sociability. For Grotius, its origins lay in God's distribution of the various products of the earth throughout different regions, which ensured that men cultivated social relations in order to satisfy their needs. Pufendorf concurred, stressing the variety of things men required to live comfortably and happily. So, too, Cumberland's editor, John Maxwell, reflected 'upon the Number of Hands that one single Garment must pass thro', before it becomes fit for use, and upon the number of curious Arts that contribute to its Perfection', to conclude that a great degree of interdependence was requisite. These views were repeated by a number of the leading defenders of the new commercial system, such as Daniel Defoe. Through the course of the eighteenth century, however, the theological elements in the division of labour gradually vanished, until only the 'invisible hand' of Smith indicated the designs of Providence.[81]

Since these arguments would later reappear in the philosophy of consumer and producer co-operation, which Owenism would both contribute to and derive inspiration from, it is worth considering the possibility that socialism attempted to combine a theory of independence which was at least partially drawn from republicanism, with a notion of mutual dependence (insofar as co-operation remained an Owenite ideal) which was largely jurisprudential in origin. Before we can examine how such contradictory views could have been reconciled, however, we must first treat the Owenite idea of independence itself in greater detail.

The chief context for Owenism's discussion of the division of labour was not the eighteenth-century debate over commercial society, but that which accompanied the rise of the manufacturing system in the early nineteenth century, and the far more extensive specialisation which this entailed. Although Smith relied upon the division of labour as one of the chief causes for the general increase of wealth, he also criticised the 'mental mutilation' resulting from the frequent repetition

---

[81] Hugo Grotius, *De Jure Belli ac Pacis*, p. 199; Samuel Pufendorf, *De Jure Naturae et Gentium*, p. 207; Richard Cumberland, *A Treatise of the Laws of Nature*, p. 92; *DeR*, 6 (1706), 5–8; see generally Jacob Viner, *The Role of Providence in the Social Order* (Philadelphia, American Philosophical Society, 1972).

of tasks, counselling the further education of the labouring classes as one means of balancing such effects. In recent years this republican dimension in his thought has been restored, notably by Donald Winch.[82] Nor did Smith's contemporaries entirely ignore such comments. Among the radical critics of the industrial system at the turn of the nineteenth century, Charles Hall made the most extensive use of Smith's critical asides, developing these into an outright condemnation of the entire system of commerce and manufacturing, and basing many of his criticisms upon the decline of martial virtues resulting from it.[83] But Owenism proposed to substitute machinery for the division of labour as the leading principle underlying increasing production, and by this means did not need, like Hall, to counsel a return to more primitive conditions.[84] How then did Owenism understand this opposition to narrow specialisation, and what ideal of unified personality lay behind its views?

Let us first consider what seems to be the Dissenting contribution to this opposition. Given the proximity of a number of important Owenite ideas to Quaker social theory, and also the derivation of much of the latter from the radical republicanism of the Commonwealth period, it is difficult to separate the religious from the republican elements in this mixture. William Penn, for example, praised the 'noble Greeks and Romans' for their antipathy to luxury, but preferred 'country life' not for specifically republican reasons, but because 'there we see the works of God'. His recommendation that Quakers 'choose God's trades before men's' and become gardeners, farmers and shepherds (though few seem to have heeded his advice) was also no doubt both religious and political in inspiration. Nonetheless, while republicans sought a militia rather than a standing army, the Quakers, at least by the restoration period, wanted to abolish the military profession entirely. To the republican objection that 'it will endanger an effeminacy by such a disuse of the trade of soldiery', Penn replied in his proposal for peace among the European nations that 'There can be no danger of effeminacy, because each sovereignty may introduce as temperate or severe a discipline in the education of youth as they please, by low living and due labour'. If instructed in 'mechanical knowledge and in natural philosophy' in particular, 'This would make them men: neither women nor lions: for soldiers are the other extreme to effeminacy'.[85] These would later also be the aims of Owen's system of education.

Within their own sect, as we have seen, the Quakers eliminated the

---

[82] Donald Winch, *Adam Smith's Politics* (Cambridge, Cambridge University Press, 1978).
[83] Charles Hall, *The Effects of Civilization on the People in European States* (1805), pp. 157–63.
[84] See *Machinery, Money and the Millennium*, pp. 39–41, 52–5.
[85] William Penn, *The Peace of Europe*, pp. 73, 80, 104, 13.

need for the professions of soldier, lawyer and priest. To these the Owenites commonly added physicians (about whom George Fox had made some uncharitable remarks) in the expectation that many of the causes of disease would be eradicated in the more healthy conditions of community life, and that all might be educated to care for their own health.[86] But if the Owenites condemned priests for fomenting opposing and nonsensical doctrines, lawyers for deliberately encouraging and extending disputes, and doctors because of their excessive charges and disinterest in prolonged health, the aim of their critique of the professions was not merely an improvement upon existing Quaker ideals. They also sought to create a new notion of the unified personality which linked republican and Quaker assumptions. For in socialism, most forms of the division of labour were seen as hostile to individual independence, to the practice of virtue, and to the exercise of human rationality. This is clear from Owen's account of how and why it was possible to unify the chief professions within each person. Listing his aims in 1848, for example, Owen argued that all should be 'so instructed that *each may be his own priest, lawyer, physician and soldier, in order that each may be the most independent of others that social arrangements can be made to admit'*. This may seem closer to the Quaker than to any other conception. But there were also epistemological grounds for superseding various occupations. For it was rational independence which Owen sought, with the aim of making possible a universally held conception of the common interest and public good. The present system educated individuals to understand only their own narrow concerns, rather than the broader well-being of all. As Owen wrote in 1845, the 'isolation of professions, trades and varied business operations' meant 'that the parties engaged in them are so strongly imbued with the knowledge of the details of some small portion of the business of life, while none are taught to comprehend the general interests of society, and these, therefore, to the great injury of all, remain unknown'. In addition, the Owenites presumed that specialisation was a cause of social antagonism generally, of class and other divisions. Here the language of independence could again be brought into play. In 1827, for example, Owen urged his followers to enjoy the advantages commerce could provide, 'but without *dependence*', meaning by this without both overproduction and the opposition of interests between producers and consumers. Thus, too, in the *New Moral World* he wrote of the goals of socialism in terms of 'combining in the same individual

---

[86] For example, William Thompson, *An Inquiry into the Causes of the Distribution of Wealth* (1824), p. 5. See generally Christopher Hill, 'The Medical Profession and its Radical Critics', in his *Change and Continuity in Seventeenth Century England* (Weidenfeld and Nicolson, 1974), pp. 157–78.

the producer, and the possessor of wealth, the communicator and the recipient of knowledge, the governor and the governed, to destroy the individious distinctions that have split up the one great family of man into sections and classes'.[87]

The very frequent use within socialism of the categories of productive and unproductive labour drawn from political economy also demonstrates the degree to which this new language was superimposed upon older notions of specialisation. Sometimes (indeed increasingly, from the 1830s onwards), this reduced the whole question to the relation between producers and non-producers, and thus collapsed the problem of the division of labour into that of class generally. But the language of political economy never monopolised mainstream Owenite discussions of specialisation. More important, especially in communitarian Owenism, was the notion of 'rational' character, which had a more specifically political than economic meaning and which underlay many socialist debates on this question. Thus Owen, in one of his clearest statements opposing specialisation, insisted that:

Society should now cease to form man to be a mere Ruler, Statesman, or Legislator, – a mere Priest, Doctor, Military Man, or Naval Man, – a mere Monied Man, – or buyer and seller for profit, – a mere agriculturalist, manufacturer, or tradesman. These are all mere fractions of a rational being. Full-formed men and women can never be made by such a mal-arrangement of the human race; – an arrangement which keeps all ignorant of their own nature and divine powers, – of society as it should be, – and of its real component parts, – all of which each man and woman should be trained and educated to comprehend, and thus each should be made to become in his or her own person a superior domestic assistant, – a superior creator and distributor of wealth, – a superior instructor or former of character, – and a superior legislator, statesman, and governor. Thus only can men and women be well-formed, and be made to be equals in promoting each other's happiness, and in living a life of rationality in strict accordance with nature and with the laws of God.[88]

This opposition to extreme specialisation was a marked departure from mainstream post-war radicalism. By the 1790s, as Isaac Kramnick has urged, many radicals had come to accept a considerable degree of specialisation as a concomitant result of commerce, while warning of the effects of corruption upon virtue. But this was hardly true of all. As we have seen, Priestley condoned a commercial division of labour, but Price was more critical, and Godwin far more so. Owenism did acknowledge the advantages of opulence to an important degree, but on the issue of specialisation Owen himself, certainly, remained much

---

[87] *SA*, no. 16 (16 November 1848), 244 (emphasis added); *NHG*, 2, no. 30 (25 April 1827), 238–9; *Robert Owen's Address to the Ministers of All Religions* (Philadelphia, 1845); *NMW*, 13, no. 48 (24 May 1845), 388.
[88] *ROMG*, 5 (15 June 1856), 11.

closer to Godwin's reaffirmation of classical dissenting ideals than to, for example, Priestley's greater embrace of commercial society.[89] But Owenism also differed on this issue from republican formulations. For the coalescence of the Dissenting search for religious independence with the language of republican virtue and self-sacrifice gave rise to an entirely new notion of independence which was both far more egalitarian and detached from property theories than most republican notions. It was also considerably more secular and socially far-reaching in its implications than most puritan ideas of independence.[90]

Where republicanism clearly gave way to puritanism within socialism was on the question of national chauvinism, particularly in relation to military affairs. Owen did not in the first instance explicitly embrace pacifism. New Lanark included military training appropriate to the formation of a militia, while New Harmony actually fielded a force of 250 men. But, as for Godwin, the crucial breaking point for republicanism came on the questions of patriotism and national ambition, for the 'character' of the new moral world would have neither a special allegiance to any country nor any propensity to warfare. This began a tradition of cosmopolitanism and intense hostility to military aggression which has, in principle, characterised virtually all subsequent forms of socialism. Patriotism, the highest virtue in the republican pantheon, was for Owen only 'another name for prejudices against, and injustice to, all other countries', and would decay because the new system would 'gradually terminate all local nationalities, and make the population of the earth into one nation, with one language, interest, and kind feeling for one another'.[91] Here was a form of cosmopolitanism which, if it corresponded to some of the early statements of Marx and Engels, was far more extreme in its opposition to nationalism than the internationalism of later nineteenth-century socialism.[92] Here 'false notions of military glory' (as John Minter Morgan termed them) were to be succeeded not by a 'politeness' which seemingly lacked a sincere and deeply-felt moral basis, but by the spirit of universal benevolence and charity which Owen would come to term his 'new

[89] Kramnick thus exaggerates somewhat in claiming that 'Specialisation for the radicals, far from a sign of corruption, was characteristic of the virtuous man' ('Republican Revisionism Revisited', 663), though his account helps to balance Pocock's tendency to stress the opposite interpretation.

[90] J. G. A. Pocock, 'Radical Criticisms of the Whig Order in the Age of Revolutions', in Margaret Jacob and James Jacob, eds., *The Origins of Anglo-American Radicalism* (George Allen and Unwin, 1984), p. 44.

[91] *ROMG*, 10 (1 January 1857), 4.

[92] See my 'Reciprocal Dependence, Virtue and Progress: Some Sources of Early Socialist Cosmopolitanism and Internationalism in Britain, 1790–1860', in F. L. van Holthoon and Marcel van der Linden, eds., *Internationalism in the Labour Movement 1830–1940* (Leiden, E. J. Brill, 1988), 1, pp. 235–58.

religion'.[93] Once again we are on the terrain of millennial Dissent, and no matter how indebted Owen was to the republican tradition for elements of his theory of independence, the ideal of republican character was roundly defeated in this crucial case of conflict with heretical Christian pacifism.

Two other points need to be made about Owen's treatment of specialisation. The first is that, besides the political and religious components we have described, these discussions addressed a specific debate about the labouring classes as well as the general question of human irrationality. It is not necessary to take up the problem of the development of the language of class and rank before Owen to see that it was very much part of his post-war assumptions. In his first substantial account of how the rational community of the future would utilise machinery to alleviate poverty, the *Report to the County of Lanark* (1820), Owen clearly demonstrated his sensitivity to the effects of the division of labour upon the working classes. In his system, he wrote:

There would at once be an end of all mere animal machines, who could only follow a plough, or turn a sod, or make some insignificant part of some insignificant manufacture or frivolous article which society could better spare than possess. Instead of the unhealthy pointer of a pin, – header of a nail, – piecer of a thread, – or clodhopper, senselessly gazing at the soil or around him, without understanding or rational reflection, there would spring up a working class full of activity and useful knowledge, with habits, information, manners, and dispositions that would place the lowest in the scale many degrees above the best of any class which has yet been formed by the circumstances of past or present society.[94]

Secondly, while we have here been mainly concerned to examine the wider implications of Owen's opposition to specialisation, it needs to be stressed that, in practice and for the short run, the Owenites usually emphasised that the means had been developed, as the *Crisis* put it, 'by which the union and division of labour may be combined to secure the peculiar advantages of both, without the evils of either'.[95] This meant that, despite the prevalence of the ideal of the unified and independent personality, the practical advantages of many types of division of labour were often recognised. Thus the rotation of tasks was occasionally suggested as a means of avoiding unpleasant consequences in cases where monotony or worse was the likely result of any activity. In fact, the more an individual Owenite was concerned with the goals of what I have elsewhere termed 'economic socialism', specifically the

---

[93] John Minter Morgan, *Hampden in the Nineteenth Century* (1834), 2, pp. 129–30. The choice of a popular republican hero as the key character in this very popular book is worth noting.
[94] Owen, *NVS*, p. 284.   [95] *Crisis*, 2, no. 18 (11 May 1833), 143.

increase of wealth, though with the means of production securely in the hands of the producing classes, the more likely it was that they would favour and praise the division of labour. This was the case, for example, with John Francis Bray. It is in such accounts, too, that we find the residual sociability arguments of natural jurisprudence, in which earlier praise for 'dependency' was now deployed in support of the new system of co-operative labour. There were thus two poles of thought within socialism with respect to the division of labour, and once again it is necessary to stress Owenism's diversity of thought and experience on this as on many other points.

The language of socialism

We have seen that one of the most important dimensions in the emphasis upon the 'social' in the eighteenth century was derived from the reinterpretation of natural law in Grotius, Pufendorf, Cumberland and others. In Britain this took both more moderate forms, for instance in the emphasis upon man's social nature of the Scottish writers, and more extreme forms, most notably in Godwin's enthusiasm for the pursuit of universal benevolence, which was based more upon the command to perform than propensity towards the duty. But there were also other foundations for the Owenite notion of sociability. 'Social' language enjoining the need for harmony and mutual aid was evident in the early nineteenth-century co-operative, guild, friendly society, and early trade union accent upon fraternity, harmony, unity and the bonds created by the voluntary association of labour. The motto of John Gast's Thames Shipwrights Provident Union studied by Iorwerth Prothero, for example, was 'Union of Sentiment in the strength of society'. As William Sewell and Maurice Agulhon have suggested with respect to France, this sense of collectivism, perhaps best understood in terms of Tönnies' opposition of *Gesellschaft* to *Gemeinschaft*, and recently developed into a general theory of artisan ideology by Antony Black, provided in its concern for brotherhood, the sharing of oaths, friendship and mutual aid a basis for the ideology of socialism.[96]

[96] *WFP*, no. 30 (5 February 1826), 477. See Maurice Agulhon, 'Working Class and Sociability in France before 1848', in Pat Thane, Geoffrey Crossick, and Roderick Floud, eds., *The Power of the Past. Essays for Eric Hobsbawm* (Cambridge, Cambridge University Press, 1984), pp. 37–66, William Sewell, *Work and Revolution in France. The Language of Labor from the Old Regime to 1848* (Cambridge, Cambridge University Press, 1980), especially pp. 143–4, 222, and Antony Black, *Guilds and Civil Society in European Political Thought from the Twelfth Century to the Present* (Methuen, 1984), especially pp. 167–81. On the ideology of sociability as expressed in friendly societies, see P. H. J. H. Gosden, *The Friendly Societies in England 1815–1875* (Manchester, Manchester University Press, 1961), pp. 134–5.

By 1800, this ethos of mutuality was increasingly aligned against the eighteenth-century development of another meaning of 'society', once again closely wedded to the distinction between the state of nature and political society, but now linked to the emergence of the concept of 'civil society' as the sphere of contract and commerce. It was from this trend, and especially from the notion of the virtual self-sufficiency of the sphere of civil society relative to government and the state, that liberal utopias from Smith to Cobden were to be constructed. Here the jurisprudential account of natural sociability and the Providential conception of trade and the division of labour were wedded to a distinctly Augustinian theory of the state. Civil society was portrayed as the sphere of the natural satisfaction of needs, while the state was derived from human evil and sinfulness, 'society' being, as a Painite radical reiterated in 1792, 'in every state . . . a blessing – but Government, even in its best state, is but a necessary evil'.[97] But unlike the Augustinian account, the state was here seen as not merely inhibiting but contributing to further evil, and thus itself requiring restraint. Here, accordingly, the strengthening of the bonds of civil society permitted a greater limitation of the functions of the state, until they could be confined to the repression of unnecessary violence. From this perspective, the increased emphasis upon human sociability derived from the jurisprudential revival underlies both modern liberalism and socialism, and accounts for the significant degree of opposition to over-government which pervades most shades of early nineteenth-century political thought.

In the first decades of the nineteenth century, however, industrialisation and economic dislocation helped to revive the notion that the self-sufficiency of civil society was impossible, and that the natural paternal duty of the governing wealthy towards the governed poor ought to be rehabilitated. This notion of 'government' was to be central to the rise of socialism, which more firmly and consistently than any other movement in this period demanded the provision of governmental relief for the poor, as well as economic regulation generally. But in socialism the demand for *more* government on the basis of the failure of natural sociability (in the form of the restraints of the moral economy) collided with a desire for *less* government resulting from the renewed socialist emphasis upon the potential scope of sociability. More than anything else, these conflicting aims were to result in the creation of a significant blind spot within many forms of socialist organisational theory. Simultaneously embracing an administrative conception of government, and removing the coercive fangs also usually assumed to be an attribute of the state, socialism groped

[97] *Patriot*, no. 1 (3 April 1792), 24–5.

towards a new definition of governance for which no real precedents existed. The search for a new form of polity in Owenism was predicated upon the conflict between two different notions of 'society'. How it developed can only be clarified, however, if we examine more closely the emergence of the vocabulary of socialism and the targetting of the language and assumptions it sought to displace. In addition, only when this confrontation within the vocabulary of 'society' is illuminated can we begin to elicit the range of meanings which became attached to 'socialism' and associated notions such as 'social science', 'social democracy' and 'democratic socialism', all of which, it was assumed, were to replace existing political concepts.

The specific constellation of ideas which became linked with the term 'socialism' had begun to form for several decades prior to the emergence of the term itself.[98] The French revolution apparently contributed two elements to this development. The collapse of the revolution, the progress of conquest and dictatorship, as well as the crushing of the British reform movement, convinced many radicals that, as the former London Corresponding Society secretary and early Owenite John Bone put it, 'this extensive failure may be attributed entirely to the political revolution having had precedency over the moral revolution. It is necessary that the circumstances of mankind be amended, and their morals, or motives for action, thoroughly changed, before they can be in a condition to preserve political institutions in all their purity'. For many, during the next forty years and longer, the precedence given to the 'social' revolution meant that a fundamental moral reform would have to precede the alteration of political and other institutions. Secondly, the French revolution was also widely perceived as 'social' in the sense that 'the new social principle ... the social compact established by the French revolution' had brought most of the population into the political process. 'Political' here implies the narrow caste hitherto permitted to enjoy the seats of power, and their sphere of activity. 'Social' refers to the rising demands of the unenfranchised majority, and the notion of popular participation generally. While 'socialism' first appeared in English in 1835, 'socialist' first occurred in print in 1827, and in manuscript some five years earlier. Both terms derived from the equation of Owen's new views with what was termed the 'social system', itself juxtaposed before 1820 to 'the individual system'. This was originally defined in

---

[98] For further details see my '"Individualism", "Socialism" and "Social Science": Further Notes on a Process of Conceptual Formation, 1800–1850', *JHI*, 47 (1986), 81–93, from which the following several pages are drawn. On the late eighteenth-century Britain see James T. Boulton, *The Language of Politics in the Age of Wilkes and Burke* (Routledge and Kegan Paul, 1963), and S. F. Wolfe, 'The Political Rhetoric of English Radicalism, 1780–1830', Ph.D., University of York (1976).

terms of what was taken to be the core teaching of the new system of political economy: the view that aggregate needs would be best satisfied by each individual following his or her own self-interest. The latter view, in turn, became by the mid-1830s identified in English with 'individualism', and was associated in its first use (which was in Owenite periodicals) with a love of money, accumulation, distinction, rank, privilege and domination. The 'social system' was principally defined by the need for social benevolence to merge with self-love (though not to supersede it), such that individual happiness could be achieved in conjunction with that of the community rather than in isolation from or opposition to it. At the basis of this view was Owen's central philosophical principle, the determination of behaviour by the environment, or belief that 'the character of man is formed *for* and not *by* him'. Connected was the correlative notion that rewards and punishments were irrational if individuals were not responsible for their own behaviour. By 1820 this conception had been added to Owen's critique of the first principles of political economy, which he summarised in a word as the doctrine of 'competition'. 'The individual system' was now defined as *'the system of individual rewards, punishments, and competition'*.[99]

For Owenite political thought, the most significant concept to be derived from this vocabulary was 'social science', which by the 1830s became synonymous with a socialist programme generally. Probably first introduced into English in the Irish Owenite William Thompson's main work, *An Inquiry into the Principles of the Distribution of Wealth Most Conducive to Human Happiness* (1824), 'social science' carried a distinctly Owenite connotation in many quarters until well into the 1840s, when it gradually took on the more neutral meaning of the largely statistical examination of civil society which would be popularised by the Social Science Association. In Thompson and for the Owenites, however, the concept had a much wider import which was broadly synonymous with the science of utility, 'the application of which becomes the art of social happiness'. Its introduction was specifically designed to provide a higher first principle to guide political economy, being nominally equivalent to 'the science of morals', but really comprising virtually all types of knowledge, since the common good was affected by so many different dimensions of both the natural and social worlds.

These, then, were the foundations of the new 'social' vocabulary which, having begun to form shortly after 1800, and becoming a widely-recognised discourse between 1835 and 1845, would be fully established as a new grammar of politics only with the revolutions of 1848. For the latter event in particular instigated the exceptionally

[99] Owen, *NVS*, p. 294.

rapid diffusion throughout Europe of such terms as 'social revolution' and 'social democracy', and the accompanying elevation of 'the social question' – the problem of poverty – to the centre of political debate.[100] By mid-century, thus, we encounter widespread confusion regarding the range of meanings of 'social' which had been accumulating since the French revolution. By now, in Britain, there were a variety of associations with the word 'socialism', including Owen's ideas on marriage, religion and property, and after 1848 also the workshop schemes of Louis Blanc. There were also many contending connotations of the word 'social', which when used in a political context brought to mind the problem of poverty, working class movements, and the condition of labour in general.

Part of the extraordinariness of the political discourse of working class radicalism in this period was the overlapping of the meanings of 'social' and its cognates in the identification, for example, of the working class as the most 'sociable' or moral class – the class created and most affected by industrialisation – as well as at the same time 'the democracy' – the largest class or the majority. This was a vocabulary whose flexibility made it an excellent rhetorical vehicle in the radical debates of the 1840s. The 'social revolution', for example, could express the aspirations of the largest class, the moral standing of that class, and the new, more sociable relations which would follow the inception of economic justice and working class accession to political power. But this ambiguity, as we will see, also created an imprecision in political argument which was to plague those who sought to wed radicalism and socialism in order to create a new form of democratic politics. For the exact way in which 'social' modified 'democracy' in the phrase 'social democracy', for example, could never be beyond contention. It could imply a more equal society, a greater degree of political and/or industrial participation, and/or the prevalence of small organisations or communities in which direct participation was achieved. How this range of meanings emerged and evolved through the various stages of the history of Owenism is the main subject of this book. We have seen in this chapter that there is strong evidence for supposing that at least some strands of Owenism can be seen as carrying forward a variety of earlier republican traditions, while a major debt to natural jurisprudence is also evident, both of these being modified in turn by millenarianism and Quaker ideals. Let us now consider in greater detail how these ideas were developed into new forms of political thinking, beginning with Robert Owen himself.

[100] On continental developments of this discourse see Eckart Pankoke, *Sociale Bewegung – Sociale Frage – Sociale Politik. Grundfragen der deutschen 'Socialwissenschaften' im 19. Jahrhundert* (Stuttgart, Ernst Klett Verlag, 1970).

2

Paternalism and democracy in the politics of Robert Owen

The fact that socialism could be understood as an attempt to extend, rather than to abolish, political participation was not always evident to its radical critics. This was particularly true in the early years of the movement, when Owen was still widely perceived as a somewhat overly enthusiastic poor law reformer whose proposals bore little resemblance to the aims of working class radicals. Whatever republican elements existed in Owen's ideas were thus scarcely acknowledged by those radicals with whom he first came into contact. More disconcerting for Owen was the fact that his plans were actually rejected by many working class leaders as antagonistic to their goal of greater social and political independence. Within a short time of the advent of his national campaign for poor law reform in 1817, Owen was thus assailed by a number of political reformers on the grounds of his apparent political conservatism. Some were mainly offended by his condescending style, for instance in his use of 'the lower orders' to describe the working classes. Others saw in Owen's plans a subtle government ploy to upset radical strategies. Among the rumours then afloat among the reformers, Richard Carlile later recalled, one was 'that Mr. Owen was an instrument of the Government, to bring forward his plan of providing for the lower classes, for the purpose of drawing their attention from Parliamentary reform'. Writing in April 1817, the radical journalist W. T. Sherwin similarly warned his readers that Owen's scheme of 'new fashioned poor houses' would insidiously 'deprive you of your political rights, in every sense of the word', while describing his educational plans as intended to form more loyal subjects of the Empire 'debarred from the enjoyment of the Rights of Man'. In his *Black Dwarf*, too, T. J. Wooler accused Owen of designing 'pauper barracks' whose 'inhabitants shall be reduced to mere automata, and all their feelings, passions and opinions are to be subjected to certain rules, which Mr. Owen, the tutelary deity of these novel elesiums, shall lay down'. The black radical Robert Wedderburn, whose mother had been a slave, went even further, terming Owen's proposals 'but an improved system of human slavery'. William Cobbett's abrasive comments on 'parallelograms of paupers' merely brought up the rear of the radical onslaught on the latest invidious scheme hatched by Old Corruption.[1]

This perspective on Owen's political intentions has also dominated scholarly opinion. From the comment of W. L. Sargant, Owen's first biographer, that his 'notions of government generally were anything but democratic, and had a rather paternal leaning' to more recent descriptions of Owen as 'essentially a conservative', 'anti-democratic', or simply 'despotic', there has been a pronounced tendency to see Owen as a 'paternal' (i.e. conservative) critic of 'democracy', whose meaning has been more often presumed than defined.[2] George Jacob Holyoake, often an opponent of Owen's, termed him a 'Conservative'. Owen's main biographer, Frank Podmore, described him as 'aristocratic in his methods and the whole cast of his mind' because 'he appears always to have conceived of reform as something imposed from . . . above'. Max Beer's standard history of British socialism dismissed Owen as 'no democrat'. Writing in 1949, R. H. Harvey noted that Owen's ideas on government 'did not run along democratic channels', while Ralph Miliband has characterised him more subtly as a 'Social Revolutionary' to whom forms of government were immaterial. Elsewhere it has been argued that Owen deplored 'democracy', which he identified with militancy, that he had little sympathy for political reform and held aloof from all popular democratic movements, that it was his American experience which confirmed Owen's rejection of political agitation, although the roots of 'his political conservatism' were evident as early as the 1790s, that Owen was a 'Tory' if 'we define Toryism as the politics of the unpolitical', that Owen was 'completely

---

[1] *Republican*, 2, no. 1 (14 January 1820), 10; *SPR*, 1, no. 4 (26 April 1817), 59–62; *BD*, 1, no. 30 (20 August 1817), 469–70; *IW*, no. 608 (24 August 1817), 116–19. Owen was also accused of employing an ex-government spy named Richmond in the New Lanark mills, though he later denied knowing anything of his previous activities. See *BD*, 1, no. 36 (1 October 1817), 603, and for Owen's denial, *CWPR*, 138 (3 January 1835), 115–22; *ibid.*, 31 (2 August 1817), 569–70. Owen later commented on the working classes in this period that 'their democratic and much mistaken leaders taught them that I was their enemy, a friend to all those in authority, and that I desired to make slaves of them in these villages of unity and mutual co-operation' (Owen, *Life*, 1, p. 160). One of the few radicals sympathetic to Owen in this period was John Gale Jones. See *MO*, no. 608 (24 August 1817), 120–22. See also Cullen's account of the radical opposition to Owen in his *Adventures in Socialism* (Glasgow, John Smith, 1910), p. 101.

[2] W. L. Sargant, *Robert Owen and his Social Philosophy* (1860), pp. 37–8; Edward Royle, *Victorian Infidels and the Origins of the Secularist Movement* (Manchester, Manchester University Press, 1974), pp. 2, 44; R. A. Soloway, *Prelates and People: Ecclesiastical Social Thought in England, 1783–1852* (Routledge and Kegan Paul, 1962), p. 224; Iorwerth Prothero, *Artisans and Politics in Early Nineteenth Century London: John Gast and His Times* (Dawson, 1979), p. 254.

indifferent' to both the 1832 and Chartist reform agitations, and finally, in E. P. Thompson's more imaginative expression, that Owen 'simply had a vacant place in his mind where most men have political responses'.[3]

This type of verdict has not been entirely unanimous, however. Lloyd Jones, Owen's only major biographer to have known him intimately and over a long period of time, described him as friendly to reform of the House of Commons, despite his dislike of temporary expedients. More recently, J. F. C. Harrison has characterised Owen's politics in terms of an ambiguous preference for both paternalism and egalitarianism. In an important comparative study, Keith Taylor has also found Owen to be more democratic than many of the early continental socialists.[4]

A judicious approach to Owen's political ideas and behaviour would thus do well to begin at a point of suspended judgement. This chapter argues that the major problem with most of the foregoing interpretations is not that they are wrong. Many accounts have indeed been erroneous or misleading. But given their frequent and usually undefined use of notoriously imprecise and historically shifting terms, the exact meaning of most descriptions of Owen's politics has often been difficult to ascertain. More importantly, however, given the complexity of the problem, no previous study has searched sufficiently widely to be able to offer any definitive assessment of the political element in Owen's work. Nor have earlier analyses either seriously examined the *unpolitical* nature of many of Owen's ideas, or placed Owen in terms of the traditions outlined in the last chapter. It is clear, therefore, that it was Owen's failure to become involved in parliamentary reform which has usually served as the chief basis for the charge of 'conservatism' against him. Nonetheless Owen's wish to

[3] G. J. Holyoake, 'Unpublished Correspondence of the Robert Owen Family', *CN*, 35 (11 June 1904), 706; Frank Podmore, *Robert Owen* (2nd edn., George Allen and Unwin, 1923), p. 427; Max Beer, *A History of British Socialism* (G. Bell, 1929), 1, p. 162; Robert Harvey, *Robert Owen: Social Idealist* (Berkeley, University of California Press, 1949), p. 87; Ralph Miliband, 'The Politics of Robert Owen', *JHI*, 15 (1954), 233–5; R. G. Garnett, *Co-operation and the Owenite Socialist Communities in Britain 1825–45* (Manchester, Manchester University Press, 1972), p. 29; C. Tsuzuki, 'Robert Owen and Revolutionary Politics', in Sidney Pollard and John Salt, eds., *Robert Owen: Prophet of the Poor* (Macmillan, 1971), p. 13; John Butt, 'Robert Owen of New Lanark: His Critique of British Society', in John Butt and J. F. Clarke, eds., *The Victorians and Social Protest* (Newton Abbot, David and Charles, 1973), p. 14; W. H. Oliver, 'Robert Owen and the English Working Class Movement', *HT*, 8 (1958), 789; James Treble, 'The Social and Economic Thought of Robert Owen', in John Butt, ed., *Robert Owen, Prince of the Cotton Spinners* (Newton Abbot, David and Charles, 1971), p. 43; E. P. Thompson, *The Making of the English Working Class* (Harmondsworth, Penguin Books, 1977), p. 861.

[4] Lloyd Jones, *The Life, Times and Labours of Robert Owen* (2nd edn., George Allen and Unwin, 1895), p. 213; J. F. C. Harrison, *Robert Owen*, p. 76; Keith Taylor, *The Political Ideas of the Utopian Socialists*, p. 99.

transcend politics was also central to his life's work. This segregates elements of his thought from most traditional categories of political analysis. Any careful study of Owen must therefore concentrate closely upon the language of his political ideas in order to establish the lines of separation between the more republican and the more transcendental or millenarian elements in his thought, which as we saw in the last chapter were also linked to jurisprudential discussions of natural society.

This chapter examines the implications of using the vocabulary of 'democracy' and 'paternalism', two of the key interpretative categories usually applied to Owen, to describe his views. Some of the problems in analysing Owen's politics can be resolved into disagreements about the meaning of these terms, whose definitions circumscribe if not dictate the conclusions often reached. We will see, however, that by contemporary standards of the meaning of 'democracy', Owen's 'despotic' tendencies have in fact been heavily overemphasised. Despite his occasional arbitrariness and overweening self-confidence, he was much more of a 'democrat' in many of his plans and organisations than has hitherto been generally assumed. That his ultimate vision of society was 'paternal' is beyond dispute, but a careful and contextual examination of the development of Owen's ideas over fifty years reveals a far more complex theory of politics than that hitherto ascribed to him. Owen did eventually adopt a household, 'paternal' model of politics which contained primitivist and republican as well as religious elements. But what this meant for both his interim and final notions of government has never been clarified, especially in terms of his ambition to resolve what he took to be the greatest problem in political thought and action of the day: the antipathy between the principles of democracy and aristocracy. Finally, it will be proposed that while Owen is best understood as a perfectionist and sectarian critic of representative democracy, he also felt that superseding such democratic procedures as elections could be understood as a positive advance upon democratic goals rather than a retreat from them. Owen did intend to abolish 'politics', but in so doing it was precisely arbitrary, 'irrational' and unwarranted power which he sought most to replace. But the schemes he advanced to substitute for existing political processes were in fact much more an integral part of traditional republican and democratic theory than has been recognised previously. Even Owen's wish to supersede politics, therefore, took place within a language and conceptual framework which was recognisably a part of contemporary political debate.

This reconstruction begins by considering the political elements in Owen's early plans, as well as the context for his initial anti-democratic reputation. Owen's search for the roots of political conflict is then characterised in terms of the language of moral and economic individualism and in reference to family and class systems. The reconstitution of a patriarchal model of politics and its extension in an aetatic or gerontocratic system of social organisation is then investigated, and interpreted primarily in terms of Owen's wish to transcend both aristocracy and democracy, or to incorporate both principles into a single scheme. The implications of the latter goal are then related to proposals for 'elective paternal government' during the years of the principal Owenite organisations. (Popular reaction to this will be discussed in a later chapter.) Finally, an account is given of the 'federalist' ideas put forward by Owen to describe an eventual world of communities, and an interpretation offered of the countervailing tendencies towards statism and centralisation in his plans.

Governing circumstances, 1816–34

It has often been remarked that Owen's experience at New Lanark gave him the confidence and inclination to revolutionise the world. The mills on the Clyde brought him wealth, and his experimental infant school and model factory village added fame. Both helped to cement an already fixed view that the educational principles he had first begun to experiment with at Manchester in the 1790s were correct, and that 'any character might be formed by applying the proper means', as he put it in 1812.[5] Two aspects of his early experience are particularly relevant to understanding Owen's political outlook. The first involves the relationship between the determination of character by circumstances, and the educator who helps to create and shape these, or who, in Owen's term, 'governs' them as their 'architect'.[6] We will later see that this doctrine could be interpreted as justifying absolute rule by Owen himself, if not others. Certainly it reflected Owen's understanding, as he put it in 1823, that 'At all times the governing power in every country has really been instrumental in forming the character of each of its inhabitants'.[7] But if the identification of 'government' with the task of education lay ultimately at the root of the paternal ideal familiarly associated with Owen, it is important to comprehend how this was translated into practice on various occasions.

[5] Owen, *A Statement Regarding the New Lanark Establishment* (Glasgow, 1812), p. 4.
[6] Owen, *A Discourse on a New System of Society* (1825, 'First Discourse'), in O. C. Johnson, ed., *Robert Owen in the United States* (New York, Humanities Press, 1972), p. 27; Owen, *Report of the Proceedings at the Several Public Meetings Held in Dublin* (Dublin, 1823), pp. 14–15.
[7] *Sun*, no. 9739 (10 November 1823), 2.

Certainly at New Lanark Owen was not equally judge and jury in all affairs, despite his potential power. By regulations laid down in 1800, the first year of his management, the village was split into groups of houses called 'neighbourhood divisions'. Once a year the heads of households in each division chose a 'principal'. These then elected twelve jurors to sit monthly for one year, hearing and judging upon all cases brought before them concerning the internal order of the community.[8] Thus despite a 'paternal' foundation – though this term would not have the same meaning in all Owen's schemes – even here a system of indirect household suffrage guaranteed a measure of self-government which would have been the envy of many democrats, and which, Owen was proud to point out, mitigated the need for the assistance of other governing authorities. These aims Owen sought to satisfy throughout his career in his 'interim' forms of government.

In his first major work, *A New View of Society, or Essays on the Formation of the Human Character* (1813), Owen asked the government to apply some of the chief principles of New Lanark to the nation at large. This entailed a more traditional variety of paternalism, and included pleas for the expansion of the legitimate sphere of governmental activity. If the end of government was to make the governed happy, Owen reasoned, gin shops, state lotteries, religious tests and other harmful laws should be ended. Duties on liquor could be raised to force the price beyond the means of ordinary consumption. Seminaries might be founded to train teachers for a new educational branch of government. Public works ought to be promoted in the event of distress, but otherwise the government was not directly to employ individuals, but only to provide training schemes in aid of private employment. However, to reform the condition of the poor was Owen's principal aim until about 1820. All other reforms, whatever these might be, would have to wait 'for some time to come'. Parts of this early programme conformed to the views of some radicals, such as the ending of religious tests and inception of a system of national education. In other areas, such as taxes upon drink, a clear divergence was evident, and Owen was closer to the evangelicals and some tories. Already he had begun to defy easy political categorisation.[9]

During the course of 1817 Owen moved rapidly towards proposing the system of universal communitarian life which would later be known as 'socialism'. His initial plans for poor law reform involved pauper communities alone. But in the face of significant resistance, much of which resulted from his antipathy to established religions,

[8] The original regulations are reprinted in Owen, *The New Existence of Man upon the Earth* (1854–55), pt 5, pp. ix–xi.
[9] Owen, *NVS*, pp. 63–90, 36.

Owen concluded that given the selfishness of the middle and upper classes, the well-being of the poor necessitated a complete social transformation in which all classes would become 'rational'. At the end of the summer he published an elaborately impractical plan for three major types of communities grouped into four class divisions, with literally hundreds of possible variations upon communities according to political and religious preference, such that Unitarians who were also Whigs, for example, would not have to begin a community with High Church Tories. Of the four classes described, the parish poor were to be directly ruled by 'properly instructed superintendents and assistants'. The second group, working classes without property, were to be employed in the 'voluntary independent associations' of the fourth class, those possessing capital of between £1,000 and £20,000 and unwilling or unable to be productively employed. The latter, like the third group (working classes with property of between £100 and £2,000) would govern themselves by electing a general committee which would then choose seven sub-committees. Propertyless employees in fourth class communities would not be eligible to elect or be elected to the general committee of these communities, but would instead nominate seven of their own number, who, with one member from each of the sub-committees, would vote to choose a head for themselves. This committee would then 'superintend all the arrangements and transactions between the employers and the employed'. Also established at this time, though its direct sources are obscure, was the principle Owen would adopt in all his plans for both future governments and the reorganisation of society generally: rule by age-group, or what Owen would later term the 'educational principle of government'. This will be discussed in greater detail below. It is clear, however, that Owen had already fixed upon this scheme as satisfying in part the need for political order. In his first description of this ideal he announced that:

Each village will ultimately be governed by a committee of its own members, from forty to fifty years of age, or should this number be too numerous, it may be composed of all from forty-five to fifty-five years of age; which would form a permanent, experienced local government, never opposed to, but always in closest union with, each individual governed. This Committee, through its oldest member, might communicate directly with the Government; and the utmost harmony be thus established between the Executive, the Legislature, and the people.[10]

During this period Owen was frequently under attack by radicals for his alleged conservatism. Soon, however, landowners, the clergy and a variety of moderate reformers also began to condemn him as a

[10] *Ibid.*, pp. 228–31, 218. John Bellers is identified with this scheme on p. 213.

levelling radical. By late 1817, Owen found himself in the unenviable position of one whom (as John Bone put it) 'the reformists call an aristocrat, the aristocrats a Jacobin'. Owen calmly and characteristically attempted to assuage both sides by suggesting that his plan would realise the hopes of each and the fears of neither. For the benefit of conservatives, he recalled his earlier suggestion that it was 'absolutely necessary to support the old systems and institutions under which we live until another system and another arrangement of society shall be proved by practice to be essentially superior'. He also reiterated that the working classes should 'still regard it as [their] duty to pay respect and submission to what is established'. Radicals, on the other hand, were informed that political changes would arrive too late to aid those already verging upon starvation. But they were also informed that the Plan, as it was now coming to be called, rather than magnifying the powers of the government, would enhance those of the people, 'because in *reality*, as well as in *theory*, every person will become qualified to chuse his own representative'.[11]

In the next few years the political aspects of the plan did not alter greatly. In the *Report to the County of Lanark* (1820) Owen was content to repeat that the management of communities depended upon their founders, and that those established by the working and middle classes should govern themselves. To the British and Foreign Philanthropic Society, established to raise funds, Owen elaborated upon the rules for government by capital investors. Until the sum spent commencing a community were repaid, a governing committee chosen annually would consist of eight members who had invested £100 or more, and four from the rest of the community. Soon afterwards, however, he suggested that in the first instance a governing committee might simply be appointed by those who had furnished the capital. This was apparently in response to the possibility that a very small number of investors might be able to underwrite the entire enterprise.[12]

The first Owenite communitarian experiment at New Harmony, Indiana (discussed below in greater detail) does seem to have confirmed Owen's dismissal of the value of immediate popular sovereignty. But it also provoked him to consider the need for eventual collective participation more carefully, and the experience (as we will see later in reference to his view of the state) helped to provide a democratic language for the framework of his ultimate communitarian

11 *AC*, no. 4 (11 April 1818), 80; Owen, *NVS*, p. 118; *MT*, no. 1 (1 October 1817), 8; no. 2 (7 November 1817), 59.
12 Owen, *NVS*, p. 287; *Proceedings of the First General Meeting of the British and Foreign Philanthropic Society* (1822), pp. 46–56; Owen, *Permanent Relief for the British Agricultural and Manufacturing Labourers and the Irish Peasantry* (n.d., c. 1822), p. 9.

plans; he would thereafter, for example, occasionally term the proposed communities 'republics'. Addressing a joint meeting of the Senate and House of Representatives in Washington DC in February 1825, prior to commencing at New Harmony, Owen was nonetheless still careful to distinguish his goals from those of political revolutionaries. But this was still phrased in such a way as to praise American political institutions, which he rarely did on British soil.[13] For as Owen explained several weeks later:

These communities are in complete union with the principles on which the constitution of this country is founded. The constitution is essentially a government of the union of the independent states, acting together for their mutual benefit. The new communities would stand in the same relation to their respective state governments, that the States now do to the General Government, and, in consequence, the arduous duties of both will be, most probably, materially diminished.[14]

But forming an interim government for communities was in many ways a more intractable matter. On his first trip to the United States, Owen published at least three plans for resolving this problem. One repeated the British and Foreign Philanthropic Society scheme of a two-thirds majority rule by holders of capital. Another suggested an elected government of those 'best qualified' to rule, and a third, a committee of twelve elected by all. The outcome of the governmental anarchy at New Harmony was that Owen was given virtually absolute power over two of the three communities then existing. His personal influence, however, failed to solve the colonies' many difficulties, and after this he returned to England.[15] Thereafter Owen's view of interim government seems often to have been coloured by his early American experience. The collapse of New Harmony probably confirmed in his mind the inadequacies of pre-existing democratic mechanisms, and more specifically the need for an equal education according to age, throughout the community, before any genuine equality could be achieved. Education was thus not only the key to the future, when the world would 'be governed through education alone, since all other government will then become useless and unnecessary'. It also seemed integral to the interim stage before the new system was securely in place.[16]

When Owen originally departed for the new world, he left behind a few determined disciples and the seeds of another community exper-

[13] Owen, *First Discourse*, p. 31; see also *NHG*, 2, no. 30 (25 April 1827), 234.
[14] Owen, *Second Discourse on a New System of Society* (1825), in Johnson ed., *Robert Owen in the United States*, pp. 53, 56; *NHG*, 2, no. 19 (7 February 1827), 145; no. 21 (21 February 1827), 161; no. 26 (28 March 1827), 206.
[15] *Ibid.*, 1, no. 48 (23 August 1826), 383; 2, no. 15 (10 January 1827), 113.
[16] *LCM*, 4, no. 3 (1 March 1830), 37.

iment at Orbiston. On his return, he found a lively and rapidly expanding co-operative movement which in some centres was already forming links with both radicals and trades' unionists, some of which we will consider in the following chapter. To its organisers, the early successes of co-operation seemed to exemplify the potential fortunes of a decentralised, essentially working class effort. It was Owen's attempt to guide this movement which led to his renewed reputation among working class leaders as a despot, and engendered a degree of mistrust which was never thereafter to be overcome.

One occasion more than any other provoked this reaction. At the third congress of co-operative societies held in April 1832, four separate but related incidents exposed the tensions between Owen's style of leadership and the co-operators' notion of democracy. Disagreement was already clear in an early discussion of strategy. Responding to Owen's 'Address to the Governments of Europe and America', a delegate named Watkins complained that co-operators were not 'indifferent to the form of government' under which their endeavours began. Two other delegates, Mandley and Petrie, interpreted this to mean that if governments would not support them, 'the working classes would do all they wanted for themselves'. Ignoring this charitable reading of his sentiments, Owen nonetheless insisted that it was the consequences of, rather than the form of government which was at issue, and that

> despotic governments were frequently found to be better than what were called democratic. In the countries where those governments existed, the industrious classes were not found in such misery and destitution as in their country; and therefore, on this ground, there was no reason to dislike despotisms. As far as the co-operative system was concerned, it was of no consequence whether governments were despotic or not. In asking for an entire change in social relations, it must be seen that change could be better effected by an existing government, than by one to be newly introduced.[17]

Most of those present failed to find this argument persuasive. But Owen had not yet finished. The main debate at the congress concerned choosing between a small-scale community plan put forward by William Thompson and a far more grandiose and expensive scheme submitted by Owen. Owen insisted that, whichever was accepted, 'to ensure success, a complete unity must pervade the whole – committees and majorities would never answer; there would be too much confusion. He had found, by thirty years' experience, that people could not act for themselves in a community. There must be some

---

[17] *Proceedings of the Third Co-operative Congress* (1832), pp. 53–4, 93; William Lovett, *Life and Struggles of William Lovett in His Pursuit of Bread, Knowledge and Freedom* (1876; rpt. McKibbon and Kee, 1967), pp. 40–1.

conducting head.' The cabinet-maker and future Chartist leader William Lovett objected that this 'savoured . . . of despotism'. Owen retorted that he opposed despotism, but nonetheless insisted that 'one mind must direct'.[18] The third incident occurred when a smaller committee rejected one of Owen's amendments to a proposed circular. Insisting upon its inclusion, Owen finally persuaded the printer to insert it after the committee had refused to do so. A delegation then went to ask Owen if this was not indeed despotic. Lovett later described Owen's reply: 'With the greatest composure he answered that it evidently was despotic; but as we, as well as the committee that sent us, were all ignorant of his plans, and of the object he had in view, we must consent to be ruled by despots till we had acquired sufficient knowledge to govern ourselves'. Much the most provocative action by Owen, however, came when a committee voted in favour of Thompson's community plans instead of his own. Lovett called Owen's response 'a bombshell', and William Carpenter even omitted it from his published report of the proceedings. For Owen insisted that if the committee accepted Thompson's plan, all existing marriage connections would have to be dissolved. Nonetheless this spiteful and senseless form of retaliation failed to have the effect Owen intended, since the committee did not alter its decision. Defiance rather than deference was already the tone of working class reaction to Owen's personality.[19]

The next few years saw little change in the perceptions established at the 1832 congress. At his Equitable Labour Exchange Bazaar, Owen gave the governor and his five directors (who were however elected from among all members by ballot) full power to hire, sack, and manage affairs as they pleased, a form of government which the London co-operator Benjamin Warden called 'of a perfectly despotic nature'.[20] During Owen's brief connection with the Grand National Consolidated Trades' Union, the zenith of his contact with large-scale independent working class organisations, he was also several times accused of dictatorial behaviour. In the name of the GNCTU executive, for example, Owen asked James Morrison, editor of the union paper, *The Pioneer*, to relinquish control over its contents to the former body, but was refused, with Morrison pointedly telling Owen that 'the sweetest despotism' was 'that of universal love'. J. E. Smith, editor of Owen's own paper, *The Crisis*, complained similarly when Owen objected to certain of his articles on the GNCTU executive, though

---

[18] *Ibid.*

[19] *Ibid.* For other accounts of Owen's behaviour at this congress see George Jacob Holyoake, *The History of Co-operation* (2 vols., T. Fisher Unwin, 1906), 1, p. 120, and Richard Pankhurst, *William Thompson* (Watts, 1954), pp. 157–79.

[20] *Rules and Regulations of the Equitable Labour Exchange* (1832), pp. 4–6; *Proceedings of the Third Co-operative Congress*, p. 47.

Smith was also clearly endeavouring to suppress Owen's writings and influence while employed on the paper. Owen's most public attempt to surpass his nominal authority came near the end of the great London demonstration in support of the 'Tolpuddle martyrs' in April 1834. Having marched some distance, he apparently left the procession and took a more direct route in order to arrive before the official GNCTU delegation to the Home Secretary, Lord Melbourne. Not being a part of the delegation, however, Owen was denied entry, and when the others finally arrived, he was ignominiously forced to leave before Melbourne admitted them.[21]

Throughout most of this period Owen also remained opposed to the immediate granting of universal suffrage in Britain, which never failed to arouse the ire of radicals like Bronterre O'Brien, future Chartist leader and at this time editor of the *Poor Man's Guardian*.[22] During the revolution of 1830, Owen had even urged the French to support the hereditary monarchy rather than the republican or other parties.[23] But his published political programmes during these years can be classified as 'liberal' in virtually every other respect except their silence on the suffrage question and their advocacy of widespread economic intervention. When proposing himself as a member of parliament in 1832, for example, Owen offered a seven point plan which encompassed a graduated property tax equal to the national expenditure, the abolition of all other taxes; free trade, national education and national employment for all who desired them; and liberty of speech, writing, and religious practice. He also promised self-government to all British dependencies.[24] As Owen's first formal political programme during the mature years of the Owenite movement, this was an important indication of his stand on a wide range of issues.

Owen was not, therefore, a 'radical reformer', in the contemporary sense of the term, during the first fifteen years of Owenite agitation. To the contrary, his behaviour in working class circles frequently generated the strong suspicion that he sought to insist upon conformity to his own inclinations, democratically or not. On occasion he was domineering and thoroughly egotistical. Yet there were also obvious democratic components in his activities and plans which must be balanced against this style of leadership. Owen often disregarded the wishes of a majority of his would-be associates. But a recent study of John

[21] *Pioneer*, no. 40 (7 June 1834), 393; *Crisis*, 4, no. 2 (19 April 1834), 12–13; *Pioneer*, no. 34 (26 April 1834), 317–19; Alexander Somerville, *The Autobiography of a Working Man* (1848), p. 286.

[22] See, for example, Owen's comments in the *PMG*, 4, no. 197 (14 March 1835), 460–1, and O'Brien's response in no. 198 (21 March 1835), 465–8.

[23] *WFP*, no. 267 (21 August 1830).

[24] Owen, *Robert Owen's Reply to the Question, 'What Would You Do If You Were Prime Minister?'* (1832), pp. 12, 3. Owen had also run for parliament twice in 1819–20. See Podmore, *Robert Owen*, p. 264 for details.

Fielden and the Regeneration Society has concluded that here Owen sanctioned the creation of an essentially autonomous working class organisation.[25] And he was also capable of insisting that his election as Grand Master of the GNCTU be approved by two-thirds of the union lodges, and of writing, with reference to communitarian government, that it was 'the natural right of man, that he should have his equal and just share in the direction and good management of these concerns'.[26] Nor were these sentiments merely rhetorical, though Owen was capable of varying his approach according to the audience he was dealing with. What exactly Owen meant by such statements, however, can only be clarified by examining his first principles of politics.

'The germ of all party': anti-politics triumphant

Owen's statements about politics only gain coherence when viewed in terms of his system as a whole. Nonetheless in the first instance we should be wary of the assumption that his political ideas can be reduced to some 'deeper', more primary or anterior principle, particularly insofar as this entails some form of economic determinism. Owen did regard political struggles as epiphenomenal manifestations of other principles of conflict. But it seriously violates the complexity of his thought to assert, as G. D. H. Cole once did, that he 'conceived of the world of politics as no more than an emanation from the real world of economic relationships'.[27] In fact Owen attempted to convey far more in his general analysis of social dissension than an economically determinist account could describe. The sources of disunion were political, moral, personal and religious as well as economic. They were grounded in ideas, culture and consciousness as well as based on class position and identity. When in 1816 Owen proclaimed his wish to 'withdraw the germ of all party from society', this referred more to an educational than an economic theory, for education underlay all forms of social behaviour, with 'original nature' (though tending to goodness) playing virtually no role at all. Only an education which could 'drown the self in an Ocean of Sociability', as Owen's New Harmony partner, William Maclure put it on first meeting him at New Lanark, could therefore create the moral environment of the new world. Economic justice, though important, was not alone sufficient.[28]

25 See Stewart Angus Weaver, *John Fielden and the Politics of Popular Radicalism 1832–1847* (Oxford, Clarendon Press, 1987), p. 107.
26 *NMW*, 1, no. 51 (17 October 1835), 40; no. 52 (24 October 1835), 409; Owen, *Robert Owen's Opening Speech, and his Reply to the Rev. Alexander Campbell* (Cincinnati, 1829), pp. 141–2.
27 G. D. H. Cole, *The Life of Robert Owen* (3rd edn., Frank Cass, 1965), p. 11.
28 Owen, *NVS*, p. 106; Maclure MSS, series 5, vol. 24, 30 July 1824, Workingmen's Institute, New Harmony.

As we have seen, by 1820 Owen had isolated two principles which he assumed underlay most human conflict: the notion that each formed his own character, and the 'principle of individual interest', or the idea that competition would provide the greatest amount of wealth and well-being for all. In opposition to these, social science asserted that character was largely formed independently of the will of the individual, and that co-operative endeavours would prove far more productive and moral than competitive systems. The following two chapters will show that the economic aspects of the new 'social' views were intended to supersede radical conceptions of the aims of political action, while in their moral philosophy, the Owenites sought to counter individualism by internalising social control, as well as extending 'police' (in the broad contemporary sense of the term) functions to the whole community. For Owen specifically, however, another aim of social science was to unite the leading traditional principles of politics, democracy and aristocracy or monarchy in a natural polity modelled upon a household conception of politics. Here his political thought was far more sophisticated than has been hitherto assumed.

All existing principles of government, Owen believed, were 'necessarily produced by the individualized state of society'. Nonetheless he did not offer a monocausal explanation for the flaws in all former political systems. Each form was defective for different reasons:

It is now evident, that no people can be virtuous, intelligent, and happy under any despotic or elective form of government, or under any modification of them. These forms must necessarily produce evil continually. Monarchy is defective in principle, on account of the uncertain character of the sovereign, as well as in the extreme inequality it produces in the condition of the governed. The elective principle is equally defective, under the old arrangements of society, on account of the corruption of morals and unceasing bad feelings which it engenders. And any combination of these two modes of government will necessarily partake of the evils of both.[29]

His need to compete with working class radicalism for support probably led Owen to concentrate upon the defects of rule by electoral majority, although he also clearly believed that 'democracy' most completely reflected the full development of the process of competition in commercial society, an assumption shared by many later socialists. His main argument against democratic forms of government did not dwell upon the goal of universal political participation, but upon the process of election or selection by which governments were chosen. Having seen the principles of democracy at work in America, Owen wrote in 1835:

[29] Owen, *Lectures on an Entire New State of Society* (1830), p. 148; Owen, *Robert Owen's Opening Speech*, p. 43.

I saw they were well calculated to mitigate some of the evils of election to office, but they produced many others, equally pernicious, by continually calling the worst feelings of our nature into constant action, proving to me, what I had long known, that there will never be a permanent, prosperous, or good state of society, as long as the election principle to the offices of government shall be maintained.

The process of electioneering was thus merely one incessant series of personal contests 'which must produce a state of never-ending confusion'.[30] If character remained unchanged, successive governors would be distinguishable only by their differing faces, no matter what their background. Nor would rule by another class fundamentally alter this process: 'if those who are poor to-day become powerful and succeed to the government to-morrow, these same individuals, who were poor, will, through their power, become rich, and they will then oppress those who may become poor by the change, and act just as the rich and the powerful have always done to the poor from the beginning to the present moment'. For this reason, because the bases of true morality were not yet widely understood, revolutions only tended to 'make democrats into aristocrats', a clear reference to the fate of the first French revolution.[31] Consequently, Owen like virtually all of his followers rejected the idea of 'party' as a model for the new society or vehicle for attaining it (the proneness of some later continental reformers to this model no doubt bore some relation to their national inexperience with the democratic process). For Owen, democratic as well as aristocratic parties were both 'the necessary effects of ignorance of human nature, of society, and of common sense'.[32]

Though some would accuse him of preferring a sectarian basis of organisation, the model of politics which Owen settled upon was essentially that of the family, with the later Owenite organisations being primarily concerned to render this ideal practicable. Owen's conception of the family, however, varied considerably from contemporary forms of family life. In the existing marriage system, motives of personal gain interfered with true affection, the wife's rights and social role were severely circumscribed, and the difficulty of obtaining a divorce, coupled with a social double standard in the treatment of infidelities, engendered both protracted mutual hostilities and pervasive duplicity. Marriage was a virtually unrivalled source of immorality which was not directly reducible to the commercial or property system:

[30] *PMG*, 4, no. 23 (7 November 1835), 731; Owen, *Public Discussion Between Robert Owen and the Rev. J. H. Roebuck* (1837), p. 115.

[31] *NMW*, 1, no. 23 (3 April 1835), 178; Owen, *A Dialogue in Three Parts Between the Founder of the AACAN and a Stranger* (1838), p. 19.

[32] *ROJ*, 3, no. 54 (8 November 1851), 12. See also no. 74 (27 March 1852), where Owen contrasts party and national interests at some length.

'there is, perhaps, now more deception expressed in look, manner, and words, all forming languages, between the husbands and wives, made such by the Priesthood of the world, than there is between any other parties throughout the whole of society, not even excepting the present buyers and sellers of goods or money for pecuniary profit'. Contemporary forms of marriage were thus responsible for all prostitution (indeed Owen often equated the two, infuriating his critics as usual) as well as a host of other vile crimes.[33]

Besides the marriage of two individuals, Owen also denounced the existing structure of the family. Here children first learned the meaning of selfishness:

the single-family arrangements are hostile to the cultivation in children of any of the superior and ennobling qualities of human nature. *They are trained by them to acquire all the most mean and ignorant selfish feelings that can be generated in the human character*. The children within these dens of selfishness and hypocrisy are taught to consider their own individual family their own world, and that it is the duty and interest of all within this little orb to do whatever they can to promote the advantages of all legitimate members of it. With these persons, it is *my* house, *my* wife, *my* estate, *my* children, or *my* husband, *our* estate, and *our* children: or *my* parents, *my* brother, *my* sisters, and *our* house and property. This family party is trained to consider it quite right, and a superior mode of acting, for each member of it to seek, by all fair means, as almost any means, except *direct* robbery, are termed, to increase the wealth, honour, and privileges of the family and of every individual member of it . . . thus is every family made a little exclusive world seeking its own advantage, regardless and to a great extent in direct opposition to all other families, having the same objects in view; and consequently, there is a more or less direct competition between families.[34]

It was in this sense that the family first nurtured the 'germ of party' by encouraging selfishness and extra-familial antagonism. By the mid-1820s, Owen had concluded that it was impossible to build a community upon such foundations. Appeals made to rational individuals were subverted by the moral claims of the family, 'as the interest of private families is quite opposed to that of a number of equally free and intelligent individuals'. Owen apparently encountered this problem at New Harmony in particular. Here, at least, in an 1826 lecture, he gave an unusually practical example of how it functioned in everyday life, while also pointing towards his own solution:

[33] Owen, *The Marriage System of the New Moral World* (Leeds, 1838), pp. 25–7. For discussion see John Saville, 'Robert Owen on the Family and Marriage System of the New Moral World', in M. Cornforth, ed., *Rebels and Their Causes* (Lawrence and Wishart, 1978), pp. 107–21, and generally Barbara Taylor, *Eve and the New Jerusalem*. The mere fact of Owenism's sexual egalitarianism and anti-patriarchalism can be understood as implying that its ideas were twice as democratic as those of most radicals, who often argued that reform should reinstate women in their rightful position in the home. For the latter, traditional view see *WTS*, no. 315 (8 September 1839), 2.

[34] *NMW*, 1, no. 9 (27 December 1834), 67.

We all know that when a family party converse together, they speak freely upon subjects which as soon as a stranger accidentally enters amongst them he never hears. Then again, there are perhaps three, four, five or six acquaintances with whom the family is intimate, and when they join the family, another little circle of ideas for conversation becomes common between the parties, but yet different from the family circle of ideas: an ordinary acquaintance appears, and that conversation also ceases: – the party begin to talk upon some general topic in which probably not one takes any real interest. But by a community education, you may all acquire the same general and particular ideas and feelings: consequently, into whatever circle you enter, you would still be in your family circle, and would converse with each other as freely as with a husband, wife, or child.[35]

Yet it was one of the paradoxes of Owen's system that to instil the feeling of 'family' into all individuals also required the cultivation of their independence from one another. As we have seen, this was primarily for epistemological reasons. Only a wholly independent consideration of the problem of individual and social interests, uninfluenced by the biases of others, would result in the voluntary, rational acceptance of the common good. The rational family thus demanded that, particularly as husbands and wives, men and women become as independent of one another as possible in order to ensure 'unions of the purest and most disinterested character'. At such points Owen's socialism had clear affinities with the radical individualism of Godwin's *Political Justice*.[36] This was to help hinder the development of too extreme a form of collectivism in Owenism.

Owen acknowledged several significant historical antecedents for the 'united-interest family'. One of these was the more closely-knit, paternal society which he nostalgically identified with pre-industrial Britain. Writing in 1850, he described a period 'eighty years ago', or just prior to the rise of the manufacturing system, when 'the real comfort of farmers and their servants living with them – of tradesmen and their apprentices and journeymen, always forming one family, was greatly beyond any now experienced; and there was confidence, attachment, and happiness between these parties, arising from their equal position and friendly daily intercourse, unknown at present'. But though Owen was inclined to romanticise preindustrial social relations, he never wished to support any principle of hierarchy – and he never doubted the class basis of past social 'harmony' – other than that of age. Future societies would be composed only of 'parents, brothers and sisters throughout the world, animated by the strongest family affections'. But such families would bear as little relation to

---

[35] Owen, *The Marriage System*, pp. 71–2; *NHG*, 1, no. 49 (30 August 1826), 390.
[36] *WB*, 1, no. 2 (27 July 1839), 10.

history as to blood. Instead they would distil what Owen took to be the best qualities of individual households as well as communities.[37]

The most distinctive characteristic of the future social family was its unity through common endeavour. Individual interest being the source of all social divisions, such competition could only be overcome 'when the whole interest of the individual, and of society is identified as one family, whose powers, faculties, properties, and possessions shall be directly applied to promote the well-being and happiness of each individual, without partiality, according to the peculiar consti-tution of each member of this large family'.[38] Owen did not suppose that the mere introduction of a 'paternal' mode of government (which would not only include women as well as men, but be based upon the diffusion of the 'feminine' virtues – charity, love, sympathy and the like – throughout society) would elicit such a sense of group identity. In particular he developed a millenarian expectation about the sudden change of behaviour which would take place in his disciples once they fully understood his system. Particularly in 1817, but sporadically in the 1830s and 1840s, too, he leaned heavily upon such millenarian imagery to describe the forthcoming transformation to the new moral world.[39] But unlike most millenarians, he never based his hopes for future social harmony upon the idea of divine intervention or even greatly increased spiritual unity, important though this was. Instead, improved social organisation would be primarily responsible for the good order of the future. Consequently the paternal *system* included not only a form of government, but also a new plan of societal arrange-ment without which the government could not survive according to the definition Owen had assigned to it. This would also guarantee to all the benefits of equal rights, equal education, and 'pure' or 'true' democracy. For it was still possible to envision the paternal form of government as nominally democratic, in the sense that all of a certain age would form the government, and hence all would eventually rule, but with other sources of divided interest remaining to undermine the mode of rule, and eventually divide the society anew.

The most important potential source of conflict was occupational distinction. An extreme division of labour did not only threaten indi-vidual rationality, though we have seen that Owen's opposition to narrow specialisation was based upon the goal of furthering the rational and independent personality. The maldistribution of labour was also a source of class distinctions, and thus underlay all political

---

37 *ROWL*, ltr 4 (1850), 33–4; *A Full Account of the Farewell Festival Given to Robert Owen on His Departure for America* (1844), p. 4.

38 Owen, *The Catechism of the New Moral World* (Leeds, 1838), p. 7.

39 See generally W. H. Oliver, *Prophets and Millennialists: The Uses of Biblical Prophecy in England from the 1790s to the 1840s* (Oxford, Oxford University Press, 1978), pp. 175–96.

and social conflict. Society was composed of those who produced wealth and value, the productive classes, and those who either shirked labour entirely, or added nothing to the social value of the product. Unless some rational scheme for assigning work were followed, political power could still be used to assist others to avoid labour, and government might still function (as Owen said the British Parliament did in 1835) as 'a complicated machine, to enable the useless nonproducer of wealth to enslave, and keep in ignorance and poverty, the actual producer of wealth'.[40] The only remedy for this was to ensure that all governors were also producers, or, in Owen's solution, *had* been producers, such that the interest of the governed and governors always coalesced, and never degenerated into conflicts between governing consumers (of taxes, hence labour) and governed producers.

Owen's final plan, matured during the mid-1830s, was for the division of society into eight age-groups, each group performing one major set of tasks at a given age, and moving on to something else at the expiry of the assigned period, thereby permitting all to do and become all. Age, the most natural and obvious principle of distinction, would thus supplant class as the basis of the organisation of labour, with the youthful, adult and mature periods of replacing what Owen took to be the functions of the working, middle and upper classes. The first 'class' (as Owen called these age-groups), from birth to age 5, would largely be occupied with being educated. So would the second (5–10 years old), which would also assist with domestic labour. In the third (10–15 years old), the first two years would be spent directing those aged 7–10 in their 'domestic exercises', while the final three years would be devoted to acquiring 'a knowledge of the principles and practices of the more advanced useful arts of life', being instructed by members of the next class (aged 15–20), who would be engaged in production as well. The fifth class (20–25) would supervise all branches of production and education, the sixth (25–30) would preserve and distribute wealth, and the seventh (30–40) would govern the 'home department' of communities. The eighth and final class, those aged 40–60, would conduct all 'foreign' affairs.[41]

The effect of this scheme, thus, was to combine producer and consumer, governor and governed, educator and educated, in order to supersede all the artificial distinctions of ranks, divisions and classes.[42] There is no evidence that Owen intended to implement this scheme at

[40] *NMW*, 1, no. 48 (26 September 1835), 382.
[41] Owen, *Six Lectures Delivered at Manchester* (Manchester, 1839), pp. 73–83; Owen, *Robert Owen's Address, Delivered at the Meeting in St. Martin's Hall* (1855), p. 17. The first statement of this scheme was probably in 1835. Se *NMW*, 1, no. 28 (9 May 1835), 221.
[42] *NMW*, 13, no. 48 (24 May 1845), 388.

the beginning of his career. It seems, rather, to have been the logical outgrowth of both his early intentions and subsequent experiences. The principle of organisation by age was first proposed (in 1817) in relation to government only, as a means of overcoming the need for elections and of providing for a fixed principle of authority. But Owen's increasing refusal to compromise with the old system, and his insistence upon equality of both education and condition as prerequisites of successful community life, transformed his initial hostility to a narrow division of labour into a general theory of the moral, social and political as well as technical division of labour. As early as 1821, Owen intimated that age and experience (the two were presumed to coincide) were the only just and natural social distinctions, and that the only inequalities of the future would be those of age.[43] It was apparently not until 1829, however, that all of the necessary elements of Owen's final theory were formally presented as a 'Universal Code of Laws' for the future organisation of society. This established that 'All shall pass through the same general routine of education, and domestic teaching, and employment' as well as government.[44] Modified only by the addition of a few minor details, this ideal was maintained, if less often adverted to, during the labour exchange and trades' union phases of Owenism during the 1830s. When Owen returned to communitarian planning after 1834, he finally elaborated what was to be his most detailed plan for the organisation of society upon the principle of age.

Owen's use of the language of politics in relation to his own 'paternal' system can now be clarified more fully. The paternal mode of government and social organisation represented the supersession of both principles – aristocracy and democracy – which Owen considered to have been the historical basis of all forms of government. Democracy (and here it was the experience of the ancient republics as well as the French revolution which Owen had in mind) had always been 'in practice essentially violent and selfish; always grasping for more territory nationally and for more wealth individually, without knowing how rationally to use the one or the other'.[45] Democracy, therefore, was merely a system of universal egoism reduced to political principle, which tended in addition to reproduce an aristocracy of new rulers with only a cosmetic change in the form of government to distinguish between the two systems. But in all of its manifestations in the old world, aristocracy too was unacceptable to Owen. The principle of rule on the basis of birth was palpably absurd, for wisdom and experience were hardly hereditary.

[43] Owen, *Permanent Relief*, p. 4; *NHG*, 2, no. 19 (7 February 1827), 146; no. 21 (21 February 1827), 161. The latter work, entitled 'The Social System', was written in 1821, though not published until 1826. See no. 8 (22 November 1826), 63.

[44] Owen, *Robert Owen's Opening Speech*, p. 49.

[45] Owen, *Life*, 1A, p. iii.

The paternal system thus synthesised the most rational aspects of both democracy and aristocracy. 'True democracy' meant 'genuine', or 'social', rather than the merely formal equality of existing republics. 'Under the best conditions of the most advanced nations', Owen wrote in 1846, 'the natural rights of mankind are talked about, but are unknown in practice; democratic constitutions are spoken of and recommended, but a true democracy has yet to be established among the nations of the earth'. But if the 'rational meaning' of democracy entailed 'equal rights at birth and through life', it could be recommended as the panacea for all social and political evils. As Owen emphasised in late 1848, 'without a full and complete equality, there can be no general permanent happiness, in fact no justice among men. It is the pure principle of democracy, carried out to its full extent in practice, that can alone carry the human race onward toward the highest degree of perfection'.[46]

'Democracy' for Owen was thus far more egalitarian than any society contemplated by the radical reformers. But the future social system would nonetheless be ruled by 'nature's genuine and unopposed aristocracy', those aged 40–60, who through their experience and interest in the happiness of the governed were naturally as well as rationally qualified to embody the 'parental principle of governing', 'the perfection of governing'. The progress of history had been towards democracy as it was commonly understood. This development could only cease, however, with the acceptance of Owen's principle of authority:

The *despotic* and the *hereditary* principles of governing are abandoned by the reflecting and intelligent Liberal, who now advocates the *representative* principle, in opposition to both; and this latter will for a time prevail; that is, until experience shall prove its evils in practice, and then it must give way to the only principle by which mankind can be well-governed. This may be called the *educational* principle, and it will supersede the despotic, hereditary, and elective – the now popular principle among the liberal reformers of society. When, however, men can have their minds formed for them, freed from the gross errors with which they have been filled by the present system, they will see clearly the everlasting evils which must attend the despotic, the hereditary, and the elective principles of governing; but it is necessary to pass through these three graduations, to arrive at the fourth, or true principle of government.[47]

Securing the final stage of rational polity entailed a variety of difficulties, however. Some of the most important of these can be best illustrated through an examination of Owen's practical handling of the

---

[46] *DU*, 11 March 1846, University of London MS. 578 (Pare Papers), fol. 147; *NMW*, 13, no. 46 (10 May 1845), 365; *SA*, no. 19 (2 December 1848), 298.

[47] Owen, *The Book of the New Moral World*, pt 6 (1844), p. 64; Owen, *Letter from Mr. Robert Owen to the New York State Convention* (Washington DC, 1846), p. 26; *NMW*, 1, no. 48 (26 September 1835), 380.

problem of transitional government, which, because of the resistance it provoked, helped considerably to undermine the socialist movement at the height of its power during the 1840s.

'Elective paternal government' and the Chartist years

Founded in 1835, the Association of All Classes of All Nations was the most important socialist organisation ever established by Owen. In it he was able to exercise considerable influence over most areas of policy making. From the outset, wrote William Galpin, one of Owen's closest associates in this period, Owen in fact 'more or less superintended the general affairs' of the AACAN.[48] Even more than the New Harmony experiment, in which he had too little control over admissions to the community, and had to share power with William Maclure and others, this was Owen's personal creation. His entire reputation (there was little left of his fortune) was staked, in turn, upon the success of the Harmony estate at Queenwood, Hampshire. During the exuberant years when its future seemed rosy, his fame once again rocketted. When all was lost in 1845, it declined equally rapidly, leaving Owen in his final years more an object of curiosity than of devotion or antipathy.

With reference to the question of organisation, Owen's influence was particularly deeply felt during this period. His scheme of 'elective paternal government', as we will see, occasioned an enormous amount of disunity, and split the socialist movement at all levels, in the leadership of the Central Board of the AACAN, at the annual congresses, in the branch organisations, and finally, doubtless hastening its demise, in the Harmony community itself. The growth of this dissension, and the impetus it gave to more traditional brands of democracy in the socialist movement, will be explored in chapter 5. Of more immediate relevance is Owen's conception of the practice of transitional government, and its relation to his plans for the final form of social organisation.

As its name implies, the 'elective paternal system' was designed by Owen to facilitate the transition between existing forms of government and the future system of paternal social organisation. To some extent, however, even the concept of a transitional form was anomalous to Owen. On occasion he reverted easily to a radical dualism similar to that which we have here earlier identified with an Augustinian position, and which reappeared in both millenarianism and the notion of moral rebirth which the Quakers, among others, associated with the process of perceiving the Light of God. The consistency of the old

[48] *NS*, no. 279 (18 March 1843), 7.

immoral and new moral worlds varied like oil and water, Owen was fond of saying. There could be 'no attempt to unite the two states of society . . . they can never amalgamate in any proportion, and it will, therefore, be useless to draw inferences on the new system from anything we see around us'.[49] Such a view was a useful defence against present failings. Yet Owen was never a fully-fledged millennialist, and always envisioned some form of practical accommodation with the needs of the present. This spirit of compromise underlay his plans for at least partial control by capital investors initially in each community, rather than anything like a class preference for capitalists, which some modern critics have mistakenly identified in his writings. Nonetheless there were important differences in the functions of interim and ulti-mate modes of organisation. While the final form of government would be mainly supervisory, with education integrated fully into all stages of the social system, the purpose of the intermediate or prepara-tory government was primarily educational. During this period a new, more moral generation would be raised, and the character of existing generations reformed. This placed a much greater burden upon in-terim forms of government, however. Only 'the individuals the most experienced and successful in governing' were capable of undertaking what Owen emphasised was '*the* most difficult task that man will ever have to perform; it is *the step* of difficulty and danger'.[50]

Before the educational process could begin, however, it was necess-ary to choose an appropriate form of interim organisation. Having considered seven modes of effecting the transition from the old to the new world in late 1834, Owen settled upon the secular equivalent of saintly rule, a union of the most rational members of society, as his personal choice. The government of the new association was to be 'paternal, and one of unity'. It would consist of a governor, called 'the Social Father of the New Moral World' (to encourage the growth of a family atmosphere), a senior council of twelve, all aged 35 or more, a junior council of twelve, aged 25–35, and an executive of six, four chosen from the senior members by themselves, and two from the junior members. The 'Social Father' was to be appointed by the unani-mous choice of the two councils, and the executive, by the unanimous concurrence of both the 'Father' and both councils. After a period of probation, members of the association would be graded into three classes, passing into each higher class after six months. In order to ensure permanent mutual sympathy, each class was to vote annually on the continuance of all its members. Any failing to receive a majority

---

[49] Owen, *The Marriage System*, p. 3.
[50] ROWL, ltr 13 (1850), 127; Owen, *The Book of the New Moral World*, pt 2 (1842), pp. 42–3; pt 6 (1844), p. 61.

would be returned to the lower class. The legislative process included careful safeguards against usurpations of power. All proposals had to be recommended unanimously by the classes to the junior council. Amendments at any stage had to be unanimously proposed upwards and then unanimously returned downwards, which clearly exemplified the adoption of Quaker and other Dissenting modes of procedure. Finally, when complete agreement was reached by the 'Father', executive, and councils, each class separately was to reconsider the proposed regulation. If a majority of the classes approved, the measure would become law. If not, it would 'be suspended until such assent shall be obtained through conviction produced by sound argument and matured judgement'. Enactment could additionally be prevented, however, if any member of any class could demonstrate, in a public assembly of the association, that the proposal was 'not in strict accordance with the laws of nature'. A more cumbersome and libertarian form of polity placing a greater degree of faith in the powers of rational argumentation could scarcely have been devised.[51]

In practice the day-to-day running of the organisation depended upon Owen and the members of the Central Board, his executive. This reflected several changes in policy during the first five years of the history of the Rational Society, as the amalgamated socialist organisations came to be called.[52] Plans for the government of future communities also altered during this period. In mid-1835, the *New Moral World*, the Society's journal and the most important source for our knowledge of socialism in this period, reprinted the British and Foreign Philanthropic Society's scheme for the government of communities by those who furnished the capital. At their second annual congress in 1837, however, the branch delegates agreed that in prin-

---

51 *NMW*, 1, no. 4 (22 November 1834), 27–8; Jones, *Life of Robert Owen*, p. 314. The other six possibilities were: a union of the great powers, of the monied aristocracy, of the landed aristocracy, of both of these, of masters and their men, plus farmers and their servants, and of operatives and peasants alone. The first full constitution of the AACAN is given in *NMW*, 1, no. 19 (7 March 1835), 145–7.

52 This was a shortened version of the Universal Community Society of Rational Religionists, the branch and financial associate of the AACAN. The two organisations merged in late 1839. See the AACAN *Minute Book*, 1838–40, MS., Internationaal Instituut voor Sociale Geschiedenis, Amsterdam, fol. 428. Among the constitutional changes during this period it was decided in 1836, for example, that the 'father' and Central Board should be elected directly by the branch delegates and congress (*NMW*, 2, no. 84, 4 June 1836, 251–3), while the earlier system was apparently reverted to in 1837 (*ibid.*, 3, no. 136, 10 June 1837, 251–2), but again rejected for the second plan in 1838 (*Proceedings of the Third Congress of the AACAN*, Leeds, 1838, p. 38), which was continued in 1839 (*The Constitution and Laws of the UCSRR*, 1839, p. 23). It is not entirely clear whether, under the new 'unity' government of 1841, Owen actually had legal control over his officers. See the *Third and Fourth Supplements to the Laws of the UCSRR* (1840). But Fleming later said that from that point on the officers of the Society certainly 'acted under his direction' (*NMW*, 11, no. 7, 13 August 1842, 52).

ciple, for at least the first two or three years, such government should be by one person only. At the 1840 congress, this system was altered again in favour of greater indirect democracy. The governor of Harmony, hitherto chosen by Owen and the Central Board, was to be elected by two-thirds of the branch delegates sitting in congress. This was nonetheless still entirely in accordance with Owen's original view. It merely happened that, on the mass application of the joint-stock principle, there were some hundreds of capitalists involved as branch members. Only when the total capital borrowed to establish the community was repaid, however, explained the editor of the *New Moral World*, George Alexander Fleming, in early 1841, could the members of the community itself be entitled to elect their own managers in every department. This provision, however, was to prove a source of continual disagreement.[53]

For the first five years of the Society's history, the joint-stock principle of management seems to have operated fairly well, with the branches providing funds and delegates, and in theory exercising control over both the president and the Central Board of the Society at the annual congresses. By the turn of the decade, however, the financial stagnation of the Society and a tendency towards 'politics' in many of the branches induced Owen to alter the governmental structure. At the 1841 congress, he proposed to introduce an 'elective paternal system' of management for both the central organisation and the branches. Lecturing on his new proposals just prior to the congress at the Egyptian Hall, Piccadilly, he argued that:

Socialism, in its present state of management among the working classes must remain in its infancy. The democratic principle is not applicable to the forming and bringing into practice a new discovery, much less an entirely new system ... the *Elective Paternal System* is alone calculated to carry out any new and complicated system successfully through the transition state. To devise and execute any great object new to society, it is necessary to be directed by an elected paternal head, who shall appoint his own officers.

In order to avoid the experience of 'divided councils, arising from the democratic principle of governing their proceedings', therefore, each branch was to choose as its 'father' one person possessed of 'the greatest number of the qualities requisite for so important a situation', and allow him or her to choose a committee or board of assistants. The central government and Harmony community would operate in the same way, with the president naming the officers rather than, as previously, having them elected by the congress. Owen also demanded that he be appointed governor of Harmony, with full power

53 *NMW*, 4, no. 176 (10 March 1838), 153; no. 195 (21 July 1838), 309; 5, no. 1 (27 October 1838), 1.

over its finances. Adopting one of his favourite ploys, he resigned as president of the Central Board in order to persuade the Congress to accept his reforms.[54]

The financial condition of the Society was certainly the chief reason behind Owen's 1841 decision concerning the best mode of intermediate government. For the previous two years, Fleming noted several months after the congress, the poverty of the classes to whom the Society primarily appealed had left it in a stationary economic condition. In proportion as Owen's new principles for internal regulation were adopted, he added, this situation would improve. Indeed, this was the case for some time after the decision was taken. Several wealthy supporters willing to stake their fortunes on the success of the new community joined the Central Board on condition that Owen retained exclusive control over the financial affairs of the Society. The most immediate result was the erection of the amazingly modern, lavishly fitted great hall on the Harmony estate, which represented the prototype of future socialist grandeur.[55]

To some extent the 'elective paternal system' also merely brought the government of the Society into line with Owen's previous experience and inclination. In both the Equitable Labour Exchange and as Grand Master of the GNCTU, Owen had been an elected leader with the right of choosing his own assistants. In principle, at least, this procedure need not have agitated too unduly the political sensibilities of more traditional democrats. In fact, as the *New Moral World* pointed out in an address to American socialists shortly after the 1841 congress, the system resembled that of the United States, where an elected President chose his cabinet officers.[56]

But insofar as 'harmony' and 'unity' were the chief aims of the new government, Owen's opponents were no doubt correct in suspecting that his proposals were intended to diminish discussion and voting at every level of the organisation, and to increase the powers of a select group of individuals to ensure the level of expenditure on the community that Owen deemed necessary to its success. Without doubt, it was true that many branches had engaged in heated discussions on a wide variety of issues. The purpose of the paternal form, as the Central Board expressed it in 1844, was thus in part to 'supersede the continual changes and frequent division in council which occurred under the old form of government', and to replace them with the feelings of kind-

---

54 *Ibid.*, 1, no. 40 (1 August 1835), 317; 3, no. 136 (10 June 1837), 247–8; 8, no. 3 (18 July 1840), 43; 9, no. 14 (3 April 1841), 211.
55 Owen, *An Address to the Socialists* (1841), pp. 11–13; *NMW*, 9, no. 23 (6 June 1841), 348, 353–5.
56 *Ibid.*, 10, no. 1 (3 July 1841), 1–2; 11, no. 7 (13 August 1842), 52, *Union*, no. 9 (1 December 1842), 366.

ness, charity and mutual good will which formed the core of Owen's 'new religion'. The Society, in other words, was to conduct itself primarily like a Dissenting sect rather than a political party. The key word associated with the new form of government, in fact, was 'unity'. Democratic executives, Owen insisted, did not admit of 'unity of principle, feeling, or action', and consequently lacked decisiveness and vigorous execution. The elective paternal system, however, combined the advantages of both aristocracy and democracy, and hence would aid in disseminating the true principles of necessity (discussed in further detail in chapter 4) upon which the new system was to be founded. As a result,

as soon as the members acquire a knowledge of the principles and their right application to practice, all anger, ill will, and division among them, must cease; the factions of the old world will die their natural death; a new mode of speaking to, and of, each other, will naturally and necessarily arise, and harmony and good feeling will be evidence in the countenance, manner, and conduct, of all.[57]

There was, nonetheless, considerable resistance in the branches both to the proposed form of government (which on the whole was rejected, as we will see), and to Owen's policies *vis-à-vis* the Tytherly community. By the combination of 'strong democratic control with an unobstructed executive power', as William Galpin described it, the recalcitrant branches still retained the power to reject Owen's proposals. Indeed he had never tried to curtail this right, asking only that branch members lend their full support to those individuals they elected to manage their affairs. But Owen himself refused to back proposals he disagreed with, and thus to cede to the branches power which was rightfully theirs.[58] In the two years from mid-1842 to May, 1844, he repeatedly resigned from various positions when his motions were defeated, and then rejoined when, amidst the growing gloom provoked by signs of the imminent crash of Harmony, the organisation turned to him as its last hope for salvation.[59]

During these years the 'elective paternal system' became the focal

---

[57] Rational Society, *Minute Book of Directors*, no. 2 (1843–5), MS. Internationaal Instituut voor Sociale Geschiedenis, Amsterdam, 18 October 1844; *NMW*, 9, no. 25 (19 June 1841), 380.

[58] *NMW*, 10, no. 25 (18 December 1841), 193–4.

[59] *Ibid.*, 10, no. 41 (9 April 1842), 322, 324; 11, no. 49 (3 June 1843), 406. Owen resigned from his positions as governor of Harmony and president of the Society in July 1842 (11, no. 5, 30 July 1842, 33, and no. 6, 6 August 1842, 41–4). He became governor of Harmony again in June 1843 (11, no. 50, 10 June 1843, 419), and president again in July (12, no. 1, 1 July 1843, 12). His final resignation came at the end of the congress of June 1844 (12, no. 50, 8 June 1844, 401–2). He departed for America in June 1844, and did not return again until June 1845, leaving again for the USA two months later (13, no. 8, 17 August 1844, 5–7, and no. 53, 28 June 1845, 433).

point for a variety of other disagreements within the socialist movement. On the one hand, it symbolised everything that the advocates of
direct democracy and increased working class participation found
wrong with the central leadership. On the other, it embodied the voice
of reason, experience and resolution to those who sought to avoid the
seeming chaos of collective decision-making. No matter how often
Owen insisted that forms of government were inconsequential, the
issue continued to haunt him. Ironically, too, the organisation of
government at Queenwood did bear a direct relation to the well-being
of the Society insofar as political debates hindered its progress, which
they did to some degree. Many members of the Rational Society thus
formed a permanent connection between issue of control and the
general progress of the movement. In the circumstances, too, this was
justifiable. Galpin complained in mid-1843 that Owen's unity form of
government had been and was being 'charged with an immense
amount of things to which it had no reference whatsoever'. But many
of the more radical Socialists also identified it with Owen's other three
major policy propositions of 1841. For now the 'transition colonies'
were to be composed of four classes: hired labourers earning £25 to £39
annually, candidates for membership (mechanics and artisans) earning an average of £65 each, full members, and independent families or
individuals. Government would be by a president elected by all
members of the third class older than 21. Opponents saw these proposals as hostile to the central tenets of socialism. G. J. Holyoake and
M. Q. Ryall, who were among Owen's most vociferous critics at this
time, argued that the plan differed 'from its predecessors in one particular, for it no longer provides that the great *political* principle of the
society should be carried out, viz. equality of age and condition'. Yet
Owen's 1841 scheme in fact largely resembled his earlier attempts to
attract the middle and upper classes as investors and community
members. Owen did originally conceive of having eight types of apart-
ments at Harmony. But it would seem that the most extensive form of
division which finally marked community life was a separation into
three age-groups.[60]

During the 1840s, Owen's political views also affected the socialist
movement in a variety of other ways. Less immediate to the daily
concerns of the Society and the community, but still of great importance to many of its members was his attitude to the Charter and its
proponents. Chapters 5 and 6 will examine relations between the
Chartist and socialist movements. In relation to Owen's own political

[60] *NMW*, 11, no. 49 (3 June 1843), 405; Owen, *A Development of the Principles and Plans*
(1841), pp. 401, 65–6; *Movement*, no. 19 (1844), 148; *NMW*, 8, no. 3 (18 July 1840), 36–7;
NS, no. 283 (15 April 1843), 7.

ideas, it is clear that while his general statements on the aims of the Charter accorded with his pronouncements on parliamentary reform in earlier years, evidence also suggests that he embraced a more catholic approach to the Chartist struggle at various times.

Owen was in fact far from averse to proposing a variety of political reforms. Both before and during the Chartist agitation, he frequently counselled parliament to adopt measures which went far beyond the search for financial aid for communities. His support for the abolition of child labour, passage of the Ten Hours' Bill, and other measures of factory and poor law reform is well known. But Owen's more political proposals, often published during election years (he offered himself as a parliamentary candidate approximately ten times) have usually been ignored. Much of this programme remained similar throughout his public career. In 1832, as we have seen, it comprised seven points: a graduated property tax equal to national expenditure, the abolition of all other taxes, free trade, national education and employment for those who desired them, and liberty of speech, writing and religion. The 1834 'Charter of the Rights of Humanity' numbered seventeen points, including the abolition of war and of the domination of religion. In the 'Charter of the Rational System' (1842), Owen added the provision of a national form of money (for example, based upon a labour rather than a gold standard), and marriage by registrar, with divorce freely available. His 'Preliminary Charter of the Rational System' (1843) consisted of twelve points, of which the most significant addition was the proviso that, following the labour exchange model, the value of goods would 'be decided by properly qualified officers, who will have no private interest to bias their judgments', which represents a fundamental intrusion by politics into economics. Throughout this period, too, Owen gradually evolved a constitutionalist programme which proposed full liberty of conscience and 'the utmost individual freedom of action, compatible with the permanent good of Society'. The use of such language, in fact, seems to have become particularly pronounced after the mid-1840s, or after Owen had faced many renewed attacks upon the potential threat of his system to individual freedom generally.[61]

But Owen's reform proposals did not necessarily predispose him towards parliamentary reform *per se*. During the first decade of Chartism, Owen never included any of the points of the Charter in his own programme. This was still the case in the 1847 election (despite Gammage's contention to the contrary), where Owen, standing at Maryle-

---

[61] Owen, *Robert Owen's Reply to the Question*, p. 12; *Crisis*, 3, no. 27 (1 March 1834), 219; *NMW*, 10, no. 43 (23 April 1842), 337; *Preliminary Charter of the Rational System* (1843); Owen, *Revolution in the Mind and Practice*, p. 60.

bone, received one vote (much to the amusement of the other candidates' supporters) out of 15,050 cast, though this was after he had stood down from the election, considerably greater support having been offered him beforehand. But Owen's views on this question finally changed soon afterwards. On 15 March 1848, after the revolution had begun in France and Germany, he published a ten-point plan which included 'Representation co-extensive with taxation, the voters to be protected by the ballot, and the representatives to be paid for their services'. Several months later he also recommended a constitutional convention chosen by universal suffrage from all European peoples, 'defective as this suffrage would be in many cases'.[62]

Had Owen finally been converted by Chartist arguments? In a sense this was the case, insofar as popular activity seemed to leave him no choice. But more precisely, he believed such changes were the only means of preventing a similar revolution in Britain. The new French revolution, he wrote, had 'like electric magic, shivered this system to atoms; it no longer exists in the minds of those who understand political movements, and who, from existing causes, can foresee future events'. In the hope of influencing the course of events, he journeyed to Paris himself, dispensing pamphlets and advice to all who would listen, and writing back that 'No nation or people ever had so promising an opportunity to establish a good government and a superior society as the French people at this crisis in their history'. And when the cause was lost, he shared in the disappointment of many more insurrectionary observers:

Had it not been for the Revolution of the three days of February in Paris, the old falsehoods and evils of society might have tormented the human race with injustice and cruelty for many years; but, fortunately for the world, Nature forced on that Revolution, which had become necessary by the crimes and oppressions of the old society, to which the industrious producers could no longer submit. And of all the murders, bloodshed, and violences following, old society is the cause; the re-action, as it is called, is to uphold the robbery, injustice, and murderous cruelty of this system of falsehood and deception.[63]

It is doubtful, however, that many Chartist leaders were over-

[62] R. G. Gammage, *History of the Chartist Movement* (1854), p. 284, also presumed in Theodore Rothstein, *From Chartism to Labourism* (Martin Lawrence, 1929), p. 8; University of London MS. 578 (Pare Papers), fol. 173; Owen, *Practical Measures Required to Prevent Greater Political Changes in Great Britain and Ireland* (1848), also printed in *NS*, no. 544 (25 March 1848), 3; *SA*, 1, no. 13 (21 October 1848), 203.

[63] Owen, *Socialism Misrepresented and Truly Represented* (1848), p. 16; Owen to Thomas Allsop, 14 April 1848, British Library Add. MS. 46344, fols. 57–8; *SA*, 1, no. 15, 4 November 1848, 235. See also Owen, *Dialogue Entre la France, le Monde, et Robert Owen* (Paris, 1848), and Owen, *Dialogue Entre les Membres de la Commission Executive* (Paris, 1848). On this episode in Owen's life see C. Tsuzuki, 'Robert Owen and Revolutionary Politics', in Sidney Pollard and John Salt, eds., *Robert Owen: Prophet of the Poor* (Macmillan, 1971), pp. 20–51, and Maximilien Rubel, 'Robert Owen à Paris en 1848', *AH*, 30 (1960), 1–12.

whelmed by Owen's change of heart in 1848, when he had little money, virtually no organisation, and few followers, considering his refusal to embrace the six points in the early 1840s, when his power and influence had been comparatively great. Many probably never forgave his hostility to the Chartist programme. In his 'Address to the Chartists' in early 1842, for example, Owen had accused those who sought the six points of vastly overrating the effects they would bring. None of the Chartist leaders, he insisted, had 'yet exhibited a knowledge of the cause of the evils now so heavily pressing on society, or of the remedies for all those evils'. The Charter, moreover, would 'make all petty politicians', with each requiring that 'his individual, crude, and undigested measures should be attended to as those of any other independent elector or member of Parliament'. The social benefits of universal suffrage, he continued, were surely evident in the USA. For while the latter possessed

in great abundance, all the materials, power, and means of prosperity and happiness for 10, 20, 30 or 40 times their present population; and yet, with all the points of the Charter secured, they are actually suffering innumerable evils with a population not exceeding eighteen or twenty millions. In fact, the territory of the United States is more than sufficient to support in high comfort all the present inhabitants of the world.[64]

It is nonetheless possible that Owen attempted some form of alliance with the Chartists. Writing in 1850, the Liverpool merchant and socialist John Finch claimed that Owen had visited the Chartist leader Feargus O'Connor while the latter was imprisoned at York Castle in 1841, and that *'union was at that time effected*, but unfortunately it was never carried out in practice'. The programme supposedly jointly agreed upon was the same as that given in Owen's 1832 address, with the addition of support for the points of the Charter. Since there was nothing particularly socialistic in these proposals, O'Connor certainly had no ideological reason to forsake such an alliance, barring the perils of being identified with Owen at all. In addition, though he was definitely opposed to Owen's views on community of property, O'Connor was so concerned with settlement on the land by 1845 that he was willing to begin 'on the "individual system" ... leaving the people to co-operate ultimately, if they saw fit'. This more compromising attitude may well have begun while he was imprisoned. The failure of the alliance instead probably had more to do with Owen, who as we have seen decided a few months later in 1841 upon a somewhat different political strategy whose economic results were more tangible than those which an alliance with the Chartists might have produced.[65]

The evidence about Owen's later position on the Charter is also

[64] *NMW*, 10, no. 44 (20 April 1843), 349.
[65] *WT*, 2, no. 56 (16 March 1850), 3; *NS*, no. 389 (26 April 1845), 6.

somewhat ambiguous. Nominated to the new Executive Committee of the National Charter Association in 1850, he refused, complaining that 'Chartism knows not how to well-employ, well-educate, or to well-govern any society'. In 1857 he was reported as receiving great applause when he supported the Charter at an NCA meeting. In 1858, the final year of his life, Owen proclaimed that he was 'in favour of the whole of the Charter', and recommended that the six points be passed 'in a liberal instalment' by 'a liberal, good, practical reform of Parliament' which would give the vote 'to all competent to make a rational use of it', which was not exactly an unequivocal statement of support for universal suffrage. However, by then, more than ever, Owen's political opinions were of little consequence to most of those around him. The Charter agitation had arisen without much assistance on his part. It equally well passed away in spite of it.[66]

Paternalism and federalism: the millennial republic

Two types of transitional government were ultimately outlined by Owen. The first, or 'elective paternal' form, combined aspects of existing representative governments with features of the future, exclusively paternal form. This was still described as a 'democratic' form of government. As Owen explained shortly before departing once again for America in 1844, leaving the shambles of Harmony behind him, there was no 'more determined enemy to inequality than himself. It was the great object of his life to destroy it'. He denied that he was 'an ingrained, thorough aristocrat'. But equality in education and social position were required before equality of participation could succeed, and it was the purpose of Owen's seemingly unequal transitional form of government to establish these prerequisites. Secondly, there was the question of the transitional form of national government to be considered. Here, in his strictures against the Chartists and elsewhere throughout most of his career, Owen adhered fairly consistently to the view that 'the existing machinery of the established governments in all countries will be found to be the best to assist to bring about this change, and conduct it, through its transition state, into all the advantages of the full new or millennial existence'.[67]

Eventually, however, the day would arrive when millennial government would be possible. At this time, as we have seen, Owen expected

---

66 *ROJ*, 1, no. 9 (28 December 1850), 65; 'Reminiscences of Thomas Dunning', in David Vincent, ed., *Testaments of Radicalism: Memoirs of Working Class Politicians* (Europa, 1977), p. 223; *PP*, no. 302 (13 February 1858), 5; *ROMG*, no. 15 (1 May 1858), 18, 40.
67 *A Full Account of the Farewell Festival*, pp. 7–8; Owen, *Lectures on the Rational System*, p. 164.

that authority based upon age would be harmoniously wielded and accepted. This plan was indebted to jurisprudential, Quaker and republican sources. But historians have also linked its 'paternal' aspects to other contemporary uses of the language of paternalism. This assumption, however, is imprecise and highly misleading. It helps us to understand some of the sources of Owen's thinking, as well as some of the resonances of his proposals. But it tells us nothing about his actual ideals of government. Instead, Owen's conception of the eventual character of the national state, rather than only the government of single communities, needs to be seen in terms of a federated national and international community structure which was probably considerably indebted to the American model. Assessing the importance of this element in Owen's thought also requires some clarification of the centralising and statist tendencies in his social theory.

The language of paternalism has long been applied to the social theory and intercourse of early nineteenth-century Britain.[68] Recently David Roberts, in particular, has explored the network of meanings and social relations associated with the term. Though he asserts that Owen ran his communities (perhaps only New Lanark was intended) 'along strictly paternalist lines', Roberts' general model of paternalism is in fact not really applicable to Owen's views. The paternalist worldview, according to Roberts, was authoritarian, hierarchic, organic and pluralistic. Paternalists typically believed 'in capital punishment, whipping, severe game laws, summary justice for delinquents, strict laws defining the duties of servants, and the imprisonment of seditious writers'. Certainly none of this is true of Owen. Closer to the latter's views is the alleged paternalist emphasis upon the preservation of small communities in which governors and governed were mutually acquainted, and reciprocal bonds of authority and deference retained. But Owen of course denied that property should be the basis of any authority, while contemporary paternalism was based precisely upon this principle. But if, as Roberts also asserts, 'paternalism' actually meant little more than a call for the protection of the poor, weak, helpless and infirm, often coupled (in Sewell, Seeley, Coleridge and Oastler, for example) with a desire for both a strong monarchy and a decentralised government, Owen did share something in common with such views.[69]

What most clearly distinguished Owen's paternalism from that of others, of course, was its grounding in the aetatic or gerontocratic

[68] On the seventeenth-century background to paternalist ideals see especially Gordon J. Schochet, *Patriarchalism in Political Thought*.

[69] David Roberts, *Paternalism in Early Victorian England* (Croom Helm, 1979), pp. 273, 2–3, 270–1, 187–9, 202–3. See also A. P. Thornton, *The Habit of Authority. Paternalism in British History* (George Allen and Unwin, 1966), especially pp. 167–228.

principle of hierarchy, and Owen's consequent condemnation of all those who sought to introduce other less rational principles in its place. This also included other types of socialism. Hence when the Saint-Simonian missionaries Fontana and Prati visited England to preach their doctrines in 1834, Owen accused their founder of having been totally ignorant of human nature, specifically pointing to Saint-Simon's ideas of hierarchy and reward according to capacity.[70]

Nor would Owen accept any justification for hierarchy or inequality on the basis of natural or physical difference. Despite the assertions of some historians, he thus rejected any ontological argument based upon the new and widely accepted doctrine of phrenology. A great many of Owen's friends and followers did embrace the science of analysing bumps on the skull, with its strong element of physical determinism.[71] From 1824, however, when the renowned phrenologist George Combe politely informed him that 'your system appears to me to originate in the peculiarities of your own cerebral development', Owen consistently opposed behavioural deductions from phrenological principles.[72] In an 1835 'Address to Phrenologists', he criticised

---

[70] *Crisis*, 2, no. 25 (15 February 1834), 207. It should be recalled, too, that other like-minded socialists did accept such principles when Owen did not. In John Goodwyn Barmby's communitorium, for example, all power was vested in the 'pater' or father. In Barmby's plan for world government, both men and women would vote, but all women would be ineligible for the position of communarch, or ruler of the earth, because 'every thing is subordinate to the prime male principle of nature' (*ECCA*, no. 2, December 1841, 11, and no. 6, May 1842, 44). Lesser writers, such as the Barnet artisan John Thimbleby, also seem to have accepted the principle of male authority. See his *Monadelphia* (1832), p. 40.

[71] The Owenite E. T. Craig apparently used phrenology to analyse applicants to the Ralahine community, though he evidently neglected to notice the underdeveloped faculty of firmness of the owner of the land, who lost the estate gambling. See generally R. G. Garnett, 'E. T. Craig: Communitarian, Educator, Phrenologist.' *VASFE*, 15 (1963), 135–50. See E. Janes, 'The Quest for the New Moral World: Changing Patterns of Owenite Thought, 1817–1870', M.A., University of Wisconsin (1963), chapters 3–4 for details and a general analysis of the relations between Owenism and phrenology, and A. C. Grant, 'New Light on an Old View', *JHI*, 29 (1968), 293–301, and generally Grant, 'George Combe and his Circle', Ph.D., University of Edinburgh (1960). The Coventry ribbon manufacturer and Owenite Charles Bray obligingly shaved the head of the young George Eliot in order to reveal her mental makeup, and himself believed, as he expressed it to George Combe, that 'the best men should be educated first'. See Bray's *Phases of Opinion and Experience During a Long Life* (1879), pp. 73–7, and his letter to Combe, National Library of Scotland MS. 7305, fol. 65.

[72] G. Combe to Owen, 28 January 1824, National Library of Scotland MS. 7382, fol. 368. See Combe's 'Phrenological Analysis of Mr. Owen's New Views of Society', *PJ*, 1 (1823–24), 218–37, for the beginnings of this debate. The commentary below the text of this article by a 'zealous and able advocate of the new views' is identified as that of Abram Combe, George's brother and one of the founders of the Orbiston community, in National Library of Scotland MS. 7383, fol. 14. Julius West wrote only of Owen's 'cordial reception of phrenology' (*A History of the Chartist Movement*, Constable, 1920, p. 41).

Combe by way of emphasising the 'all-surmounting power of education'. Elsewhere he denounced the phrenologists as 'leading the public much astray' by reducing the question of private property to mere operations of the organ of acquisitiveness, and assuming that the present condition of man was 'his natural and fixed state'.[73]

Nor did Owen's paternalist principles ever take the form of any plan for temporary political dictatorship. In the mid-1830s he confronted such a policy (remote though its implementation may have been) through his association with an eccentric Tory and fellow of King's College, Cambridge, James B. Bernard. The latter sought to ally farmers, the aristocracy, and working class radicals in order to eradicate the manufacturing interest and restore (with certain novelties – such as an elective monarchy) the preponderance of the landed gentry. For about a year Owen associated with and paid quite close attention to Bernard. But though he shared the latter's views on the need for the predominant influence of one individual during the transition period, Owen departed from Bernard on the issue of the necessity for violent revolution, which in turn was closely linked to the form such leadership would take. J. E. Smith, one of Owen's other main associates in this period, did alter his views (as we will see) to accord more closely with Bernard's. But Owen does not appear to have conceded much in this regard.[74]

It has also been argued, both by George Jacob Holyoake, who knew Owen fairly well (though usually as an opponent) and some later commentators, that Owen's 'paternal' concerns were so much with social condition and so little with personal liberty that he 'saw no objection to slavery, when beneficially controlled'. This exceedingly impolite fiction apparently originated in Owen's remark, returning from a visit to the West Indies, that its slaves were generally more comfortable than were Irish or English day-labourers. In 1829 this was probably true in many cases. But such comparisons were in any case a commonplace in the rhetoric of factory reformers like Oastler, Fielden and Bull, as well as Chartists like O'Connor, who, following upon the successes of Wilberforce, Clarkson and others in securing the abolition of slavery in the British empire, found the idea of 'white slavery' to be a powerful symbol of the degradation of free-born British operatives. It is absurd to presume that Owen intended more than this by such remarks. He always asserted that 'tyrants and slaves are never rational', and that any future society must be devoid of 'slavery and

---

[73] *NMW*, 1, no. 23 (3 April 1835), 180–3; no. 25 (18 April 1835), 200; Owen, *A Dialogue in Three Parts*, p. 13.

[74] See my 'A Utopian Tory Revolutionary at Cambridge: the Political Ideas and Schemes of James B. Bernard, 1834–39', *HJ*, 25 (1982), 583–603.

servitude, that no inferior impressions may be made upon any of our faculties'. Closer to the end of his life, too, he cited the abandonment of slavery as a condition of America becoming the country where the transition to the future could take place.[75]

If we examine the social and political ideas of leading 'paternalist' factory reformers like Michael Sadler and Richard Oastler, with whom Owen has often been compared, far greater differences than similarities emerge. Like Owen, both Oastler and Sadler were implacably hostile to Malthusian political economy and its legislative offspring, the New Poor Law, and to the crude application of *laissez-faire* and the social dislocation and pauperisation which accompanied the widespread introduction of machinery. Sadler's biographer termed his system 'paternal' by comparison with the prevailing 'selfish' system. Oastler, too, cried for *'paternal* government', and believed in *'the social state'*. But what this meant was a properly maintained hierarchy of rank and station based upon the holy trinity of 'the Altar, the Throne, and the Cottage'.[76]

With the political ideas of such men and others like them Owen did share a profound mistrust of contemporary political radicalism (though some of them were involved with it as well to a degree), and especially a disbelief in the ostensible benefits to the social condition of Britain of the immediate passage of universal suffrage. Owen, too, admitted that some principle of social hierarchy was necessary. But this had nothing to do with economic class, hereditary privilege, or even in the last instance, with virtue, since this too was susceptible of conflicting interpretations. The paternal character of the 'educational principle of government' ultimately bore almost no resemblance to the paternalism embraced by and associated with many of Owen's contemporaries in other branches of the reform movement. Owen was

---

[75] G. J. Holyoake, *The Life of Joseph Rayner Stephens* (1881), p. 188; see W. L. Sargant, *Robert Owen*, p. 267, and R. H. Harvey, *Robert Owen*, p. 137; Owen, *Robert Owen's Opening Speech*, p. 189; Owen, *Book of the New Moral World*, pt 1 (1836), pp. 65, 63; *ROJ*, 3, no. 54 (8 November 1851), 14–15.

[76] Owen, for instance, could never have commented, as Oastler did, 'Do I then say that there should be no grades in society, that there are not to be servants and master? No! But I do say that servitude and labour ought not to be oppressive. I know from my own experience, for I am but a servant – that I have as much pleasure in serving my master as my master can have in receiving my services. No master has the right to demand the services of any human being unless the reward of those services will be a comfortable living. And that is, I verily believe, all the working classes want' (Cecil Driver, *Tory Radical: the Life of Richard Oastler*, Oxford, Oxford University Press, 1946, pp. 130, 203, 427). On Oastler's emphasis upon paternal government see *FP*, 31 July 1841, 247. On Sadler see the *Memoirs of the Life and Writings of Michael Thomas Sadler* (1842), pp. 33, 67–8, 379, 447. See also R. L. Hill, *Toryism and the People, 1832–46* (Constable, 1929), p. 178, for a discussion of Owen which terms him 'the very incarnation of benevolent Toryism applied to industry'.

simply much more radical and far-reaching in his assumptions of what 'paternalism' entailed. Even the specific concept of 'elective paternal government' had far less to do with any broad ideal of paternalism than it did with Owen's preference for American-style cabinet government as the interim form of rule, as against demands for a greater prevalence of direct democracy.

A final aspect of Owen's political ideas relevant to any assessment of the democratic character of his thought concerns the relationship between the statist and decentralist tendencies in his conception of the government. Owen is often assumed to have proposed a voluntarist, peaceful, and decentralised conception of socialism in contrast to earlier and later systems of centralised state management preceded by either insurrection, or a more clearly class-based revolution. Despite his communitarian emphases, Owen would be ill placed, however, in a history of anarchism. He clearly never succumbed so far to radical anti-political dualism as to identify 'government' with 'politics', as Godwin for instance had done. This prevented him from ever seeking to abolish 'government' *per se*. Writing in 1850, Owen specifically distanced himself from Pierre-Joseph Proudhon, whose ideas were becoming well known in Britain, and who, in Owen's description, desired 'the world to govern itself without a government':

M. Proudhon has discovered that all past and proposed governments, as all have been based on the old error of society, are bad, and unequal to make man and society what both should be for the happiness of our race. And he is right: adopt any form of government based on the old error of the world respecting man and society, and failure and disappointment are sure to ensue. But it does not follow that the population of any country can do without governing arrangements; or that a good government cannot be devised, and beneficially carried into execution. This would be going from one extreme of error to another, and to act on the supposition that a good government cannot be formed for the human race.[77]

Rather than anarchism, Owen envisioned a world government built upon a federal structure, with communities as the basic units of organisation. Much of the federalist rhetoric in Owen's writing occurs after 1845. But it is possible to trace his initial acceptance of such concepts to his early experience at New Harmony. Here, in the mid-1820s, Owen first began to speak of his communities as standing 'in the same relation to their respective state governments, that the states now do to the general government'. The germ of such ideas had been present, in

---

[77] *ROWL*, 11 (1850), 99. Alexander Herzen went so far as to imply that Owen wanted no government at all, and compared Babeuf (unfavourably) as the 'surgeon' of history intending state supervision and organisation, to Owen as the 'man-midwife' opposing to force the rule of reason (*My Past and Thoughts*, New York, Alfred Knopf, 1968), 3, pp. 1236, 1240.

fact, since at least 1817. But in any case they were bound to be associated independently with his community plans. Certainly as early as 1821 we find a writer in the *Economist* referring to a proposed member of such colonies as 'a co-operative federalist'.[78]

It seems probable that Owen also derived some inspiration for his federalist ideas from other quarters. His partner at New Harmony, the philosopher, teacher and inventor William Maclure, who eventually seceded from the main community in order to govern a smaller one (modestly called 'Macluria'), was one likely source. Maclure's republican conviction was that 'the smaller the political society, the better every thing is administered for the interest of the many; the corruption and maladministration of all nations is in exact proportion to the extent of territory and number of beings over whom their rulers domineer'. His plan, accordingly, was to pay political labour at the same rate as all other forms, and to ensure that every office of power was elective, rotated as often and delegated as infrequently as possible. Besides a general social equality which would 'force every consumer to be at some time a producer', the only sure way to reconcile the interests of governors and governed was to divide power as far as possible, 'alternating and reciprocating authority, so as to make the governed of this day, month, or year, the governors of the following day, month, or year'. Another possible contributor to Owen's federalist notions was the Irish socialist William Thompson, whose *Labor Rewarded* included a detailed plan (discussed below) for a national government which was essentially federalist in character.[79]

Thompson's plan, however, and most others like it, relied upon the use of widespread and frequent elections. For Owen, however, demands for frequent rotation remained one of the central problems of democracy. Nonetheless federalism could be developed into a fully-fledged theory of world government without implying the need for elections. In one of his first statements along these lines, Owen proposed that the youngest individual whose service in the general council of a community was completed might be delegated to the united council of a circle of ten communities, the second youngest, to the council of a hundred communities, and the eldest to the council of a thousand communities. The oldest members of the latter council would form another council representing a hundred thousand, a million, or more communities. Details were added to this plan at various times, but its shape remained unchanged. By this means further

---

[78] *NHG*, 2, no. 34 (23 May 1827), 265; *Economist*, 2, no. 30 (18 August 1821), 66.
[79] William Maclure, *Opinions on Various Subjects* (New Harmony, 1831), 1, pp. 33, 83; 2, pp. 317, 452; William Thompson, *Labor Rewarded* (1827), pp. 121–4.

elections were disposed of, no matter how complex administration became. Some national basis would be required for this system in the first instance. Especially after Queenwood seemed lost, Owen became increasingly persuaded that the United States ought to be the 'Central Power' of the union of nations, and went so far as to helpfully design a draft 'Provisional treaty of federative union' between Great Britain and America. But this was only intended as a means of beginning the process of community-building, for ultimately all national boundaries were to disappear inside of an organisation of state, national and continental federations.[80]

Owen's federalist emphasis was usually described less in terms of a hostility to great states than a belief in the specific virtues of small societies. Communities should contain no more than 3,000 people

for very many important reasons respecting education, training, occupation, wealth, amusements, and the general enjoyment of life; but especially because by this simple arrangement *every one from birth to death* will have his physical, intellectual, moral, practical and spiritual character well formed for him, and will be without difficulty well cared for through life by society.[81]

Nonetheless Owen's discussion of 'government' often involved a clear tension between his ultimate decentralised communitarian millennium and the demands he placed upon the existing state to engage in social and economic reform, and indeed, to extend its powers considerably. This apparent paradox – the need for greater centralisation in order to establish a more federal society – has not been unfamiliar to the subsequent history of socialism. For all of his insistence upon the virtues of community life, almost every practical proposal Owen made in his long career, especially after the final demise of Harmony in 1845, was in fact calculated to increase the power of the state. The need for increased governmental powers and greater administrative centralisation as a consequence of his reform proposals was already evident in 1817, when Owen first spoke of 'nationalizing' the problem of the poor. It did not abate through the labour exchange, factory reform, short time and other movements to which Owen lent his plea for legislative interference. Throughout his life, Owen also always seemed to feel that one more argument voiced in a minister's ear at an opportune moment would be sufficient to set the machinery of government in motion on his behalf. Besides predisposing him to seek reforms from existing regimes, such elements also prevented Owen from losing faith

[80] Owen, *Robert Owen's Opening Speech*, pp. 139–40; *ROJ*, 3, no. 54 (8 November 1851), 14; no. 71 (6 March 1852), 149; *SA*, 1, no. 11 (7 October 1848), 171.
[81] Owen, *The Millennium in Practice* (1855), p. 20.

in the virtues of centralised government, no matter how deep his love of 'community'.[82]

Owen suffered a lifetime of disappointments as a result of his desire to introduce reforms through existing governments. In 1851, recalling the mutilation of his proposed childhood employment bill at the hands of a parliamentary committee, he reflected that 'I saw so much sacrifice of truth and correct feeling, for supposed personal or class advantages, that I became thoroughly cured of my veneration and high opinion of our legislators'. There is probably less self-delusion in this than might be supposed. But increasingly, and especially after 1845, Owen had to call upon the state to bring about socialism. Private philanthropy had failed him miserably, and perhaps inevitably would have done so, since he kept increasing the sums required to make a success of his projects. Class-based pressure by labourers and artisans was out of the question after 1835, and had never been his preference anyway. Few other options were available.[83]

The consequences of this tendency were to be of fundamental importance to the history of socialism in the next decade. By 1846, Owen had come to deny what up to a year earlier he had insisted upon, that individuals should buy land for communities, 'because that would be to retain all the present evils of private ownership of land, and nothing could be gained to forward the object sought for – that is, to make the land the property of the population, for its use, without alienation, from generation to generation'. To effect this object, he now decided that 'the land must be purchased by the Governments, in the first instance'. Several years later, Owen added that governments should not only purchase the land, but also build, furnish and stock the individual townships.[84]

Yet to some extent the problem of beginning communities became national much earlier, when Owen defined the solution as requiring momentous exertions of which only governments were really capable. If the relief of the parish poor, Owen's starting point, required a national solution, the salvation of the country could scarcely be accomplished by lesser efforts. Placing the solution in the hands of the state in this sense merely represented the working out of the logic of

---

[82] Owen, *NVS*, p. 184. Herzen once asked Owen why the latter continued to petition autocrats such as Nicholas of Russia. He replied: 'While a man is alive one must not despair of him. There are so many kinds of happening that may lay open the soul. Well, and if my letter doesn't work and he throws it away, where's the harm? I shall have done what I could. It is not his fault that his upbringing and the environment in which he lives have made him incapable of understanding the truth. In such a case, one must not be angry but feel pity' (*My Past and Thoughts*, 3, pp. 1207–8).

[83] *ROJ*, 1, no. 14 (1 February 1851), 108.

[84] Owen, *Letter from Mr. Robert Owen to the New York State Convention*, p. 27; *ROJ*, 3, no. 65 (17 January 1852), 108.

existing positions. Certainly from early on, Owen believed that governments had, or ought to have, full responsibility for all of the 'circumstances' within their sphere of competence, and having ascertained their best use, had the duty 'to form the whole social arrangements in such a manner as to induce, or morally compel, all men to act in conformity with this knowledge'. Even if this compulsion would not require a police of the usual type, the need for a rational interim education provided a centralising tendency of its own: 'The creation of the circumstances to well educate man, is a national work, to be directed by national wisdom, and executed by national capital ... in order that the education for all should be the most useful and the best that national means can give, and that there should be harmony throughout the nation, and with other nations'. The ideals of rationality and uniformity thus compelled a centralising bias of their own.[85]

Another centralising tendency in Owen's thought had an economic source. Owen's opposition to *laissez-faire* came not only from the consciousness of what he took to be its immediately harmful effects, but also, from a managerial and administrative point of view, from a simple belief in its inefficiency. *Laissez-faire*, he wrote to his long-time friend Lord Brougham in 1855, might be

very well for ignorant governments, who by their active measures would injure their subjects, but the worst possible advice for those who have to govern the improving populations of Europe and America. For the time has now arrived, especially in Great Britain, filled as it now is with scientific powers of production, when individuals without the aid of government can do nothing effectual to relieve the country from its daily accumulating difficulties.

Nonetheless Owen does not seem to have felt that too much of an extra-community administrative apparatus would be required once the communitarian system had become universal. At least he never planned for such an eventuality. Other socialists in this period, notably John Gray, did offer plans for much more centralised state economic management. But Owen never carried such ideas so far. On the whole his mind was too imbued with the virtues of community ever to become fully caught up in the logic of a national and international economic system, despite the implications of many of his own theories and reform demands. In this aspect of his theory, rather, the logic of the paternal state tended to give way before that of the federal state, even if in his writings Owen did not manifest that vehement opposition to the principle of centralisation which was characteristic of men like Oastler and Stephens, as well as later radicals like Joshua Toulmin

[85] Owen, *Book of the New Moral World*, pt 1 (1836), p. 52, pt 2 (1842), pp. 32–3.

Smith, son of the Birmingham Owenite William Hawkes Smith (on whom see chapter 8 below).[86]

Owen's views were thus substantially different from those of men like Oastler and Stephens. He was a 'paternalist', but yet synthesised and developed this principle in an egalitarian framework as foreign to 'Altar, Throne, and Cottage', or any other landmark of what is usually termed 'paternalism', as it was possible to be without losing sight of the concept completely. Owen believed in the principle of hierarchy as the basis of a benevolent, kind and watchful government. But his expression of this principle derived more from primitivism and the sectarian practices of radical Dissent than any form of doctrinaire conservatism.

For all of this, too, Owen was also a 'democrat'. Doubtless his ideas lay outside of the mainstream tradition of democratic theory in their opposition to elective representative governments. But Owen was nonetheless deeply committed to a conception of equality which he believed materially fulfilled what were otherwise empty rhetorical claims about equal rights. In this sense, too, Owen was also a 'republican', seeking both the cultivation of the public virtues and universal civic participation, as well as a more traditionally Platonic community of property, though conceiving of these goals in terms of organisations which had never existed anywhere.

Owen's views cannot be characterised as reducing radical political claims to their ostensibly 'real' or 'rational' social or economic content. His concern was never solely with the standard of living of the working classes, irrespective of the form of government under which they lived, no matter how misleading some of his statements on this theme may seem. This misinterpretation is based upon debates concerning political changes *prior* to the introduction of the co-operative system, where Owen denied that political reforms must precede the foundation of communities, and not to its eventual mode of operation. Owen believed that all human beings, ideally educated to the same standard, held the same right to govern. Indeed, the plasticity imputed by him to human nature could lead to no other conclusion. He realised, too, that those who inhabited his communities, however misled they were as to the importance of political forms in the interim period, would share democratic concerns, and would not cease agitating until all participated in government. And he concluded that his system could never succeed if nonproducers governed and producers obeyed.

[86] Owen to Brougham, 1855, Owen Collection, Holyoake House, Manchester, letter 2533. Stephens was also hostile to centralisation. See his *Champion*, 1, no. 1 (10 November 1849), 13. He nonetheless also believed that home colonies could only proceed on a national basis. See his *PM*, no. 11 (November 1841), 324–5; *FP*, 17 April 1841, 122.

Not only were all nonproducers a burden upon the producers. It was only just that all share in necessary labour. Any form of government might prove an equal burden, unless it were closely linked to the interests of the producers themselves.

Owen's 'democratic' ideal rejected the compromises of republicanism with commercial society by which large republics could exist through the medium of representative institutions, but at the cost of losing much direct individual political participation. Owen did concede the need for more extensive forms of organisation, however, and believed that a federal system would permit whole nations, even the world, to embrace communitarianism. His rational millenarianism, moreover, allowed him to conceive of one world with one language, one form of social organisation, and a unity of sentiment. This eccentric mixture of ancient, primitive, religious and modern political components was not recognisably a part of contemporary democratic thought, but nonetheless clearly anticipated the new forms of democratic theory which would thereafter be associated with socialism.

Owen's millennial expectations were not, however, shared by many of those who otherwise subscribed to his views. For these, socialism could be wedded to a more traditional radical form of democratic theory to produce a political ideal which did not require the unity of saints to succeed, but might rely upon a more widely accepted notion of citizenship. In their hands was created a conception of democratic socialism more amenable to the prejudices of the old world, yet still entailing a revolution in radical political thought which extended the concept of democracy far more widely than had ever been previously attempted. Much of this development would take place in the working class movement. In 'community' itself, however, Owen's ideas were extended, put to the test, and modified in a variety of ways. Before we consider the retreat from Utopia, therefore, let us examine how communitarianism sought to create an ideal polity in which virtue was to govern over a considerable sphere of behaviour.

PART II

Social science, polity and economy

3

The 'eye of the community': social science as communitarian government

A deep faith in the tendency of small groups united by a common purpose to regulate their members' conduct was the cornerstone of the Owenite communitarian utopia. However many social problems might simply dissolve with greater production and a more just distribution, it was always felt that some regulation of human behaviour would still be required. But this small burden, it was argued, could be assumed by the community as a whole, without the need for complex institutional mechanisms. If this confidence were misplaced, however, laws and lawyers, judges and courts, prisons and armies would eventually render the new world little more than a pale imitation of the old, with only the name of 'socialist' to distinguish them. But if it were well-founded, 'government' and 'society' would become synonymous, and natural order would supersede the artificial constraints of existing governments. Later forms of socialism inherited much of this moral optimism regarding the abolition of conflict, while tacitly shifting the context of its operation to the sphere of the nation-state. To Owenism, however, this combination of assumptions was contradictory. The community was central because only here was 'community' possible. Here family and sect alike extended to all, and mutual supervision and regulation would ensure that more alien and oppressive forms of social control would not be necessary.

Explaining how such natural principles of order operated was one of the chief aims of the new social science. Four aspects of this ideal of communitarian government will especially concern us here. Firstly, the sources of Owenite moral philosophy are reviewed, with particular emphasis being given to the role of utilitarianism and sociability in the socialist account of the effects of public opinion on individual conduct. The central and hitherto largely underestimated function of necessitarianism in providing both a future ideology and direct source of behaviour are then described. Thirdly, the conception of individual, civil and constitutional liberties in Owenism is explored, especially in

109

relation to the charge of 'totalitarianism' levelled by Talmon and others against many forms of early nineteenth-century socialism, though never seriously applied to Owenism. Finally, Owenite constitutionalism and the actual governmental experience of the early communities are reviewed briefly in order to give us some sense of how far practice corresponded to theory.

Social control and natural psychology

Communitarian life required that several thousand individuals co-exist harmoniously without the need for any substantial or continuous external police intervention. Central to this aim was the belief that public opinion would serve as an informal governing power in circumstances where most behaviour was observable by others. If it were not to be backed by strongly coercive sanctions, however, public opinion had to rely upon the existence of deeper principles of natural order. The assumption that it could do so rested in part on the view that natural sociability, eroded during the course of historical development, would be revived in community. The Scottish printer, political economist and Orbistonian George Mudie, for example, adopted aspects of contemporary Scottish social theory in his argument that during the agricultural stage of history, 'the pernicious consequences of the principles of separation and disunion, that is, of the *opposition* of interests, and the consequent misapplication of productive powers, began to be manifest'. Consequently 'so unnatural a state soon required severe laws, or the terrors of punishments, to hold societies together'. Consonant with ideas of a 'Golden Age' or natural society, the weakening of instinctive social bonds in early societies was here linked to the origins of property.[1]

But it was not only the recaptured bonds of a society long gone which were to maintain order in community. There was also some evidence that other forces, particularly co-operative labour, would help to ensure that the progress of society was 'to union', as Owen once put it. Moreover, the notion of returning to the laws of nature was only partially Arcadian in inspiration, though it derived much sustenance from an ideal of rural community. For Owenism also inherited a Christian and jurisprudential distinction between human and natural or divine laws, where the latter were assumed to embody the working out of Providence through the naturally social tendency of human nature, aided by the progress of reason. This was interpreted in particular in light of the underlying dualism of parts of the Christian

[1] *Economist*, 1, no. 2 (3 February 1821), 20; no. 4 (17 February 1821), 55–6; no. 17 (19 May 1821), 258. For a later, similar view see the *Deist*, no. 6 (1842), 1–4.

tradition. Sustained by the common Dissenting assumption that the laws of society held no legitimate sway over the individual's relation to God, Owen and many socialists thus juxtaposed 'the laws of God and nature' (as Owen termed them by the late 1850s) to 'the ever-changing, wicked and absurd artificial laws of men, made to endeavour to oppose these divine laws', and contrasted the 'general *social* law of *Nature*' to 'the general *selfish* law' of man's 'unwise contrivance'.[2]

On this interpretation of the laws of nature, no physical force would be needed to compel conformity to accepted rules in community, just as, it was assumed, none had been required in the original condition of mankind. The ideal of community also had roots, however, in existing organisations formed for mutual benefit, such as friendly societies and joint-stock charitable institutions. It was these, indeed, that Owen had principally in mind when he sought evidence of growing 'union' in society around him. But this notion of a voluntary association rendered universal promised a society superior not only to all existing organis-ations but also to any previous form of polity. For the light of reason and advantages of association were now to be extended to all corners of society. However, this required an appreciably greater degree of rationality than that demonstrated in existing mutual aid or other voluntary associations. 'In a rational state there can be no compul-sions', confided one early socialist, 'since every degree of force implies a corresponding weakness in reason, not only in the individual com-pelled, but in those also who use the compelling power'. Traditional forms of organised coercion therefore had no role to play in com-munity. Instead, the art of persuasion was to be refined to an excep-tionally high degree. Public opinion, trusted James Elishama Smith, one of Owen's chief lieutenants during the mid-1830s, would therefore become 'the only magistrate' of the future, with the press as 'the only executioner'. This could be understood, in fact, as only an extension of a process already at work in an age of rapidly-expanding literacy and the increasing power of journalism. In 1831 for example, Owen claimed that 'the very existence of government now depended upon public opinion'.[3] What could be more natural than to presume this trend was inherent in the progress of society?

In community itself, the extension of the role of public opinion also

---

[2] *BNR*, no. 9 (4 March 1837), 67–8; Owen, *Life*, 1, p. xliv (this was written in 1857, after Owen began to use 'God' as a synonym for 'nature'); *Economist*, 1, no. 21 (16 June 1821), 332. On the Protestant background to this distinction see Ursula Henriques, *Religious Toleration in England, 1787–1833* (Routledge and Kegan Paul, 1961), pp. 50, 88, 264.

[3] *NMW*, 2, no. 86 (18 June 1836), 265–6; *Crisis*, 2, no. 27 (13 July 1833), 210; *Proceedings of the Third Co-operative Congress* (1832), p. 41. There is an excellent analysis of why no government founded upon the laws of human nature could be compulsory in *ComS* (11 December 1830), 18, under the heading of 'Science of Society'.

relied upon the vital psychological premise that public esteem was an essential source of human motivation and object of behaviour. A number of major Scottish philosophers in the previous century had defended this view. Adopting a broadly utilitarian psychology, most Owenites also assumed that the chief sources of happiness derived from satisfying the need for sociability rather than from relations to objects. Here the search for affection and the respect of others constituted a kind of secret history of motivation generally. As one Owenite put it:

The most prolific source of pleasure or pain which can operate on a human being, is the relation in which he stands with his fellow creatures. On this relation all his happiness depends, and to maintain it is the end of all his exertions. Why does he seek to obtain riches? Is it for their own intrinsic value? Does the man of business forego all present enjoyment, and devote all his early life to confinement and anxiety, that he may in his old age gratify his palate and encompass himself in luxury? Such, indeed, seem the objects of his ambition, but not for themselves are they prized: it is because they draw the esteem of the world on their possessors.[4]

This desire for esteem was, with other forms of ambition, believed to be susceptible of being 'directed to produce either good or evil'. Guiding it in a beneficial direction required merely that 'individuals know the nature of the impressions which their conduct makes upon the community'. Natural sociability would then furnish its own scheme of rewards and punishments suitable to the fine tuning of behaviour, since the community would gently indicate all transgressions and evoke embarrassment and regret as an appropriate penalty. Just as jurisprudential writers like Pufendorf had indicated that bad conscience resulted from violating the laws of nature (and most Christians would say the same for the laws of God), the Owenites presumed that 'the painful emotions which arise in the mind, from the sense of being an object of pity' were 'the natural punishment of vice', while 'the esteem and affection of the wise and good' were 'the natural reward of virtue'.[5]

These benefits could only be realised, however, in 'circumstances where the actions of every individual will be known'. In such intimacy alone, 'when all were as friends and brothers, known to each other', would it be impossible to 'resist such moral sanctions' and substitute

---

[4] *An Essay in Answer to the Question* (1834), p. 5. The great force of the desire for esteem was a familiar theme amongst the Scottish writers. See for example, Adam Smith, *Theory of Moral Sentiments* (1759; rpt. Oxford, Oxford University Press, 1976), pp. 50–66 (cited in the *Essay* quoted here), Dugald Stewart, *Outlines of Moral Philosophy* (Edinburgh, 1793), pp. 84–5, Adam Ferguson, *Principles of Moral and Political Science* (Edinburgh, 1792), 1, p. 150.

[5] Pufendorf, *De Jure*, pp. 222–3; Abram Combe, *The Sphere for Joint-Stock Companies* (Edinburgh, 1825), pp. 45, 47, 37.

(as was reported of a Shaker community) 'distance or neglect' for coerciveness of a more forceful nature. This ideal simply could not be grafted upon existing social arrangements or made co-extensive with the nation-state, just as the virtues of ancient republics, as even radical writers conceded, could not be reproduced in large, representative democracies. In great states, socialists contended, moral police were often ineffective, for the 'vicious' could

hide themselves deep in the dregs of society, in the haunts of crowded cities, where the public opinion that acts upon them is that of their associates, congenial spirits from whom their own vices are reflected; from such sinks of infamy arise deleterious influences, corrupting the moral atmosphere even as fevers are generated by physical impurities.[6]

Owenites deeply interested in establishing co-operative communities thus agreed with Owen's recommendation that the cities would have to be 'gradually abandoned, and the population of the world ... formed into manageable masses'. Owen was fond of saying that he hoped to live to see grass growing over the streets of London. Nor was this perspective identified only with a 'paternal' ideal or Owen's own political ideas. William Thompson, too, acknowledged that 'in a large metropolis public opinion loses all control over private morals: the private conduct of individuals is beneath its notice; it is lost in the ocean of actions, and no time nor pens could register private conduct'. George Alexander Fleming's *The Union* also later agreed that it had been 'found by experience, that public opinion loses its force, in proportion as its operation is diffused over a larger space and population', while conceding that, 'on the other hand, when acting in too limited a sphere, its tyranny becomes intolerable'. Thus the exact size of communities was a matter of great moral and political consequence. Amongst Owen's direct associates, in fact, only James Elishama Smith was so bold as to deny that the social system was necessarily 'incompatible with the existence of large and splendid cities'. This occurred, however, after his break from Owen in the mid-1830s. Then he admitted that while the size of cities might have to be limited, this did not entail their destruction. He also now condemned Owen's 'system of uniform and everlasting parallelograms' as based exclusively upon a calculation of economic principles rather than higher moral values.[7]

The desirability of small communities, however, was not solely as a

[6] Abram Combe, *Metaphorical Sketches* (Edinburgh, 1823), p. 154; William Hebert, *A Visit to the Colony of Harmony* (1825), pp. 3–4; Charles Bray, *Philosophy of Necessity* (1841), 2, p. 464.

[7] Edward Higginson, *Human Equality* (Hull, 1840), p. 5; *ROMG*, no. 8 (1 October 1856), 3; William Thompson, *An Inquiry into the Principles of the Distribution of Wealth* (1824), p. 505; *Union*, no. 5 (1 August 1842), 135–6; James Elishama Smith, *Lecture on a Christian Community* (1833), p. 17; *Shepherd*, 3, no. 19 (4 November 1837), 146.

result of the efficacy of moral police within them. An ecological element was also present which is not usually associated with early socialism. Though he was a cotton manufacturer, Owen intensely disliked the overconcentration of industry. He had seen, in the last decade of the eighteenth century, what results this could have in Manchester. As a factory village, thus, New Lanark – a model in turn for much Owenite communitarianism – ideally united the virtues of rural and urban life for Owen. Industry was to be located in the countryside in order to avoid both the extermination of nature via overconcentration, and as well the loss of contact with natural surroundings for those engaged in production. As Owen pointed out in 1814, the inhabitants of New Lanark had benefited greatly from having

their gardens and potato grounds to cultivate; they have their walks laid out to give them health and the habit of being gratified with the ever-changing scenes of nature; – for those scenes afford not only the most economical, but also the most innocent pleasures which man can enjoy; and all men may be easily trained to enjoy them.

Such opportunities were lacking in cities. Courts, alleys, lanes and streets were 'injurious to health, and destructive of almost all the natural comforts of life'. Large cities, towns and manufactories, therefore, should be abandoned if for no other reason than 'to ensure the enjoyment of pure air'. But it was the existing system of retail shops and warehouses which made towns necessary, Owen thought, and which thus excluded their inhabitants 'from the health and pleasure of the benefits and delights of the country'. Here moral and ecological considerations clearly overlapped, and strengthened the need for socialism to take a communitarian form.[8]

'Community' could also be too small, however. If modern states were so extensive as to dilute the intensity and displace the objects of virtue, many more communitarian Owenites conceded that the individual family was too confined to serve as a focus of moral identity. Consequently the loyalties it involved would have to be transferred elsewhere. The prospect of abolishing existing forms of the family and marriage alienated many potential supporters of the Owenite system, however, and led others to attempt to reconceptualise the goals of socialism. To James Elishama Smith, the problem of the family and marriage system of the old world was in fact 'the pivot upon which the whole political question of a social and anti-social system must turn – "*Whether should mankind be one family or many families?*"' Each system posed separate problems. At present fervent devotion to the common good was difficult to achieve because each family remained an island of

---

[8] Owen, *NVS*, pp. 43, 267; Owen, *The Book of the New Moral World*, pt 3, p. 15, pt 2, p. 25.

selfishness isolated from the rest of society. In community, however, as Charles Bray expressed it, 'The members would be as one family, each bringing what he possessed to the common stock for the general good; each employing the talents with which Nature had endowed him, not for his own personal advancement, but for the good of all'. A variety of means were to be used to achieve this ideal, in particular the Platonic scheme of educating children in the care of the entire community rather than relying upon their natural parents, which was attempted at Orbiston, New Harmony and elsewhere. In combination with Owen's plan for government by age, such devices represented an ideal of Christian as well as republican fraternity which was intended (in John Francis Bray's words) 'to extend universally that love which is now pent up within the narrow circle of a family'.[9] But this emotion could only operate within certain very clearly defined physical parameters. Once the natural boundaries for the exercise of sociability were surpassed, the psychological assumptions upon which socialism was based would cease to be valid.

The illocutionary force of necessitarianism

A second means of ensuring civic virtue in the future society lay in the inculcation of a system of beliefs which it was proposed to substitute for what came to be known by the mid-1830s as individualism, and which centred on the notion that each individual formed his or her own character. Juxtaposed to the theories of individual responsibility and freedom of will as the central doctrine of their philosophy was the socialist interpretation of necessitarianism, whose first premise was that character was formed *for* rather than by the individual. To the Owenites, necessitarianism meant that all human actions could be traced to motives and intentions which themselves originated in upbringing and environment. No-one could be termed a 'free agent', since all acted according to the strongest impulse affecting their will at any one time. Some Owenites consequently believed, as Godwin had done, that there would be neither promises nor contracts in the new moral world, since these interfered with the spontaneous dictation of behaviour. But although this was the single most important dogma of the Owenite canon, its significance has never been fully appreciated. For 'necessity' was not merely a crude environmentalist explanation and argument against the apportioning of blame and punishment (and particularly divine retribution) for poverty and moral failure when these could never be deserved. In an age when the poor were widely

[9] *Shepherd*, 3, no. 5 (29 July 1837), 35–6; Charles Bray, *Philosophy of Necessity*, 2, p. 435; John Francis Bray, *Labour's Wrongs and Labour's Remedy* (1839), p. 123.

blamed for their own condition, particularly after Malthus described a lack of sexual restraint as the underlying cause of social distress, this Owenite response was clearly comprehensible. But the necessitarian philosophy was also designed to function *practically* as a pacifying element among Owen's followers. Correctly understood, it could be a major means of avoiding conflict. Its illocutionary meaning was therefore as vital as its explanatory claims. In fact, necessitarianism directly supplanted the role of the divinity, or knowledge of the divine, in Christian systems such as that of the Quakers. Rather than the 'Inner Light', or knowledge of God, producing a revolution in behaviour, an appreciation of the principles of necessity would do so.[10]

Three deductions from philosophical necessity were particularly significant in this respect. Held in conjunction with hedonistic psychological views, necessitarianism reinforced the belief that individuals inevitably pursued pleasure and avoided pain. If happiness, for example, resulted from treating others with care, respect and love, as would hopefully be the case in community, these actions would be repeated. If virtue were rewarded by society, its manifestations would also increase. An intellectual corollary of this view (commonly held by the Dissenters respecting their own religious views) was that if the pursuit of truth were given sufficient approbation and 'true views' disseminated, then no individual could (as the Scottish Owenite and Orbistonian Abram Combe put it) 'willingly hold erroneous ideas'.[11]

Even more importantly, as far as the question of immediate social order was concerned, if individuals were not responsible for their actions because character and motives were environmentally formed, this would exhibit 'the irrationality of being angry with an individual

---

[10] *NMW*, 2, no. 53 (31 October 1835), 1–2. On the development of necessitarianism see Thomas Hobbes, *A Letter about Liberty and Necessity* (1677), Anthony Collins, *A Philosophical Inquiry Concerning Human Liberty* (4th edn., Glasgow, 1749), David Hartley, *Observations on Man* (1749), especially 1, pp. 85–114, 268–367, David Hume, *Enquiries concerning Human Understanding and concerning the Principles of Morals* (1748–51; rpt. Oxford, Clarendon Press, 1975), pp. 80–103, Jonathan Edwards, *A Careful and Strict Enquiry into the Modern Prevailing Notion of that Freedom of the Will* (1754; rpt. New Haven, Yale University Press, 1957), Joseph Priestley, *The Doctrine of Philosophical Necessity Illustrated* (1777), William Godwin, *Enquiry Concerning Political Justice*, pp. 336–59, 378–400. The most extensive Owenite treatment of the subject is Charles Bray's *Philosophy of Necessity*. The 'Essays on the Formation of Human Character' published by Owen in 1813–14 contain little else but deductions from the doctrine of necessity. A general discussion of eighteenth-century debates is given in Aram Vartanian, 'Necessity or Freedom? The Politics of an Eighteenth Century Metaphysical Debate', *SEC*, 7 (1978), 153–74.

[11] Owen, *NVS*, p. 23; Abram Combe, *The Religious Creed of the New System* (Edinburgh, 1825), p. 16. For antecedents of this idea see for example A. Collins, *Philosophical Inquiry*, pp. 86–8; J. Priestley, *Philosophical Necessity*, pp. 97–9. For a similar contemporary use of necessity to justify freedom of the press see Samuel Bailey, *Essays on the Formation and Publication of Opinions* (1821), pp. 63, 69, 79.

for possessing qualities which, as a passive being during the formation of these qualities, he had not the means of preventing'. Praise and blame, reward and punishment, would be repudiated immediately as both useless and harmful (some debt to Stoicism is evident here). The delusion of self-formation made individuals 'proud, vain, jealous, malicious, covetous, selfish, ambitious, irritable, angry, uncharitable, and religious'. Its negation would engender exactly the opposite effects. Anger, revenge and ill feeling would cease the moment the doctrine of irresponsibility was accepted. The socialist lecturer C. J. Haslam expressed this characteristically optimistic Owenite deduction from necessity (which separated the socialists from most earlier necessitarians) in claiming that 'The moment a man embraces our principles, that moment he is stripped of anger and revenge for ever. That moment his feelings are reversed, and this is effected by him believing in the *irresponsibility of man*, which, they say, is a doctrine so dangerous'.[12] Necessitarianism, consequently, was to become the basis of socialist toleration, and was the core of Owen's 'new religion of charity' by the end of the 1820s.

A further influential corollary of necessitarianism was the notion that if personal responsibility could not be assigned for behaviour, neither could particular individuals be blamed for maintaining a degrading and inhumane social system. This deduction distinguished the practical language of socialism sharply from that of most radical discourse. For a fundamental distinction had to be drawn, on the Owenite account, between recognising the empirical existence of a struggle between classes (principally conceived as producers and non-producers) and blaming anyone for perpetuating it. Most Owenites ascribed blame instead to a '*system*' which created rich and poor alike, rather than to any specific category of its subjective embodiments. The wealthy were no more responsible for their behaviour, after all, than anyone else. For, with great equity, the environment fashioned the behaviour of the rich as well as the poor. 'The capitalists are not our enemy, *but the money*', wrote the labour exchange socialist William King of London, echoing Owenite views, and adding that 'the capitalists are made what they are by the money. We war not with men but with systems'. Owen's explanation was that:

In the existing order, or rather disorder, of things, the rich, as a necessary consequence of their riches, must oppress the poor – and every rich man, whatever may be his assumption to piety and humanity, is an unjust man, and a grievous oppressor of the industrious poor. But it is not the rich man who has

---

[12] Owen, *NVS*, p. 23; Owen, *Robert Owen's Opening Speech*, p. 159; C. J. Haslam, *A Defence of the Social Principles* (1837), p. 8. For antecedents see especially Priestley, *Philosophical Necessity*, pp. 111–12.

wealth, and who desires to accumulate more, or the poor man who exerts himself to become rich, and who, if successful, would act precisely as the rich man has always done and will always do, that is to blame, or that ought to be punished or despitefully used; because individual riches and poverty will always produce the oppressor and the oppressed in mutual contention. It is the system itself which generates and supports this inequality of wealth and poverty, that has made them, and now makes them, the idiots which they are.[13]

The impossibility of assigning blame to anything but an abstract 'system' (of property, classes, beliefs and practices) made any conception of class warfare as a mode of progressing towards the new moral world virtually impossible. As we will see, this led to many clashes with the Chartists and others who did attempt to develop and utilise class antagonisms. But while this aspect of the doctrine would become much more important, it was not cental to the original purpose underlying Owen's continuous stress upon the doctrine of the formation of character. For necessitarianism also overtly denied that the poor had anything to do with creating their own fate. It made sense for Owen to emphasise this when we consider not merely the immense influence of Malthusianism, but also the considerable religiosity of much of his audience. The notions of Original Sin, good works as a means of salvation, and poverty as a mark of damnation were therefore clearly Owen's original target for the doctrine. But as historians have increasingly conceded, these ideals also in some respects underpinned the ideological basis of the entire social order. For this reason, as Paine for one had unfortunately discovered, attacks upon the established religion were taken even more seriously by all authorities than assaults upon the monarchy, aristocracy, or parliamentary corruption. In an age in which religion and the work ethic (as well as the duty to obey all constituted authority) were still intimately connected, Owenism explicitly rejected the moralising discourse which, in nominally rewarding prudence, diligence, and abstemiousness and punishing their opposite vices, underlay the Malthusian assumptions of the new Poor Law, certain extreme forms of the ethos of self-help, and the crude moral homilies of popularised classical political economy.

Nonetheless the Owenites still retained the possibility of applying discrete moral pressure to those whom they regarded as benefiting from the existing social system. For necessitarianism could also be interpreted as prohibiting the excoriation of *individual* capitalists for the fate of the poor, but allowing some condemnation of all who acted as the embodiments of class interest. Emerging towards the end of the 1820s, this compromise permitted a limited conception of class

---

[13] 'K' [W. King], *The Useful Working Population*, p. 2; NMW, 1, no. 19 (7 March 1835), 148.

opposition to arise in Owenite circles. During the labour exchange period, this was directed in particular at unproductive shopkeepers and 'middlemen' (who however often included capitalists in the Owenite view), who it was assumed were to be swept away by the successes of the co-operative economic system. This assisted in concentrating the idea of a 'system' upon classes rather than, for example, sets of beliefs (e.g. about character), thus helping to focus Owenism upon the real world rather than merely ideological antagonism.[14]

Communitarianism and personal liberty

Many radicals, as we have seen, feared that Owen's communities would merely apply the discipline of the workhouse while denying political rights to working class members. Some of Owen's own followers would also accuse him, though usually not his system, of being prone to despotic tendencies. But how far did Owenite communitarianism anticipate that some loss of personal liberty would be part of the price paid for greater social harmony and prosperity? Or for that matter, how far did it fail to explore such implications? This question is clearly central to any effort to place early British socialism within the wider context of the history of political thought, and especially the history of democratic theory. Taking the origins of statist socialism as their point of departure, however, most historians sympathetic to early nineteenth-century socialism have simply passed over any wider political implications of communitarianism in this period. Nor have these areas been more carefully scrutinised by those markedly hostile to socialism. Conservative critics such as J. L. Talmon have ignored British developments at this time as well as communitarianism generally, while broadly attacking nineteenth-century socialism for having laid the foundations for later socialist dictatorships. This omission is perhaps partly a result of realising the inadequacy of the model of 'totalitarian democracy' to explain many aspects of pre-Marxist socialism. But Talmon and others have nonetheless implied that the sources of twentieth-century 'totalitarianism' can be found in virtually all

---

[14] See for example, *PMG*, 3, no. 155 (24 May 1834), 123, which claimed that 'slavery is the work, not of individuals, but of classes, and . . . Governments are but the tools of these classes, for purposes of aggression and robbery'. Middlemen were thus not to be blamed for being such 'by accident or necessity', but only if they supported oppressive governments. An interesting and obviously entirely unintended side effect of Owen's denial that the expenses of government were the chief causes of distress was that some radicals like Cobbett mistakenly thought Owen's writings tended 'to cause it be believed, that the miseries of the people arise out of *their own indiscretions, and not out of the acts of the government*' (*CWPR*, 114, 17 November 1827, 499).

forms of early socialism, and have even described this, from the viewpoint of the history of democratic theory, as their central distinguishing characteristic.

Given the prevalence of such charges in some circles, as well as the need to confront resolutely the problem of socialist dictatorship and expose its roots and assumptions, the 'totalitarian' hypothesis merits some brief consideration here. For Talmon, 'totalitarian democracy' can be defined by 'the assumption of a sole and exclusive truth in politics'. Also known as 'Political Messianism', it postulates 'a preordained, harmonious and perfect scheme of things, to which men are irresistibly driven, and at which they are bound to arrive'. It recognises 'ultimately only one plane of existence, the political', and widens 'the scope of politics to embrace the whole of human existence. It treats all human thought and action as having social significance, and therefore as falling within the orbit of political action'.[15] Inevitably, therefore, it seeks to govern all aspects of social existence, and to ensure that all conform to its historical expectations. Let us consider whether Owenite communitarianism might on balance have been secretly guilty of such ambitions, or at least represented a threat to liberty unforeseen at the time.

One plausible approach to this question is through the political implications of Owen's epistemology. Did Owen's belief in only one true view of the world – a conception he undoubtedly held – require or imply at least the interim introduction of the new world under the direction of a dictator or a few 'saints'? We have already seen that Owen rejected the idea of dictatorship as a means of inaugurating the new system, while admitting the great value of rule by one individual until government by age could be instituted. This period of rule could also be understood as coinciding with the formation of a new generation raised upon socialist moral principles. Owen doubtless saw himself principally as an educator, and believed that governments strongly influenced the development of individual character. He also identified the sphere of government with that of education, and did extend its scope to all social life (though not, of course, by broadening the meaning of the term 'politics'). Education, however, was eventually to end the unconscious determination of character by circumstances. Owen conceived of the passage of mankind from a state of passive, mechanical necessity to one of collective, voluntary control, as a movement from 'the present state of society, *governed by circum-*

---

[15] Talmon, *Origins of Totalitarian Democracy*, pp. 1–2. See also Talmon, *Political Messianism: The Romantic Phase* (Secker and Warburg, 1960). For a useful discussion of this definition, see John Dunn, *Rethinking Modern Political Theory* (Cambridge, Cambridge University Press, 1985), pp. 87–102.

stances' to 'that which will arise when society shall be taught to *govern circumstances'*. But, in this sense, all who lived under existing circumstances were certainly imprisoned within them. Owen saw himself, however, as the first active legislator of modern history, though he doubtless understood this in terms of what has recently been described, in reference to a tradition of Nonconformist utopianism familiar to Owen, as an 'absconding legislator' able to establish a new social order and then leave it intact.[16] He often conceived his work at New Lanark in these terms: 'Having discovered that individuals were always formed by circumstances by means imperceptible and unknown to the individuals, I formed them, to the extent I could control the circumstances, into what I wished them to become; and in this manner were the beneficial changes effected in the population under my care'.[17]

For Owen, at least, the creation of the new moral world would entail the re-education of most of the population. But there were still two ways of construing the political import of this process. On the mechanical interpretation of education usually invoked by Owen, new circumstances would be introduced until the legislator was satisfied with the results. This tended to assume that most would be passive receptacles for new impressions, whose cumulative effects would eventually modify their behaviour. New character might even be produced via a quasi-millennial conversion over a brief period akin to the passage from night to day. This might be said to be the religious model of the formation of new character. On the other hand, it was also possible to see this process as a series of gradually ascending steps, where each stage of amelioration extended the knowledge and capacity of the individual, hence potentially allowing for an increasing measure of popular control and activity almost from the beginning. This was a more properly educational notion of character formation. Such an explanation was preferable if democracy was to be a goal of the new system, and if an active conception of personality was to underly popular participation. But Owen himself did not give great stress to this interpretation, seeing democratic participation as a future ideal rather than as a necessary means of reaching the new society. Quite rightly, he was thus often accused of having too passive a conception of the formation of new behaviour.[18] But the more passive others were presumed to be, the more active a role was thrust upon Owen himself,

---

[16] See James Holstun, *A Rational Millennium. Puritan Utopias of Seventeenth-Century England and America* (Oxford, Oxford University Press, 1987), pp. 91–101.

[17] Owen, *NVS*, p. 273; Owen, *First Discourse*, p. 27. On the dichotomy of voluntary–mechanical see Godwin, *Enquiry Concerning Political Justice*, pp. 361–76.

[18] See the later discussion of this issue in *StS*, 1, no. 7 (October 1862), 53–4.

or those who might be considered as 'educators'. Hence Owen was criticised by Marx in the third of the 'Theses on Feuerbach', which stated that:

The materialist doctrine that men are products of circumstances and up-bringing, and that, therefore, changed men are products of other circum-stances and changed upbringing, forgets that it is men who change circumstances and that the educator must himself be educated. Hence, this doctrine is bound to divide society into two parts, one of which is superior to society (in Robert Owen, for example).[19]

Owen thus left himself open to the charge (here made by J. E. Smith in 1840), that he had in fact consequently nominated himself as the 'God of the New Moral World':

Your characteristic doctrine of the influence of *external* circumstances contains one important truth, which the old world has despised. It is the sum and substance of your system – 'Man is the creature of circumstances'. It is your *first fact*, yet it is not a first principle, for it makes man the creature of things which are themselves creatures, and directs the mind to no organic principle of creation. Being your *first fact*, therefore, and the beginning of your system, your system is *without* an organic principle, unless that organic principle be yourself. For, according to your own doctrine, the creators of men, the old circumstances, have not created them *well*. You propose to create *new* circum-stances, which will create men better. You, yourself, therefore, are the God of your own system, and above yourself there is no organic principle acknowledged.

There was much justice in this accusation. Insofar as Owen would continue to insist that 'the governing powers among all people form, or may form, the character of the population', the educational side of the doctrine of circumstances can be said to have been amongst the pri-mary sources of his 'paternalism'. This was a clear departure from, for example, his mentor Godwin's antipathy to the legislative creation of character. Nonetheless, Owen never used such ideas to justify a more strictly political form of dictatorship. Nor did any of his followers. Owen did seek a 'total' transformation of personality and behaviour in the new world. But in this process he never conceived that violence could play any useful or reformatory role. This was, indeed, a contra-diction in terms for Owen, given the type of character which was to be created in the new world. Certain forms of moral coercion were commensurable with this ideal. But violence, beyond legitimate self-defence, was not. The right to life itself was simply much too

[19] *MECW*, 5, p. 7. Marx added that 'The coincidence of the changing of circumstances and of human activity can be conceived and rationally understood only as revol-utionising practice.'

highly valued. For this reason, in particular, Owen cannot be situated in any history of the precursors of modern 'totalitarianism'.[20]

Contemporary liberals such as J. S. Mill and Alexis de Tocqueville nonetheless found an equally grave threat to liberty in the degree of control which the public opinion of the majority would have in any democratic community. In 'community', however, this power was to be increased considerably. Was there no perception of the dangers this might entail? In fact it was often assumed that this represented a much milder form of coercion than the existing police, army and other civil authorities provided, certainly as far as the working classes were concerned. In addition, it was believed that such control would operate almost subliminally, without the need either for eternal vigilance or an agency of police. A prototype of such restraint had been Owen's use of 'coloured monitors' at New Lanark. There, blocks of wood with different colours on each side were suspended over the workplace of each employee and rotated according to performance, such that each knew how the others were graded. But most Owenites also felt that the public opinion of the future would be exerted very differently from that of the past. William Thompson for example trusted that the motive for prying would dissolve, since all would have an interest in freedom of expression and thought. The Owenite lecturer T. S. Mackintosh concurred, and here we see how important necessitarianism was to such confidence:

The influence of public opinion, so far from being weakened or destroyed in a social community, will have its strength augmented in a ten-fold degree. This, indeed, will be its chief security; but it will be a public opinion very different from that which exists at present. The bitter principle – the spirit of savage justice – revenge, which infects the public opinion of civil society, will be extracted. The frown of disapprobation will have more of pity than of anger, and the smile of approval will partake more of the spirit of congratulation, than the vain mockery of adulation, so often and so falsely exhibited at present.[21]

Efforts to establish such forms of control were attempted in at least a few instances. George Mudie's Co-operative and Economical Society

---

[20] James Elishama Smith, *The Little Book* (1840), p. 12; *NMW*, 13, no. 9 (24 August 1844), 65. Godwinian biases against virtually all forms of association were probably best preserved by Richard Carlile. See for example *CPR*, no. 1 (19 October 1839), 2. For an explanation of how men could be created by circumstances and yet control them see the *Report of the Discussion between Robert Owen and the Rev. William Legge* (1839), p. 34. Owen was not always consistent in his descriptions of who precisely was chiefly responsible for forming character, though he usually accorded this honour to 'those who have influence in the affairs of men' (especially ministers and legislators) and 'the learned' (Owen, *NVS*, pp. 14, 107).

[21] William Thompson, *Practical Directions* (1830), pp. 33–4; T. S. Mackintosh, *An Inquiry into the Nature of Responsibility* (Birmingham, 1840), pp. 84–5. See also *An Address to the Members of Trades' Societies* (1833), p. 28.

at Spa Fields, London, in the early 1820s appears for instance to have agreed upon the propriety of introducing a quasi-Dissenting system of mutual control. Each member had 'his own friendly Monitor', whose task it was 'to notice to his appointer such errors of conduct, temper or language' which endangered the harmony, good will and mutual esteem of the community, no other channel being available to convey complaints or admonitions. At Orbiston, Abram Combe worried only that '*publicity* forms a punishment rather too severe', which therefore

ought never to be resorted to unless in cases of necessity; that is, when the individuals *persevere* in doing wrong and refuse to alter. In such cases we have only to let their conduct be known as it is manifested, and we may rely with the utmost confidence on the result. The Eye of the Community, and the inward feeling produced, will soon either create a change of conduct, or make the individual retire from the Society.[22]

Some distinction between public control over actions and over opinions was recognised, however. One of the best-known aphorisms in the movement (it appeared on the masthead of the *New Harmony Gazette*, the *Crisis*, the *New Moral World*, and George Alexander Fleming's *Union* as well as other papers) was 'If we cannot *reconcile all opinions*, let us endeavour to unite all hearts'. This was connected with the suggestion that 'It is not unreasonable to hope that *hostility* may cease, even where *perfect agreement cannot be established*'.[23] Such sentiments to some extent identify Owenism with a romantic reaction against the pursuit of universal benevolence through the powers of the intellect alone, and with the belief that disinterested morality could be based upon the sentiments and feelings. Godwin was well known, in fact, for having embraced this view against his own earlier theories, and in this Shelley followed him.[24] A distinction between hearts and minds also implied that the feelings which formed and emanated from the most essential social bonds (such as sympathy and a desire for the esteem of others) might prove sufficiently strong to unite a community even where opinions still divided it. This also permitted a defence of intellectual freedom despite the need for harmony and union in community. Some no doubt believed, however, that many forms of intellectual difference were in fact reducible to feelings anyway. Social Hymn No. 45, sung at some Owenite meetings in the 1840s, encouraged such a view:

22 *Economist*, 2, no. 50 (10 January 1822), 379–80; *RO*, 2, no. 1 (17 January 1827), 10.
23 This phrase was originally cited in Owen's second 'Essay on the Principle of the Formation of Human Character' and was taken from 'Mr. Vansittart's Letter to the Rev. Dr. Herbert Marsh' (Owen, *NVS*, p. 22).
24 See the useful discussion in Judith Shklar, *After Utopia* (Princeton, Princeton University Press, 1957), p. 44.

O let no sect or party feeling find
A resting place within the human mind
Feelings unsocial from mankind be gone
Let self and social love unite as one.[25]

In communitarian practice, unity proved more difficult to achieve. At Orbiston Abram Combe commenced with the assumption that 'If it be at all possible to unite hearts, *without* reconciling opinions, it must be by allowing *equal* liberty to all'. Scarcely a month later, however, he resolved that 'the hearts of mankind can never be completely united until their opinions be reconciled, and as this reconciliation cannot take place until a *fixed standard* of comparison be established, which all are willing to acknowledge, it must be a matter of great importance to introduce such a standard'. This Combe attempted by fixing the definitions of key terms, comparing their limited, prejudiced 'local sense' with their 'general sense' as it would prevail in the new world. 'Error', for example, was in a 'local sense' defined as 'any thing contrary to the notions imbibed in infancy, and opposed to the generally admitted notions of the community'. Its 'general sense' was 'any thing which, of itself, neither can be demonstrated, nor shown to be consistent with that which can be demonstrated'. More pointedly, 'Radical Reform' in the 'local sense' was 'a reformation, or beneficial change, in the constitution of the legislative, and executive branches of government'. In the 'general sense', however, it was 'a reformation in the morals and habits of the people, and in the system for supplying their wants'.[26]

Thus despite the fact that Owen had claimed that his original intention was only to reveal the sources of opinions, 'and thence to bring the right of private judgement into general practice', this 'right' for some socialists did not usually include a notion of conflict with the universal truths of reason. Some pressure towards intellectual conformity was exhibited on occasion, particularly by Combe at Orbiston, and during the 'sectarian' phase of Owenite organisation between 1835 and 1845. The latter period also witnessed at least one attempt by the chief Owenite organisation – the Association of All Classes of All Nations or Rational Society – to evade contention through fixing the meaning of important terms. Here the 'natural system' was for example defined as 'such as requires no factitious aid; but contains its own sanctions; always producing, when its laws are obeyed, sensations of pleasure; and when disobeyed, sensations of pain'. 'Artificial Rewards and Punishments' were described as 'pleasures and pains denounced by governments, corporations, and individuals, to

[25] *Social Hymns* (Leeds, 1838), p. 35.
[26] *RO*, 1, no. 4 (1 December 1825), 27; no. 9 (12 January 1826), 66; Combe, *An Address to the Conductors of the Periodical Press* (Edinburgh, 1823), pp. 11, 18.

support exclusive interests; not in accordance with nature'. The initial act of conformity by new members to the AACAN to the 'Catechism of the New Moral World' during the latter period, while in practice it entailed no more than a public reading of the text, doubtless contributed to this tendency towards uniformity.[27]

Nonetheless many saw little harm in the greater trend towards homogeneity implied by socialised life. 'Philo J.', for example, conceded in 1821 that while all would 'have more of real freedom and independence than the mass of mankind have in their present state', they would 'nevertheless be under greater moral restraint in all that vitiates and degrades their nature ... they will be under a more complete control from reason'. It could therefore be anticipated 'that greater unanimity would exist as greater knowledge would prevail'. It was Owen, however, who carried the logic of uniformity to its greatest extreme, and projected a puritan and enlightenment cosmopolitanism onto a new plane. Having by the late 1830s concluded that all members of society should pass through the same general routine, Owen proposed that 'there should be throughout the hemisphere the fewest languages, governments, laws, and opposing interests, prejudices, habits, and manners'. National boundaries and identities would therefore have to be abolished, or submerged into one model of rational identity which would pervade the earth. Owen now emphasised that there could 'be no difference of opinion among those who are permitted to think for themselves, and who have been taught to observe facts with attention, and to reason accurately from those facts'. In his final years, too, he came to insist that only one language was to be taught to all from birth, 'Anglo-Saxon' (and it might be worth recalling in this context his own youthful difficulties in overcoming his provincial Welsh accent and becoming fully anglicised). But despite these conformist tendencies, Owen still insisted that 'A just equality of the family of man, will not consist in making all alike'. Never forced to face this inconsistency, he made no independent effort to resolve it.[28]

Most Owenites were considerably less extreme in their demands for uniformity. But virtually all agreed that whatever diversity did enter into the future society, it would not take traditional political forms. 'The first step to a permanent improvement is the forbearance of all parties', was Owen's oft-repeated view on the matter. To G. A. Fleming, the existing social system engendered 'a fatal misapprehen-

---

[27] Owen, *NVS*, p. 100; *NMW*, 5, no. 24 (6 April 1839), 380–1.

[28] *Economist*, 2, no. 44 (24 November 1821), 288; Owen, *Manifesto of Robert Owen* (Washington DC, 1844), p. 5; Owen, *The Future of the Human Race* (1853), p. 19; Owen, *The Coming Millennium* (1855), p. 20; *ROMG*, no. 11 (1 August 1857), 127; *ROWL*, letter 10 (1850), 49.

sion of the true interests of man' because 'Measures of amelioration or changes are beheld through the distorted and false medium of party, and their bearings considered not in relation to the national welfare, but sectional interests'. 'Once admitted as a principle into any state', echoed an Owenite lecturer, 'party spirit immediately seeks to extend itself, and speedily surrounds with a dense atmosphere of exclusion every individual'. 'All parties are tyrants', thought J. E. Smith, though later agreeing that 'Divisions are necessary at first to bring men to a common understanding', such that 'A party may complain against the powers that be, without aiming at their overthrow; the complaint may be made on purpose to stimulate and do good'.[29] For some Owenites the rule of the virtuous few meant that partisanship could simply never emerge. One W. Hopkins, for example, informed the *Social Pioneer* that in the future 'there would be no such thing as faction, but men of the greatest capacity would of course have the chief direction of affairs yielded to them, and would share the power amongst each other without envy'. But to others it was precisely democratic rotation for all which would render party unnecessary. To 'Philo J.', thus, democratic procedures alone would inhibit the sources of partisanship:

The only distinction of *rank* would arise from superior talents, virtue, and benevolence; and if one station was deemed more exalted than another, the party filling the station, being appointed by a majority of opinion, upon the propriety of entering upon the more important duties, there could be no gradation felt, particularly as the various offices would be fulfilled periodically, and the officers would have no *reward*, but the consciousness of doing their duty, and the approbation of their co-associates.[30]

This view anticipated those later Owenites who were inclined to combine socialism and radicalism.

The wish to abolish all parties, politics and even laws in community did permit an element of arbitrariness in those few practical examples of which we have any knowledge. At Orbiston, Abram Combe instituted a 'New Court' for the 'extinction of disputes', where only 'undisputed *facts*' were to be admitted as evidence. 'In the New Court', Combe declared, 'Common Sense sits as presiding Judge'. But in the only case known to have been heard there, when a group of Orbistonians argued against Combe's official designation of the inhabitants of the community as 'Adherents to Divine Revelation', Combe himself

---

[29] *NMW*, 2, no. 68 (13 February 1836), 122; 5, no. 37 (6 July 1839), 584; 1, no. 49 (3 October 1835), 391; *Crisis*, 2, no. 28 (20 July 1833), 217; 4, no. 7 (24 May 1834), 51.

[30] *Pioneer*, no. 28 (15 March 1834), 245, 247; *SP*, no. 5 (6 April 1839), 37; *Economist*, 2, no. 43 (17 November 1821), 269–70. Occasionally allied to an opposition to party was the view that the working classes required no leaders. See Lovett's comments on this, quoted in Henry Solly, *James Woodford, Carpenter and Chartist* (1881), 1, p. 81.

represented common sense, and though twelve witnesses were called, it was his opinion which prevailed.[31]

Nonetheless there are very few instances in the literature of Owenism when the future was described in terms of *less* civil or political liberty. Charles Bray commented in the midst of widespread distress in 1842 that 'We talk of liberty, while the multitudes are slaves to work and want; we must give up such liberty, which means chance, that we may possess the only real liberty dependent on law. Each man as he comes into the world must be shown his place and work, and not left to find it, or starve'. But this assault upon *laissez-faire* did not refer specifically to civil and political liberty at all, except insofar as it was often pointed out that such liberties declined or were meaningless when the material well-being of the people was insufficient (as Mudie claimed in 1821).[32]

Much more often, in fact, socialism was associated with an extension rather than a diminution of liberties. In those communities for which evidence remains, the free play of ideas seems to have been emphasised. The New Harmonite William Pelham, for example, stressed that

I enjoy mental liberty, after having long been deprived of it. I can speak my sentiments without fear of bad consequences, and others do the same – here are no political or religious quarrels, though there is a great diversity of opinion in matters of religion. Each says what he thinks, and mutual respect for the sentiments of each other seems to pervade all our intercourse.

Accompanying such assertions was again often the language of the Protestant right of individual conscience, which was adopted to suit socialist purposes. Owen had called for full liberty of conscience on all matters of religion to be established in his communities from the beginning. Moreover, the call to abolish 'that futility – human legislation' (as the *New Moral World* put it) did not express an appeal to anarchy, but the belief that 'governing by violence' could be supplanted by a superior mode of polity. In turn, government by 'human nature' meant that 'executive government' might be dispensed with. The complete eradication of 'responsibility', the Manchester lecturer John Watts also declared, echoing a long tradition of Protestant antinomianism, would come about 'by making man a law unto himself'. Still another form of freedom, some believed, would result from society's 'emancipation from the tyranny of custom and fashion', when needs would become as rational as their possessors, though this view became increasingly unpopular in the 1840s. Some *types* of freedom, therefore, and particularly the economic 'liberty' which benefited only

---

31 [Abram Combe], *The New Court* (n.p., n.d.), pp. 2–11.
32 Charles Bray, *An Essay Upon the Union of Agriculture and Manufactures and Upon the Organisation of Industry* (1844), pp. 104–5; *Economist*, 1, no. 4 (17 February 1821), 62.

the few, would be surrendered, but others more valuable would be acquired.[33]

Constitutionalism and early communitarianism

If we consider briefly the experience which the early Owenite communities had with government and management, it is clear that no community lasted long enough for anything like a 'final' form of rule to be implemented, much less for the dissolution of coercive power into the community at large to be genuinely tested. Consequently there is little evidence of divisions occurring over threats to civil or personal liberty *per se*. Of far greater importance was the relationship between the inhabitants of a community and those who founded it, and whose position was consequently so influential that it was not even necessary to relegate all power to them constitutionally.

Virtually all of the early communities, as well as those which were planned but never established, were in fact constitutional democracies of one type or another in which popular sovereignty was fixed in a founding document. This was evident from the earliest Owenite experiments. The regulations for the first of these – George Mudie's London Co-operative and Economical Society – were drawn up by Mudie at the request of a committee of artisans (mainly journeyman printers) which included the young Henry Hetherington. This resulted in government by a committee which rotated monthly and was composed, in principle, of all of the members of the Spa Fields community (some twenty-two families), who evidently lived communally for about two years.[34]

Far more important as a prototype for later socialist activities, particularly for Owen's own ideas on government, was the New Harmony community, with which Owen was intensively involved for some four years, and which at one point numbered about a thousand members. Governing the community was an issue which here, as elsewhere, provoked considerable conflict among the members, and can only be described, to follow Arthur Bestor's term, as an exercise in 'dissonance'. The Preliminary Society of the community, formed on 1 May 1825, was nominally administered by a committee originally named by

---

[33] 'Letters of William Pelham', in Harlow Lindley, ed., *Indiana as Seen by Early Travellers* (Indianapolis, Indiana Historical Commission, 1916), p. 373; *NMW*, 4, no. 161 (25 November 1837), 34; *ComS*, no. 3 (11 December 1830), 18; *NMW*, 8, no. 2 (11 July 1840), 21; 4, no. 159 (11 November 1837), 17.

[34] *Report of the Committee Appointed at a Meeting of Journeymen* (2nd edn., 1821), p. 27; *Economist*, 2, no. 51 (2 March 1822), 399. On British Owenite communitarianism generally see J. F. C. Harrison, *Robert Owen*, pp. 47–63, R. G. Garnett, *Co-operation and the Owenite Socialist Communities*, and W. H. G. Armytage, *Heavens Below* (Routledge and Kegan Paul, 1961), pp. 77–167.

Owen. According to his constitution the whole community was then to be permitted to elect three further members of the managing committee a year later, the delay being to allow the members time to become acquainted with the character of those they would name as governors. One year after, Owen proposed, the community could then choose half the committee, and a year after this, institute a full community of goods, presumably including complete democracy. Accordingly the community did name new members to the committee, as well as confirming Owen's appointments. The weekly meetings of the whole population also had the right to make non-binding recommendations to the committee. During the first seven months of the society Owen was absent, and was replaced by his son William, who seems, as representative of the owner of the property, to have taken the major economic decisions himself. Some members were quite unhappy with this arrangement, terming it an 'aristocracy' and even a 'despotism', and complaining that members who criticised the system were threatened with expulsion. But this was also the only penalty which could be wielded against those who became deeply indebted to the Society and then threatened simply to leave, as one storekeeper did. On Owen's return in 1826, the members decided to begin the transition to full community immediately. 'By constant efforts' Owen encouraged every one to 'speak his *real* sentiments favorable or unfavorable to the proposal'. A constitutional committee was formed which soon disagreed on a number of fundamental issues, with Owen himself pressing for the creation of a hierarchy of officials who would report on the conduct and industriousness of each member, Robert Dale Owen advising the creation of a greater number of deliberative bodies, and Owen's friend and travelling companion Donald Macdonald urging the relinquishment of all laws and constitutions in favour of decision-making by 'open family assembly'.[35]

The final constitution of the new Community of Equality fixed the power of decision-making in assemblies of all resident adult members. The relationship between Owen and the members remained undefined in the constitution. But faith in his restorative powers was undiminished. After several weeks of disastrous administrative chaos, therefore, it was agreed that Owen himself, with four trustees appointed by him, should govern the community for at least one year,

35 Arthur Bestor, *Backwoods Utopias: The Sectarian and Owenite Phases of Communitarian Socialism in America, 1663–1829* (Philadelphia, University of Pennsylvania Press, 1950), p. 160, and generally 160–201; *NHG*, 1, no. 1 (1 October 1825), 2; 'Letters of William Pelham', in Harlow Lindley, ed., *Indiana as Seen by Early Travellers*, pp. 383, 411; T. C. Pears, ed., *New Harmony* (Clifton, Kelley, 1973), p. 40; George Lockwood, *The New Harmony Communities* (Marion, Chronicle Co., 1920), pp. 105–10.

and until two-thirds of the community felt they could govern themselves. Growing divisions, and the realisation that productivity was unacceptably low, soon added to the burden of the community. A group of backwoodsmen who were opponents of Owen's religious views (though they also apparently disliked rule by one individual) broke away to form a new community, Macluria, to which Owen agreed to grant a large tract of uncleared land. This instigated the secession of another group, this time of English farmers who had come together from Morris Birkbeck's Illinois settlement, and who in April 1826 received another grant of land from Owen to form 'Feiba Peveli' (whose name was taken from its geographical co-ordinates; New Harmony was to be appealingly renamed 'Ipba Veinul'). A fourth community of the 'Literati' also planned to enter into orbit around the mother association, but Owen's opposition prevented its formation. Anxious to remedy his precarious financial situation, Owen then selected 24 members to form the nucleus of the first community, giving them responsibility for repayment of the land, as well as the right to admit new members and establish various grades of membership. But he retained governing power himself until two-thirds of the members wanted self-government, provided this did not occur within the first year. In May 1826 the community was further subdivided on the basis of occupation, being now organised into educational, agricultural and mechanical sections. Nonetheless malingering remained substantial and productivity was inadequate, the cause later primarily being ascribed to 'carelessness in many members regarding community property'. In the autumn, after the expulsion of a number of members, the segments were reunited, except for the school, over which Owen's current partner, William Maclure, assumed full control, expressing his considerable distrust of Owen's practical abilities. Further divisions continued, with Owen attempting to curtail the former Quaker Paul Brown – the leader of the 'republican' party seeking immediate community of property in all goods – by tearing down his advertisements for meetings, accusing him of seeking communism because he was himself poor, and censoring his ideas in the *New Harmony Gazette*. Subdivided again in January 1827 by Owen, New Harmony collapsed by April, with Owen returning to Britain in June lamenting the premature adoption of equality and community of goods. Maclure remained to assist the school, but Owen, having lost some $100,000 of his fortune, resolved to begin again elsewhere. Within the next few years, New Harmony spawned some nineteen branches or imitators, many of which were in Indiana or adjacent states. Some details of the administrative arrangements of these remain. Emissaries from New Harmony, including Paul Brown and Josiah Warren, visited the small settlement of Kendal, Ohio some time in 1825 and persuaded it to form a community on Owen's principles. This governed itself by general meeting and lasted from the spring of 1826 until early 1829. The Blue Spring community, among others, suffered a similar fate, evidently breaking up over the issue of what colour homespun trousers were to be dyed. Here universal male suffrage prevailed, with only women who were also heads of families being permitted to vote. An Owenite community was also planned for Valley Forge, Pennsylvania, which was to be governed by a weekly meeting of men and women alike, but it seems never to have been founded.[36]

The early British communities were no more successful. Established near Motherwell during Owen's absence at New Harmony, the Orbiston community originated from the six hundred families who had formed the Edinburgh Practical Society during the early 1820s, some of whom had also gone to New Harmony after embezzlement cut short the life of the Society. The lands on the Orbiston estate belonged to the Owenite Archibald James Hamilton, who was anxious to imitate the great success of New Lanark. The early stages of the development of the community were also intended to be overseen by a committee of the fund-raising organisation – the British and Foreign Philanthropic Society – but the latter collapsed too quickly to perform this service. Begun by Hamilton and the Edinburgh tanner Abram Combe, the community was first occupied in April 1826 by about a hundred trades-men and labourers, who as at New Harmony were accepted as they applied and lacked fervent dedication to the new principles. At the outset the form of government was not fixed, with some preferring a committee, and Combe himself, as the resident representative of the owners, urging rule by one, removeable director. In late March, the members agreed unanimously to allow Combe to guide their affairs as long as they were pleased with his performance. By August, however, Combe complained that the operatives of the community opposed his system of one-man rule, and denied that he had the right to compel obedience from them. The question arose again several months later when some of the more militant Orbistonians led by Alexander Camp-bell (who would remain associated with Owen for the next forty years)

---

[36] *NHG*, 1, no. 21 (15 February 1826), 161–3; no. 23 (1 March 1826), 175; no. 27 (29 March 1826), 209; no. 29 (12 April 1826), 225; 2, no. 26 (28 March 1827), 206–7; Paul Brown, *Twelve Months at New Harmony* (Cincinnati, 1827), pp. 15–25, 56–8, 71; A. E. Bestor, ed., *Education and Reform at New Harmony* (Clifton, Kelley, 1973), pp. 365–8, 373–97; T. C. Pears, ed., *New Harmony*, pp. 172–200. On the Kendal community, see Wendall Fox, 'The Kendal Community', *OAHQ*, 20 (1911), 176–219, and *NHG*, 3, no. 18 (13 February 1828), 141. On Blue Spring see Richard Simons, 'A Utopian Failure', *IHB*, 18 (1941), 98–115. On the Valley Forge community, see the *Preamble and Constitution of the Friendly Association for Mutual Interests* (Philadelphia, 1826).

proposed the institution of a full community of goods. At this time all members also voted on one another's readmission to the community, a process which lasted four hours and ultimately rejected none, 'though some underwent a severe trial' despite the fact that negative criticisms were supposed to be excluded from the process.[37]

After some deliberation, the proprietors of 'Babylon', as the locals now termed the community, agreed to give all power over the buildings and land to the inhabitants, in return for the repayment of the capital plus 5% interest. A new form of government was set up, composed of one representative for each ten community members, plus the heads of the various production departments. The latter were themselves chosen by their own members, though their positions were ratified by the whole community at quarterly meetings. Combe became the President of the Executive Committee, though now sharing power with a 'General Secretary'. At the end of the year the community, now some 250 strong, was still divided on the issue of community of goods, with a small but vocal majority approving the measure at least until early 1827. Combe's illness forced the election of a Vice-President (his brother William Combe) responsible for ensuring the enforcement of the committee's resolutions. Upon his accession, however, a new outbreak of egalitarian enthusiasm took place. Mounting disagreements, an increasing financial burden and inadequate productivity provoked Combe to propose that the President be appointed by the proprietors, who if they disagreed could have their votes weighted according to their investment. Pressure upon the tenants by the local clergy as well as their own friends and relatives did not help. Nor did a trade depression, which resulted in the interest on their capital being raised. Thefts from communal stocks necessitated the stationing of guards armed with guns and assisted by dogs. The community collapsed when subscribers failed to forward their capital, and Combe died in August after over-exerting himself at spade husbandry. The last members departed in December 1827, with two, including Campbell, spending most of the next year in Hamilton Jail, having inadvertently become partially liable for some of the debts of the community.[38]

Midway through the Orbiston experiment, William Thompson also attempted to found a community near Cork with the assistance of the London Co-operative Society. This colony, which was to begin with

---

[37] Lockwood, *The New Harmony Communities*, p. 129; Alexander Cullen, *Adventures in Socialism*, pp. 171–322; *RO*, 1, no. 13 (2 March 1826), 102; no. 15 (30 March 1826), 116; no. 17 (26 August 1826), 132–3; no. 21 (7 October 1826), 155–61.

[38] *RO*, 1, no. 22 (1 November 1826), 163–5; no. 25 (27 December 1826), 187–9; no. 29 (14 March 1827), 26–7, 32; no. 34 (19 September 1827), 65; Garnett, *Co-operation and the Owenite Socialist Communities*, pp. 65–100.

the principle of equal distribution and ultimately to have some 2,000 inhabitants, was to be managed by eight or more committees in charge of various aspects of production and administration, with one member of each committee leaving every three months and remaining ineligible for office for a similar period. As at Orbiston and New Harmony, 'entire freedom of thought and expression on all subjects, and entire freedom of action not interfering with the feelings of others' were to be guaranteed. Sufficient subscriptions were not received to allow the community to commence, however.[39]

A more successful attempt to found an Irish community took place on the estate of John Scott Vandeleur, a convert to Owen's views at the Dublin meetings of 1823, which was located at Ralahine in Co. Clare. Much of the enthusiasm generated in this community was also the result of the efforts of the working class co-operator, E. T. Craig, who became Vandeleur's steward and schoolmaster of the community. Though Vandeleur was both the owner and manager of the association, a constitution of late 1831 established a committee of nine out of fifty-two members elected by half-yearly ballot of all members, male and female, and including four members from the previous committee. Its primary task was the daily assignment of work to all. As in earlier communities, Vandeleur and Craig initially had no real choice over the admission of members, who included only 18 'efficient labourers', but had to accept those already employed on the estate. As at Orbiston, however, members initially admitted and later readmitted one another by ballot (and others were later rejected upon application for admission). By the constitution, which remained unaltered during the society's two year life, Vandeleur retained the power of expulsion for the first year of the community, and chose his own secretary, treasurer, and storekeeper. Recourse to lawyers and courts being prohibited, arbitration in the event of disputes between members lay with the full community, a majority of which could settle any case. At a time of considerable economic distress and social upheaval in the area (Vandeleur's earlier steward had been murdered shortly before the community began), Ralahine without doubt made a considerable contribution to social justice, abolishing the hated office of steward and offering a reasonable reward for labour as well as education for children. It prospered, growing to some eighty members by the autumn of its second year. Insofar as the committee was elected by universal suffrage, it was also a remarkable experiment in democracy. Full freedom of opinion and religious practice were allowed. Weekly meetings discussed the distribution of labour, and occasionally, the conduct of members. The relationship between master and servant was evidently

[39] *LCM*, 1, no. 10 (October 1826), 314–20.

largely superseded, and John Finch claimed that 'no permanent classification, but that of age' actually operated. Quarrelling was regarded as
a 'high crime' which could bring expulsion (one 'trial' by the 'Ralahine
Parliament' of twenty-nine men and seventeen women resulted in a
warning being issued to the argumentative parties). But Ralahine was
a comparatively unpolitical experiment in other respects, and there is
some indication that this was quite deliberate; Craig was pleased, for
example, that several members gave up attending the great repeal
meetings of Daniel O'Connell. More importantly, there is no evidence
that Vandeleur's authority was ever really shared or challenged. Correspondingly, Vandeleur's flight after losing the estate in his Dublin
club (rumour had it that he later became a locomotive engineer in
America) left the inhabitants stranded and helpless. His agreement
with them was not even recognised as a legal document. He had
chaired all meetings of the community, acting as what Finch called
'king and father of his people', and though there is no evidence that he
ever abused his powers, his capacity for moral suasion was certainly
greater than Owen's had been at New Lanark, or Combe's at
Orbiston.[40]

A not dissimilar, though more egalitarian, relationship between
proprietor and tenants also emerged at the Manea Fen estate of William Hodson near March, Cambridgeshire, which became known as
the Hodsonian community. This was also set up without the official
sanction of Owen or any Socialist organisation, though a variety of
efforts were made to integrate the community into the official Association, at this time seeking a new location for a community. More
generous than Vandeleur as well as more dedicated to Owen's principles, William Hodson conveyed his 200 acre estate to some forty
members in the autumn of 1839, with the aim of achieving 'united
exertion' and full equality of rights. In November a committee of
management was set up composed of six members, four nominated by
the community and two by Hodson, who chose those who had the
next highest proportion of votes as an expression of his confidence in
the community. The constitution stipulated that Hodson was to
remain President from 1840 to 1845. Three directors – two of the
community's, one of Hodson's – were to be rotated out annually. After
August 1845, or if Hodson was no longer a member, the community
was to elect a board of seven persons, who would choose their own
president. Unfortunately the community lasted only until early 1841.

[40] *NMW*, 4, no. 181 (14 April 1838), 198; no. 182 (21 April 1838), 207; no. 183 (28 April
1838), 214; no. 192 (30 June 1838), 196; E. T. Craig, *An Irish Commune* (Dublin, Irish
Academic Press, 1983), pp. 25–47, 66, 98, 108; Garnett, *Co-operation and the Owenite
Socialist Communities*, pp. 100–29.

The opposition of the local clergy and others, deep personal divisions between many members, and the inability to find a market for its produce, rendered life difficult for the inhabitants, who had initially made considerable steps towards repaying Hodson for the value of the land. Well might Hodson claim that the community was no longer dependent upon him, since a majority vote was required to alter any of its rules. Such contentions were simply not meaningful in conditions of distress. Evidently in financial difficulties in late 1840, Hodson was strongly criticised by the colonists, who were however still wholly dependent upon his largesse. When the members decided to assume management after Hodson had ordered meat deliveries stopped, he in turn seized the books of the community. Pro- and anti-Hodson parties were formed, and on 30 February 1841 matters had deteriorated so far that the anti-Hodson leader was shot at by one of his opponents. Groups of the latter also seem to have gone about armed with bludgeons, and to have pillaged what they could from community stocks. Once again, as the Owenites were wont to insist, democratic rights had proven insufficient in the face of social and economic power.[41]

From this extremely brief survey of the governmental arrangements of the early Owenite communities it is clear that every community sought ultimately to introduce universal suffrage and power-sharing, often including rotation of offices, as well as social equality. Members of the communities clearly believed that they were engaging in an experiment in democracy as well as in collective ownership. It is also evident, however, that proprietorship was the central fact of moral and political power in every community. Until the value of the land had been repaid, the worth of democratic control was clearly extremely limited, and the claims of the members against those of the owners were bound to be a certain source of contention. This, we will see, was also to be the case at Queenwood.

How does the internal management of these communities affect the question of authoritarianism in early socialism? Most communities devised some form of mutual surveillance, particularly of working habits, and members were liable to be criticised publicly, and even expelled, for shirking their duties. On the other hand, freedom of religion and the expression of opinion were usually guaranteed constitutionally, and were certainly more clearly spelt out and readily available than was true for the working classes in the society at large. For the most part, too (though records are sadly lacking in this respect), the adjudication process seems to have functioned fairly well in most

---

[41] *WB*, 1, no. 6 (24 August 1839), 53; no. 18 (16 November 1839), 147–8; no. 20 (30 November 1839), 167; W. H. G. Armytage, 'Manea Fen', *BJRL*, 38 (1956), 288–310.

communities, though constant disagreements, particularly about the question of community of goods, seem to have plagued most. No community survived long enough to guarantee that police, judges, courts and prisons would surely disappear from the landscape of the new moral world. But all claimed, and not without justification, to have made a reasonable step in this direction.

It is not evident, therefore, that the sectarian impulse in many early communities would have produced anything like the theocratic authoritarianism of the Shakers, much less a more repressive regime. Throughout early Owenism, the ideology of personal and political liberty was too clearly present to permit any very considerable infringement upon the perceived rights of community inhabitants. Economic freedom, of course, was to be curtailed in the interests of the common good. But the restriction of liberty otherwise was not an issue in early community planning and organisation. Mutual supervision, without the right of violent coercion, was seen as an attribute of the most advanced of the Christian sects, and as vastly superior to the existing system of repressive, class-based order and police. But there is no hint in Owenism as a whole of the excesses of seventeenth-century puritanism, any more than those of the French revolution. The strongly voluntary emphasis of communitarianism, with the coalescence of republican and radical ideals, simply prevented such a threat from emerging.

It is worth bearing in mind, too, that there was nothing unusual in many of the separate opinions we have examined here. A reluctance to allow factions to develop was obviously entailed by the tremendous emphasis given to 'harmony' and 'unity' in community life. But hostility to 'party' pervaded working class radicalism as it had much political rhetoric in the previous century. Whether the higher form of the common good was the Dissenting Interest, the Cause of the People, or some similar collectivity, partisanship lacked respectability for most who found themselves outside of traditional party boundaries. Some radicals, like Samuel Bamford, for instance, conceived 'THE NATION' as 'the only party' to be served, and wanted a moral 'bond of union' to 'put down all demagoguism, – all trading agitation, – all jealousies, – all dissensions, – all recriminations. It would bring together good men and true of all grades, and would create a common brotherhood'. More religious radicals were also more likely to place great stress upon the importance of brotherhood and moral union. Occasionally such ideals were expressed in overtly religious terms, though without the explicitly sectarian overtones which Owenism often invoked. A 'CHRISTIANITY OF POLITICS' combining 'common brotherhood of feeling and sentiment' was thus what the progress of popular reform required, argued 'Roger Radical' in 1820.[42]

Yet it could be objected justly that, outside of the socialist system of ideas, these were relatively isolated sentiments with no particularly threatening political import. They did not seem to imply the abrogation of republican or representative institutions, as Owen himself planned, much less curtailing the system of civil liberties which the radicals sought to restore and extend. Radicals also tended to deny the value of partisanship in favour of unity, and to de-emphasise the form of the government they sought by comparison with the spirit of union and political equality with which it was to be conducted or the social and economic ends expected of it. This resulted for instance in Richard Carlile's claim (following Paine) that 'republicanism' did not imply any particular form of government, but rather meant that

the interest of a whole people is considered in preference to individual or party interest. An absolute monarchy might be a more perfect Republican form of Government than the present British Government, and if that absolute monarch was a mild and intelligent man, and had no principle or particular interest at heart but that of the country and the whole people, that state of society would be perfectly republican.[43]

Such views were common among writers who combined Owenite and radical views in the 1830s and 1840s. They are also closely associated with the use of the term 'democracy' to describe the working classes generally, where the focus was often upon the interests of a class rather than any political mechanisms by which these were to be represented. No doubt some of the more perfectionist, sectarian Owenites did take such views further than most radicals would have considered prudent. But communitarian Owenism as a whole did not, for the simple reason that it remained too close to radicalism and the working class movement to abandon democratic ideals which had not yet been won in the society at large.

The politics of perfection in early nineteenth century social theory only anticipated modern totalitarianism to the degree that it permitted

---

[42] Samuel Bamford, *Passages in the Life of a Radical* (1844), pp. 417, 420; 'Roger Radical', *Why are We Poor?*, p. 20. See also Christopher Thomson, *Autobiography* (1847), p. 169, where it is argued that without a 'deep spirituality', the passage of measures like the Charter would be 'useless' and 'rent in twain by the machinations of the political partisans and well-paid demagogues', and Alexander Somerville's remarks along the same lines in *PS*, no. 1 (7 December 1833), 2.

[43] *Republican*, 5, no. 1 (4 January 1822), 1. For a similar, co-operative view of this question see *HTA*, no. 5 (23 October 1830), 66, where it is argued that the type of government was unimportant once a radical reform had taken place. See also Cobbett's disclaimer that the form of government was of special interest to him, in *CWPR*, 15 (29 December 1821), 1546, and 120 (6 November 1830), 618.

the virtual abolition of privacy, suppressed freedom of opinion, and established coercive mechanisms to enforce regulations. Privacy, however, was highly valued in most communities; it was often emphasised that no-one could enter members' rooms without their permission. Despite conflicts over essential issues, freedom of opinion was never, in principle, threatened in any community. Had the extreme perfectionism of a few Owenites ever come to dominate a community, this might have altered in favour of a more traditional sectarian model. This could have involved widespread arbitrariness, and an almost complete system of mutual behavioural supervision which made no sufficiently subtle distinction between acts and opinions. The most optimistic, millenarian Owenites did indeed expect that moral perfection was possible, and considered that their principles embraced all aspects of human existence, even if they preferred the term 'social' to 'political' to describe this universal quality. To the extent that Owenism emulated not only a Dissenting sect, but an extremely perfectionist one at that, it fearlessly abandoned the constraints of political prudence, and pointed towards a regimen of considerable conformity.

Nonetheless the trend in the development in Owenite thought in the 1830s and 1840s ran in the opposite direction. The accusation that personal liberties might be threatened in the short term, but even worse, a uniformity of slave-like character would be created in the long term, had been present from Owen's first efforts to popularise his plans, and persisted throughout the early community experiments. In reaction to this charge, socialists by the early 1840s gave greater stress to personal liberty than they had twenty years earlier. Despite the Rational Society's attempt to enforce a degree of conformity upon its members, this trend began to dissipate by the 1840s. Some of the socialists, and notably Holyoake, were extremely hostile to what they regarded as the creation of an inordinately passive character as a result of the doctrine of non-responsibility. (Holyoake later complained that 'an audience of English communists who eschew praise and blame, are as free from animation as Egyptian mummies. They are very obliging but are very mute. Truth and falsehood, right and wrong, are received by them with the same respectful attention'.) As a result of such criticisms, an 'individualism of socialism', as the *New Moral World* put it in mid-1844, came to be recognised as a legitimate and integral element of Owenite philosophy. Self-cultivation could thus be seen as a perfectly acceptable goal, provided it was possible for all, and it was understood that character was formed within circumstances determined by society. It was therefore plausible to argue that while all were born essentially similar, a considerable 'variety of natural character and capability' was nonetheless possible.[44] This, in turn, would open the door to the defence of eccentricity within the socialist movement, which became more prevalent in the mid-1840s. Nonetheless in the most extreme formulations of the rationalist ideal of one interest, most of which emerged in the early years of the communitarian movement, the seeds of a virtually complete social uniformity were doubtless clearly present. If differing opinions upon subjects other than religion were to be 'tolerated', this was not as a result of the possibility of their correctness, but only because Owenism's emphasis upon the voluntariness of its entire endeavour made any other course of action almost impossible.

But even here, this rigorous pacifism nonetheless *centrally* distinguished communitarian Owenism from many later forms of socialism, and placed it much closer to Dissenting sectarianism than to social or political radicalism generally of any type. Perfectionism may have helped to drive Owenism towards uniformity, but it also made the forcible implementation of such beliefs impossible, or at least very difficult. For the model of a voluntary, non-coercive society was qualitatively enormously different from those regimes based upon all-encompassing fear and force which are usually termed 'totalitarian'. The distance between fear of one's neighbour's disapproving stare and the terror of the guillotine is vast indeed. Whether Owenism could eventually have spurned all physical force in a society composed solely of communities is a moot point. But it was very strongly committed to non-violence. For this reason, in particular, it would be inaccurate to enrol Owenism among the early proto-totalitarians. Non-violence meant that no revolutionary seizure of power was necessary, and no dictatorship of one class over another permissible. Nor did Owenite perfectionism allow a single party to monopolise power, for this was an irrational principle of rule. Owenism also lies outside any history of 'totalitarianism' because of its historical development, for this was markedly different from the genealogies described by Talmon, for whom the transition from a Rousseauist general will to the Jacobin terror and Babouvist conspiracy is an essential lineage in this history. Instead, as we have seen, the conformist trends in Owenism were based in particular upon enlightenment and Christian cosmopolitanism, and notions of a single discoverable truth and of moral perfectibility. Finally, Owenism also produced a school of socialists much more committed to a more traditional ideal of republicanism and democracy than Owen himself was. As we will now see, these sought to extend the notion of popular representation well beyond its traditional bound-

[44] G. J. Holyoake, *Rationalism* (1845), p. 42; *NMW*, 12, no. 51 (15 June 1844), 410; no. 52 (22 June 1844), 421-2.

aries, indeed beyond 'politics' entirely and into 'society', and especially into the organisation of the workplace. Here democracy was not therefore to be superseded, but rather rendered far more widely accessible.

4

'A mere trifle by comparison': social science, republicanism and political economy

The notion of 'social science' did not only encompass an account of how society might be organised so as to supersede the more punitive and coercive functions of government. Social science was indeed to replace the art of government as it had been hitherto practised. But the concept was also intended as an explanation for the insufficiency of existing theories of political reform, and of the science of government as it had been previously understood. In particular, social science aimed to demonstrate that radicalism relied far too heavily upon an outmoded conception of the relationship between government and the economy. The radical reformers' central economic assumption was that prosperity would ensue once the burden of governmental taxation imposed by 'Corruption' was eased. This approach, the Owenites insisted, had been surpassed by wartime economic developments, which demanded new theories of economic activity, and a greater role for government in guiding the economy. Without a new analysis of the economy, radicalism would be simply unable to conceptualise large-scale and permanent unemployment, mechanisation, and commercial and monetary crises, or to propose appropriate political responses to them.

The desire for a new approach to politics from an economic perspective was shared in part by the classical political economists. Many of these agreed that an alleviation of taxation would be economically beneficial, but argued that traditional theories of government paid far too little heed to the existence of natural laws of economic development which, far from requiring greater intervention and regulation in favour of the poor, demanded as little interference with the market mechanism by political authorities as possible. During the immediate post-war years, the intellectual ascendancy of political economy paralleled the development of Owen's plans. Both forms of thought, indeed, had a number of important assumptions in common. Given their commitment to competition, private property and social in equality, however, the classical economists quickly became Owen's most hostile critics.

The Owenites responded by articulating their own doctrines of political economy, which developed into a fully-fledged alternative economic system by the mid-1820s. Socialist economic thinking was rent, however, into two contending, but rarely clearly juxtaposed, schools. One tendency in socialist theory centred upon the desirability of maintaining limited needs and subsistence agricultural production in communities, though some manufacturing capacity was still to be developed at a local level. Another, however, aimed to harness industrial capacity to socialist goals in order both to expand production well beyond its present limits and to ensure a just distribution of its results. These parameters corresponded to some degree with the boundaries of Owenite political thought. The most perfectionist, optimistic assertions about the potential absence of conflict in the new moral world tended to occur in the context of that type of communitarian planning which insisted upon keeping needs simple and rendering the economic and administrative system correspondingly uncomplicated. To the theories of commercial development which I have elsewhere termed 'economic socialism', however, corresponded a set of assumptions which might be termed 'political socialism'. Those who sought greater state intervention and the encouragement of production by public enterprises, and who agreed with the political economists as to the legitimacy of expanded needs, increasing consumption, and the desirability of a rising standard of living, in other words, also tended to assume that more traditional modes of political rule exercised primarily at the level of the nation-state would prevail, though these would be democratised and might assume new forms.[1]

The impact of Owenite economic thought on socialist political ideas paralleled that of classical political economy upon liberalism in a variety of ways. One of the accomplishments of classical doctrines was to usurp many of the analytical and policy functions which formerly belonged to the sciences out of which its own first principles emerged, namely moral philosophy, natural jurisprudence, and political philosophy.[2] In the degree to which it accepted some of the perspective of political economy, socialism would share the assumption that many of the traditional concerns of political thought were now more correctly assigned to the field of political economy. If it is too early to speak of a 'displacement' of the sciences of government by those of the economy at the end of the eighteenth century, some conflict of aims was already

---

[1] See generally my *Machinery, Money and the Millennium*.
[2] See Stefan Collini, Donald Winch and John Burrow, *That Noble Science of Politics*, pp. 23–126.

evident between different modes of conceiving public well-being, and the beginnings of a shift in favour of political economy was certainly evident by the 1790s.

An important transmitter of the new preference for the science of political economy over the traditional sciences of government was Dugald Stewart, who interpreted Smith to a generation of influential students, including the future editors of the *Edinburgh Review*, the most important popularising vehicle of political economy in the early years of the nineteenth century. Stewart's views, however, were also well known to the first Owenites, who often cited them in their early periodicals and pamphlets. For Stewart the new science aimed centrally to provide public happiness. If this, rather than liberty, for example, was the true aim of government generally, much existing speculation about forms of government and rights and duties could be set aside, and political thinking refashioned around the idea of utility. This perspective, we will see, was also central to Owenite notions of the aims of government. For Stewart, a new method for the science of politics was clearly called for. Chastising those who were led 'to direct their efforts much more to improve the theory of Government, than to ascertain the just principles of *Political Economy*', Stewart for example insisted that happiness was 'in truth, the only object of legislation . . . of *intrinsic value*' while 'what is called *Political Liberty*, is only one of the means of obtaining this end'.[3] From this utilitarian perspective on public welfare, thus, forms of government were largely immaterial, provided they did not interfere with the process of economic development. What was central instead was the creation of wealth. To this end, the classical political economists, who also largely adopted this perspective on government, usually argued that a main task of governments was simply to avoid interfering with the balancing mechanism of the market.

Though the direct and immediate impact of *laissez-faire* ideals upon contemporary legislation has probably been exaggerated, the rapid ascendancy of political economy as a social and political philosophy remains undisputed. For much of the nineteenth century, political economy successfully dictated the terms of debate about such vital issues as the poor laws, trades' unions, hours and conditions of labour, emigration, the morals of the poor, and the extension of the factory system. Amongst many others, the Owenites observed that by the 1840s it often seemed as if the dogmas of the new science had swept aside all previous notions of government. The Christian Owenite John Minter Morgan, for instance, questioned rhetorically whether the nation was 'governed by State and Church – meaning, by State, the

3 Dugald Stewart, *Collected Works*, ed. W. Hamilton (Edinburgh, 1855), 8, pp. 22–3.

axioms of political economy, inculcating the sacrifice of every humane consideration and noble sentiment to the accumulation of wealth'. But this trend was by no means seen as an entirely negative development, and represented, as we will see, an approach to politics with which socialism could also at least partially concur. Insisting in 1842 that wages had fallen in proportion to the influence of political economy on parliament, George Alexander Fleming, for example, agreed that politics *could* only be categorised as a branch of 'policy or social economy'. When it was not so classified, 'Politics, separated from economy', was 'a mere selfish struggle of aristocratic placemen and their dependents, of section against section, of class against class'. The radical Richard Carlile's definition of political economy as 'the good divested of the evil of politics' also helps to capture this sense of the value-freedom, but yet moral superiority, which even some working class radicals imputed to the new science.[4] In some respects, thus, it was conceded on all sides by the 1840s that economic policy constituted the 'essence' of what 'politics' was properly about, if it was not merely to be understood as the pursuit and retention of power. The extension of this idea to working class radicalism generally, we will see, owed much to Owenism's constant, critical barrage against all varieties of reformers who failed to acknowledge these new truths.

The socialist notion of economic thought and development was to have an impact upon its own conception of politics which thus both paralleled, but also significantly departed from, that which political economy had upon liberal political thought. This chapter will consider five aspects of the relationship between economic and political ideas in Owenism: 'the machinery question', or the extent to which the concept of a harmonious unpolitical society was predicated upon an industrial conception of opulence; the emphasis upon exchange as a central social activity, and the corresponding displacement of issues of justice and rights to the exchange process; the rejection of the predominant economic assumptions of political radicalism, which described taxation as the principal cause of economic distress; the use by Owenites of the American model as the central example of the inadequacy of mere republican political institutions to provide substantial well-being; and finally, the re-emergence of political ideas within Owenite economic theory and of quasi-political plans for future economic organisation.

---

[4] John Minter Morgan, 'Letter to the Rt. Hon. Lord Ashley' (n.d.), *Tracts* (2nd edn., 1849), p. 190; *Union*, no. 3 (1 June 1842), 66; no. 1 (1 April 1842), 3; *Republican*, 14, no. 14 (13 October 1826), 417. On the separation of politics from economy in popular accounts of political economy see R. K. Webb, *The British Working Class Reader* (George Allen and Unwin, 1955), pp. 83–102.

Machinery and the progress of opulence

For the socialists, machinery was both the greatest cause of contemporary distress and the most important potential source of liberation from debilitating labour. But the harnessing of steam also had profound political implications. Mechanisation was an essential element in the vision of a harmonious future because the extension of opulence through new forms of production, rather than a restriction of needs, came (albeit gradually) to be seen by the Owenites as the best means of resolving the struggle for the means of subsistence. In earlier historical stages, individuals had always been nagged by a pervasive fear 'of being over-reached by others, and, without great care to secure their individual interests, of being deprived of the means of existence'. This had 'created a universal selfishness of the most ignorant nature'. Moreover, prior to the age of manufacturing, manual and natural means of production had been unable to supply 'the wealth and the leisure requisite for an equality of a superior education and condition of the human race'. Nonetheless, the need for historical progress had required that 'Until this new scientific power was secured to be applied on the most extensive scale for the universal service and benefit of man, slaves and servants were necessary to give leisure to some to discover, invent and improve'. But by the early nineteenth century, the Owenites believed, the new mechanical powers, combined with new agricultural techniques, were 'far more than are required to terminate all slavery and servitude among the human race, and to attain and secure a superior education and condition for all'. The existing organisation of society, then, was designed only to 'counteract the evils of *under-production*', which reinforced a system of gross social inequality. As Owen put it in discussing the new communities in 1823:

The arrangements under which they will live, will enable them, by pleasant, healthy, and desirable occupations, easily to produce a surplus beyond their own wants and wishes, and thus afford them the means of extending much aid to others, until every portion of society around them shall be as independent as themselves. Thus, in a short time, there will be no clashing of pecuniary interests, no unsocial differences on the subject of religion; every motive to individual or national contests will be withdrawn.[5]

If subordination occurred solely to produce a surplus, then, it could now be terminated. For this reason it is incorrect to assert with Engels (though it is still widely assumed) that the Owenites believed that their utopia could be introduced at any time, or when a sufficient percentage

[5] Owen, *Life*, 1A, p. 302; Owen, *Book of the New Moral World*, pt 7 (1844), pp. 24–5; NMW, 2, no. 62 (2 January 1836), 75; *Sun*, no. 9651 (30 July 1823), 1–2. Some of these issues are discussed in Alan Ryan, *Property and Political Theory* (Oxford, Basil Blackwell, 1984), pp. 169–71. Also useful is Andrew Reeve, *Property* (Macmillan, 1986), pp. 77–111.

of the population had become possessed of 'rational' beliefs. The progress of machinery alone made socialism possible. This aspect of Owenism, at least, exemplified a clearly materialist philosophy of history.

Thus, the advancement of machinery had several kinds of political consequences. Opulence superseded the need for individual selfishness and social division, as well as the necessity for a small progressive elite, because leisure for the inventive few alone was no longer required. In addition, machinery helped to resolve the Scottish paradox by which the increasing opulence of society entailed an ever narrower division of labour, which confined the mental capacities and, broadly, 'civilisation', of all those touched by it. Consequently no stultifyingly narrow task needed to be assigned exclusively to any one again. We have already seen the implications this had for Owenism's recasting of republican and Dissenting notions of independence.

In community, agriculture and manufacturing were to be blended so as to ensure both scientific progress and variation in individual work. But Owen did not, as we have seen, reject a minute division of labour because of its psychological effects alone. Its impairment and narrowing of the faculty of judgement also engendered a division of interests based on occupation which severely restricted the prospects of social harmony by obscuring the true interests of society as a whole. Consequently social and individual improvement were both analogous and interdependent. Without the universal development of all the human faculties, social divisions would continue to prevail, and individual culture would also be inhibited. With the notion of 'all-rounded development', a similar view would emerge, linked with the tradition of *Bildung* but also clearly drawing upon Owen, Fourier and others, in the writings of Marx and Engels. This perspective on the division of labour was thus amongst the most significant elements of the early socialist inheritance passed to modern socialism.

This approach to the machinery question set Owenism markedly apart from contemporary radicalism. Republicans like Charles Hall, socialists argued, were wrong to blame economic distress upon the draining of labour from agricultural production to the new manufactories. The curse of machinery was not that it existed but that it was wrongly applied. It would not be an exaggeration, in fact, to claim that the basis of Owen's proposals for community of goods was not essentially Platonic, utopian or early Christian in inspiration, but rested largely upon a notion of the manufacturing process. This, at least, was the opinion of the American Owenite Lewis Masquerier, afterwards an individualist critic of socialism, who concluded many years later about Owen and others who followed him on this question that

It is the saving of certain kinds of labor and the manufacturing of machinery that seems to lead to the error of communism of property and labor, and to the sentiment that it is the natural form of society. Reformers, urging the communitizing and nationalizing principle of rights and property, seem to overlook the fact that nine-tenths of labor and production are agricultural and mechanical, and also performed with small and ordinary tools – leaving only the other tenth, perhaps, to be done by machinery. They seem to plan reform so much upon it, that it shows they think machine-labor everything. Hence, they plan large palaces to keep the communists together to annoy and infect the whole. This plan tends to the employment of officers or managers, which put their sovereignty or power of self-government into a state of alienation and monopoly.[6]

Such a threat to democracy from the organisational forms which would accompany widespread mechanisation was rarely conceded by the socialists, however. The liberating aspects of machinery were far more obvious in this early period, when the problems of the large-scale management of production had not yet become widely evident. But the problem of hierarchy within the labour process was recognised by the 1830s, and a variety of solutions to it put forward.

The concentration of the problems of social conflict in the economic sphere is also evident in the Owenite treatment of exchange. Political concepts were retained in some areas of the Owenite analysis of exchange, as we will see later in this chapter. But we must first consider how the investment of exchange with moral qualities linked it to the wider problem of sociability, the way in which social divisions were understood to emanate from the exchange process, and the effects such notions had on a language of rights.

That existing modes of exchanging commodities were among the primary sources of human dissension had already been clearly expressed by Owen in the *Report to the County of Lanark*. Here the principle of the exchange of labour for labour was first proposed as a means of eliminating 'the present demoralizing system of bargaining between individuals', since 'no practice perhaps tends more than this to deteriorate and degrade the human character'. Social harmony was impossible until the exchange relation had been placed upon a new and wholly just basis because exchange affected so many other areas of human activity. To William Thompson, for example, just exchange was a fundamental aspect of sociability generally. John Gray's *Lecture on Human Happiness* (1825) also demonstrated how the exchange relation was used to supplant more political explanations of social distress:

---

[6] Masquerier, *Sociology* (New York, 1877), p. 52. See my 'Lewis Masquerier and the Later Development of American Owenism, 1835–45', *LabH*, 29 (1988), 230–40.

the propensity to exchange labour for labour . . . is the original principle, by which [man] is enabled to leave, at such an immeasurable distance below him, all the brute creation. Why then do we so frequently attribute our miseries to the defects of governments, since it is exclusively by barter, that the power, by which individuals are enabled to tyrannize over nations, is introduced into the world? . . . barter, *and barter alone*, is the basis of society, and . . . *all other institutions amongst men* are built wholly and solely upon it.[7]

Consequently Owenite theories of exchange tended to concentrate that part of the socialist language of rights which did not refer to freedom of conscience upon economic rather than political relationships. Owen's comment in 1839 was characteristic: 'every individual has FULL EQUAL RIGHT to the earth, and to the services of others in return for his own, and there is no other right inherent in the human race'. Here the duty to labour was seen as even more central than the right to the produce of labour, as might be expected from an essentially Protestant discourse on work. After about 1820, Owen himself no longer appealed to the duties the wealthy owed the poor as the stewards of God's earth. Instead he resurrected the 'genuine principle of barter' as a natural standard of value based upon 'common justice'. This was a dramatic departure from the usual jurisprudential conception of right and duty in exchange, however. For justice was here defined by the right to receive *equal* exchanges, as John Gray emphasised, and not merely the duty to fulfil all contractual obligations, no matter how unjust the terms of the contract. Rights were here subordinated to the internal, substantial justice of labour relationships, not limited by the formal constraints of freedom of contract in civil society.

Of course, not all notions of political and civil rights were subsumed under the right to just exchange. Owen and others sometimes spoke of a 'natural right' of all to govern, for example, but only very rarely inferred further from this that political rights emanated from pre-existing civil rights, or had been established by some form of social contract. Such arguments, and indeed this whole form of jurisprudential discourse, were central to radicalism from Locke through Paine and long after, but were in fact almost entirely eliminated in socialism. Instead such assumptions were usually subsumed under the category of economic justice, on the one hand, and on the other, under the quasi-republican demand for universal democratic participation, which no longer required 'rights' to be lodged against any alien form of authority. H. S. Foxwell was thus certainly wrong to claim that Owen never raised any claims of rights at all. But beyond the issue of religious

---

[7] Owen, *NVS*, pp. 251, 262–3; John Gray, *A Lecture on Human Happiness* (1825), p. 3.

toleration, Owenite discussions of rights were usually confined to the question of rights and duties in relation to labour, rather than the relationship between individual and government.[8] This was a trend which would also predominate in later forms of socialism.

The case against the taxation analysis

The Owenite treatment of the questions of machinery and exchange helped to displace discussions of conflict from the political to the economic sphere. A more frontal assault upon the political thought of contemporary radicalism occurred, however, over the taxation question. Late eighteenth- and early nineteenth-century parliamentary reformers agreed almost unanimously that excessive taxation was the primary cause of economic distress. 'We will venture to affirm', wrote the radical journalist John Wade in 1818, 'there does not remain an individual, unless he is a devourer of taxes, who ascribes the misfortunes of the country to any other causes, than the enormous burdens under which the people groan [and] the measures of our weak and incapable rulers'. Writing a year later, his fellow reformer W. T. Sherwin specified that

> *Forty-four millions of dead taxes, where there used to be but nine*, accounts for the whole of what we feel, and what we complain of. It explains everything. And as these forty-four millions are the principal cause of all our sufferings, we can never be any better off, unless, at least, a part of them are removed. They have created, and they constitute the whole of our misery; and when they are lessened, and not until then, can we calculate upon any other alleviation.

This, then, was the battle-cry of the radicals. 'The *only cause* of the distress is *taxation*' insisted T. J. Wooler. Taxation was 'the great mill-stone around the neck of the country' echoed the radical *White Hat*. '*Taxation* is the *father*, the *paper system* the *mother*, and pauperism is the *offspring* of their union ... *Taxation, created and supported* by the Boroughmonger, is the root of the worse than Egyptian plagues with which poor England is afflicted' was Richard Carlile's formulation.[9]

'Taxation' thus symbolised all of the loathsome consequences of aristocratic misrule. Placemen, tythes, pensioners, the civil list, the national debt, the standing army: all were so many deductions from

---

[8] Owen, *Six Lectures* (Manchester, 1839), p. 61. See *Crisis*, 1, no. 31 (6 October 1832), 122, and 2, no. 35 (17 August 1833), 261, on morals and labour exchanges; Owen, *NVS*, pp. 261–2, 250; Gray, *Lecture*, p. 32; Anton Menger, *The Right to the Whole Produce of Labour* (1899), p. lxxiv. For a clear example of Owen's use of natural rights language see *NMW*, 4, no. 186 (19 May 1838), 235.

[9] *Gorgon*, 1, no. 1 (23 May 1818), 1–2; *SPR*, 1, no. 1 (5 April 1817), 2; *BD*, 8, no. 4 (23 January 1822), 134; *WH*, no. 1 (16 October 1819), 3; *Republican*, 2, no. 4 (11 February 1820), 135. See also the *Briton*, no. 7 (6 November 1819), 52.

labourers' wages, and all had corrupt government as their source and parliamentary reform as their antidote. This had been self-understood to some extent ever since the revival of the parliamentary reform movement in the late eighteenth century. 'What is the object of Political Reform', asked a Sheffield radical in 1793:

But by suitable regulations to guard more effectually against oppression, to produce more general comfort and happiness, to prevent future unnecessary burdens on the subject, and gradually, as well as rationally, and with due respect to safety as well as justice, to diminish those which already exist? To the industrious, oeconomical, regular and orderly mechanic, such a reform would be an essential benefit, as he could then by moderate but constant labour, enjoy more comfort, maintain his family better, and be able to provide a sufficiency for sickness and old age.[10]

Those post-war radicals who dissented from this emphasis did so largely because they embraced certain of the fundamental assumptions of classical political economy, which ascribed low wages principally to a surplus of labourers. This view Owenism of course disputed. But it did concur in seeing the labour market, rather than state expenditure, as the site of greatest economic importance. When Richard Carlile became one of the first important working class radicals (Thomas Hodgskin was not an active parliamentary reformer) virtually to convert to political economy in the late 1820s, he began to attack Cobbett's exclusive emphasis upon taxation, arguing that the supply and demand of labour played a greater role in the determination of wages. However, most radicals continued to focus primarily upon state expenditure, and considered its reduction as the first measure of any reformed parliament. Even the abuse of paper currency, particularly important to Cobbett, for example, was seen as resulting directly from a corrupt parliament, rather than as deriving from any natural economic laws.[11]

This concept of the sources of distress was Owenism's main target among radical doctrines. The taxation argument represented an essentially political model of economic activity which assumed that the market operated consistently and favourably when undue governmental interference did not occur. Radicalism did not address the issue of the validity of Say's Law concerning the natural balance of supply and demand. Political economy, in turn, paid little attention to the costs of government in its own account of distress (and also attacked working class radicals on this issue), concentrating instead upon the persistence of aristocratic land monopoly and absence of freedom of

[10] *MH*, no. 43 (19 January 1793), 3.
[11] *BD*, 5, no. 24 (13 December 1820), 846–8; *Lion*, 1, no. 1 (4 January 1828), 5–7; *CWPR*, 108 (6 May 1826), 329. For examples of the taxation analysis in the 1830s see *BH*, no. 8 (30 July 1836), 29, and *Demagogue*, no. 2 (5 July 1834), 12.

trade. Consistent with his own adoption of the standpoint of classical political economy on this question, Owen disavowed the taxation analysis as early as August 1817, at a meeting where many radicals were present. It did not help to endear him to them. Over the next thirty years, Owenism without doubt contributed significantly to decline in popularity of the taxation argument in radical circles. A large part of this debate revolved around the specific example of America, as we will see shortly. But even in relation to the laws of the market generally, the Owenites maintained that an alleviation of taxation would not produce the effects desired unless the co-operative system were first adopted. Hence Alexander Campbell, after Orbiston a trades' unionist, and soon to become an Owenite lecturer, informed a meeting of Glasgow operatives in 1831 that

> Regarding taxation, I endeavoured to show [in my last lecture] that, while you had no wealth of your own, no means of employing each other, but entirely depending for your subsistence on the demand for your labour from capitalists, – and while the productive power of machinery was brought in competition with your labour in the market, – that every attempt to reduce the taxes would have a tendency to lessen consumption, and throw more individuals into the already-overstocked labour market; the effect of which would be, to reduce your wages in proportion . . . but as soon as you can better your present circumstances, and become your own capitalist and employers, every reduction of taxes will be a benefit.

The most the Owenites thus ever conceded to decreased taxation under the existing economic system was that it might (in J. E. Smith's words) restore the working classes 'to the condition of their forefathers, without preventing the possibility of a recurrence of the evil'.[12] What made this most abundantly clear, and what more than anything else lent increasing support to the socialist critique of mere republicanism, was the economic development of the United States, that 'beacon of freedom' which had been so central to the confidence of the radical reformers after the shattering defeat of late eighteenth-century British colonial policy.

The American model

Their dogma was social, as opposed to political, reform – their argument, that political reform would not effect one important change in the condition of the people – their instance, America.[13]

---

[12] *Champion*, no. 242 (24 August 1817), 265–7; Alexander Campbell, *Address on the Progress of the Co-operative System* (Glasgow, 1831), p. 2; James Elishama Smith, *Lecture on a Christian Community* (1833), pp. 19–20. Similar sentiments are in the *Remarks on the Rational System of Society* (1832), p. 6, *MUK*, no. 1 (1 October 1830), 4, and, relative to the Corn Laws, *BCG*, no. 3 (1 June 1829), 9.

[13] *FM*, no. 7 (1 February 1850), 200, describing the Owenites' attitude towards politics generally.

No argument against parliamentary reform came to be as telling as the example of the United States, though it was almost three decades after the advent of Owenism before serious distress in America was widely acknowledged by British radicals. It has often been noted that America was a profound inspiration for British radicals, supplanting Sparta and to some extent even the ancient Anglo-Saxon constitution as an ideal to be emulated after the 1780s and (seemingly unaffected by the French revolution) remaining popular until well after 1850.[14] For English Jacobins like 'Citizen' Richard Lee, writing in the 1790s, the newly founded United States was 'a bright and immortal example to all colonies groaning under a foreign yoke, proving the invincible energy and virtue of freedom, and enjoying a state of prosperity, since she has thrown off her dependence on Great Britain, hitherto unknown in the nations of Europe.' To his fellow radical Joseph Gerrald, what was remarkable about this 'Eden of the new world' was that 'Above all, a baneful luxury, which engenders diseases, that not only embitter life, but poison the very source of it, is there unknown. They have no wants but such as nature gives, and which may be easily supplied by a moderate degree of labour. Life is simple, and therefore it is happy'. Invested in the new nation, then, were the aspirations of natural society, the ancient republics, and modern radicalism. Such a powerful symbol of virtue would indeed prove difficult to sully.[15]

This vision was consequently of enormous importance to the radical movement. As Cobbett once put it, 'while the *example of America remained*, there was no safety for what Castlereagh called the SOCIAL SYSTEM', the ancient aristocracy of Great Britain. Optimism about the success of the American experiment had not been tempered much by 1815. A Glasgow reformer reflected in 1819, for example, that the radicals held out the American 'government and people as the models of every perfection'. Some radicals did see American prosperity more

---

[14] On the Spartan in relation to the American ideal, see Elizabeth Rawson, *The Spartan Tradition in European Thought* (Oxford, Clarendon Press, 1969), p. 270. On the Anglo-Saxon model in this period see Colin Bonwick, *English Radicals and the American Revolution* (Chapel Hill, University of North Carolina Press, 1977), pp. 262–3. See also Harold Parker, *The Cult of Antiquity and the French Revolutionaries* (Chicago, University of Chicago Press, 1937). On the radicals' view of America generally see *CWPR*, 36 (29 July 1820), 69 and R. R. Palmer, 'The Fading Dream: How European Revolutionaries have seen the American Revolution', in: Stanley Palmer *et al.*, eds., *Essays on Modern European Revolutionary History* (Austin, University of Texas Press, 1977), pp. 89–104, and D. M. Clark, *British Opinion and the American Revolution* (New Haven, Yale University Press, 1930), pp. 152–80, Frank Thistlethwaite, *The Anglo-American Connection* (Philadelphia, University of Pennsylvania Press, 1959), pp. 39–75, D. P. Crook, *American Democracy in English Politics* (Oxford, Clarendon Press, 1965), especially pp. 69–93. Continuities between the American revolution and British Jacobinism are explored in Arthur Sheps, 'The Edinburgh Reform Convention of 1793 and the American Revolution', *ScT*, 5 (1975), 23–37.

[15] Richard Lee, *Rights of Man* (1795), p. 1; Joseph Gerrald, *A Convention the Only Means of Saving Us from Ruin* (3rd edn., 1794), pp. 23–4, 75–6.

in terms of specific economic conditions than as resulting from the
political system. The *Reformists' Register*, for example, argued that
wages were high in the USA because 'the quantity of marketable
labour is comparatively small'. Others were willing to acknowledge
that America did not enjoy universal opulence. The *Black Dwarf* admitted that there was some economic hardship in the USA, though it
insisted that the combination of full political rights and maturing
industry would ultimately furnish a comfortable existence for all. T. J.
Wooler even conceded that distress had 'pressed heavily upon the
Americans. Their trade has experienced a severe revulsion. Their
agricultural produce has wanted markets; and also the evils of a paper
system have been felt in the United States'. But most importantly,
Wooler also added that

No-one there thought of blaming the government, because every one knew the
government was blameless. It had neither *caused* the evils by unnecessary and
destructive wars, or by enormous taxation, nor had it *aggravated* them, by a
total neglect of economy; or by the insult of those who petitioned it for
redress.[16]

Such confidence still prevailed in some quarters in the 1840s, too.
Nonetheless, it was becoming increasingly rare. Radicals like the
young John Francis Bray were rudely shocked, in fact, when reality
and ideal collided. Bray began his *Labour's Wrongs and Labour's Remedy*
in 1833 with the intention of demonstrating the superiority of the
republican system. He realised the difficulties of this approach, however, when he recollected his own earlier visit to America and asked
himself the question, 'Did you ever see any beggars, or poor, or
unemployed people in Boston?' and answered, 'Yes, plenty of them!'.
This led him to rewrite the book completely, and to conclude that

the equality of rights which is thought to be enjoyed by the people of the
United States is so enjoyed only in imagination. There is the same inequality of
rights amongst them as amongst us; for they, like ourselves, are divided into
rich and poor – into capitalists and producers – and the last are there, as they
are here, at the mercy of the first . . . The citizens of the United States, it is true,
are exempted, by their republican form of government, from some of the
grievous burdens and restrictions which the monarchical form imposes upon
the people of the United Kingdom; but these are mere trifles in comparison
with that vast social burthen which the working class has sustained in all
countries for so many ages, – and even those advantages, trivial as they are,
will not always be enjoyed by the Americans. Their present exemption arises

[16] *RR*, no. 20 (7 June 1817), 623–4; *CWPR*, 37 (29 July 1820), 69; *Hints Addressed to the
Radical Reformers* (Glasgow, 1819), p. 26; *BD*, 2, no. 2 (14 January 1818), 22; *WBG*, 2, no.
17 (23 April 1820), 129. Sherwin held it to be a 'base fabrication' that provisions were
dear in America and work not available (*SPR*, 4, no. 1, 7 November 1818, 7–9). See also
WH, no. 8 (8 December 1819), 126–7.

from the peculiar circumstances by which they are surrounded, in respect to time and place, and has but little connection with the form of their government.[17]

If radical confidence in the connection between republicanism and economic prosperity had begun to wane during the intervening twenty years, this was not only because American social conditions had manifestly worsened, but also because Owenite criticisms thereby gained credibility. Piercing the illusion of universal American prosperity was likely to provoke popular disapprobation, however. The Owenite and Chartist William Lovett, for example, was greeted by hissing when he alluded to American ills at a Chartist meeting in 1838, and even Feargus O'Connor later found himself assailed for his 'harsh treatment' of America. For the federal, republican United States of America was the modern radical ideal institutionalised and incarnate. Any defamation of it therefore reflected badly upon the parliamentary reform movement generally.[18]

As in other schools of early socialism, and later for Marx and Engels, America became the apotheosis of untrammelled *laissez-faire* for the Owenites. Several elements in their use of America as a negative example merit special emphasis here. The first is simply that we know how jarring a blow against simple republicanism the discovery of American destitution was for a number of influential Owenite writers. To Bray and Thompson, for instance, it was perhaps the single most convincing argument for socialism. But it is also worth noting that Owenite reasoning was not levelled against the United States alone. It was also applied, for example, to the French revolution of 1830.[19] Nor was it designed to indicate that social conditions in a republic were *worse* than elsewhere. The point was that the wealthy (Owen added priests and lawyers) had come to govern in America *despite* universal suffrage and cheap government, not as the inevitable consequence of the political system.[20] The critical issue was thus freedom of commerce rather than popular political participation. G. A. Fleming hence declared that social evils would be comparable in a democratic, mixed or despotic government. The worst state was simply one 'where popular political economy has been most generally reduced to practice'.[21]

17 British Library of Political and Economic Science MS. R. (SR) 208 (Bray Papers), 7; John Francis Bray, *Labour's Wrongs and Labour's Remedy*, pp. 18–19.
18 *NS*, no. 59 (29 December 1838), 8; no. 594 (10 March 1849), 1.
19 *HTA*, no. 3 (9 October 1830), 41. On the image of America in other early socialist schools, see A. S. Tillett, 'Some Saint-Simonian Criticism of the United States before 1835', *RoR*, 52 (1961), 3–16. Marx's views are detailed in Robert Weiner, 'Karl Marx's Vision of America: A Biographical and Bibliographical Sketch', *RP*, 42 (1980), 465–503.
20 See Owen's comments in *LCM*, 3, no. 5 (July 1828), 127.
21 *Union*, no. 4 (July 1842), 97.

Probably the most important effect of the Owenite use of the American example was that it pinpointed the radicals' tendency to associate economic well-being with governmental institutions. Nor were the socialists alone in indicating this proclivity. It was also assailed by conservative critics of radicalism, a coincidence which did little to serve Owenite aims. Reflecting upon the 'rise and progress of popular disaffection' at the end of the eighteenth century, for example, Robert Southey (later a supporter of some forms of co-operation) noted in 1817 that 'men fell into the strange mistake of believing that the facilities of subsistence in America were owing to its form of government, and that the abolition of the privileged orders was all that was needful for placing us in the same condition with the inhabitants of the new country'. Another ex-Jacobin and Pantisocrat, Samuel Taylor Coleridge, also referred to 'that error ... of attributing to Governments a talismanic influence over our virtues and our happiness – as if Governments were not rather effects than causes'. In this case, it was a commonplace of late eighteenth- and early nineteenth-century political thought that Owenism sought to replace by the notion that economic systems were relatively autonomous with respect to forms of government, and depended instead upon the mode of distribution of labour.[22]

But the belief that republican governments promoted prosperity was extremely widespread amongst the working classes and parliamentary reformers, and its erosion marks a crucial turning point in the entire history of modern radicalism. At stake was the validity of some of the essential concepts of eighteenth-century republicanism, which had passed into early nineteenth-century radical political thought. The classical political debate about forms of government had also centrally concerned the relationship between commercial expansion and national virtue. Here the latter had been defined in terms of an inclination to participate for the public good, as the strength of the spirit of liberty in any particular nation, and as individual moral fortitude. Eighteenth-century British writers such as Hume had often reiterated that commercial freedom tended to promote political liberty. Where personal liberty and relative equality existed, it was also believed,

---

[22] *QR*, 16 (January 1817), 534; Leslie Chard, *Dissenting Republican* (The Hague, Mouton, 1972), p. 258. Similar sentiments were not infrequently voiced by the Tory radical factory reformers. See the Rev. George Stringer Bull's remarks quoted in J. C. Gill, *The Ten Hours Parson* (SPCK, 1954), pp. 140–1, and *HRI*, no. 11 (19 April 1834), 85, Oastler's comments as discussed in Cecil Driver, *Tory Radical*, pp. 295, 303, and J. R. Stephens' analysis in the *Champion*, no. 21 (30 September 1838), 6, and in *SMM* (January 1840), 14–15. Some more respectable radicals with their own schemes for reform also pointed to American distress by the late 1830s. See for example, Attwood's criticisms in C. M. Wakefield, *Life of Thomas Attwood* (1885), pp. 362–4.

freedom of commerce was more likely to arise. The form of a government and a nation's opulence were thus clearly assumed to be interdependent. Many examples seemed to support such a conclusion. Certainly Britain, Holland and other mixed governments had been widely envied during the seventeenth and eighteenth centuries, and here governmental form and commercial opulence seemed obviously linked. The success of the American revolution, in which, Paine had insisted, 'the representative system of government' had enabled the new nation 'to conquer' and 'enabled her also to recover', had merely reinforced this association.[23]

Owenism proposed a quite different conception of the relationship between polity and economy in contending that opulence or poverty resulted from the relatively independent operations of natural economic laws rather than the specific form of government. Most eighteenth-century radicals believed that republican institutions facilitated liberty of commerce, which in turn generated wealth. It might be inferred from this both that freedom of commerce *alone* could provide opulence, if non-democratic governments permitted its operations, and that democratic institutions were required to safeguard the progress of commerce in order to ensure a just distribution of its benefits, and an avoidance of encroaching monopoly. The first of these positions was broadly speaking that of the more unpolitical varieties of classical political economy. The latter was voiced by those radicals (who included many political economists, however) for whom corrupt monarchies and aristocratic governments restrained the natural distribution resulting from free commerce. In the 1820s and 1830s, Thomas Hodgskin popularised this argument most successfully, if also more extremely than most of its proponents. The novelty of the Owenite position was that it accepted the theory that economic laws functioned independently of forms of polity, that both governments and capitalists were 'blind instruments of the irresistible laws which direct the progress of society', while rejecting any faith in the natural tendency of these laws to supply wealth to most of those who laboured. For this reason, though the Owenites were insistent about the existence of objective social and economic laws operating outside of the consciousness of their participants, they had little interest in exploring their operations. Having established to their own satisfaction that freedom of trade engendered increasing monopoly and would eventuate in economic catastrophe through overproduction, underconsumption, and the separation of society into a small wealthy class and a mass of labouring poor, the socialists saw little sense in plotting the

[23] Thomas Paine, *Complete Writings*, 2, p. 449.

exact course by which this would occur.[24] Instead, Owenism pressed home its attack upon what might be termed the 'fallacy of economic consequences' doggedly held by most political radicals. Just as in the Chartist years, when some of the economic results which it was avowed would follow the passage of the Charter were well-nigh miraculous, many earlier radicals failed to distinguish sufficiently between direct consequences of parliamentary reform in the alleviation of taxation alone, and those which necessitated far more advanced economic strategies and programmes. This left them open to a variety of attacks from the socialist camp.[25]

It could be objected, however, that no moderately educated parliamentary reformer expected the diminution of taxation *alone* to ensure economic recovery, despite some of the comments cited earlier on taxation. Radical reform also implied a popular government jealously mindful of the interests of the majority, such that the suitable extension of further economic regulation and/or freedom for the common good could simply be assumed to be part of any reform programme. Yet it is precisely this act of presumption which was a weak link in radical and republican arguments. Such measures were very often left tacit until well into the 1840s, and it was this lack of a sophisticated economic programme, and conception of the relationship between political and economic reform, to which Owenite arguments were often directed.

The American model thus bore much of the brunt of the Owenite offensive upon the ostensible economic naiveté of the political reformers. But the socialists themselves were not entirely consistent in their use of America as a negative example, and failed to draw deterministic conclusions from their own arguments against the inability of legislation to cure economic evils when this did not suit them. As we have seen, federalist notions derived from the American system of government were of some importance to Owen's own political thought. Other early Owenites such as Alexander Campbell also considered the North American form of government to be the best model for communities. Moreover, particularly when he was in America, Owen granted that America had certain advantages, relative to the potential progress of his system, which did not derive solely from its natural setting. In 1825, for example, he informed the Americans that

In your industry, mechanical knowledge, and general enterprize, in the quality and cheapness of your soil, in the extent and variety of your climate, in your

---

[24] *NMW*, 1, no. 5 (29 November 1834), 36.
[25] See for example the extensive list of benefits which Carlile claimed parliamentary reform ('or properly speaking, a Revolution in the affairs of Great Britain and Ireland') would bring, in the *Republican*, 1, no. 5 (24 September 1819), 79–80.

liberation, in particular, from the prejudices of the old world, *but more particularly in the freedom of your government*, you amply possess the means to secure immediately the most important private and national benefits to yourselves and to your prosperity.[26]

Owenite arguments cannot be interpreted as embracing a crude economic determinism for another reason. For even if parliamentary reform were held to be a lesser goal than direct economic reconstruction, the socialists, too, often appealed for legislative interference on behalf of their own plans and measures such as factory reform.[27] This was a contradiction which some radicals would later hurl back. No matter how often Owen and others insisted that economic distress was unconnected with the particular persons who governed, that the evil lay 'deeper, much deeper' than this, it was increasingly conceded that the socialist system, too, required national resources in order to commence. But a total surrender of this point by the Owenites was only evident after 1845. Although American social distress seemed to subvert a republican argument, thus, it was only when the Owenites could convincingly claim that they had no need of government whatsoever (e.g., to some extent during the GNCTU and labour exchange bazaar periods during the 1830s) that they could wholly escape a trap of their own devising. Nonetheless, by the mid-1840s an increasing number of radicals had begun reluctantly to confront the political and economic implications of American economic distress.[28]

However, a few Owenites also held doggedly to the notion that greater democracy was bound to have beneficial economic consequences. Particularly in the case of the young William Thompson, efforts were made to reconceptualise this relationship. Thompson was especially concerned to introduce a political component into an Owenite account of the process of wealth abstraction. This in turn, he believed, would help to make Owenite economic thought more acceptable to radical reformers. In the most common Owenite account of exchange, injustice occurred when equal amounts of labour were not exchanged. For Thompson, however, it was not only or even primarily the equality of the exchanges which was at issue in ascertaining fairness, but their *voluntary* character. This conception of 'voluntary exchange' derived both from Godwin's emphasis upon voluntariness of activity as the perfection of society, and Bentham's notion of the value

[26] *LCM*, 1, no. 11 (November 1826), 348; *NWR*, 29, no. 732 (12 November 1825), 175, emphasis added. For similar comments by Owen see the *Communitist*, no. 18 (12 February 1845), 69; Owen, *Manifesto of Robert Owen* (Washington, DC, 1844), p. 5, *ROWL*, letter 10 (1850), 90. Robert Dale Owen also implied that his father's principles could be applied most successfully in a republic (*Crisis*, 1, no. 36, 16 November 1832, 144).   [27] *MT*, no. 2 (7 November 1817), 38.
[28] For example, *NS*, no. 337 (27 April 1844), 4; no. 338 (4 May 1844), 1.

of the security of each labourer's possessing his or her produce. Exchanges therefore ought to be founded upon reason or persuasion, which taught sympathy and a mutual interest in joint endeavours. Otherwise exchange was merely brute force and robbery.[29]

'Forced exchange' therefore described a transfer imposed by 'the stronger party' when one party denied that an equivalent had been given. Such exchanges could be perpetrated by the capitalist, middleman, landlord, slaveholder, even hypothetically the labourer who, lacking sufficient competition, could dictate terms to his or her master. But Thompson's explanation of this concept clearly included a political dimension. 'Forced abstractions' had as their antithesis those natural laws of distribution which required 'no factitious aid, which demand the removal or non-imposition of restraint'. These, Thompson believed, were most clearly exemplified in the United States of America. For while it wrongly oppressed slaves and women, America embodied one sound principle, 'no representation, no taxation'. Consequently all exchanges were voluntary there, and involved no element of force, though within a few years Thompson would retract this argument.[30]

'Forced exchange' thus represented the taxation, monopolies and restraints established by an unrepresentative government. This definition comprised what the radicals termed 'class legislation', which was assumed to affect market relations. 'Forced wages', for example, were defined as 'regulated at the caprice of those whose interests are opposed to that of the labourer'. This conception ultimately rested upon an assumption of the economic results of various forms of government, and the theory of voluntary exchange was thus at bottom a sophisticated critique of non-representative government. 'So intimately connected and dependent upon each other are these two great blessings, equal security and representative or self-government', Thompson went on to claim, 'that the establishment of the one necessarily includes that of the other'. Representative government would therefore have to be implemented everywhere. Unjust exchanges could take place either by 'direct operation of law, or by indirect operation of unwise social arrangements', but these were deeply and intimately connected. In accordance with his radical background, Thompson consequently pursued an overtly political explanation of social distress, though by 1827 he withdrew somewhat from this conclusion in proposing that co-operation could proceed without political reform. But even then, he still insisted that 'until political institutions shall be supported without standing armies, without force of any sort;

29 Godwin, *Enquiry Concerning Political Justice*, p. 127; Thompson, *Inquiry*, pp. 49–51. See *Machinery, Money and the Millennium*, pp. 94–8.
30 Thompson, *Inquiry*, pp. 52, 3, 44, 99, 101.

until all taxes are voluntarily paid, 'tis idle to talk of free competition, of the freedom of labor'.[31]

Such comments, in fact, enabled Thompson to lead the first group of Owenites who sought to combine political radicalism and co-operative economy. For, to these socialists, like Thompson, Owen's plan cardinally signified economic justice rather than the supersession of the political institutions of the old immoral world.

Intervention and administration

The political economist has superseded the soldier in the government of society. He is the great reservoir of mundane wisdom. The Philosopher is merely a parasite of the statesman. The Divine is merely his chaplain and his toad-eater. The General is merely his subordinate officer or lieutenant.[32]

An acceptance of the market-centred analytic emphasis of classical political economy was paramount to the Owenite refutation of the government-centred arguments of the radicals, and in particular to the view that parliamentary reform would substantially mitigate economic distress. Nonetheless the regulatory assumptions of socialist political economy implied that new forms of public or political institutions would have to be created in order to ensure economic justice and fair distribution. Having largely rejected the idea of a system of natural liberty, or the validity of Say's Law, the Owenites in effect massively repoliticised economic relations by substituting conscious public choice for market allocation. The implications of this shift for the evolution of political thought were momentous. Every other contemporary form of radicalism retained considerable faith in the beneficial effects of a commerce freed from monopoly and excessive taxation. Some Owenites, and particularly William Thompson in his early writings, did vacillate on this question. Given the compelling simplicity of free trade arguments, and their widespread popularity, this was not surprising. But one of Owenism's general distinguishing characteristics was its rejection of such views. In fact, most socialists understood *laissez-faire* to mean only 'that the strong should oppress the weak, or that the merchants, the brokers, the shipping interest, and all the other interested parties . . . should still be permitted to do so to any extent they please'.[33]

Instead of the anarchy of free commerce, Owenites such as George Mudie began as early as 1821 to call for the management of the national economy 'upon a well-devised plan or system of arrangements', as

---

[31] *Ibid.*, pp. 109, 267, 488; Thompson, *Labor Rewarded*, pp. 12, 40–2.
[32] *Union*, no. 7 (1 October 1842), 300–1.   [33] *Crisis*, 3, no. 24 (8 February 1834), 197.

current manufacturing institutions seemed to be organised.[34] But Owenism's overriding concern with the establishment of communities, and its eventual intention of superseding the existing system of government by a nation of such communities, generally prevented (at least up to 1848) any serious wedding of the planning principle with a new conception of national administration within mainstream British socialism. From Owen's earliest calls for factory reform onward, the Owenites instead always demanded piecemeal intervention to reduce hours of labour, introduce workers' education, alter factory conditions, and ensure greater poor relief.[35] We have seen, however, that it was only after repeated failures that Owen finally became convinced that *only* the state could commence the new moral world, by buying land and building communities. Even if, in its labour exchange phase, various socialist plans for a national bank and bazaars were published, no conception of centralised state planning really took hold between 1820 and 1845.[36] Mainstream Owenism was, in fact, incapable of theorising a state whose economic role was to be consistently and widely interventionist. This would have involved seeing socialism primarily in national terms, and being able to conceptualise a new administrative apparatus operating within what would be, in effect, a far more highly politicised state. Most socialists were simply not prepared to take the implications of interventionist thinking this far. Their biases were overwhelmingly federalist and communitarian so long as Owen himself dominated the movement. But William Thompson's emphases in this regard would not have been much different either. Moreover, to have discussed the state in such terms would also have required conceding some ground to those radicals who argued that a reformed state could alleviate the economic conditions of the working classes.

The foremost exception to this tendency nonetheless still provided an important undercurrent in Owenite thought, and was to become quite important by the late 1840s. This was the scheme for centralised economic management first outlined in John Gray's *The Social System* (1831), and subsequently refined in John Francis Bray's *Labour's Wrongs and Labour's Remedy* (1839).[37] In the *Social System*, all necessary production (a sphere of free enterprise for the production of luxuries was also to be permitted) was to be managed by an elected 'National Chamber

---

[34] *Economist*, 1, no. 6 (3 March 1821), 88–9.

[35] Sherwin commented on Owen in 1817 that 'His idea of government appears to me to be this: that it is a *something* whose duty it is to watch over the happiness and morality of a Nation', and added that 'This . . . is beginning at the wrong end . . . It is not in the power of any Government to *make a People happy*; – all that it can do, is *to avoid everything which can make them otherwise*' (*SPR*, 1, no. 8, 24 May 1817, 128).

[36] See for example *NMW*, 1, no. 9 (27 December 1834), 72, no. 10 (3 January 1835), 78–9.

[37] See *Machinery, Money and the Millennium*, pp. 117–25, 146–7.

of Commerce' consisting of a president and a certain number of representatives. These officers, who were to 'be invested with supreme power, during the time they may be in office', were not however identical to state officials. Indeed, they were to 'abstain from all political and religious discussions', and to 'treat, with equal justice, men of every political opinion, and of every religious creed'. Thus they were 'to submit themselves, in all things, without complaints, to the established authorities of the country', who, however, required the Chamber's consent to alter fundamental commercial laws. Gray took great pains to point out that his commercial system was compatible 'with all forms of political government having the least resemblance to fairness or freedom'. But since the system was designed to abolish the vast majority of unproductive labourers, including many government officials, it seems unlikely that he assumed that the present government would adopt his plan. Nonetheless Gray's '*thoroughly organised plan* of producing, exchanging, and distributing the wealth of the country' (which he later denied was influenced by Saint-Simon) was in fact the first British socialist attempt to outline a dual system of national political and economic administration. This involved conceptualising a balance of power between the two types of government, and a weakening of the political branch, which would be forced to seek the agreement of the Chamber of Commerce on important policy questions, while the Chamber would manage most aspects of the economy. 'Administration' by no means completely superseded political 'government' here. But the recognition of a separate sphere of competence and activity was an important step in the direction of a new form of governmental economic activity.[38]

In Bray's *Labour's Wrongs* the role of politics in social transformation was much more in evidence, since Bray was both a Chartist and Owenite. Far more than Gray, to whom he was otherwise heavily indebted, Bray thus conceived of the political and economic administrations of the future as united. The owner of the land and the means of production was to be the nation, guided by the working classes. Following the example of the GNCTU, whose plans had inspired Bray, economic management would take place through a hierarchy of local and general branches of trade. Members of these organisations would be elected by local communities, with produce being distributed through large markets or bazaars. For Bray this system was not, however, compatible with a monarchy, or for that matter with any government in which the non-producers, including capitalists, pre-

---

[38] John Gray, *The Social System: A Treatise on the Principle of Exchange* (Edinburgh, 1831), pp. 31–2, 37, 95, 341; Gray, *An Efficient Remedy for the Distress of Nations* (Edinburgh, 1842), p. 176.

dominated. But he nonetheless warned the radicals that no political reform 'engrafted upon the present social system' would be successful. His dislike of violence was also great, and his preferred mode of change was therefore typically Owenite. Even a penny a week from each member of the working classes could set the new social system in motion, though Bray confessed that only if the working classes had themselves alone to maintain could they buy all of the fixed capital in the kingdom within seventeen years.[39]

If universal suffrage did install a new regime, however, it would not for Bray resemble past forms of government. Here the ostensibly higher moral purpose and politically untainted character of both radicalism and Owenism was crucial to Bray's assumption of less conflict and political disagreement in the future. The existing social movement had no 'evanescent and exclusive character . . . no leaders, and no class and caste interests to subserve', and could not be 'established by a particular party today, and subverted by another party tomorrow'. In his optimism about moral and political unity Bray was thus a great deal more Owenite than Gray (in the *Social System*), and accordingly felt that politics would be superseded by administration for the common good to a larger degree. Yet he also stressed the democratic nature of this administration more clearly than Gray, emphasising, for example, the election of regulatory boards, rather than leaving this process to 'an equitable principle'. But if the latter phrase did mean universal suffrage for Gray, it is easy to see why he felt the election of such a democratic economic administration was compatible with nearly any form of government, since the latter would be virtually powerless in many areas of domestic policy once the new social system was established.[40]

If some Owenite opposition to *laissez-faire* implied a general, if vaguely conceived, system of collective management, other socialists alluded to more specific economic tasks to be undertaken democratically in the future. Such discussions were uncommon, however, because the implementation of basic doctrines seemed fairly simple. If all produce were divided in community, or all work rewarded according to labour-time (perhaps in relation to production costs), little possibility of dispute could arise. If differential rewards were to be admitted, however, or some choice between future production and more free

---

[39] John Francis Bray, *Labour's Wrongs and Labour's Remedy*, pp. 82, 127, 180, 74–5, 69, 171. The best study of Bray remains H. J. Carr, 'A Critical Exposition of the Social and Economic Ideas of John Francis Bray; and an Estimate of his Influence upon Karl Marx', Ph.D., University of London (1943), especially pp. 93–170, from which one article was published ('John Francis Bray', *Economica*, 7, 1940, 397–415). Also useful is M. F. Jolliffe, 'John Francis Bray', *IRSH*, 4 (1939), 1–36.

[40] Bray, *Labour's Wrongs*, p. 191.

time became necessary, or if the standard of value itself were not fixed, some means of assessing these would have to be provided. The central question was precisely what kinds of problems were to be left to public decision-making. Most socialists agreed that the division of labour was of primary importance in this regard. John Gray's early plans, for example, argued that it was a matter of 'social' determination how many workers should be admitted to any occupation. Even amongst 'productive labourers', some were uselessly employed, while others in some unproductive but necessary tasks (such as distribution) could be more usefully employed.[41] In itself the allocation of labour power was clearly an exceedingly complex problem. If no fixed standard of value by which the reward of labour could be estimated was agreed upon, decisions of this type would correspondingly be more numerous.

But many Owenites were loath to venture too far into this matter. The popular Manchester socialist lecturer John Watts, for example, insisted that labour was 'the source of all wealth'. But he offered no assistance as to how this would help in determining future wages or production. It was easy to advise that the 'greatest happiness of the greatest number' ought to prevail. But this was hardly a precise principle of administrative direction. It did imply that children and those legitimately unable to labour should be supported, thought Watts, while the interests of the whole required the production of 'the greatest amount of necessities and desirable wealth'. Rule by the principle of utility, however, meant primarily that 'the interests of the mass must be consulted, and prosperity will follow'. Ignoring a range of complex issues raised by previous socialist writers, Watts here simply reinforced the confident but naive assumptions of the political radicals.[42]

In Owenite political economy the substitution of human control for market determination thus implied the creation of a new sphere of public decision-making. With a few exceptions, however, the specific character of this sphere was nowhere carefully delineated. The lack of a sophisticated theory of government, a simplistic faith (not of course shared by Owen himself) in the ability of democratic participation to resolve all important conflicts, popular prejudices in favour of non-interference and free trade, and a bias against centralisation, all contributed to this lacuna in Owenite theory. It is evident that those socialists who sought the further extension of industry and production of a widening range of goods also tended to accept more traditional conceptions of democracy, rather than seeking the perfectionist supersession of all social conflict. Despite the coalescence of 'economic socialism' and 'political socialism', however, no clear model of the

---

41 Gray, *A Lecture*, pp. 51, 58.
42 John Watts, *The Facts and Fictions of Political Economists* (Manchester, 1842), pp. 5, 16, 28.

administration of the economics of control ever emerged. Given the connections between certain radical 'mercantilists' (notably John Bellers) and Owenism, and the well-known regulatory aims of seventeenth- and early eighteenth-century political economy, it is surprising that more discussions of such precedents are not encountered in socialist works. But there are virtually none at all. Earlier legislation, particularly on the Poor Laws, was regarded as evidence of the wisdom of a previous 'paternal' approach. But speculation about the form of government which such legislation had required or created did not take place. Aggressive monarchies, such as that of Elizabeth I, under whom the old Poor Law was established, held little attraction to socialists. Some of the bureaucratic apparatus suggested by the eighteenth-century French economists might well have been useful to the Owenites. But the politics associated with such states were also wholly unappealing.[43] More likely, as we will now see, it was an extension of a democratic, republican form of government which many socialists imagined when they considered how production was to be managed in the future. For from the early 1820s onwards, Owen's communitarian ideas and co-operative economic doctrines were also taken up by working class radicals who agreed that his ideas pointed to many inadequacies in radicalism, but who saw no reason to sacrifice more traditional forms of democracy in the pursuit of economic justice and social equality. For these socialists, to the contrary, Owenism came to represent a new principle of democracy whereby popular participation was to be extended beyond the sphere of parliamentary politics, and into economic and social organisations never previously considered as potentially subject to democratic management.

[43] See generally Philip W. Buck, *The Politics of Mercantilism* (New York, Henry Holt, 1942), especially pp. 133–43. Buck simply terms totalitarianism 'neo-mercantilism', as if the economics of control automatically implied political repression, a simplistic trend of thought lamentably still argued at present. There are also useful comments in Gunnar Myrdal, *The Political Element in the Development of Economic Theory* (Routledge and Kegan Paul, 1953).

PART III

The origins of social radicalism

5

Owenism and the emergence of social radicalism, 1820–35

Given Owen's predominance over the early socialist movement and the relative orthodoxy of many of his chief lieutenants, it is not always easy to surmise how much disagreement existed among socialists on a range of important issues, such as religion, marriage and private property. Nonetheless Owenism obviously embraced a much wider spectrum of beliefs than those Owen himself was pleased to term 'rational'. When, in the midst of the considerable clamour Owen had caused in the late summer of 1817, 'a Plebeian' informed W. T. Sherwin that 'very few have ventured to claim the title of "*Owenite*"', religious controversy was assumed to be responsible for such reluctance. Twenty years later, others would decline the title of 'socialist' because it was by now also widely identified with Owen's ostensibly licentious views on marriage. Nonetheless, Owen's opinions on these and other questions were also contested by many who otherwise remained loyal to the general trend of his thinking. This process continued even after the Rational Society, which officially adopted the name 'Socialist' in 1841, succeeded in enforcing a degree of orthodoxy upon its members.[1]

Political thought and practice proved to be one of the areas which excited the greatest controversy within Owenism. A socialist heterodoxy in politics began to emerge in the mid-1820s around a variety of issues. Particularly contentious was the choice as to whether radical parliamentary reform should precede community-building or be understood as the chief means of attaining other socialist economic measures, or whether parliamentary reform itself should be regarded as insignificant compared to the need to supersede more traditional

---

[1] SPR, 1, no. 25 (20 September 1817), 355–7. On attempts to distinguish socialism from Owenism, see for example, SE, 1, no. 110 (20 October 1838), 42; NMW, 8, no. 22 (28 November 1840), 349, 9, no. 14 (3 April 1841), 210; NS, no. 48 (13 October 1838), 8, no. 51 (3 November 1838), 6; no. 54 (24 November 1838), 3; Robert Buchanan, *An Exposure of the Falsehoods of a Pamphlet Entitled 'The Abominations of Socialism Exposed'* (Manchester, 1840), p. 6; *Reasoner*, 24 (1859), 201; Mary Hennell, *An Outline of the Various Social Systems* (1844), p. 170; TS, 1, no. 56 (9 November 1839), 4; *Report of the Discussion between Messrs. Lloyd Jones and C. Leckie* (Glasgow, 1839), p. 39.

forms of democratic organisation. In fact, Owen's insistence upon the futility of parliamentary reform was repudiated by many of his working class followers by the late 1820s. A select group of these attempted in a successive number of organisations to unite radical objectives with an Owenite programme of co-operation and community-building. The specifically Owenite contribution to the radicalism of these years, however, has never been detailed and categorised adequately. A demonstration of its character entails re-examining the debates and programmes of the first important working class Owenite organisation, the British Association for the Promotion of Co-operative Knowledge (BAPCK, 1829–34), the more radical National Union of the Working Classes (NUWC, 1831–34), and the social radicalism of the leading working class journalist James Bronterre O'Brien, as well as the relation of Owen's political and organisational views to the development of the GNCTU, and to the trades' union democracy of James Morrison and James Elishama Smith. From the mid-1820s through the mid-1830s, we will see, many of those who accepted Owen's co-operative and communitarian goals set out to wed these to a programme for radical parliamentary reform, creating in the process a new, major strand within the reform movement which will here be termed 'social radicalism'. In addition, Owen's influence on a number of trades' union leaders inspired a new, quasi-syndicalist conception of trades' union co-operation as well as a series of important debates about the proper scope of working class participation and consequently the correct definition of democracy itself.

The 'unpolitical' years, 1820–29

Initial suspicion about Owen's communitarian ideas by radicals did not quickly abate after 1817, and it was not until the emergence of the extra-communitarian co-operative movement after 1825 that the more radical conception of Owenism began to be popularised more widely. The search for a primarily working class audience was certainly not among Owen's leading aims at this point. Until 1827–28, he was mainly interested in the success of his first colony at New Harmony, for which he sought only wealthy supporters. Owen certainly already intended to secure the salvation of the working classes, but at this time, as he later admitted, this involved virtually no contact with them.[2]

In these years, most of Owen's followers also evaded discussions of some of the political implications of his plans. With the Six Acts, Peterloo and the Spencean scare still fresh in the public mind, this was

[2] Owen, *Life*, p. 60.

clearly prudent. Until the mid-1820s, Owen's ideas were all too readily linked in the public mind with Spence's, and Owen would later relate an apocryphal story about discussing his opinions with a stranger on a coach journey, after which his fellow passenger replied that he must be either Spence or Owen. A number of radical papers also connected the two, and found it curious that Owen continued to seek aristocratic support from a class which increasingly felt that such an identification was not altogether misplaced. It was not the most auspicious time to add a political dimension to a movement for moral, social and economic regeneration.[3]

Nonetheless the early Owenites were hardly devoid of political opinions, though these initial discussions are difficult to recreate. George Mudie's Co-operative and Economical Society at Spa Fields, London, resolved for instance to abstain from all such debates, and very few occurred in Mudie's *Economist* (1821–22). The second major source for this period, the *London Co-operative Magazine* (1826–30) similarly declined to engage in political or theological speculations. Individual Owenites were also quite circumspect. Owen's friend, the India House administrator and socialist Benjamin Scott Jones, for example, wrote nothing political for the *Economist*, but informed the Unitarian *Monthly Repository* that all members of communities would elect their own officers. By comparison with the controversies of the Chartist years, political inquiry and debate in the early period appear to be virtually non-existent.[4]

Despite the more utopian aspects of some early communities, the vast majority of Owen's early working and middle class followers nonetheless probably regarded communitarian practice as an extension of the principles of democratic and particularly local self-government. Owen had written that the communities would eventually be self-governing. This goal was repeated in the 'Articles of Agreement' which bound Mudie's Spa Fields group, (and was republished by the *London Co-operative Magazine* as a model for others), as well as in plans for and discussions about the Orbiston community.[5] A number of the early Owenites also had backgrounds of radical reform activity dating from the 1790s and even earlier. Jones, for example, emphasised his 'love of true liberty and . . . readiness to withstand arbitrary and despotic rule, in whatsoever shape they may appear', and invoked

---

[3] See T. J. Wooler's comments on the change in Lauderdale's view of Owen in *BD*, 12, no. 15 (1 June 1824), 446–8.

[4] *Economist*, 2, no. 39 (20 November 1821), 208; *LCM*, 1, no. 1 (January 1826), 10; *MoR*, 18 (1823), 452.

[5] *Articles of Agreement for the Formation of a Community on Principles of Mutual Co-operation* (1825), pp. 4–5; *RO*, 1, no. 1 (10 November 1825), 1. For similar views at a slightly later period, see the *Associate*, no. 9 (January 1830), 51 and no. 10 (February 1830), 54.

Cartwright and Burke from the days of his youthful involvement with parliamentary reform.[6] One of the main founders of Orbiston, A. J. Hamilton, also had radical sympathies.[7]

The best-known of the early socialists to have entertained such sentiments, as well as the most active in continuing to propound them, was William Thompson, who may rightfully be considered the founder of a more traditionally republican form of British democratic socialism. Thompson, too, as we have seen, invested much hope in the moderating tendency of public opinion in communities, and the capacity of shame to permit laws virtually to 'execute themselves'. But he also wasted few opportunities to emphasise the benefits of popular political participation and the pressing necessity for representative self-government.[8] Between 1824 and his early death in 1831, Thompson wrote and lectured extensively in favour of a decentralised and more participatory form of socialism. His *Inquiry into the Principles of the Distribution of Wealth* (1824) united a plea for self-government with an argument for increasing returns of wealth. Democracy would provide security to the producer, thus augmenting production through increasing confidence that the produce of labour would not be forcibly and unjustly abstracted by nonproducers.[9]

Thompson's supreme confidence in republican institutions did not survive the 1820s, however. *Labor Rewarded* (1825) still praised representative government, but certain doubts now crept into the argument. 'Free competition' and 'the freedom of labour' were still held to be contingent upon 'equal political institutions', meaning, ideally, a single house of representatives, the abolition of all privileged classes and standing armies, and the voluntary payment of taxes. But by now Thompson's political concerns had begun to shift in other directions. Centralisation of government was now particularly strongly criticised, and a brief plan was appended to correct the American constitution, which Thompson now felt had failed to prevent the domination over the nation as a whole of 'the caprices of a few hundred persons' inhabiting the capital. Thompson conceded, however, that 'federalization' was also liable to certain evils, such as the retention of slavery in the southern states. The problems of both extreme forms of government were to be corrected by reorganising society around parishes or

[6] *Economist*, 2, no. 33 (8 September 1821), 109; no. 42 (10 November 1821), 261–2.
[7] See the Hamilton Papers, Motherwell Public Library, vol. 1, fol. 8 and vol. 16, fol. 159. The latter contains a petition by Hamilton to the MP for Lanark concerning the restoration of triennial parliaments. See also Hamilton's *Prospectus of a Plan for Establishing an Institution on Mr. Owen's System* (1822).
[8] Thompson, *Inquiry*, pp. 231, 234, 226. On Thompson's politics generally, see Richard Pankhurst, *William Thompson*, pp. 102–17.
[9] Thompson, *Inquiry*, pp. xiii–xiv, 44, 212–13, 267.

communes, which by universal male and female adult suffrage would elect representatives for one year terms to county, state and national legislatures. Measures passed by the national assembly would then be ratified not only by three-quarters of their own members, but by the state assemblies as well, with no executive officer being granted veto powers over such legislation. Furthermore, any commune, province or state which objected to legislation by other units (concerning slavery, for example) would have the right to complain to the national assembly, which could suspend such legislation if it agreed that the interests of others besides those who passed it were affected. A single civil and criminal code would also be introduced throughout the union. Communes would not be allowed to enforce their own internal regulations by any punishment except expulsion, while the death penalty and any infliction of pain as a form of punishment were to be banned. These measures, Thompson felt, would thus remove the dual evils of both 'local barbarism' and excessive centralisation.[10]

Together with Anna Wheeler, Thompson published in 1825 a well-reasoned plea for female suffrage and women's equality. This denied that even the granting of equal civil and political rights to women would give them a genuine equality of happiness in the existing system, since under competition a premium was given to strength, while no compensation was allowed for women's special burden of nurturing children. If a co-operative system was not quickly achieved, however, it was conceded that equal political rights for women would at least afford them the maximum capacity for happiness which the present system permitted. To this end, Thompson and Wheeler focussed in particular upon the arguments against women's suffrage in James Mill's 'Essay on Government' (and their view helped sway the young John Mill against his father). Denying that the interests of women were ever necessarily identical with those of their husbands or fathers, Thompson and Wheeler lambasted the fictitious 'family interest' implied by such a view. Condemning the vows of dependency and slavery forced upon married women, they demonstrated that the despotic effects of the institution of marriage degraded the husband while also retarding progress generally. Society was also weakened because women, whose mental capacities were as great as men's, were unable to contribute to the political and legislative process. No system of suffrage which did not include women, then, could possibly be just. This charge the Owenites would often later level at the Chartists, who usually restricted their demands to universal male suffrage.[11]

10 Thompson, *Labor Rewarded*, pp. 15, 42–3, 121–4.
11 Thompson, *An Appeal of One-Half the Human Race* (1825).

In the next six years these and other aspects of Thompson's democratic creed were extremely influential in the rapidly-expanding co-operative movement. In his last work, published in 1830, Thompson again reiterated the desirability of obtaining assent to any communal arrangements, extending this even to 'children capable of forming an opinion'. External governments, he also stressed, should play only the minimal role of granting loans in the formation of communities, while the latter were warned to take every precaution to avoid the predominance of a few individuals. Thompson did, however, agree with Owen that the initial government of the communities should be by those who had subscribed the capital, or their representatives. But to balance this control he also recommended that labourers in each economic department choose their own leaders 'with the assent of the general director if thought necessary'.[12]

Though Thompson did not actively promote immediate parliamentary reform as a means of obtaining co-operative communities, he doubtless encouraged efforts in this direction. G. D. H. Cole exaggerated somewhat in writing that Thompson never invoked the assistance of government, but saw it as upholding monopoly, and thus was 'the principal contributor of the new, working class version of Owenism'. Thompson did consider the possibility of government loans, and at this time Owen himself actually asked no more. Both Owen and most Owenites saw existing governments as creatures of class privilege which would eventually, but gradually, have to be abolished. Nonetheless Thompson's popularity among working class co-operators is undoubted, and it was a great symbol of the trust they placed in him, that when in 1831 it was decided that one man should govern the initial community, he was their choice.[13] To understand the context of this decision, however, we must consider the character of the existing co-operative movement, which by now to some extent already consciously sought to fuse Owenite goals with radical means.

Socialism politicised, 1829–35

Both the British Association for the Promotion of Co-operative Knowledge (founded in May 1829) and the organisation which partially succeeded it, the National Union of the Working Classes (founded in 1831 and abandoned in 1835) have earned an honourable mention in virtually all histories of Chartism, early British socialism and the early labour movement. Many members of these associations –

[12] *LCM*, 1, no. 1 (January 1826), 23; Thompson, *Practical Directions for the Establishment of Communities* (1830), pp. iv, 9, 12, 226.
[13] Cole, *History of Socialist Thought*, 1, p. 117; *CPL*, 6 May 1831, 16.

men such as Hetherington, Cleave, Lovett and Watson – had been co-operators since the mid-1820s, and went on to become Chartist organisers and leaders. In this milieu, the most intellectually active of the major Chartist leaders, Bronterre O'Brien, first emerged, quickly began the process of adapting Owenite to radical goals, and soon became one of the principal teachers of many of those around him. To historians of socialism, in particular, the significance of these organisations has long been recognised as lying in their 'fusion' (in the words of J. F. C. Harrison) or 'link' (in W. H. Oliver's term) of the co-operative and radical movements.[14]

Rather than repeating a general institutional and social history whose outlines are well known, we will concentrate here upon the character of the analysis espoused by the members of these organisations, which has been the subject of considerable contention. This is the only way of ascertaining adequately how far Owenite ideas contributed to the novel mixture of doctrines usually associated with this union and what this implied. What is controversial about these organisations in this period, it is usually assumed, is the degree to which they established for the first time the rudiments of a radical, political socialism which is a recognisable antecedent both to Marxism and later nineteenth-century British socialism. Nonetheless it is clear that especially in relation to theories of property and competition, an older, more teleological approach to this question is no longer tenable. Co-operation did not simply evolve from an unpolitical to a radical standpoint which was analytically more mature and sophisticated. A process of evolution did take place, but it entailed a variety of disjunctures, the recourse to earlier positions, and the co-existence without resolution of contradictory social analyses. It is argued here, in particular, that the co-operative embrace of radicalism involved the renewed use of older radical arguments (for example, that the main cause of distress was taxation) which, if they were juxtaposed with relative ease in this context, had been avoided in the economic analyses of an earlier and less political variety of Owenism. Moreover, while a relatively coherent union of political means and socialist ends was often articulated by BAPCK members, the NUWC, composed as it was far more of radicals than socialists, watered down this programme considerably. Thus it was on the whole – at least in its official pronouncements, and perhaps partly for tactical reasons – quite orthodox in its views of property. No

---

[14] Harrison, *Robert Owen*, p. 215 (in reference to the NUWC and the *Poor Man's Guardian*); Oliver, 'Organisations and Ideas Behind the Efforts to Achieve a General Union of the Working Classes in England in the Early 1830s', D.Phil., University of Oxford (1954), p. ii (in reference to the BAPCK). The latter work, unfortunately never published, contains the most extensive previous account of these organisations. See especially pp. 39–80.

increasingly sophisticated political socialism grew continuously through these organisations, therefore, though this has often been contended.

When the BAPCK was founded by members of the London Co-operative and Union Exchange Societies in 1829, its objects and attitudes were already clearly demarcated from those of other existing working class political and economic associations. At its first meeting, one opponent was already indicated: 'the whole project of joint-stock co-operation', or the use of dividend schemes, which according to Lovett (at least in the report of Richard Carlile, who satirised some of the proceedings) 'were but systems of competition'. The method and aim of labour exchanges were also already discussed from the outset.[15] Following the failures of Orbiston and New Harmony, a co-operative turning towards politics was also a logical step, and from the early days of the BAPCK attempts to unite political and economic reform were understood as part of the rationale of the organisation. The young Cornish cabinet-maker William Lovett, for example, was among the most prominent members to weave radical and Owenite themes together. It seems clear that the main problem in this respect was convincing radicals of the veracity of Owen's economic analysis, for many co-operators seem to have agreed upon the desirability of political reform. Rendering Owenism acceptable to the radicals entailed familiarising them with a new language whose chief concept focussed upon issues of economic development and justice. One means of making this language more immediately accessible was to connect it to assumptions which the radicals already shared, for example about the nature of human behaviour generally. At a BAPCK meeting of October 1829, for example, we can see that Lovett's interpretation of 'competition', the central concept in Owenite economic analysis, was essentially moral rather than economic. But this was also more clearly adaptable to working class audiences than a more narrowly economic conception, which did not resonate with any key concept in the radical vocabulary:

The selfish feeling in man may fairly be called the competitive principle, since it causes him to compete with others, for the gratification of his wants and propensities. Whereas the co-operative may be said to be the social feeling that prompts him to acts of benevolence and brotherly affection. Competition, the child of selfishness, nursed by Avarice and Self-Interest, and educated in the school of Ambition, has been the demon whose path has been marked by the blood of nations, whose withering influence has blasted nature's best produc-

---

[15] *Lion*, 3, no. 20 (15 May 1829), 610–13. For a description of individual wealth as the cause of all social evils, see the short address by the London Co-operative Trading Fund Association entitled *To the Operative Classes* (1828).

tions, and made man worse than the brute – to prey with the vulture's rapacity on his fellow man.

Lovett then moved to more traditional radical concerns. But he clearly aimed to express these in a new way. Connecting competition to the issue of political reform, he explained that 'with respect to equality of power, co-operators conceive that the power to govern or to punish all, should be delegated by all; otherwise, the selfish feeling prevailing, society will soon be brought to a state . . . when one party will become so opulent as to be able to purchase the other, and the other so poor as to sell themselves'. Moral selfishness, economic power and political monopoly were thus causally linked in Lovett's analysis. But this combination of factors was also intended to persuade non-political co-operators as well as radicals of their errors. Thus political reform could now be recommended to co-operators:

As to politics, you say, what have 'I to do with politics?' It has to do with you; it forms part of your existence, and it is to the neglect of the important duty of watching over your public interests, that you have been brought to such a condition as to have few private ones to attend to . . . Co-operators are of the opinion, that most of those evils have been occasioned by the unequal division of labour; by men living too much on the labour of others (this of course proceeding from the selfish feeling), instead of labouring themselves.[16]

This process of adaptation of radical to Owenite ideas in the BAPCK probably was aided by the strongly moral emphasis of co-operators such as Lovett. Though almost any discussion of 'competition' was characteristically Owenite, a moral description of its attributes was much more identifiable with an analysis in which the direct actions of government were the cause of distress than any more narrowly economic explanation. In the latter view, competition originated in the principle of profit upon price, but was aggravated by growing numbers of distributors and a declining market for produce. The most immediate cause of working class distress was held to be competition between machinery and manual labour, in which the costs of government, so important to the radicals, played no apparent role. But it was obviously much easier to castigate class behaviour as subjectively selfish, and to link this to a traditional radical analysis of Old Corruption, than it was to analyse it in terms of objective economic necessities. Still, there were other means of making the new economic analysis more palatable. Co-operators could lambast 'the aristocracy', for example, but then emphasise that what they meant by this term was 'all those whose interests are separated or removed from those of the democracy, or the

---

[16] *Report of the Second Quarterly Meeting of the Society for Promoting Co-operative Knowledge* (1829), pp. 9–14.

people at large, no matter in however slight a degree'. Others assailed 'taxation', but then added that 'we working classes are drained of the products of our labour, by taxes imposed upon us under the name of profit, and which give birth to a system of individual competition'. The specific notion of 'living on the labour of others' also seems to have been particularly useful in facilitating a wedding of the radical analysis of taxation, in which payments to priests, aristocrats, placemen and the like made taxes burdensome, and the Owenite conception of the abstraction of the produce of labour, which accentuated non-partici-pation in necessary work ('instead of labouring themselves'). Here, in other words, a general duty to labour supplanted complaints about specific forms of avoiding labour.[17]

This may appear to be only a matter of emphasis. The radical view focussed on the positive, unjust appropriation of wealth-as-money, while the socialist view condemned the negative, unjust noncontri-bution of wealth-as-labour. In fact, an enormous gulf separated the two conceptions. For the radical theory could only be fully directed at the recipients of taxation, who as 'idlers' and 'parasites' did no work at all. The Owenite analysis, however, was based upon a material defi-nition of wealth and, very often, an activist conception of production in which actual exertion was required in order to be accounted a genuine 'productive labourer'. These categories implicated all of the non-pro-ducing classes, but especially middlemen and capitalists, who did not create material wealth directly, and who, even if they did labour, could not claim an unequal reward according to Owenite theory.[18] The rad-ical conception of living upon the labour of others virtually excluded any consideration of capitalists and investors, particularly in manu-facturing (though fundholders could be criticised since taxes were paid to service the national debt). The Owenite notion, however, easily encompassed such groups. When these classes were not named in these discussions, the rhetoric of parasitism formed an excellent bridge between the radical and socialist views of society. When they were, the penetration of Owenism was quite evident.

Another good example of this creative interaction between radical and Owenite language appeared in the report of a speech by a co-operator named Foskett at the third quarterly meeting of the BAPCK in the first week of January 1830. Foskett spoke on this occasion about the various manifestations of competition, which in his view embraced enmity between governors and governed, taxation, and the misdirec-

17 *PPP*, 14 October 1830, 2; *ComS*, 25 December 1830, 33. For a different but nonetheless common emphasis upon competition which held it to originate in the existence of too many distributors, see [William Pare], *An Address Delivered at the Opening of the Birmingham Co-operative Society* (Birmingham, 1829), p. 9.
18 *Machinery, Money and the Millennium*, pp. 135–6.

tion of productive powers as well. Here we also encounter an extension of the Owenite idea of 'competition' to encompass problems already defined as central in radical discourse:

A competition of wealth and poverty, manifested itself in the unequal distribution of the former, creating a rapid decline in our natural resources, and an increasing poverty amongst the people, first by an unnatural and barbarous corn law, imposing a tax of sixty millions a year upon the people for this single article . . . A tax of ten millions a year for the clergy, besides a dead weight of twenty millions a year, to pay the interest on the debt, and innumerable other taxes. This excessive taxation has a tendency to make a few rich and a multitude poor, and to destroy that sympathy and identity of interests, which should exist in every nation between the governors and the governed. A competition between wealth and poverty was again strikingly manifested in the employment of machinery aided by capital, to the great injury of the working classes.

Here, too, though taxation was a potent weapon wielded by wealth against poverty, so was the abstraction of profit as the Owenites conceived it:

One cause of this state was, that the exchangers and distributors of wealth were paid for their services, not on the principle of wages, but upon that of profit; the amount of profit in the year 1812, being sixty millions more than the wages of labour, although the number of labourers was more than twice the number of distributors. There seemed to be a grand error in our commercial institutions. The workmen, for the future, must become the employers, as well as the employed, and must pay themselves. Profit was one of the principal channels through which the wealth of labourers was drained out of their possession; and the occupation of distribution rendered the most lucrative and reputable. Hence originated the principle of competition in trade, and this rendered machinery a curse instead of a blessing to mankind.[19]

This passage is interesting for several additional reasons. It demonstrates that, in a crude statistical account (based on Colquhoun, whose 1812 figures were still cited on occasion in the 1840s), the taxation analysis could seem quantitatively as convincing (if not more so) as that based on profit. 'Competition' also functions here in an extremely broad manner to embrace all forms of abstraction. Finally, 'profit' is explained as the basis of competition in trade, which in turn caused manual labour to suffer the affliction of machinery. 'Taxation', therefore, while it was an aspect of 'competition', was quite separate from 'competition in trade'. 'Taxation' could be completely removed, but much distress would remain: 'profit' and oppression via machinery would be untouched. Here, then, we see the successful alliance of the radical and Owenite analyses of distress, with neither dominating the other. All of the abstracting classes were condemned, and both parlia-

19 *Report of the Third Quarterly Meeting of the BAPCK* (1830), pp. 16–17.

mentary change and radical economic reform were enjoined. This mixture of views was not necessarily held by all members of the organisation. Nor did it inevitably become a dogma of the leaders of the political co-operators. But it did demonstrate that conscious efforts were being made to reconcile radical and Owenite world-views.

About a year was required to reach this particular blend of radical and Owenite ingredients in the BAPCK. A variety of possible compromises between conflicting aims were reflected in successive statements of its goals. According to the laws of the Association in early 1830, its object was the creation of capital 'to be employed in the establishment of an agricultural, manufacturing, or trading community'. Brighton-style consumer co-operation was clearly excluded in Lovett's proposals several months later, which reiterated that

all plans of Co-operation that fall short in their ultimate objects of equality of rights, of equal labour in the production of wealth, of equal participation in the enjoyment, together without a system of education adapted to such a state of things, are mere expedients, futile in their effects, calculated to prop up a defective system, and will not be permanently beneficial to the wealth-producing classes.

At this meeting the BAPCK also issued its first petition to parliament, and working class co-operation now emerged into the world of politics proper. Explicitly disregarding the opinion that co-operators should not meddle in politics (an obvious reference to Owen), the Association stated that objects of co-operation were as much political as moral, with Lovett insisting that equality of rights included equality in labour and of enjoyments. The King and parliament could become co-operative pioneers, it was suggested, by repealing taxes on comforts and necessaries, substituting a comprehensive graduated tax on property, abolishing primogeniture, shortening the duration of parliaments, and granting universal suffrage. Significant for further debates, too, was a motion by Henry Hetherington and John Gast which appeared to render the success of co-operation contingent upon parliamentary reform:

Your petitioners further conceive, that they should be able to place themselves in comparative comfort and independence by the plans of CO-OPERATION propounded by Mr. Robert Owen, and adopted by themselves and many thousands of the most intelligent and industrious of their fellow-workmen, if the burdens that press on the elastic springs of industry, – namely excessive taxation and unjust and partial enactments [are removed].[20]

[20] *Ibid.*, p. 11; *Report of the Fourth Quarterly Meeting of the BAPCK* (1830), pp. 12–15. The petition was also printed in the *WFP*, no. 248 (10 April 1830). A gradual rapprochement between co-operative and radical views in the Midlands can be seen in the pages of the *Voice of the People*. See especially no. 20 (14 May 1831), 156, and no. 25 (18 June 1831), 196–7. For Scotland see Alexander Campbell's comments in *STUG*, no. 7 (26 October 1833), 55, where a turning away from politics is also already evident.

The BAPCK's attempt to combine Owenism and politics was thus both conscious and reasonably successful. Francis Place, a devotee of Ricardianism and generally unsympathetic observer of these proceedings, commented that the co-operators, taking advantage of Owen's absence in America, had resolved

to take up such points of his system as they believed would be appreciated by the working classes, and to be the means of uniting them for specific purposes, taking care that these purposes should not interfere more than was possible with opinions in the proceedings to be adopted, in matters on which great differences of opinion existed. Leaving these to time they expected those who associated having experienced the advantages of those parts of Mr. Owen's system, they might be induced to investigate the whole.

According to Place this had the result not only of widely disseminating Owen's views, but also of specifically attracting radicals to them, hence convincing 'many of those who had held aloof from co-operators, as persons who retarded political reforms. The speeches of the members henceforth partook, as did also their resolutions, much more of a co-operative character, and the extremes of radicalism were somewhat modified thereby, in the violence of feeling which had pervaded them'. Such effects anticipated much of the interaction between the two movements in the coming years.[21]

Place also pointed out, however, that there was some resistance by radicals to this mollifying tendency in Owenism. This was especially true of the choleric William Benbow, who blasted Owen with a volley of articles in his short-lived *Tribune of the People* (1831).[22] Other members of the BAPCK, too, Lovett later recalled, had also attended meetings held by Owen in which he had condemned 'through his usual philanthropy, the Radical Reformers', and had consequently carried resolutions against him. On his return from America, Owen, with his usual aplomb in such matters, in fact only further complicated the BAPCK's efforts to reconcile co-operators and radicals. Indeed, he might well be said to have deliberately sabotaged such efforts. In early 1830 Jenneson, the chairman of the BAPCK, found himself forced to disclaim all connection with Owen's now regular Sunday lectures, which seemed clearly designed to upset the BAPCK's strategy of articulating an acceptable working class and political form of Owenism. Nonetheless, some members still voiced their appreciation of

[21] British Library Add. MS. 27791, fols. 244–5, 248.

[22] Prewar descriptions of the *Tribune of the People* are being followed here, as the original and apparently unique copy was destroyed. It is likely that these articles were reprinted in Benbow's *The Delusion, or Owenism Unmasked* (1832), which remains lost. The *Tribune* apparently lasted only four numbers, as Benbow failed to pay the printer, R. E. Lee, who brought the matter before the public in *Victimization, or Benbowism Exposed* (1832). On Benbow's Central Co-operative Society, see Prothero, *Artisans and Politics*, p. 246. Benbow continued his criticisms of Owen in the *Agitator and Political Anatomist* – for example December 1833, 4–7.

Owen's labours. In an address of late December 1830, for example, it was claimed that while it was not necessary to adhere to all of Owen's opinions, he had first proclaimed the need for *'total change'*, and had impressed upon the working classes the conviction of their importance through emphasising the value of productive labour. The notion that the working classes generally could employ themselves was also widely associated with his name.[23]

It was Owen's moral and economic analysis rather than his political ideas which was thus of primary interest to the BAPCK. What the co-operators effected was the translation of such ideas into a radical discourse familiar to a much wider audience. This process was often vague and somewhat haphazard. Making taxation appear to emanate from 'selfish competition' was not the most compelling way of revealing a convincing alternative to the usual radical analyses, even if such caution was regarded as tactically necessary. At other times, however, the BAPCK made the novelty of its Owenite views strikingly evident. At a meeting in early 1831, for example, it was claimed that 'Those who do not labour are burdens on those who do, and are burdens heavier or lighter in proportion to the income that each possesses . . . all shop-keepers, wholesale dealers, master manufacturers, merchants, etc. gain their income by the sale of the produce of the producers (which the producers ought not to allow)'. This manualist definition of the distinction between productive and unproductive labour was new to political radicalism (and in part to Owen as well). It therefore constituted the first and most crucial logical component in the construction of working class Owenism.[24]

The significance of the BAPCK, therefore, has not hitherto been clearly understood. The most detailed previous interpretation of these questions, by W. H. Oliver, errs on two points in particular. Clearly, it is not appropriate to describe the 'right to all he produced' as the co-operative socialist proposition newly offered to, and accepted by, the working classes. This is a common misinterpretation which dates from Anton Menger's *The Right to the Whole Produce of Labour* (1899). The language of the radical analysis of taxation also acknowledged such a right, except that here the 'whole produce' comprised the inclusion of that proportion abstracted by the government, whereas for the Owenites it comprehended abstraction by *all* other classes. Secondly, the ideological importance of the BAPCK did not result from the fact that co-operative ideas were 'injected' with class consciousness, but that they were now linked to political reform. The complex question of the

[23] British Library Add. MS. 27822, fol. 17; *WFP*, no. 253 (15 May 1830), 38; *CPL*, 'A Letter to the Right Hon. Wilmot Horton' (31 December 1830), 16.
[24] *Ibid.*, 'A Letter to Lord Brougham' (11 March 1831), 126.

language of class and class consciousness in this period cannot be explored at length here. But it is clear that both Owenites and radicals acknowledged a gulf and antipathy between a variety of social groups. Without doubt, however, the Owenites addressed the abstractions of capitalists and the middle classes far more than the radicals, and referred more to economic position than political power in so doing. In an economic sense, then, the class consciousness of the BAPCK originated on the Owenite rather than the radical side. The Owenites did not of course encourage class antagonisms. Nor did they exhibit a detailed grasp of the relationship between political and economic power. But they refined the language of class to a much greater degree than the radicals, and this, after all, is what 'class consciousness' is also about, rather than only the formulation of class-based programmes aiming at revolution. Consequently the standard account of the reformulation of class consciousness in Britain during these years, which too often relies upon a teleological ideal in which true class consciousness is *only* definable by the demand for proletarian revolution, needs substantial revision.[25]

The National Union of the Working Classes, 1831–35

Throughout 1830 the BAPCK stepped up its campaign for parliamentary reform. 'The cause must prosper so long as Robert Owen is its supporter', enthused Henry Hetherington, editor of the first widely circulated social radical journal, the *Penny Papers for the People*, adding that 'We are but his disciples: and only differ with him in considering that the end which we aspire to attain, must be promoted at first by the very means which are opposed to it – force; but we are younger, and, therefore, should bow to his superior judgment, did not, perhaps, in this instance, our animal feelings interfere.' 'Force' in this instance implied moral, extra-parliamentary pressure of a type which Owen found unacceptable even if it fell well short of the actual threat of revolution. Nonetheless, Owenism and radicalism were here clearly recognised as interlocking means and ends: 'REFORM AND CO-OPERATION – these shall be the saviours of mankind; these two blessed weapons shall restore mankind to happiness – to justice ... first, therefore, CO-OPERATE, then claim your rights, and the foremost is

---

[25] Oliver, 'Organisations', pp. vi, 55. For parallel developments in Scotland see Fiona Montgomery, 'Glasgow Radicalism, 1830–1848', Ph.D., University of Glasgow (1974), p. 266. For a similar argument that 'class consciousness' in this period did not necessarily imply greater radicalism, see Craig Calhoun, *The Question of Class Struggle. Social Foundations of Popular Radicalism during the Industrial Revolution* (Oxford, Basil Blackwell, 1982), p. 223, and my discussion in 'The Triumph of Class Conscious Reformism in British Radicalism, 1790–1860', *HJ*, 26 (1983), 969–85.

REFORM in Parliament'. In 1831 these claims were combined once again, at least partially, in a new organisation. The National Union of the Working Classes was soon to become one of the most important working class political organisations of the pre-Chartist period. Its roots lay in a number of earlier groups, including the Association for Civil and Political Liberty (1828) and the London Irish for Catholic Emancipation (1829). The formation of a new organisation was timely, of course, given the veritable frenzy of parliamentary reform agitation which seized the London working and middle classes from early 1831 onwards. This surge of activity also encouraged various BAPCK members to expand into other areas. In March, for example, Benjamin Warden and others formed the Metropolitan Trades' Union, which sought to raise the value of labour by diminishing hours of employment and to attain parliamentary representation for the working classes.[26]

Most of the energies of the BAPCK, however, were funnelled into the new radical political union. First projected in late March, possibly as a result of William Lovett's efforts in particular, its general objectives were announced as being 'to enhance the value of labour, to afford support and protection to all who depend upon their labour for subsistence, and to adopt such measures as may be deemed necessary to increase the domestic comforts of working men'. Added by Foskett in a subsequent address was the co-operative aim that the working classes seek capital by keeping their own shops, buying land, manufacturing their own clothing, and exchanging amongst themselves. These policies, however, were not a part of the official founding programme of the NUWC. In a 'Declaration of the Rights of Man', published in late May, the new organisation professed to seek liberty, equality before the law, security of the individual, and 'the full enjoyment of the produce of ... labour'. So stated, of course, such aims did not vary from those of previous radical associations. Tactically, no doubt, this was wise, considering the damage done to the reform movement in the past by the charge that it sought equality of property. But the Owenite members of the group naturally found all such statements outmoded and inadequate. Consequently this document was treated quite critically by a number of the more socialist members, one of whom complained that 'we should have man's *right* declared to be *equality* in EVERY *situation* – in every respect'. Another co-operative member, too, rejected the Union's views on property as

---

26 *PPP*, 16 October 1830, 2; 8 January 1831, 1–2; 26 March 1831, 3. There is a good review of developments in this period in Prothero, *Artisans and Politics*, pp. 267–326. For an earlier account see Beer, *A History of British Socialism*, 1, pp. 299–313.

not being consistent with a state of *general equality*; for man is capable of producing, by his daily labour, a by far greater quantity of the necessaries of life than would be his fair proportion, and than he could possibly enjoy ... we should always find many willing to produce more than they required, and many on the other hand, as willing to produce less – little or nothing; [but] no man can possibly have the right to enjoy or monopolize more than he can possibly require.[27]

It is difficult to judge how widespread such uncompromising co-operative Owenism was in the NUWC. The association's list of objectives was carried almost unanimously at an early meeting, and reprinted in virtually identical form throughout much of the next four years as it expanded in branches across the country. Heterodox views on property and commerce were certainly never a part of its official pronouncements. An 1831 NUWC broadside reiterated that 'individual property of every description, acquired by honest industry, or under the sanction of laws (however unjustly enacted)' was 'SACRED AND INVIOLABLE'. Nor is there any reason to suppose this was a merely tactical declaration. When the Manchester branch was opened, its aims were stated only to be universal suffrage, annual parliaments, the ballot, and no property qualifications. Some members were not even willing to go this far. John Derisley, for example, who seems later to have defected to the Place-supported National Political Union, wrote a pamphlet addressed to the Union opposing both annual parliaments and removal of property qualifications.[28]

Why then should the NUWC be treated as anything other than a working class, radical reform organisation, important in its own right, but not significant for the emergence of that form of social radicalism which concerns us here? Clearly its ideological centre was much closer to orthodox radicalism than it was to the hybrid, political Owenism of the BAPCK. Contemporary accounts to the contrary are in fact somewhat suspect. It was Francis Place, both as a politician and historian, who gave vent to his phobia about all extreme views of property and tried to visit the sins of the small Owenite wing upon the entire NUWC as a means of undermining the popularity of the organisation. Even the more moderate, if still semi-hysterical, pamphlet written against

[27] *Ibid.*, 1 April 1831, 7–8; 27 May 1831, 1–5. George Howell gave Lovett credit for founding the NUWC (*A History of the Working Men's Association from 1836 to 1850*, Newcastle upon Tyne, Frank Graham, 1973, p. 20). Howell, however, also associated Lovett with the followers of Henry Hunt in this period (p. 17), which seems to be contradicted by more recent accounts. See John Belchem, *'Orator' Hunt. Henry Hunt and English Working Class Radicalism* (Oxford, Clarendon Press, 1985), p. 214.

[28] Francis Place, *Proceedings Relating to the NUWC*, October or November 1831; *CMPM*, January 1832, 182; *PMA*, 10 November 1832, 8; John Derisley, *An Address to the NUWC* (HO 64/18). See also the *Union*, no. 1 (26 November 1831), 16, for details of the proposed NUWC/NPU merger.

the NUWC by Edward Gibbon Wakefield concluded that its members comprised far more Huntites than Owenites, an opinion in which those who leaned towards Owen's views concurred.[29]

Nonetheless the Owenites did make some converts in the new organisation. This was despite the opposition of outsiders such as Place as well as NUWC members like one Duffey, who was cheered at a meeting for terming Owen one 'of the greatest political impostors of the day' for his 'mystification' of the paper money issue, and for carrying on 'some sinister design' which remained otherwise unde-fined but clearly echoed the radical fears of 1817. Other members, however, such as the radical publisher Lorymer, indicated wider sup-port for Owen in claiming that 'if any party in England admire the system of citizen (or *Mister*, should he not like that honourable desig-nation) *Owen*, and co-operation in general . . . the Republicans are not excelled in that respect. They not only admire, they almost adore, the co-operative system, and only wish it were universally and *immediately* practicable'.[30] But it is still unclear how far this was really true for the NUWC as a whole.

Of course, we should not treat the question of social radicalism in the NUWC as only the one-sided attempt of co-operators to convince radicals of the limitations of mere political reform. The Owenites, as well, were capable of changing their minds on both strategic issues and the ultimate value of Owen's views on property, commerce and other matters. Some former BAPCK members appear to have retained their Owenite orthodoxy during this period, and perhaps, by virtue of their oppositional status, to have increased their faith in it. Others, caught up in the intensely political atmosphere of the period, and perhaps beginning to query the wisdom of Owen's ultimate aims, no doubt came to concede not only the utility but also the primacy of parlia-mentary reform. This point is extremely significant given the osten-sibly 'purely political' origins of Chartism by a group which included former NUWC members and Owenite co-operators. William Lovett, for instance, who was amongst those who helped to found the London Working Men's Association (LWMA), still argued at this time that competition was a great evil 'resulting from machinery', and insisted, even more importantly, that individual competition in the pursuit of wealth would be unknown in the future. James Watson, another

---

29 British Library Add. MS. 27797, fols. 252, 290; E. G. Wakefield, *Householders in Danger from the Populace* (1831).
30 Place, *Proceedings Relating to the NUWC*, 28 July 1832; *Republican*, 2, no. 3 (May 1832), 46–7; 1, no. 31 (January 1832), 211–12. For other comments on the new sympathy of the radicals for co-operation, see *Isis*, no. 30 (8 September 1832), 468–9; *Radical*, no. 8 (8 October 1831), 32 (where co-operation but not living in communities was supported) and *Cosmopolite*, no. 21 (28 July 1832).

co-operator and early Chartist, seconded these propositions at a meeting. But he also reflected several months later that what was requisite
was 'something like' Owen's plan 'which had for its object the security
of the proceeds of industry for its own advantage . . . they wanted a
system which would give the working man the produce of his own
labour to do as he pleased with, before feeding a thousand *cormorants*'.
This is certainly more a radical than an Owenite phrasing of the matter,
though it is dangerous to signify too much by it. Nonetheless, some
Owenites in this period did begin to renounce their belief in 'community' as well as community of goods, spurred on by Owen's early
failures as well as his obvious stubbornness about adapting the plan to
meet other contingencies, such as the creation of urban communities.[31]

How, then, should we categorise the social radical component in the
NUWC? Lovett, whose views began to shift towards liberalism at the
end of the 1830s, certainly believed that the organisation differed from
other contemporary groups 'in its advocating of first principles and
abstract opinions of right and justice'. Officially, at least, it did not
uphold his own principles, however, and must ultimately be classified
as closer to the 'confused medley' of socialism, trades' unionism, and
radicalism of Arthur Shadwell's description than anything like a coherent unity of the theory or programmes of the co-operative and radical
movements. It can plausibly be argued, in fact, that the probable effect
of the NUWC (and the period of reform agitation) upon a number of
erstwhile co-operators was to weaken their socialist beliefs. Watson is
again a good case in point. Strongly drawn to co-operation in the late
1820s, a few years later he nonetheless proclaimed that the main source
of distress was the abstraction of too much labour from the working
classes for government expenses.[32]

The renewed concern with parliamentary representation also
resulted in an increasing tendency among many types of co-operators
to insist that economic change was contingent upon political reform,
an emphasis which would foreshadow Owenite–Chartist debates
during the 1840s. Some socialists (the term was now beginning to
circulate more freely) of course still felt that communities could be

---

[31] Place, *Proceedings Relating to the NUWC*, 24 December 1831, 4 March 1832; *PMG*, 1, no.
3 (23 July 1831), 22. At the third co-operative congress Watson termed himself both a
co-operator and a political agitator (*Proceedings*, p. 71). He had been acquainted with
Owenite ideas since 1825 (W. J. Linton, *James Watson*, 1879; rpt. Clifton, Augustus M.
Kelly, 1969, pp. 18–20). For other instances of support for Owen's ideas in the NUWC,
see the *Union*, no. 3 (10 December 1831), 37, where a carpenter named Velor spoke in
support of Owen's plan, and no. 4 (17 December 1831), 59, where a Mr. Maunsell
eulogised Owen highly, and the *Isis*, no. 6 (17 March 1832), 92, where Julian Hibbert
said that the radicals would act as pioneers for Owen's system.

[32] British Library Add. MS. 27822, fol. 17; Arthur Shadwell, *The Socialist Movement*
(Phillip Allan, 1924), p. 29; *WMF*, no. 14 (23 March 1833), 105; no. 15 (30 March 1833), 116.

established, and indeed society refashioned, without the need for undue partisan pressure or upsetting governmental reforms. These threw themselves wholeheartedly into the labour exchange and trades' union movements during these years, assailing radical strategies with renewed vigour once the severe disappointments of 1832 were widely conceded. However, before the passage of the Reform Act, others, including some who had supported co-operation since the early 1820s, clearly began to tilt towards seeing political reform as primary. These included some who would be working class leaders for most of the next twenty years. When James Tucker wrote to the *Poor Man's Guardian* that co-operative trading associations would 'hasten our political emancipation', Henry Hetherington, for one, replied that Owen exhibited

a strange perversity of mind in expecting to realise his political millennium before working men are placed on an equal footing with the other classes of the community with regard to political rights; and I consider him, on this point, in almost as hopeless a condition, as the individual who believed he was made of glass; it was useless to knock his head against the wall to convince him to the contrary – the notion was immoveable. So it is with Mr. Owen – he entertains an absurd idea, that with the aid of a plundering aristocracy he shall be able to establish Co-operative principles, notwithstanding the unjust and iniquitous laws which at present exist in this country. In his case, experience is unavailing, for after more than twenty years' exertion he is not a jot nearer the attainment of his object. His mental vision must have some peculiar defect, or he would perceive that he was 'dipping water into empty wells, and growing old in drawing nothing up'.

This was a theme repeated many times in the *Poor Man's Guardian*, the first major organ of the new mixture of social and political radicalism.[33]

The emergence of a new group advocating the ballot first and fundamental social change thereafter in effect split both the radical and Owenite movements. By the mid-1830s, the spectrum of reformers comprised socialists with little or no faith in political reform, radicals who found Owen's eccentric ideas about community of property abhorrent, and a new group of social radicals dedicated to using political power to achieve relatively specific socialist ends. The latter, in turn, were subdivided according to their attitude towards private property and competition. In the first rehearsal for a hundred similar meetings during the Chartist years, a public discussion on 'Owenism vs. Political Reform' found all three points of view represented in September 1832.[34]

33 *PMG*, 1, no. 31 (14 January 1832), 245; see also no. 28 (24 December 1831), 221; 2, no. 64 (1 September 1832), 513–14; no. 67 (22 September 1832), 537–8; no. 68 (29 September 1832), 545–6, 551; 3, no. 98 (20 April 1833), 121; 4, no. 198 (21 March 1835), 473–6.
34 *PMG*, 2, no. 67 (22 September 1832), 537–8.

Such divisions of opinion cannot have profited the NUWC. Disappointed with the results of the Reform Act, many members apparently departed for the seemingly greener pastures of the GNCTU. By the end of 1834 the NUWC was virtually defunct. It had played an important role in the reform movement, but not in the dissemination of Owenite views. On the whole, Iorwerth Prothero is thus correct in seeing the NUWC as Jacobin rather than working class and republican rather than Owenite in its orientation. Certainly it was far less committed to Owenite ideas than the BAPCK. Earlier interpretations of these organisations, however, most notably by W. H. Oliver, who has argued that through the NUWC co-operative socialism became revolutionary in politics, should not be too quickly dismissed. Instead they require further refinement. For even if Owenism hardly predominated as a whole in the NUWC, it is clear that a variety of ideologies circulated among its individual members. Some radicals clearly did come to follow James Bronterre O'Brien's lead in seeing political socialism, the combination of parliamentary reform with some type of collective ownership, as the only possible programme of reform.[35] By the end of the 1830s, however, O'Brien too had repudiated Owen's views on property and embraced John Gray's approach. This rejected communitarianism and permitted the accumulation of justly earned property through labour, though seeking the regulation of production at the national level. This type of co-operative but non-communitarian Owenism, as we will now see, represented a fourth form of social radicalism during the late 1830s and 1840s, in addition to those much less influential varieties of Spenceanism which survived into this period.[36]

The social radicalism of James Bronterre O'Brien

From the perspective of the 1840s, when he emerged as the most important Chartist leader after Feargus O'Connor, James Bronterre O'Brien's conversion to co-operation was one of Owen's great successes in the previous decade. The impossibility of attaining fundamental social change without political reforms was one of O'Brien's chief messages as editor of the *Poor Man's Guardian* and 'Schoolmaster'

---

[35] On the decline of the NUWC see William Lovett, *Struggles*, p. 40; British Library Add. MS. 27797 fol. 251; Prothero, 'Chartism in London', *P&P*, 44 (1969), 76–105; Oliver, 'Organisations', p. 66. Cole and Filson somewhat confusingly noted of the artisans of the NUWC that 'The labour theory of value led them to a political conception of class society, and a demand for a share of state power by their class' (*British Working Class Movements: Select Documents 1789–1875* (Macmillan, 1951), p. 228.

[36] On Spencean survivals in this period see *Machinery, Money and the Millennium*, pp. 156–8, and generally Terry M. Parsinnen, 'Thomas Spence and the Spenceans', Ph.D., Brandeis University (1968).

(as O'Connor later termed him) to a rising generation of Chartists. Nonetheless O'Brien was the first important radical journalist of this period to break decisively from the tenets of liberal political economy. That he already sought some type of Owenite co-operation by the early 1830s is also undoubted. Against Charles Knight's defense of classical political economy, *The Results of Machinery* (1831), O'Brien insisted that co-operation, not emigration, was the only alternative to further unemployment. Denegrating the limited aims of trades' unions, who were *'combining as servants'*, he urged them to 'co-operate as men'. At the second co-operative congress in April 1831, O'Brien reiterated his opposition to competition, and in a letter to Owen the following spring spoke of 'my brother co-operators'. Like Owen, too, he fully supported the inviolability of both public and private property *'as long as the individual competitive system prevails in the world'*. A number of times in the *Poor Man's Guardian*, O'Brien also described Owen's principles as basically true, and requiring only political power to become practical. When, in 1836, O'Brien catalogued the growing divisions amongst the radicals, he again identified with Owen (but now Babeuf as well) on the end sought, and aligned himself with Owen's followers against the 'Sham Radicals' who consorted with the middle classes and regurgitated their political economy. In the Chartist years, too, he acknowledged a preference for Owen over Cartwright, Cobbett, Volney and Paine, writing that Owen

with all his hallucinations, is the only one of the lot that is worthy of the name *Reformer*. Owen is right, at any rate, as to the end, but his means are delusive. The others seem to me to have mistaken both the *end* and the *means*. Were all the practical reforms proposed by Paine, Cartwright and Co. to be carried into complete effect tomorrow, they would not realise any of the results anticipated by their authors. They would leave the *radix* or root of the evil where they found it, and consequently cause no substantial change in the condition of the bulk of society.[37]

In Chartist circles such recommendations may have helped Owen's cause considerably in the early 1840s. Nonetheless by then O'Brien had also come to renounce Owen's views on community of goods in favour of a system which emphasised justice over equality. Exactly when this occurred is unclear, though it was evidently linked not only to previous communitarian failures, but also to debates about the operations of labour exchanges. For here a central issue had been the return of the product of labour to the individual producer in a system in

[37] *MRBH*, no. 4 (14 May 1831); no. 6 (28 May 1831); *Proceedings of the Second Co-operative Congress*; Owen Collection, Holyoake House, Manchester, letter 546, 27 May 1832; CPL, 'A Political Herald' (21 January 1831), 4; *PMG*, 2, no. 64 (1 September 1832), 513–14; no. 67 (22 September 1832), 545–6; *Buonarroti's History of Babeuf's Conspiracy* (1836), pp. 55n, 213–14n; *NS*, no. 176 (27 March 1841), 1.

which competition had been abolished, but no community of goods established. The grand evil of property, O'Brien stated in an editorial in the *Poor Man's Guardian* late in 1834, was not its unequal distribution, or unjust protection by law, but its unfair acquisition in the first place. To this extent O'Brien could be understood as still agreeing with Owen, who only several weeks earlier had again emphasised to a meeting of operatives that 'not the *amount* of capital but the principle of its accumulation' and misdirection was at fault. But O'Brien, now departing irrevocably from Owen, concluded that since it seemed impossible for men to co-operate by living in common, the next best thing would be for them to acquire property fairly, upon the principle that those who contributed the most should become the wealthiest. This, O'Brien emphasised, was the true application of the 'democratic principle' to all departments of economic life. At present, by contrast, he insisted that 'the monarchic principle prevails in all, and as a consequence, all are slaves except a few great capitalists'.[38]

This introduction of political terminology to describe economic organisation is important, for it demarcates the working out of a debate which had grown in momentum since the co-operative movement in the mid-1820s first began practically to develop the implications of Owen's ideas about collective economic management. Several things can be said about O'Brien's use of language in this respect. His specific emphasis upon the extension of the principle of democracy on this occasion appears to have been instigated by his recent debate (considered in greater detail below) with James Morrison, editor of a GNCTU paper, the *Pioneer*. Morrison was strongly smitten with Owen's personality and teachings, writing to Owen in mid-1833, 'let me be a Drummer in your service – drill me as a sergeant drills his recruit. Above all things teach me charity'. In the *Pioneer* he argued, in characteristically Owenite fashion, that as the working classes were insufficiently educated to be immediately suited to make good use of universal suffrage, they should commence practical political training within their own trades. By this process a slow accession to the responsible use of power was possible, in which the most important areas of social administration would also be the first to fall under working class control.[39]

However, this entailed an overt rejection of the radical strategy of seeking the immediate extension of the suffrage. 'We have determined', insisted Morrison, 'that REFORM shall commence from within. We govern within ourselves, and conceive it to be a duty to acquaint

[38] *PMG*, 3, no. 175 (11 October 1834), 281–2; no. 172 (20 September 1834), 257.
[39] Morrison to Owen, 23 July 1833, National Library of Wales MS. 14352C; *Pioneer*, no. 17 (28 December 1833), 129.

ourselves with the principles of government, consisting simply in good internal regulations. We feel that to regulate trade, or the several branches of labour by which we live, will most speedily regulate government'. The Union, therefore, rather than parliament, was to be used to achieve universal suffrage. What Morrison termed the 'system of the division of labour' was now to be applied to politics, instead of the ideas of the 'old republicans'. O'Brien was not willing to countenance such a clear repudiation of radical strategy, however, and responded that he could not counsel direct legislation by the people, but still found universal delegation entirely acceptable (a view he would alter two years later). Working people were intelligent enough to govern the nation. Thus, compared to the 'peddling transactions of Union shops or Co-operative Bazaars', universal suffrage would render the land the property of all (with full compensation to existing landlords), while establishing collective control over the supply and value of money. This debate thus prompted O'Brien to sketch the reform plan he would preach for the next thirty years. He was willing to adopt some of Morrison's conception of extending democracy beyond parliament, but interpreted this primarily in terms of the rights of labour rather than any theory of organisation:

The democratic principle once introduced into the workshop will extend itself to the farm and every other industrial department. Then will the reign of fraud and usury have to end. Then, for the first time, will industry and wealth be seen hand in hand, while idleness shall be clothed in rags. Then will aristocracy disappear from the earth with its ghastly train of sorrows. Then will man meet man erect, and the language of truth become as respectable as that of falsehood is now rendered by the plundering classes.[40]

What O'Brien meant by 'democracy' therefore, was not the extension of popular control to the sphere of production, as Morrison intended, but the reward of labour according to effort and acceptance of accumulation on the basis of work. Owen had conceded the utility of temporarily accepting this principle in the labour exchanges, as a means of superseding competition. But he never saw labour exchanges as anything but a means of preparing for an eventual community of goods. O'Brien, however, now saw this process as an end in itself.

Two other interpretations of the innovations in O'Brien's ideas in this period also require revision, particularly since these reflect a

---

[40] *Pioneer*, no. 39 (31 May 1834), 377–8; no. 40 (7 June 1834), 385–6; *PMG*, no. 158 (14 June 1834), 145–6; no. 168 (23 August 1834), 227. There is a very detailed analysis of this debate in Oliver's 'Organisations', chapters 23–24, which does not, however, suggest that it produced any change in O'Brien's later preference for direct democracy by the whole people. See *Buonarroti's History of Babeuf's Conspiracy*, pp. 213–14n, where O'Brien wrote that parliament should be abolished altogether, and the approval of the entire population solicited for the passage of every law.

common view of the presumed unification of working class social and political radicalism during this period. Clearly, it is mistaken to argue, as Oliver has done, that 'the key-note of co-operation used as a theory of revolution [was that] political tyranny and economic injustice became a single social phenomenon'. This was equally true in the radical analysis generally, where taxation was accounted the cause of economic malaise. Individual employers were sometimes criticised by radicals for being 'unjust', but their policies were not believed responsible for a decline in the standard of living, which was attributed instead to governmental expenses. Such burdens were imposed because the government did not represent the people. Its tyranny therefore lay both in its refusal to permit such representation, and in maintaining parasitical dependents at the expense of the rest of the population.[41]

Equally misleading is the common view – here quoted from Theodore Rothstein – that O'Brien was probably the first to articulate 'the conception of Government as the executive committee and watchman of the interests of the ruling classes', and that he consequently saw political activity as substantially a function of economic interests. That O'Brien held such a notion is correct, though, expressed so vaguely, so had virtually all previous radicals as well as most Owenites. A more precise, related error is made in imputing to O'Brien the belief that government was exclusively in the hands of the *'bourgeoisie'*. Setting aside the obvious objection to anachronism, since this term had not yet entered into British radical discourse, we can see that O'Brien's emphasis upon the need to nationalise the land *as well as* to introduce 'equitable exchanges' meant that while he did assert that the government after 1832 was largely in the hands of the middle classes, he had by no means adopted an exclusively two-class, bourgeoisie-versus-proletariat model of either economic exploitation or political oppression. The real cause of distress for O'Brien was *'the robbery of the productive classes by the upper and middle classes through the medium of rents, tithes, profits, and the like impositions'*. He did not believe that only the middle classes were the 'possessing classes', as Rothstein assumed. Had he done so, the entire framework of his analyses and proposed reforms would have been quite different. Instead of juxtaposing bourgeoisie and proletariat, his theory evolved from the Owenite distinction between productive and unproductive labour, which counted both agricultural labour among the oppressed, and landlords among the oppressors. Although O'Brien's recognition of widespread abstraction through manufacturing profits did much to alert a new generation of radicals to this process, we should avoid once again too

41 Oliver, 'Organisations', p. 73.

teleological a treatment of this development. The aristocracy retained tremendous economic as well as social power after 1832, as O'Brien was well aware.[42]

Union without politics: the Grand National Consolidated Trades' Union and radicalism, 1833–34

Disgust with the meagre fruits of immense political exertions did not dampen the desire for reform after 1832. For the next several years, the trades' union, co-operative, radical reform and Owenite movements intermingled and discussed common strategies to a greater degree than they would throughout most of the rest of the nineteenth century. Extensive debates now occurred about the relevance of co-operation to democratic processes and trades' unions, and the relationship of all of these to government and parliament. Many GNCTU leaders rejected the primacy of the political reform movement, and argued for the extension of union organisation towards a national regulation of trades. Without recapitulating the brief history of the GNCTU as a whole, we must now consider in greater detail how far these 'syndicalist' ideas, as they have often been termed, owed something to Owenite views of politics, and what this implied for their significance.[43]

It is well known that much of the enthusiasm which fuelled the GNCTU resulted from the sense of failure after 1832. As Richard Carlile commented, 'One of the consequences of the disgust created by the present Parliament has been the wonderful formation of Trades' Unions'. For the same reasons, the latter also drew sustenance from the collapse of the political unions, which after two years of virtually continuous agitation (as R. E. Lee reminded O'Brien in late 1833) had failed to gain universal suffrage. This was widely blamed upon middle

[42] Theodore Rothstein, *From Chartism to Labourism*, pp. 107–15; *PMG*, 2, no. 123 (12 October 1833), 327; 3, no. 146 (22 March 1834), 49–50; no. 155 (24 May 1834), 123; 4, no. 230 (31 October 1835), 722.

[43] On the GNCTU generally see W. H. Oliver, 'The Consolidated Trades' Union of 1834', *EconHR*, ser. 2, 17 (1965), 77–95, as well as the earlier accounts in Raymond Postgate, *The Builders' History* (Labour Publishing Co., 1923), pp. 93–111, and G. D. H. Cole, *Attempts at a General Union. A Study in British Trade Union History, 1818–1834* (Macmillan, 1953), pp. 90–154. On the decline of the union see also J. Marlow, *The Tolpuddle Martyrs* (Panther, 1974). The question of Owen and Owenism's influence on the political ideas of the unionists is quite separate from that of Owen's general influence in guiding the union, which has been quite justifiably de-emphasised in recent accounts. Contemporary support for this is given in *WP*, no. 58 (1834), 665, where Owen's theoretical emphases were condemned at a builders' meeting. A corrective account of Owen's influence is offered in Iorwerth Prothero's 'London Working Class Movements, 1825–1848', Ph.D., University of Cambridge (1966), p. 153, and R. G. Kirby and A. E. Musson, *The Voice of the People: John Doherty, 1798–1854* (Manchester, Manchester University Press, 1975), pp. 320–1.

class betrayal. Trades' unionists were therefore quick to indicate that an important difference between the two forms of organisation was that 'Political unions were composed of various classes in society, but the Trades' Unions are composed of the working people only'. For these and other reasons, then, the strategy of the GNCTU was explicitly anti-political. In keeping with trades' union traditions, political debate was generally excluded from its proceedings; one unionist boasted, for example, that 'politics, that care-worm of the heart, never yet lurked into our lodges'. The abjuring of politics extended even to the avoidance of certain terms when describing union activities. One member, for example, urged that the use of words such as 'convention' should be avoided, since they insinuated 'politics into a system which ought to be strictly social'. This insistence upon the need for internal harmony also took other forms. The 'Derby Union Song', for example, encouraged such sentiments: 'Both Whig and Tory I now curse / Because they both curse me / Their blest amendments make me worse; with them I can't agree / All party factions I resign / With all their roughish pelf / In Union sweet I'll now combine, / and so protect myself'.[44]

Clearly the anti-political bias of the unionists helped to make Owenism attractive to them, and vice-versa. But while this may in some respects have been necessary, it was hardly a sufficient precondition for the extraordinary, even revolutionary doctrines espoused jointly by James Morrison and J. E. Smith in the well-known letters on 'Associated Labour' written in the *Pioneer* under the pseudonym of 'Senex'. In some respects, in fact, the Senex letters directly contravened the previous spirit of union management. Their main aim was to set forth an analysis of the existing social structure and its weaknesses, explaining that 'hireling labour' employed by the capitalist had succeeded systems of 'enslaved, or compulsory labour', but could now, through 'associated labour', secure to all a fair share of their labour and abolish competition. This was to be accomplished by the trades' unions forming large 'partnership manufactories' and trading amongst themselves 'upon a pure republican principle'. Pressure was to be exerted to help ensure the election of a Commons favourable to the interests of the productive classes. But the franchise would be useful only when labour was independent. In the meantime, the industrial and agricultural management of the nation could be accomplished by the election of a 'House of Trades' representing all unions at a national level. These proposals, as Oliver has rightly indicated, were not 'anti-political' except in a very limited sense, for the scheme of representation by trades was presumed to be one of universal suffrage, and the

---

[44] *Gauntlet* (March 1834), iii; *Man*, no. 23 (15 December 1833), 180; *Destructive*, no. 65 (26 April 1834), 93; *Pioneer*, no. 28 (15 March 1834), 247; no. 23 (8 February 1834), 194.

ultimate capture of parliamentary power was still an expressed goal.[45]

Morrison's defence of this plan did, however, clearly echo Owenite complaints about the insufficient education of the working classes given the need for responsible use of the parliamentary ballot. Rather than asking, as the 'old republicans' did, that the suffrage 'be granted to our humiliating and degrading intercession, or petition, or extorted by our thundering or blustering threats', Morrison thought it better that the people 'begin and serve apprenticeship of Trades' Union, in order to qualify themselves for action'. This was a 'noble and independent manner' of gaining the suffrage markedly superior to the radicals' 'fawning, crouching, humbling, petitioning, and praying'. Most importantly, a central element of the preparatory, union exercise of the suffrage was that it educated the worker in participation, 'training men by practice as well as mere theory'. It recognised that political wisdom required a gradual and extensive process of both experience and education. By contrast the national, republican ideal, involving 'mere theory only', was

a system which involves the mind of the working man in all the mazes of political economy, without giving him an opportunity of exerting his bodily activity in the management of that productive industry which is the basis of all national wealth ... By teaching him at first to direct his attention to general politics his mind is bewildered in that unbounded field, where the greatest minds have lost their way, and ruined the country. But by directing each trade to its particular department, we adopt the system of the *division of labour*, and have some assurance that the affairs of each will be conducted well; and if each trade is well conducted, there can be little danger of the whole.

This striking contrast of views revealed another highly important distinction between the unionist and republican approaches. This related to the commercial policies of both systems, and their associated ideas of work and expertise. The republicans, Morrison asserted, were prone to 'despise the system of the division of labour: they would set one man to the making of a pin, which would cost him perhaps a week to accomplish'. The unionists, however, 'would divide the labour among many, and produce the article by hundreds in an hour'. The unionist system was thus, 'the system of the division of labour brought to bear upon the great field of social policy', while 'the old republican system is the old-fashioned Jack-of-all-trades' system, which would make every man Jack-of-all-trades and master of none'. This view of the republican attitude towards the division of labour, while something of a caricature by the 1830s, is nonetheless still revealing in

[45] *Pioneer*, no. 28 (15 March 1834), 243; no. 29 (22 March 1834), 259; no. 31 (5 April 1834), 283; no. 37 (17 May 1834), 354; no. 38 (24 May 1834), 363; no. 40 (7 June 1834), 388; Oliver, 'Organisations', pp. 431–2, and 'The Consolidated Trades' Union of 1834', 91–4.

demonstrating the distance between some kinds of radicalism and trades' unionism. It also indicates that for Morrison, and probably many others, no conflict was perceived between maintaining a relatively narrow division of labour while adopting elements of Owen's system. As with co-operation in the mid-1820s and later, thus, this type of socialism accepted the jurisprudential, political economic defence of dependency and the division of labour. It did not aim at a more republican, much less a millenarian republican, unified personality in which independence was the supreme value. Here it was the co-operative system rather than Owen's ultimate goals which thus found favour amongst the working classes.[46]

Despite Oliver's contention to the contrary, Owen did profoundly influence Morrison's political ideas in a more institutional respect.[47] The notion of the 'House of Trades', first used by Smith in April 1834 and by Morrison in May,[48] in my view is taken directly from the plan for the extension of the union on a national basis publicised widely the previous autumn by Owen. This scheme clearly shows how far Owen was prepared to admit the principle of representative democracy into the process of production. Owen's plan was that the union branches

would form themselves into two lines of parochial, country, and provincial lodges; the first consisting of parochial lodges of builders, shoemakers, tailors, etc etc, respectively appointing a delegate to represent them in the provincial lodge (of which there will be four). The second line of lodges will consist of the united trades formed into provincial, county, and parochial lodges, as with those of the respective trades, whose business it will be to superintend the interests of the various workmen in their respective communities ... The superintendents, who will supply the place of masters, will be men elected for their skill and integrity.[49]

---

[46] *Pioneer*, no. 39 (31 May 1834), 378. Morrison described Owen as being on 'the *extreme left*, both in theology and politics', because he had 'put a decided negative upon the hopes which religion inspires, and represented the whole of the human race as capable of being moulded by education after any model', adding that 'these are the only two points upon which we are disposed to differ with our amiable friend'. He doubted that sectarian education could be overcome as easily as Owen believed, however, and argued that 'any plan for the formation of human character is impracticable, until unanimity of opinion upon moral and religious subjects be created in the public mind' (*ibid.*, no. 40, 7 June 1834, 394–5). On Morrison generally see John Sever, *James Morrison of the 'Pioneer'. Notes on His Life and Background* (Typescript, Cambridge University Library, 1963).

[47] Oliver's view on this question is somewhat unclear, however, since he argues that Morrison's notions of class and political organisation 'can hardly be considered Owenite except in origin' ('The Consolidated Trades' Union', 93).

[48] *Crisis*, 4, no. 1 (12 April 1834), 2; *Pioneer*, no. 39 (31 May 1834), 377–9. Smith anticipated this notion as early as February; see the *Crisis*, 3, no. 26 (22 February 1834), 214. But Owen's plan was published in the previous October.

[49] *Man*, no. 14 (13 October 1833), 108. Oliver states only that the idea of a 'House of Trades' 'really arises inevitably from a plan for universal co-operative production. There need be no other ancestry' ('Organisations', p. 430).

Here Owen advocated an ascending series of councils, in which *all* delegates and officials were to be selected by ballot, a remarkable concession on his part to the prejudices of the old immoral world. His proposal that masters be replaced by elected superintendents was also a far more radical suggestion than virtually any unionists had countenanced to date. Such proposals make it difficult to assume that the effect of Owenism upon the GNCTU was to inhibit the growth of class consciousness, as is often assumed, unless we take an overly constricted definition of this term and assume it to entail only the belief in the necessity for the violent overthrow of existing inequalities. Owen's notion was in fact extremely close to the idea of extra-parliamentary 'workers' control' of the means of production usually associated with the term 'syndicalism', which Oliver has refused to apply to the GNCTU on the basis of insufficient evidence.[50]

This misconception stems from a neglect of Owen's early plans and overemphasis on his later, frequently cited opinion that a union of both masters and men based upon their fundamental identity of interests was required. This view has led to some wildly mistaken assertions about Owen's ultimate intentions. Yet there was no contradiction between Owen's initial proposals and the unionist idea, expressed against O'Brien, that the GNCTU could provide annual parliaments, universal suffrage, no property qualifications, and the like.[51] It is certainly true that Owen encouraged a prototype of the 'unity' form of government in the proceedings of the GNCTU. As early as May 1833 he proposed that the branches of the National Equitable Labour Exchange renounce 'all law proceedings in our transactions with each other' by forming 'arrangements to adjust whatever differences may arise between individuals, or associations of individuals, by the decision of three persons selected for their superior knowledge and experience in the new principles, and their known love of justice; these individuals to be annually chosen by the elders of their district'. This

---

[50] M. J. Haynes, 'Class and Class Conflict in the Early Nineteenth Century: Northampton Shoemakers and the Grand National Consolidated Trades' Union', *LH*, 5 (1977), 90; Oliver, 'Organisations', p. 431. Owen himself wrote to Henry Brougham that he had joined the union to 'if possible prevent that collision between the very rich and the very poor, which the gross errors of the present system have rendered next to being unavoidable' (Brougham Collection, University of London, 14065, c. May 1834). 'Functional state' is Oliver's description of plans for the GNCTU. Morrison's view that government must be composed of men who either laboured or had laboured was also virtually identical with Owen's, as we have seen. See the *Pioneer*, no. 17 (28 December 1833), 129. On the evolution of the idea of extra-parliamentary working class political organisations in this period see T. M. Parsinnen, 'Association, Convention and Anti-Parliament in British Radical Politics, 1771–1848', *EHR*, 88 (1973), 504–33.

[51] *Man*, no. 24 (22 December 1833), 191–2.

plan, derived, as we have seen and Owen acknowledged, from the Quakers, was suggested later to the GNCTU. Each local trades' union was also urged by Owen to 'let the men best qualified to give the cause their effectual assistance, be sought out, and let the others give them their entire confidence.'[52]

The more influence Owen gained in the GNCTU, in fact, the further his sentiments on 'kind feelings', 'charity', and the reconciliation of employers and employed were extended. But even in June 1834, he still insisted that 'the system of masters and servants must be super- seded', and that the object of the union was not to create new masters but to abolish their class entirely, as well as to end all poverty and warfare. An inclination to see Morrison's conception of the class struggle as a 'notable advance . . . on Owen's purely persuasive, ex- clusively rationalist, prescription for change' should not be allowed to obscure other aspects of Owen's contribution to the ideas associated with the GNCTU. Even if Owen never explicitly said that the union was to replace parliament, his position was nonetheless much closer to this (considering that he regarded the organisation of production as the chief task of government, next to education), and much more egalitarian, than historians have hitherto indicated.[53]

The political odyssey of James Elishama Smith

The case of James Elishama Smith, Owen's editor at the *Crisis*, is slightly different from that of Morrison. Many striking elements in Smith's early views could easily have been derived, or differ very little from, those of Owen. Smith asserted, for example, that 'neither mon- archy, aristocracy, nor democracy, is practicable. The only practicable species of government is a mixture of all three', or one which combined leadership, advisers and at least the indirect influence of the people upon both. Agreeing that it was necessary to seek universal suffrage because 'no other system is consistent with the idea of liberty', Smith nonetheless insisted that 'universal suffrage could never be of great practical utility, unless bestowed upon a well-informed and intelligent public'. Though the people might legislate well on some questions if given the opportunity (for example, on behalf of the poor), they might not on others (such as religious reform). Nor would 'universal suffrage

---

[52] *Address of Robert Owen at the National Equitable Labour Exchange* (1833); *WTS*, ns no. 36 (4 May 1834), 286; no. 31 (30 March 1834), 246, also printed in the *Destructive*, no. 67 (10 May 1834), 105–6; *Rules and Regulations of the GNCTU* (1834). A letter from 'W.L.' to the *Poor Man's Guardian* suggested that the unionists use the Quakers and Moravians as examples of care and good feeling (3, no. 156, 31 May 1834, 132).

[53] *OGTU*, no. 1 (7 June 1834), 1–2; no. 2 (15 June 1834), 14; Oliver, 'The Consolidated Trades' Union', 94.

at present produce any salutory or successful change in the fundamental principles of government'. In particular, the 'Trades' Union, or
Co-operative system' would probably 'find no place' in the discussions
and legislation of any parliament elected on the conventional 'Old
Radical' platform of universal male suffrage (influenced by Saint-Simonian as well as Owenite feminism, Smith complained that 'no one ever
proposes to give the women a vote'). A new House of Commons might
'humble the church, humble the pensioners, and reduce the burden of
taxation', therefore, but it would accomplish no more. It might fulfil
'the principal use of government', which was to provide public tranquillity. But it would not satisfy the 'higher and more important duty
than that of government', the regulation of production.[54]

Instead of plotting a radical course, Smith argued in mid-1834 that
the GNCTU should constitute itself as a 'House of Trades', with the
separate trades being equivalent to boroughs. The trades could then
supervise production, this being an area 'in which the people ought to
have some skill', and which they could 'attend without any sacrifice of
time or of interest [and] without proving detrimental to the interests of
the rest of the community: it is the people's department.' Here universal suffrage would also eventually make the working classes fit for
government generally:

> it is a suffrage which does not at first extend to the government, but merely
> confines itself within their own sphere of duty; a suffrage which gives every
> man a share in the government of his own particular trade; and in the govern-
> ment of the trades in general, but does not divert and confound his mind with
> the extraneous matters of civil politics, until he has become thoroughly versed
> in the elementary principles of discipline and good order. There is only one
> way of learning, and that is, by beginning at the elements, taking the simplest
> tasks first, and then proceeding to the most difficult . . . and what can be a more
> simple lesson in government to a tradesman than the government of his own
> trade? Let him first learn to manage his own affairs well before he attempts to
> rule the destiny of the whole country. If the people cannot rule the trades, they
> cannot rule the country at large, in which there are a thousand interests of
> which they have no idea, and of which they have never heard the names
> mentioned, nor the nature described.

In these proposals, there was little to distinguish the views of Morrison
and Smith. But the latter also attempted to extend the application of

---

[54] *Crisis*, 4, no. 7 (24 May 1834), 50. On James Elishama Smith, see also J. Knipe,
'Owenite Ideas and Institutions, 1828–1834', M.A., University of Wisconsin (1967),
pp. 135–87, D. Cook, 'Reverend James Elishama Smith: Socialist Prophet of the
Millennium', M.A., University of Iowa (1961), 148–91; Raymond Postgate, *Out of the
Past: Some Revolutionary Sketches* (New York, Vanguard Press, 1926), pp. 97–106; J. F.
C. Harrison, *Robert Owen*, pp. 109–22, and John Saville, 'J. E. Smith and the Owenite
Movement, 1833–4', in Pollard and Salt, eds., *Robert Owen*, pp. 115–44.

Owenism to trades' union organisation in a direction unexplored by Morrison. For the trades themselves, Smith suggested, might well assume not only the regulation of production, but also the supervision of morality and public order. This was a function which in Owenism had been previously restricted to communities. Smith now allowed, however, not only that each trade might become 'a species of police', but that this was 'the only system of police which is practicable'. Thus 'Each union, each trade would ... know all its own members, their character, their employment, their place of residence; so that every man who could not give an account of himself, would be regarded as a suspicious character. It is the most perfect system of government which can be adopted.'[55]

Smith's equation of private property with 'private government' and public property with 'public government' at this time also doubtless met with both Morrison's and Owen's approval.[56] But whatever identity of opinions Smith shared with Morrison in the 'Senex' letters, he had by mid-1834 moved towards a new position which, in its strong emphasis upon the necessity of temporary dictatorship, probably derived from the ideas of the eccentric agrarian conservative James Bernard, who held Owen's attention for some time during this period.[57] Bernard was a Tory willing to provoke revolution, if need be, in order to restore the power of the landed aristocracy. He became associated with Owen in mid-1834, when Bernard's curious *Theory of the Constitution* attracted the attention of GNCTU leaders anxious to garner support for the union among agricultural labourers (for he appeared to have the backing of some farmers). Owen noted of King's, Bernard's college, that it was 'a place of all others the least likely to produce a plan for the complete reform of the evils of society', but termed Bernard 'the most learned practical man he had hitherto met with'. Enthusiastically introducing him to his circle of London acquaintances, Owen informed his friend Henry Brougham that Bernard's work was 'full of startling matter of the highest import'. The initial appeal of Bernard's *Constitution* to Owen probably lay in its vehement attack upon the manufacturing and commercial middle classes. Much of the work concerned the historical decline of the monarchy, territorial aristocracy and system of agricultural preference. But Bernard did not seek simply to restore the monarchy to its former glory. He admitted, in fact, that as a mode of rule it was 'full of anomalies' and 'a very bungling and imperfect contrivance for ruling mankind'. What he proposed, there-

[55] *Ibid.*, no. 1 (12 April 1834), 1. [56] *Ibid.*, no. 2 (19 April 1834), 11.

[57] *Crisis*, 4, no. 13 (5 July 1834), 97. On Smith's hostility to Owen in this period see W. A. Smith, *'Shepherd' Smith the Universalist* (Sampson Low and Co., 1892), p. 104. A Saint-Simonian element is probable in Smith's emphasis on the need to maintain hierarchy, though Owen did not oppose hierarchy in principle either.

fore, was an elective monarchy which would represent the true national interest. Since the aristocracy, parliament and the press were all devoted to the cause of money, moreover, such a reform would have to commence with the working people. These were to be led, however, by a great leader 'possessed of powers sufficient to enforce his decrees', and modelled on Cromwell, Napoleon and Julius Caesar. Since these were all dead, Bernard offered his own services to the cause, while Owen called for a 'Moral Napoleon . . . to effect what the physical Napoleon failed to accomplish', also doubtless hoping to cast himself in the role.[58]

These proposals were fairly intensively discussed by Owen and Smith in 1834 and 1835. The *Official Gazette of the Trades' Unions* of the GNCTU as well as early issues of the *New Moral World* serialised unpublished chapters from the second volume of Bernard's *Theory*, which expanded upon his political plans. He now denied that he sought universal suffrage, not as a matter of principle, but because 'the certain effect of any scheme for vesting government in the hands of a numerical majority of the people' was always the reverse of that intended, and would 'put the government into the virtual possession of those very classes who are ever found to be their greatest enemies'. In Britain, this meant that the entire working population would 'gradually come to be infected with doctrines that are favourable to the commercial and monied classes.' Accordingly, landowners worth £100–£150 annually and some house owners would possess the franchise, with twice as many MPs coming from counties as towns. But since the working classes could not be depended upon to vote independently of the shopkeepers, Bernard reasoned, town elections could even be put 'directly into the hands' of the latter, 'to be managed as they like best'. Local government was also to be reorganised, with censors now being elected in each county with a rank equal to lord lieutenant, and with powers to search out all offences against public morality. In the House of Lords, moreover, peerages were to be normally limited to life, and forfeited for gambling, evading payment of debts, or advocating trading, commercial or democratic privileges.[59]

What Owen and Smith probably found most interesting about the

[58] *Crisis*, 4, no. 16 (26 July 1834), 123–4; Brougham Collection, University College, London, 43454, Owen to Brougham, 19 July 1834; James Bernard, *A Theory of the Constitution* (1834), pp. 198–9, 510–11, 506–9, 140; Brougham Collection, 17868, Owen to Brougham, 18 March 1835. For further details see my 'James B. Bernard'. A similar scheme for the alliance of the landed and working classes had earlier been proposed by George Mudie. See *AWC*, no. 4 (17 March 1827), 79.

[59] *NMW*, 1, no. 13 (24 January 1835), 103–4; no. 15 (7 February 1835), 118–20; no. 16 (14 February 1835), 126–8; no. 17 (21 February 1835), 135–6; no. 19 (7 March 1835), 150–2; no. 20 (14 March 1835), 158–60; no. 22 (28 March 1835), 174–6.

political elements in Bernard's plans was their attempt to unite the principles of monarchy, aristocracy and democracy. Smith in particular supported Bernard's call for a temporary dictatorship, and accepted the idea that an elective king or queen was the 'perfect monarchy'. Pure democracy, he agreed, was impossible; 'the people, without a leader', were 'like particles of dust in a whirlwind'. The best system of government would thus unite 'the popularity and justice of the Radical system with the subordination, regularity and determination of the system of Toryism'. Only a democratic monarchy could accomplish this by maintaining the sovereign will of the people while concentrating all power and authority in a single individual who would legislate without the aid of any parliament. One of the Owenites' greatest faults, Smith said, was that they had not recognised the need for such authority, and had indeed tried to reject it.[60]

Smith's views on political matters in the years following his break with Owen in 1834 demonstrate a working out of these problems, and a reconsideration of what he regarded as the failure of Owen's political ideas. Many of Smith's reflections in this regard concern the principle of authority and the need for hierarchy. By comparison with the Owenites, he had earlier remarked, the Saint-Simonians had sought the same co-operative end, 'only it has assumed with them a monarchical or hierarchical, but with us a republican aspect; there all the difference lies. They have a visible head or father, a sort of pope; we have '*no head*' at all, and are determined to live without one; each man with us has a head of his own'. The trend towards democracy increasingly dismayed Smith, and clearly helped to drive him towards Bernard. It also led him to evolve a new theory about the relations between theology and politics, whose application to Owenism is in some respects quite revealing, since it suggests another possible source of Owenite egalitarianism. 'Atheism', for example, by which Smith clearly meant Owenism, corresponded to 'mere republicanism or democracy, without the principle of monarchy to control and give unity of design ... The atheist has no supreme ruler at all; he has formed all nature into a pure republic, and refused to admit even of an elective presidency'. Now it was necessary, Smith insisted, to reorganise society such that the principles of both 'individual supremacy' and 'universal sovereignty' triumphed. This could be accomplished by abolishing parliament and electing a king and council directly. The 'useful trades', moreover, could be reorganised on the same lines, although the 'fine arts' were to be 'purely atheistic and democratic'. For while all the necessary arts were social and co-operative, the imagi-

---

[60] *Shepherd*, 1, no. 16 (13 December 1834), 121–2; no. 17 (20 December 1834), 129–30; no. 43 (20 June 1835), 344; 3, no. 2 (8 July 1837), 19; no. 4 (22 July 1837), 25–7.

native arts were unsocial and individualistic. Smith therefore termed his new scheme 'THE SOCIAL AND ANTISOCIAL SYSTEM'.[61]

By the end of late 1834, Smith also became increasingly convinced that a central flaw in Owenism was its insufficent attention to the individual. Owenism had failed, he stressed in early 1835, to realise that 'Individualism, or the love of self' was 'the first movement of Nature; and the extreme limit of its progress outward is universalism, or the love of all . . . Self-love and social love therefore are one and the same thing, when under the influence of an enlightened mind.' In order to reconcile these two great principles, therefore, and to eradicate this error in socialism, Smith now proposed a system termed 'political universalism'. This would eliminate that type of individualism which permitted virtually complete freedom of action, and failed to teach any to consider themselves as 'servants of the public'. Such extreme individualism had resulted in the fact that the population was divided into slaves and tyrants, the latter being the possessors of land or moveable property prohibited to the use of the rest. 'True liberty', Smith insisted instead, was 'that state of refined sensibility in which the will of individual selfishness becomes identified with the love of our neighbour'. At present, there was thus 'too much liberty . . . the moral tie that ought to bind together . . . is not sufficiently strong, and on that account we are obliged to employ a substitute for the moral law, namely the law of the magistrate and the police-officer, to supply its place'. Nonetheless, the final antinomian utopia would never be reached:

The moral law is the goal to which society is progressing. The perfection of society consists in a complete abandonment of the political or magisterial law. But perfection is unattainable: it can only be held up as a model for our imitation, a standard for estimating the degree of progress to which we have attained.

'Political universalism' would therefore represent a far more perfect system of social control and mutual police, because it would virtually eliminate the possibility of criminality, not by making each a law unto himself or herself, but by ensuring a system of adequate moral supervision. Here, once again, the proximity of militant dissent and a relatively complete system of social regulation is evident:

It is necessary to number the people, to gather them into tribes like the children of Israel, according to their respective modes of life, and to keep an exact register of all their names, so that no man shall be lost in society; no man be without a tribe, without a class, without a department of industry, in which his character is known, and to which he is ever responsible for the employment of

---

[61] *Crisis*, 3, no. 12 (16 November 1833), 92–3; *Shepherd*, 1, no. 16 (13 December 1834), 121; no. 17 (20 December 1834), 129–30.

his time. But by this registry he loses his liberty; he is no more his own master, to roam abroad over hill and dale, through cities and towns, to haunt the lurking-places of depravity, and plunder unseen the produce of industry. He can no longer act the part of an impostor; for in every town, every city which he frequents, his name and character is as well known as it is in his native village. He can only travel as an honest man; disguise must be attended with immediate detection and infamy.

Smith confessed that this system, in which passports would be required to travel anywhere (a similar scheme had been proposed by the magistrate Henry Fielding in 1753), was indeed a 'moral inquisition'. But such an intensified scheme of moral police was not meant to produce more forceful coercion. In cases where 'the behaviour of tradesman to tradesman, or merchant to merchant, and of each to the public in general would be strictly scrutinised' (that he chose such examples is important), and acts of turpitude detected, 'no other punishment would be required than merely publication of the evidence in the public journals. The moral law requires no more. It lets the prisoner loose upon society ... which must, as it improves, become more and more a prison to the detected scoundrel.'[62] In reality, therefore, this was to be the communitarian system extended, as Owen never assumed could be done, on a national scale. Existing towns and cities would be retained, but the communitarian ideal of regulation by moral coercion would be greatly broadened in its scope. Smith's was the only real effort ever made to expand Owen's ideas in this way by envisioning the nation governed like a sect of godly believers. What brings it close to more modern versions of authoritarian socialism, clearly, are the mechanisms of control required, because the scope was now the nation rather than the community. But even here, of course, there is no indication that Smith thought that physical coercion would play any significant role in such a system. In this sense his model remained religious rather than political.

It is not surprising, then, to find Smith in this period also calling for a return to a more spiritual notion of government. The Owenites and infidels, he complained in 1837, sought to do without authority generally. But he now acknowledged the divine authority of Moses and Christ, seeking to build upon this and 'employ the authority' they provided. Smith still insisted, too, that a single leader was necessary, claiming that the Owenites might unite with the Hicksites, the rapidly-spreading American Quaker followers of Elias Hicks, who could together form 'The Church universal, represented by an individual, selected for the office by the general will, and possessing in that capacity, divine authority, in every thing he does, by the expressed or

---

[62] *Ibid.*, no. 33 (11 April 1835), 257; no. 34 (18 April 1835), 265–6.

tacit consent of the Church'. Shortly after this, too, Smith concluded that 'The State must finally become a Church, and the Church a state, and this takes place when ever the State becomes a moral, instead of a political, government'. In this event, taxes having been abolished, 'the legislative council shall be exclusively employed in devising means for moralizing the people, teaching them, directing them, counselling them, kindly entreating them, and never offending them because never taking a penny from them'. Smith's later emphasis was thus more upon paternal care than the gradual elevation of the working classes. A decade later, he had lost virtually all influence in the socialist movement, but was still warning against 'carrying liberty to a vicious excess', and invoking the patriarchal principle of supervision or pastoral care to balance the existing system.[63]

The experience of the GNCTU thus provoked considerable reflection by Owen and his close associates on alternative forms of democracy. In these years, the general trend of Owen's own thinking on government was much closer to that of Smith and Morrison, and theirs to him, than has been assumed. Owen did not of course condone a class struggle of operatives against masters, but continuously hastened to instil that 'spirit of peace and charity by which alone the regeneration of mankind can ever be effected'.[64] This was consistent with his lifelong outlook, as was his attempt to mix electoral democracy with Quaker modes of administrative conduct. But Owen's proposal that the Union take over guidance of the entire process of production was not inconsistent with his economic theory, nor was his attempt to eliminate masters entirely incommensurate with his earlier views. Owen did hope in this period for the widespread extension of representative democracy into institutions in which such practices had never been applied, and this, for the history of socialism, is ultimately the most significant aspect of the GNCTU. But Owen, of course, also regarded such solutions as merely temporary, which others of his associates at this time clearly did not. For them, Owen's ideas had helped inspire an entirely new conception of trades' union organisation which was in some respects far more radical than, and certainly dramatically different from, anything that working class radicalism had ever conceived. Socialism at this point thus inspired a new conception of democracy altogether, which was to prove of enormous importance in the future.

However, the GNCTU was a relatively brief if exhilarating moment in the chronicle of Owenism. By 1835 Owen had already laid the foundations for a new organisation which proved to be the most

---

[63] *Shepherd*, 3, no. 4 (22 July 1837), 26; no. 25 (16 December 1837), 193; *FH*, 5 (1847), 347–8, and 6 (1848–9), 11–12.
[64] *Pioneer*, no. 19 (11 January 1834), 149.

powerful and long-lasting of any of the manifestations of early socialism. Within a year after the demise of the union, the first stirrings of
Chartism were also evident. From the failure of social reform, once
again, sprang an interest in politics. Let us now turn, then, to the
complex and often unhappy relationship between these two
movements.

6

Owenism and Chartism, 1836–45

Any study of the relations between Owenism and Chartism is hampered by a variety of obstacles. Though easily susceptible to caricature, neither movement, in fact, was monolithic. Each spanned a considerable range of activities and embraced a broad spectrum of opinion. This was particularly true for the social and political theories debated within each camp. Though two ideals marked the extremity of views dividing the two groups – anti-Chartist Owenism on the one hand, 'purely political' Chartism on the other – the region between these incorporated a considerable range of political ideals, including various forms of liberalism and tory radicalism. Formidable historiographical gaps nonetheless inhibit our sense of the subtlety of opinion expressed in both movements. Given the absence of local studies of Owenism in particular, it is extremely difficult to offer an adequate taxonomy of variations in opinion, much less, among the shifting sands of popular participation on both sides, to account adequately for the processes underlying their origins and development. For despite the inspiring work of J. F. C. Harrison, Owenite studies remain far less developed than was the historiography of Chartism prior to Asa Briggs' edition of *Chartist Studies* (1962), which disclosed the rich variety of Chartist phenomena made accessible by detailed local studies. This has been succeeded in the last quarter century by a shelfload of excellent biographies, further local studies, general overviews of the subject, and methodological reconsiderations. These have shed very little light upon Chartist–Owenite relations in particular. But they have ensured that Chartism remains one of the best studied – and controversial – areas of British labour history.

Owenism, by contrast, has virtually no good biographies on anyone other than Owen and Thompson upon which to draw, and has generated too little theoretical controversy from which to commence a debate similar to that in Chartist historiography about its character as a social and intellectual movement in the late 1830s and 1840s. Given its considerable strength at the end of the 1830s, its momentous exertions as a propaganda machine, and the recognised participation of a number of Chartist leaders in communitarianism or co-operation, such omissions are surprising. But there are still further barriers to any rectification of this state of affairs. Matters are complicated by the fact that the leading journals of both the political and social reformers cannot be trusted to have reported accurately their own members' opinions on the other movement, or on dissident tendencies within their own. Moreover, much of the remaining evidence is scattered, piecemeal, and often suggestive rather than corroboratory.

Such limitations considerably circumscribe the nature of the conclusions we can draw about a relationship which was, in fact, of much greater importance to Owenism and Chartism alike than has been previously assumed. My aim here is accordingly limited to delineating the range of contacts between Owenites and Chartists before 1846, ascertaining the issues which divided them, examining how a few individuals – such as the socialist lecturer James Napier Bailey – sought to unite Chartist and Owenite convictions in a single programme, and analysing the resurgence of democratic Owenism over the Queenwood issue. No attempt will be made here to tackle fully the complex question of the 'social' character of Chartism, the affinity between its class bases and its ideologies, and the relation between economic and political arguments among the various sections of the movement and between individual Chartists, though many aspects of these issues will be touched upon tangentially.[1] Nor will the more specific problem of the 'socialist' character of Chartism be explored here, though the following chapter will consider this with respect to the 1846–52 period. However, it is still necessary to examine briefly how the intersection of 'Socialism' (which term, capitalised, will from here on be used to designate the organised Owenite movement, following contemporary usage) and Chartism has been approached previously by historians in order to clarify the types of questions which such an inquiry must broach.

Considering the enduring popularity of Chartism, and the socialist sympathies of many of its chroniclers, it is surprising how tangentially and unsystematically the Chartist–Owenite relationship has been treated. In 1854, the first historian of Chartism, R. G. Gammage, though aligned with O'Brien (whose writings he held to have 'laid the

---

[1] See in particular Gareth Stedman Jones, 'Rethinking Chartism', in *Languages of Class*, pp. 90–178.

foundations' for Chartism), had nothing specific to say about the Socialists, except in relation to the post-1848 socialistic programme. Writing somewhat later, Henry Solly observed only that the Socialists generally were somewhat conservative in their politics. Opposing Frank Podmore in 1908, however, Joseph McCabe found that most of Owen's followers 'were not at all indifferent' to the Chartists, but fraternised with them everywhere, a verdict virtually ignored thereafter. Writing in 1916, Frank Rosenblatt deduced that 'unlike most of his Chartist colleagues' Feargus O'Connor was 'a strenuous opponent of the current Socialist theories' – that is, communism. In the same year, Preston Slosson concluded that while all of the Chartist leaders wanted a greater distribution of property, few sought a socialistic programme. Shortly afterwards, Mark Hovell distinguished between a few Chartists who were 'downright Socialists', and the majority who disregarded Owen because of his communism. In 1920, Julius West made one of the strongest claims on this issue, calling the Chartists 'permeated with Socialist ideas' because of their commitment to state interference in the economy. Refining such suggestions, Theodore Rothstein soon after juxtaposed O'Brien's socialism, which he described as having laid the foundations for proletarian socialism, and Owenism, which was characterised as having opposed Chartism.[2]

Postwar historians have been more concerned with extending the social history of Chartism, or examining selected aspects of the movement, than offering broad generalisations on this question. Cumulatively this has provided a much more fragmented picture of Chartism as a whole than existed earlier. But there has also been some reaction against interpretations which argued in favour of a fairly extensive impact of Socialism upon the Charter agitation, notably by J. T. Ward ('Socialist theories never influenced O'Connor – or most of his followers') and Alexander Wilson. Asa Briggs, too, has inferred that 'Socialists of the Owenite variety often had no more sympathy with Chartism than Owen himself'. David Jones has summarised these developments in terms of an overreaction against those earlier historians who sought to draw a firm connection between the two

[2] R. G. Gammage, *History of the Chartist Movement* (1854), p. 76; Henry Solly, *James Woodford, Carpenter and Chartist* (1881), 1, p. 21; J. McCabe, *Life and Letters of G. J. Holyoake* (Watts and Co., 1908), 1, p. 47; Frank Rosenblatt, *The Chartist Movement in its Social and Economic Aspects* (New York, Columbia University Press, 1916), p. 109; Preston Slosson, *The Decline of the Chartist Movement* (New York, Columbia University Press, 1916), p. 31; Mark Hovell, *The Chartist Movement* (3rd edn., Manchester, Manchester University Press, 1966), p. 32; Julius West, *A History of the Chartist Movement* (Constable, 1920), p. 176; T. Rothstein, *From Chartism to Labourism*, pp. 35–7.

movements. R. G. Garnett, however, has claimed that many Chartists accepted Owenite social criticisms while rejecting the more eccentric socialist dogmas.[3]

A number of studies have augmented our knowledge of the local connections between Owenites and Chartists. Examining Scottish Chartism, Alexander Wilson has noted the existence of a Chartist co-operative shop which appears to have been Socialist, while Leslie Wright has emphasised Owenism's 'strong Scottish connections' and the presence of several excellent Owenite lecturers touring in Scotland. Peter Searby has alluded to links between both movements in Coventry, as has John Foster in relation to Oldham. J. F. C. Harrison unearthed several individuals in Leicester who were both Chartists and Owenites, and has confirmed the leading roles played by Joshua Hobson and J. F. Bray in both movements. Ray Boston discovered at least one American emigré who had been both a Chartist and an Owenite. Dwindling support for the Bradford Radical Association led to its conversion into a Socialist organisation in May 1838, according to A. J. Peacock. But a study of working class movements in Barnsley and the Black Country has concluded that no Socialist there was involved in either political or trades' union activities. An examination of Brighton Chartism has also found that the two movements kept aloof from one another for the most part. The two hundred Owenites active at Yarmouth in 1839, however, found a section of the local Chartists happy to work with them.[4] Many other local Chartist studies simply fail to mention Socialism, though no meaningful conclusion can be drawn from this omission.

[3] J. T. Ward, *Chartism* (Batsford, 1973), pp. 180, 33–4; A. Wilson, 'Chartism', in J. T. Ward, ed., *Popular Movements, c. 1830–1850* (Macmillan, 1972), pp. 124–6; Asa Briggs, 'National Bearings', in Briggs, ed., *Chartist Studies* (Macmillan, 1962), p. 295n; David Jones, *Chartism and the Chartists* (Allen Lane, 1975), pp. 27–8 (Jones' work is nonetheless virtually unique in detailing some of the debates between Chartists and Socialists and naming individuals who belonged to both camps); R. G. Garnett, *Co-operation and the Owenite Socialist Communities*, p. 143. Other post-war writers have also de-emphasised the relationship between Chartism and Socialism. See, for example, George Lichtheim, *The Origins of Socialism*, p. 138.

[4] Alexander Wilson, *The Chartist Movement in Scotland* (Manchester, Manchester University Press, 1970), p. 128; L. C. Wright, *Scottish Chartism* (Edinburgh, Oliver and Boyd, 1953), pp. 97, 132–3; Peter Searby, *Coventry Politics in the Age of the Chartists* (Historical Association, 1965), pp. 14–15; John Foster, *Class Struggle and the Industrial Revolution* (Methuen, 1974), pp. 207, 309; J. F. C. Harrison, 'Chartism in Leicester', in A. Briggs, ed., *Chartist Studies*, pp. 132, 65, 68; Ray Boston, *British Chartists in America* (Manchester, Manchester University Press, 1971), p. 18; A. J. Peacock, *Bradford Chartism, 1838–1840* (York, St. Anthony's Press, 1969), p. 15; George Barnsby, *Robert Owen and the First Socialists in the Black Country* (Wolverhampton, Integrated Publishing Services, 1984), pp. 21–2; Barnsby, 'The Dudley Working Class Movement, 1832–60', typescript, p. 10; T. M. Kemnitz, 'Chartism in Brighton', Ph.D., University of Sussex, 1969, p. 46; A. F. J. Brown, *Chartism in Essex and Suffolk* (Essex Record Office, 1982), p. 118.

Such as it is, this brief catalogue represents much of our knowledge of the social history of the connections between Owenites and Chartists. Considering the meagre historiography of Owenism, and the fact that, amidst many hundreds of thousands of Chartists, there were perhaps no more than 4,000 to 10,000 Owenites active at the height of the movement (though the rate of turnover may have been fairly high, and the diffusion of Owenite ideas was vastly more extensive), the contradictory character of the evidence is unsurprising. Given the breadth of the subject, my account here will not focus upon expanding in detail the social historical aspects of the links between the two movements. Some of these connections will be embellished in order to contextualise the arguments offered. But my concentration will be upon presenting a representative account, not an exhaustive history, of what the Owenites and Chartists said to and about one another, in debates, editorials, brief asides, in moments of anger and in a spirit of mutual conciliation. We will consider the Chartist view of Socialism first.

Chartist complaints

When the Chartist press denounced the Owenites and their views, one or more of four subjects was usually involved. The most significant of these, property, will receive the greatest attention here. The other three – the question of religion, Socialist optimism about the malleability of human nature, and attacks upon the Chartists by some Socialists – will be introduced only briefly in order to give some sense of the spectrum of disagreement between the two camps.

The subject of religious faith was, of course, one on which the Chartists were themselves divided, although efforts were clearly exerted to prevent tensions between Chartist Christianity and Chartist infidelity from splitting the political movement further.[5] That Socialism and infidelity were nearly synonymous in the public mind was stressed earlier here. This fact probably more than any other continuously impeded the popularity of the new views. Owenite blasphemy, not fear of Owenite communism, led to the debate on Socialism in the House of Lords in 1840, to the organisation of a series of anti-Socialist lectures in London and elsewhere, and to the extensive lecture tours and barrage of publications of the rabid anti-Socialist John Brindley

---

[5] On Chartism and religion see H. Faulkner, *Chartism and the Churches* (New York, Columbia University Press, 1916), and E. Yeo, 'Christianity in Chartist Struggle', *P&P*, 91 (1981), 109–39.

and his imitators. This identification must also have been made by many Chartists. It almost certainly accounts for the tory radical Joseph Rayner Stephens' expression of his 'strong feelings' against Socialism, despite his knowledge of and even liking for Owen personally (and even if Stephens himself was not precisely a supporter of the Charter, he exerted a considerable influence on the movement up to 1840). When Feargus O'Connor, too, heard someone in a crowd call him a Socialist, his first response was to turn and reply that, no, he believed in God. As editor of the *Northern Star*, Joshua Hobson (a sympathiser of Owen), knowing full well how distracting such debates could be, refused to entertain Socialist discussions of theology in the paper, and recalled that many radicals had turned against Paine on account of the latter's theological beliefs. Most Chartist leaders sought to arouse no more unproductive prejudice against the movement than necessary. It was probably chiefly because of religion that Peter McDouall (referring generally to alarming the public) argued that Chartism was more practicable than Socialism. In some of the Chartist–Socialist debates, too, the Owenite dogma of the formation of character was assailed by their Chartist opponents. At a Rochdale meeting on 1 May 1841 between the Manchester Chartist lecturer James Leach and the Liverpool Socialist Missionary William Spier, for example, Leach vowed that 'The Charter declares all beings responsible; the law of responsibility is necessary; it was asserted that the law of responsibility had produced a great amount of evil in the world; he denied it: the law of responsibility never had been carried into practice'. Whereupon the chairman of the meeting called him to order, deeming this question worthy of an entire evening's further discussion.[6]

A second line of criticism from the Chartist side was that Socialism had been tried already and found wanting, and that its impotence resulted from imperfections in human nature. Formerly an active co-operator himself, William Carpenter noted of Owen in 1840 that

---

[6] *NS*, no. 198 (28 August 1841), 4; no. 225 (5 March 1842), 6; no. 67 (23 February 1839), 7; *MCJ*, no. 22 (28 August 1841), 170–1; *NMW*, 9, no. 20 (15 May 1841), 312. See also *OF*, no. 59 (15 February 1840) 26, and the letter in *ECC*, 2, no. 56 (1842), 13–14, which accused certain 'malicious people' of trying to link Chartism with Socialism and infidelity in order to awaken religious animosities. Also in this vein see the *Champion*, no. 184 (22 March 1840), 7, where at his trial a Sheffield Chartist admitted attending some Socialist meetings but denied he was a Socialist, explaining that he had 'never said I did not believe in the Bible or Testaments. I never said I did not care a d--n for an oath'. See also *TS*, 2, no. 93 (25 July 1840), 3, on opposition to Chartist infidelity. There is some evidence that the Owenites mitigated their theological criticisms after this period, much to the chagrin of some die-hard freethinkers. See the *Beacon*, no. 2 (9 March 1844), 32, for their reaction.

'For at least a quarter of a century he has been drawing bills on futurity at short dates, which have all been dishonoured', adding that 'The Socialist Philosophers assume a power in external circumstances over humanity, which circumstances have never exercised; and a power in humanity over circumstances, which humanity has never attained.' The idea that men would be 'rational' in communities the Chartist *True Scotsman* also found wholly unconvincing. Commenting (with some regret) upon the imminent demise of Queenwood in 1845, too, the *Northern Star* remarked that 'if there be any truth in the system of the Socialists, or any chance of that system being reduced to practice, experience has proved that it can only be by committing its working to a race trained free from the prejudices and habits of the present generation', which was in most respects a polite way of asserting its impossibility.[7]

Some Chartists also grew to dislike or oppose the Socialists simply because the latter attacked them so sharply on occasion. An observer at a Manchester debate in late 1840 between representatives of the two parties found the Owenites somewhat less than charitable, and reported that

These Socialists were full of contradictions to each other, and as full of spleen, scoffs, sneers, and ridicule, as the most inveterate enemies we have to deal with; pointing to our prisons being full of Chartists, and making many scurrilous remarks on the Convention, with as much consequence and affectation as the most long-faced, oily-tongued saint we have in Christendom.

About a year later, opposition of this type was still noticeable enough to be mentioned in a general address of the Chartist Executive Council. Thomas Cooper, too, later conveyed the sense of betrayal and insult many Chartists probably felt when he recalled that the leading Leicester Socialists appeared at times to have misrepresented deliberately what took place in their discussions with the Chartists. Not only, he recollected, had the Socialists misconstrued their opponents' position, but in the case of a debate between the Socialist Missionary J. C. Farn and Bronterre O'Brien at Newcastle, they had even claimed a 'victory' over the Chartists when (according to O'Brien) in reality Farn and half a dozen of his friends had been booed, hissed and obliged to leave the platform. But the Chartist press, and particularly the *Northern Star* (as O'Brien himself knew all too well), was certainly no

---

[7] *Charter*, 2, no. 60 (15 March 1840), 16; *TS*, 2, no. 55 (2 November 1839), 3; *NS*, no. 409 (13 September 1840), 3.

more trustworthy in the matter of treating its opponents fairly.[8]

These were points which provoked tension on both sides. But with the partial exception of religion, which was of course often taken very seriously by working class radicals, nothing was more important to the problem of programmatic accommodation between the two movements than the question of property. Owen's desire for a community of goods often met with considerable scepticism in radical circles from 1817 onwards, as we have seen. Communal living in general never had much appeal to reformers of the post-Waterloo era. Nor did it to the Chartists. 'An *amiable* delusion' (in the words of the radical *Odd Fellow*) was a more generous description than that usually volunteered by the Chartist press. George Julian Harney's defence of his own conception of radicalism was probably the more common reaction to this (usually misrepresented) aspect of Owenism:

The Charter was the means to an end, the means their political rights, and the end social equality. Did he mean that they all should have their food dressed alike, their houses built in parallelograms, their coats having one uniform cut? God bless you, no such thing. He only meant that all men should have what they earned, and that the man who 'did not work, neither shall he eat' (cheers).

Specific economic arguments were also used against communities. Lovett's and Hetherington's *National Association Gazette* promoted the introduction of some modification of the co-operative principle in the production and distribution of wealth, but pointedly added that the idea 'that Home Colonies can ever entirely supersede individual competition – nay, that they themselves will ever thrive without competition – is about as rational an expectation as the advent of the millennium or the discovery of the elixir of life'. Such asides were an important measure of the distance some social radicals had travelled since the mid-1830s, though Hetherington did not stray as far afield as Lovett. Elsewhere, the stock argument which the Owenites had heard since 1820 (but which had been levelled against schemes for com-

---

[8] *NS*, no. 159 (28 November 1840), 2; *ECC*, 1, no. 46 (1841), 181; Thomas Cooper, *The Life of Thomas Cooper* (4th edn., 1883), p. 174; *Charter*, 1, no. 32 (1 September 1839), 498; *BS*, no. 27 (10 September 1842), 6. The early editors of the *Northern Star* were well known for re-writing reports in order to enhance their significance. Up to the late 1840s, certainly, it is possible that Socialist views were deliberately excluded on many occasions when they might have occurred in local reports. On this editorial policy see H. Solly, *James Woodford*, 1, pp. 146–8, *CPR*, no. 1 (19 October 1839), 9, where Carlile accused O'Connor of overestimating by tenfold the numbers at a meeting both had attended, and R. G. Gammage, *History of the Chartist Movement*, p. 17. On a case of misrepresentation of anti-Chartist views by the *New Moral World*, see the *Charter*, no. 32 (1 September 1839), 498.

munity of goods since Aristotle) was reiterated: if a common fund supplied all then any incentive to produce would be exterminated.[9]

Chartist views on property embraced a spectrum defined by the O'Brienites at one extreme, and committed economic liberals like Henry Vincent, who denied that the government had any right to interfere with commerce, on the other. Whatever the views of individual reformers, it was usually official Chartist policy to declare private property sacred and inviolable. This was established in the 29-point 'Declaration of Rights' at the 1839 Convention, and was not often publicly departed from thereafter. Even Bronterre O'Brien could recite from this platform without being entirely inconsistent, for much the same reason that Owen could: the rich would retain the entire value of what they owned because it was the *future* production of wealth which would be more fairly distributed. To some extent such affirmations were a tactical necessity, since many of the Chartists' opponents suspected that the rhetoric of political reform only masked a fervent desire to confiscate the possessions of the middle and upper classes. Hence Thomas Cooper was forced to respond to the *Morning Chronicle* that the Chartists did not support Socialist doctrines – such as a wish to distribute property and abolish middlemen and capitalists – their goal being only the Charter, with all other questions left to its successful operation. Similarly, too, the editor of the Chartist *Brighton Patriot* asserted that 'There are no politico-economical differences about the Charter. It simply proposes that the representative principle should be carried out'.[10]

Such views did not of course preclude Chartist sympathy for and experimentation with co-operation, though, as Dorothy Thompson has recently concluded, this was largely of the retail variety, and did not aim at collective control over the manufacturing process. Reducing distribution costs did not threaten to bring down the entire social edifice. Many Chartists, in fact, were probably either ignorant of, or genuinely opposed to, anything like communitarian equality. 'I never knew levelling advocated among Chartists, neither in public or private, for they did not believe in it', recalled Benjamin Wilson half a century after the movement had begun:

What they wanted was a voice in making the laws they were called upon to obey; they believed that taxation without representation was tyranny, and ought to be resisted; they took a leading part in agitating in favour of the ten hours question, the repeal of the taxes on knowledge, education, co-operation,

---

[9] *OF*, no. 60 (22 February 1840), 30; *NL*, no. 86 (8 June 1839), 4; *NAG*, no. 24 (11 June 1842), 190–1; *TS*, 1, no. 46 (31 August 1839), 361.

[10] *Nonconformist*, no. 38 (29 December 1841), 629; *ECC*, 1, no. 18 (1841), 69; no. 31 (16 June 1838), 4; *MCI*, no. 12 (1 May 1841), 46; *BP*, no. 211 (5 March 1839), 4.

civil and religious liberty, and the land question, for they were the true pioneers in all the great movements of the time.

O'Connor, too, was recognised as an opponent of equal property, although his language was frequently, and in part no doubt deliberately, imprecise. Defining justice as 'the pure source of social and political equality, not equality as to property and luxury, but equality as to their respective enjoyments' was an elusive means of satisfying demands for greater equality without appearing to be a socialist. What most radicals probably took such statements to imply, however, was the creation of a society in which gradations still existed (as one Captain Wood put it at Wakefield), but in which all property would be protected. But at the same time the few would not be allowed 'to live and fatten on the industry of the many' (as it was expressed at a meeting of Ipswich radicals). And the sacredness of private property would be applied to labour as well as capital, as the editors of both the *Northern Liberator* and *Northern Star* emphasised, the latter citing Locke on the labourer being worthy of his hire.[11]

The Chartist attitude towards property rights was encapsulated in one phrase more frequently than any other. The ubiquitous 'fair day's wages for a fair day's work', which O'Connor described after his trial in 1843 as being 'the aim and end of the People's Charter', represented the popular inheritance of an earlier moral economy tradition associated with expressions like 'live and let live' and 'the just price and the fair wage'. Such slogans were neither intrinsically opposed nor favourable to *laissez-faire* or intervention *per se*, but referred more to the desire to retain a customary standard of living than the economic means of doing so. Their appeal was succinctly symbolised in Feargus O'Connor's claim to be 'a beef-and-mutton a pork and butter and milk and honey radical ... an open air, a work-when-I'm-able-and-work-for-myself-and-my-family Radical'. The obstacles preventing a 'fair day's wages' were still sometimes described only in terms of taxation, especially by the *Northern Liberator*, the most Cobbettite of the major Chartist journals. When many Chartists claimed a right to the 'whole produce of labour', a reduction in state expenditure was often all they meant to imply. Chartist rallies not infrequently heard demands, thus, for the reinstatement of 'the absolute and entire controul, which every Englishman possessed over the produce of his labour, no particle of which could, on any pretence, be taken from him, until he and his

---

[11] Thompson, *The Chartists* (Temple Smith, 1984), p. 301; Wilson, 'The Struggles of an Old Chartist', in David Vincent, ed., *Testaments of Radicalism* (Europa, 1977), p. 210; *NS*, no. 59 (29 December 1838), 2; no. 37 (28 July 1838), 8; no. 41 (25 August 1838), 8; *NL*, no. 136 (16 May 1840), 4; *NS*, no. 129 (2 May 1840), 4. For an example of Chartist co-operation, see *NS*, no. 137 (27 June 1840), 5, and for one explanation of its rationale, Robert Lowery, *Address to the Fathers and Mothers* (Newcastle upon Tyne, 1839).

brother labourers had signified their assent to such abstraction, by delegates chosen from their body'.[12]

When most Chartists used the word 'equality', then, they probably had in mind something like A. H. Beaumont's conception of 'an equal opportunity to every man of obtaining all the advantages of society: no one having a monopoly, and each exclusively enjoying the produce of his own industry and intellect'. This was a radical liberal, but not a socialist, ideal. Nonetheless, we cannot be sure how wide dissent from such views may have been. For tactical reasons, it was felt unwise to identify with the 'levelling' property theories of the Socialists, and hence prudent to deny any association at all with the latter. There were, as we will see, exceptions to this rule. But there is little doubt that while many Chartists were opposed to Socialist theological attitudes, and others found Owenite proposals hare-brained, or (in the case of communities) vaguely coercive and overly conformist, it was the question of property which, from the Chartist side, was the most imposing obstacle to any genuine alignment between the two movements. Let us now consider what many Socialists felt divided them from the Chartists.[13]

Owenite grievances

The greatest single source of Owenite opposition to Chartism was probably Owen himself, for the sympathies of many Owenite leaders and a fairly large proportion of the membership in Owenite branch organisations ran mostly in the other direction (as we will see shortly). Nonetheless, the rationale behind many of Owen's arguments was also conceded by Socialists who supported (at least at some point) the passage of the Charter. In fact, such objections were bound up with the analytic claims of Owenism as an intellectual enterprise, not personal antipathy to the Chartists or steadfast loyalty to Owen himself.

As might be expected, property relations were most frequently at issue when the Socialists dissected Chartist plans and ideas. There were, however, also other matters criticised by the Socialists which ought briefly to be touched upon here. Perhaps the most important of these concerned what the Owenites felt was an unduly hostile, class antagonistic style by which the Chartists sought reform, 'the bitter discontent gone fierce and mad', as Carlyle termed it, born of hunger

---

[12] *The Trial of Feargus O'Connor* (Manchester, 1843), p. viii; *NS*, no. 139 (11 July 1840), 7; *NL*, no. 92 (20 July 1839), 4; *NS*, no. 59 (29 December 1838), 6; *NL*, no. 126 (14 March 1840), 7.
[13] *NL*, no. 8 (9 December 1837), 1.

and the anger of outraged indignation rather than the dulcit charity of necessitarian omniscience. Now, more than ever, the reform movement seemed to require the stability which necessity promised. Socialism tended to mollify the passions, a London Owenite named Turner reminded a Chartist meeting at the John Street Institute, castigating the radicals for using 'such strong language, calling the men in power bloody despots, tyrants, etc. He thought it was calculated to create evil feelings, indeed, he objected to all harsh names'. The use of 'violent and vituperative feelings and expressions', another Socialist wrote,

so far from conciliating, irritates, naturally irritates the privileged classes, and disposes them to use active measures for the repression of individuals and designs so inimical to what they deem their rights and happiness; the combatants are mutually repelled from each other; and instead of meeting for the consideration and adjustment of differences, or reciprocal concession, are induced to keep aloof from all occasions of meeting, or when they are unavoidably compelled to meet, indulge in the most unmeasured hostility to each other; superciliousness, and contempt, and dislike, on the one hand, being met by angry invective, keen sarcasm, or undisguised hatred, on the other.[14]

Such sentiments were connected to the ambivalent attitude of many Socialists towards politics generally. Not merely the Chartist agitation, but the normal conduct of the electoral process, was repugnant to those who sought to implement a new conception of social order. This was reflected in one explanation for why the Socialists did not participate officially in the 1837 elections, though criticism on this occasion was clearly directed more at the Tories than the Whigs:

Deeply impressed with the irrationality of such proceedings, the socialists have taken no part in the contest now waged around them. Their kingdom is emphatically 'not of this world'. They see with feelings of the most pregnant regret the most debasing influences let loose upon an already ignorant and degraded portion of the population, to add fresh force to the ordinary evil tendencies of our general institutions. We speak not merely of the excitement which, by destroying that equability of temper necessary to a well-regulated mind, takes away the primary constituent of mental enjoyment and all true morality; but of the vitiating and inhumanizing power of the gin-shop and beer-tap; by which, as of old, the supporters of 'Church and State' seek to maintain that power over the minds and bodies of men, which the progressive spirit of the age denies them, and will shortly annihilate.

[14] Thomas Carlyle, 'Chartism', *Critical and Miscellaneous Essays* (1899), 4, p. 19; NS, no. 205 (16 October 1841), 2; NMW, 4, no. 162 (2 December 1837), 46. In a series of petitions written in 1840 to the Home Office, about ten Socialist branches (in uniform statements, suggesting the instigation of the Central Board) deprecated 'the late violence in Wales', but insisted that nothing would change until social conditions did. These petitions are preserved in HO 44/38. In at least one case (Bethnal Green), the Socialists claimed that they had directly inhibited the Chartists' propensity to violence. See the *Statement to the Marquess of Normandy* (1840), pp. 14–15.

With these attitudes, many Socialists inevitably found the political process distasteful. Politics had 'become a mere selfish struggle of aristocratic placement and their dependents, of sections against sections, class against class'. What reason was there to suppose, some Socialists demanded, that the Charter would improve things rather than creating what one wag termed 'universal suffering and animal parliaments'? Owen's charge that it would merely 'make all petty politicians' was widely repeated. Instead of the 'Robespierre spirit' which Robert Dale Owen had accused the *Poor Man's Guardian* of perpetrating in 1832, those Socialists who decried such methods pointed to the conduct of their own proceedings, which were designed to foresake the

formidable muster of prejudiced, prepossessed and hostile parties, each prepared to battle for place and power, to sacrifice individual and conscientious opinion at the shrine of party, to lose sight of the general welfare in the universal paltry and selfish struggle for individual aggrandizement, and keep up an empty war of words, while misery and destitution implore a proper direction of the natural resources. 'The truth' has 'made us free' from these irrationalities.[15]

This sort of self-righteousness many Chartists doubtless found particularly galling. Nor do they seem to have taken the criticisms it implied with a great degree of seriousness. The accusation that their own struggle was sectarian and pursued the benefit of one class alone, and that their aims were incomplete because they neglected female suffrage, also do not seem to have worried many.[16]

The Socialists not only criticised the Chartists, but also sought to persuade them that their energies were misplaced and that their ends were attainable by other means. An extreme formulation of the Owenite case against Chartist political strategy was that socialism simply superseded the need for radical reform. There were several variations on this theme, some of which stressed political, and others more economic, factors. One argument, urged by the ex-radical reformer William Hawkes Smith but echoing a line commonly adopted by Owen, considered that 'In truth, provided personal freedom be permitted in a country, it matters but little to the success of the co-operative scheme, what particular forms and institutions prevail. A community of mutual interests, be the Government what it might, must be, within itself, essentially and practically a democracy'. Another proposition of this type, offered at times against some of the

[15] *NMW*, 3, no. 144 (29 July 1837), 326; *Union*, no. 1 (1 April 1842), 3; *NMW*, 10, no. 44 (30 April 1842), 348–9; *FE*, ser. 2, 4, no. 45 (1 September 1832), 359; *NMW*, 4, no. 184 (5 May 1838), 221.
[16] *NS*, no. 207 (30 October 1841), 6; *NMW*, 9, no. 20 (15 May 1841), 312–13; 10, no. 9 (28 August 1841), 65.

more socialistic Chartists who still considered that universal suffrage was necessary first, denied that the government would interfere with successful communitarian development. Instead, the wealth of communities would confer the suffrage upon their members, and no government would dare to interfere with private property so far as to demolish existing communities.[17]

More than anything else, however, it was their perception of the Chartists' failure to confront the actual workings of the economic system which formed the basis of Socialist denunciations. Considerably more than in the 1820s, the Socialists could display 'the startling anomaly of a political constitution in America, framed on the principles of radical politicans, co-existing with commercial embarrassment – a distressed labouring population and a continual struggle between the wealthy and the poorer classes of society, as to who shall be master, and who the slave'. Here the problem with the Chartists was not that they were *too* radical but that, in failing to penetrate below the surface of society and in not comprehending how the powers of production, distribution and consumption had to be harmonised in order to ensure the happiness of all, they were not radical enough. Compared to the need to supersede all social systems based on class, the value of the suffrage was negligible:

such has been the system of society hitherto, a system involving the distinctions of classes, the rich and poor, the master and servant, the employer and the unemployed, that the mere political distinctions of eligibility for power and right of suffrage, however much they may be liberalized, sink into comparative insignificance before the exclusions, the petty tyrannies, the privations and retired cruelties necessarily inflicted during a continuance, under any species of competitive government, of a separation of classes, and a subdivision of interests.[18]

These sentiments were often translated into attacks upon Chartist obscurity in formulations of their economic programme. 'Of what use will it be to elect the men of your choice and cheer them through the street, if they do nothing afterwards?' was a typical comment by Socialists in their debates with Chartist opponents. Nor were dogeared slogans invoking an outmoded and rapidly disappearing social and economic system of any appeal against Socialist arguments. 'A fair day's wages for a fair day's work' won few converts from Owenism to Chartism. Most Socialists refused to believe that the Charter alone, usually taken to include the repeal of the Corn Laws and other unfair taxation, could possibly provide even short-term opulence. Even

---

[17] *NMW*, 4, no. 169 (20 January 1838), 99; *NS*, no. 102 (26 October 1839), 7; *NMW*, 4, no. 161 (25 November 1837), 37; *HF*, no. 4 (4 January 1840), 52–3; *SE*, no. 99 (4 August 1838).

[18] *NMW*, 4, no. 161 (25 November 1837), 37; 2, no. 96 (27 August 1836), 349.

before the Chartist agitation was seriously underway, the *New Moral World*, in discussing a meeting chaired by O'Connor, analysed the economic consequences of the radical reforms then being proposed. The editor presumed everything most Chartists would have sought: the Charter granted, a monarch or president satisfied with £5,000 annually, the separation of Church and State, the abolition of tithes, pensions and other useless places and sinecures as political rewards, the dissolution of the standing army, and the general reduction of taxation to American levels within two years. What would the result be?

If the interests of all the population were the same, then a reduction of the general expenditure would be a reduction of the necessity for so much labour, and all would, to a certain extent, be relieved. But, with our *separate* and *opposing* interests, the reduction of expenditure is equivalent to the discharge of so many labourers which is the same thing as a reduction in the price paid for labour; and this would go on, until the wages of labour would be reduced to the same relative scale as at present; that is, *to the mere subsisting price*; which, as the political economists tell us, is the natural reward for labour: and notwithstanding all this change, therefore, in the two years after, the industrious classes would find that they were in just the same state as before.

Such reforms, therefore, rather than alleviating, would merely deepen the extensive national suffering already existing.[19] These arguments were widely employed by Socialists to discourage the Chartist agitation, or to warn that the benefits to be anticipated from such reforms would very likely be a great disappointment to those who reckoned upon a heavily laden table, cheap ale, warm hearths and everything else which O'Connor and others proclaimed the Charter would supply.

In examining the Chartists' and Socialists' views of each other so far, a stereotype has been relied upon from which we must now depart. The idea that most Socialists were uninterested in or hostile to the struggle for the Charter, and that most Chartists who had any acquaintance with them saw the Socialists as ridiculous, utopian, or heretical does have some historical foundation. As a caricature it circulated from the outset of the Chartist movement, and merely confirmed earlier radical suspicions of Owen which dated from his first public meetings in London in 1817. Considerable credence was thus added to the anti-political image of the Socialists.[20] The extent to which the Chartists conformed to the extreme portrait drawn in some Socialist accounts, however, lies beyond the boundaries of the present

[19] *NS*, no. 205 (16 October 1841), 7; see also *ES*, no. 48 (17 September 1842), 3; *NMW*, 6, no. 43 (17 August 1839), 686–7; 1, no. 50 (10 October 1835), 396–7; 3, no. 139 (24 June 1837), 285.
[20] See for instance *OF*, no. 49 (7 December 1839), 2.

discussion. This is primarily a question of the imputed economic efficacy attached to a range of reforms (of taxes, the Poor Laws, the Corn Laws and so forth). For the notion that any Chartist sought parliamentary reform simply for a change in the form of government is obviously unconvincing. Chartism clearly was a 'knife and fork' movement. But if we cannot explore more deeply how the relationship between parliamentary and economic reform was understood by the Chartists, there is little doubt that most Chartists had a far less sophisticated grasp of political economy than most Owenites. In the next section, we will consider how this affected Owenite involvement with Chartism, and what attempts were made to unite radical means with socialist ends.

Charter Socialism

Chartists were of many sorts. There were moral-force Chartists and physical-force Chartists; there were Chartists and something more; there were whole-hog Chartists, bristles and all; and there were Chartists who cried aloud, 'The Charter today, and roast beef the day after!' Indeed, the divisions amongst them were almost endless – at least as endless as the men who set up as leaders, for every little leader had his little following, while the bigger leaders had bigger followings.

We have Sacred Socialists, *Secret* Socialists, Scientific Socialists, Christian Socialists, Radical Socialists, and now . . . Church Socialists.[21]

While no-one has yet rediscovered a Sacred Socialist with bristles, it is instructive to recall, when considering both the stereotypes which then existed and those which to some extent we must ourselves necessarily impose upon the past, just how much variety and fluidity there was in the Chartist and Socialist movements.[22] Both carried forward their own sense of organisational, personal and ideological history, and developed according to their own internal logic as well as in relation to the society around them, to the fits and starts of industrial growth and depression, the actions of churches, the state and police, and the course of public opinion generally. With respect to many questions which interest us here, each was additionally bound to some extent to the actions and reactions of the other. This was certainly true, for example, of the exchange of individuals between the organisations and activities of both. The attractions of each varied according to time

<hr />

[21] W. E. Adams, *Memoirs of a Social Atom* (Hutchinson, 1903), 1, p. 174; *NMW*, 8, no. 15 (10 October 1840), 226.
[22] A 'Sacred Socialist' adhered to the views of James Pierrepont Greaves, whose followers were amongst the founders of the Ham Common Concordium.

and place, and the accession of a better Chartist lecturer or the opening
of a new Owenite Hall of Science certainly had the capacity not only to
attract newcomers but also to draw support from rival organisations.
People did not simply enlist in Chartist and Socialist associations to
manifest their deeply-felt adherence to certain principles. The passage
of time, moreover, could remove their original reasons for so doing.
Both Chartism and Socialism suffered a variety of defeats which
carried away many thousands of their supporters. But other developments also affected the mobility and interest of their members. Some
became respectable, and others poorer and increasingly hopeless.
Many became disappointed with the lack of progress in their movement. The Socialists, in particular, seem to have experimented widely,
frequently moving on to something else besides 'pure Owenism', or
combining it with their Socialism. Some adopted a new gospel, others
water-cures or laughing gas (frequently enjoyed at Social Festivals).
Numbers enlisted in mechanics' institutes, returned to their old
church, puzzled over phrenology and mesmerism, or embraced nud-
ism. Hundreds emigrated. Owenite views were consequently more
widely diffused, and mixed with a variety of other, non-political
reform and self-improvement campaigns. But the Socialists were also
apparently unable to hold the long-term attention of thousands of
potential or temporary adherents. Francis Place, among others, was
struck by the fact that while there often seemed to be the same number
of Owenites, the rate of turn-over was fairly high, though this may
have been truer for London than elsewhere.[23]

In such circumstances, it would have been surprising if there had not
been frequent contact between Owenites and Chartists, beyond their
debates, which actually resulted in mutual conversions to varying
degrees. The form and appeal of both groups may appear widely
divergent today, particularly for those who would dismiss Owenism
as a middle class movement. But it should be recalled that each provided cultural facilities, ways of life, and modes of identity linked to
what was largely understood as a common ideal, a world in which all
were accorded dignity, a decent standard of living, and a full range of
civil, religious and political liberties, privileges which far too many
were denied under the existing system. This widely shared vision
lessened the distance between both movements. From one perspective, Owenism could be understood as concentrating primarily upon
social equality rather than moral perfectionism, while Chartism could

---

[23] British Library Add. MS. 35150, fol. 90. The Socialists' enemies were fond of saying
that many of Owen's followers were primarily interested in the copious amusements
provided at the Social Festivals. See for example, J. Mather, *Socialism Exposed* (1839), p.
22.

be interpreted as guided more by a notion of economic well-being and general social equality than a concern with the specific mechanisms of government which would bring this about. Given this apparent middle ground, both could be understood as roads to the same end. This coalescence was to become increasingly evident in the early 1840s.

Attempts from both sides to supersede the principal differences between the two groups, and particularly to incorporate Owenite goals and analyses into the larger radical movement, did not, however, proceed as a logical development and extension of the earlier elements of unity achieved in varying degrees by the BAPCK and NUWC. In fact, the latter organisation, which was far more strongly engaged politically than the BAPCK, made as we have seen no attempt to bring about such a unification of goals or principles, although some members continued to purvey the social analysis adopted by the BAPCK. It is generally agreed that a small group of London radicals who had also been co-operators laid the foundations of London as well as moral force Chartism. But the increasing influence of this group, far from proceeding from their ability to unite radical and Owenite pro-grammes, actually corresponded to their own de-emphasis upon Owenite arguments and plans, and to an adjustment of these to the goals and language of radicalism. This process of adaptation probably proceeded from a wish to salvage from Owen's views what was more widely attractive, such as an emphasis upon education, rather than a widespread renunciation by former co-operators of the less popular elements in his plans. It is this strategic consideration, then, rather than merely their increasing doubts about the realism of Owen's plans, which helps to explain the relatively easy passage of Lovett, Cleave, Hetherington and others into Chartism in the mid and late 1830s.

Nonetheless the creation of gradualist, moral force, educational Chartism was a complex process which cannot be adequately examined here, since it would lead us too far into the problem of the origins of Chartism itself. In addition to the careful study of the writings of Lovett and others, such an investigation demands the consideration of other evidence not yet adequately examined elsewhere, but which falls outside our scope here as well. The influence of Place, for example, is clearly germane here, as is the process by which classical political economy was embraced by some radicals, and even more importantly, also eventually accepted by a few socialists. It would be interesting to know, too, how and why Lovett came to attempt to dispense with all forms of leadership generally, and how Owenism might have influenced this idea. Julius West is probably correct in assuming that most of the members of this key group which overlapped both movements between 1835 and 1840 – especially Lovett, Cleave and Hetherington – in this period came to discard certain Owenite assumptions, while strongly embracing working class political action. Owenism was still accepted to the extent that *laissez-faire* was not regarded as the epitome of political wisdom, and moral force alone was regarded as the legitimate means of social change. How far such moral force beliefs hindered Chartism from setting a more revolutionary course in the late 1830s and early 1840s, however, is extremely difficult to gauge. We will see, though, that there is some evidence that this occurred.[24]

The group around Lovett – for he was certainly their leading spokesman – was also important for another reason. Despite frequent expressions of fraternal sympathy with radical, national, independence, or working class efforts in other countries in the reformist press, there was little organised internationalism in the British working class prior to the mid-1830s. The London Corresponding Society and similar organisations in the 1790s had expressed considerable approbation for the democratic, revolutionary cause in France, abrogating the traditional enmity between the two countries on the basis of the shared interest of both peoples in republicanism, or at least, in greater social justice. The years between Waterloo and Chartism saw the creation of a new conception of shared identity which was based more upon the economic role of the working classes than the exclusion of 'the people' from the political process. Owenism's economic analysis contributed significantly to this change by popularising an interpretation of the productive/unproductive distinction. Still G. D. H. Cole has been one of the few historians to contend that the Lovettite Chartists might be termed more 'class conscious' than the O'Connorites, but as a consequence of their greater insistence upon working class leadership. Nonetheless the specific nature of their analysis can also be used in support of such a position.[25]

But the social Chartist internationalism of the late 1830s also varied considerably from the anti-nationalist and anti-patriotic views of some early socialists. Owen himself, as we have seen, was properly speaking an extreme cosmopolitan, seeking the eradication of all national boundaries and supersession of national differences in favour of a homogeneous, unified world. By the mid-1840s, however, plebeian Owenism had moved much closer to that branch of internationalism

---

[24] West, *History of the Chartist Movement*, p. 49. On Lovett's opposition to leadership, see George Howell, *A History of the Working Men's Association*, p. 26. Henry Solly also reported that Lovett told a young Chartist, when asked how he could serve him, that 'we don't want leaders and chiefs among working men. Do your duty and serve your fellow countrymen, and don't trouble your head about me' (*James Woodford*, vol. 1, p. 81).

[25] Cole, *Chartist Portraits* (Macmillan, 1941), p. 313.

which most socialists would embrace in the last third of the century. Through organisations like the Democratic Friends of All Nations, and also in the LWMA, the Lovett circle in particular extended their fraternal greetings to their Belgian, French, Polish and other working class brethren, but also attempted to explain what bound their interests together, namely their economic position as the true producers of wealth. A collective perception of this interest, it was believed, would assist in eradicating 'those national prejudices and bigotted feelings which the selfish and despotic rulers of mankind have implanted and perpetrated for their own advantage'. When the working classes became aware, as Lovett stressed in an address to the French workers in 1844, that there was an *'identity of interest'* between them, and when 'the majority of our brethren have knowledge to perceive it, the advocates of national strife will be few, and the trade of war will fail to bring either glory, honour or fame'. To meet such ends, it was suggested, a 'Conference of Nations' should meet annually to resolve all national disputes by arbitration, all English colonies should become self-governing, and the recent British wars in Afghanistan and China, and French adventures in Algeria, should be condemned as unjust. Many of these views were close to those voiced in the later International, whose English members included a number of O'Brienites. The proximity of these proposals to Owen's own programme is worth noting. But generally, it is evident that the pacifistic elements in Owenism were extended to the wider working class movement, and the first serious efforts at socialist working class non-aggression begun in Britain.[26]

At some point many members of the Lovett circle began to drift even further away from, and then decisively to break with, their former socialist views. Lovett's own enthusiasm for Owenism began to wane gradually at the end of the 1830s. Eventually he abandoned his faith in community of property completely, later stating that communities would invite 'a kind of social despotism far worse than any that now exists'. Though not yet so pessimistic, Lovett argued for free trade at a Complete Suffrage meeting in 1842, and concluded that competition was beneficial insofar as it assisted in 'keeping up man's energies to the

---

[26] *NMW*, 3, no. 109 (26 November 1836), 35. There is some discussion of these issues in Henry Weisser, *British Working Class Movements and Europe, 1815–48* (Manchester, Manchester University Press, 1975), pp. 53–7. Parallel sentiments in the International are revealed in *The General Council of the First International* (Moscow, Foreign Languages Publishing House, n.d.), p. 431. For further discussion, see my 'Some Sources of Early Socialist Cosmopolitanism and Internationalism in Britain, 1790–1860', in F. L. van Holthoon and Marcel van der Linden, eds., *Internationalism in the Labour Movement 1830–1940*, 1, pp. 235–58. On the Democratic Friends, see Christine Lattek, 'The Beginnings of Socialist Internationalism in the 1840s: The Democratic Friends of All Nations', in *ibid.*, 1, pp. 259–82.

tension point'. But Lovett nonetheless also upheld the desirability of some form of co-operation in production to the end of his life.[27] Important Owenite elements certainly persisted in his writings after the founding of the LWMA in 1836, too, and thus clearly contributed to making the tone of this organisation more social radical than traditionally radical. An early 'Address to the Citizens of the American Republic', for example, devoted several paragraphs to American monopoly of property, a theme otherwise fairly unusual in radical circles even in the mid-1840s. In September 1836, Lovett also delivered a scathing attack upon the causes of human degradation, which he described as the right of individual property in land, machinery and productive power, the right of individual accumulation of wealth, and the buying and selling of human labour. At this time, too, he still asserted that

individual *property leads to* individual interests, and a tendency *under any form of government* to acquire an undue influence in the making and execution of laws ... Whatever local or general corruption springing from this source stand in the way of inquiry or improvement, the evil originated in the allowing of *private property in the lands and productive powers of the country*, which has generated private interests, partial legislation, and the plunder and oppression of the millions.[28]

By 1842, however, Lovett described distress as having two somewhat different sources: 'the great POLITICAL CAUSE, in my opinion, is irresponsible legislation – the great SOCIAL CAUSE is defective education'. This view had been anticipated in *Chartism: a New Organisation for the People* (1839), written jointly in prison with John Collins. This work, while it owed something to Socialist ideas of organisation, failed to advertise much of their programme besides reiterating the need to educate those who would one day govern. But it also stressed the duty to teach the right of property as part of any system of education, as a means of helping to prevent 'pilfering and dishonesty', and further emphasised the legitimacy of 'acquisitions of honest industry'. These were closer to orthodox Chartist than to Owenite formulations (though *Chartism* may have assisted gaining Lovett and others the label of 'pharasaical Chartists' for seeming to think themselves better than the common working man). It is possible, at any rate, that by this point

---

[27] Lovett, *Life and Struggles*, pp. 36–7; (1876 edn.), pp. 407, 428–30; *Nonconformist*, no. 45 (16 February 1842), 108. On the origins of the London Working Men's Association see D. J. Rowe, 'The London Working Men's Association and the People's Charter', *P&P*, 36 (1967), 73–86; Prothero, 'The London Working Men's Association and the People's Charter', *P&P*, 38 (1967), 169–73; and Prothero, 'Chartism in London', *P&P*, 44 (1969), 76–105. For Place's opinion of Lovett's beliefs, see British Library Add. MS. 27791, fols. 67, 241.

[28] Lovett, *Life and Struggles*, p. 108; *HTD*, 10 September 1836.

Lovett had already had a genuine change of opinion about much of the Owenite canon, perhaps in conjunction with his trial and imprisonment. A similar conclusion may have overtaken James Watson. But we cannot be sure that this was the case.[29]

Henry Hetherington, however, and probably John Cleave as well, remained much less sceptical about the ultimate aims of Owenism. An increasing concern with moral reform did not prevent Hetherington from frequently commenting on the major themes of Owenite political economy in his *Halfpenny Magazine* (1840–41), and still propounding the contingency of moral upon economic innovation. The Chartists professed to be political reformers and the Socialists moral reformers, he complained at this time, but the first took 'little notice of morals, and the second disclaim politics'. In the *National Association Gazette* (1842), he and Lovett generally took Bronterre O'Brien's side against Feargus O'Connor and the 'insane balderdash addressed to the Chartists in their chief organ'. The journal also included remarks (probably by Lovett) sceptical of the claim that communities could ever entirely supersede competition. In 1844 we find Hetherington still giving news of the Owenite movement, and in the following year he attended the final Rational Society congress as a delegate. In a remarkable 'Last Will and Testament' written as he was dying of cholera in 1849, too, Hetherington reaffirmed his faith in Owenism:

I quit this world with the firm conviction that his system is the only true road to human emancipation: that is, the only just system for regulating the affairs of honest, intelligent human beings – the only one yet made known to the world, that is based on truth, justice, and equality. While the land, machines, tools, implements of production, and the produce of man's toil, are exclusively the possession of do-nothings; and labour is the sole possession of the wealth-producers – a marketable commodity, bought up and directed by wealthy idlers, – never ending misery must be their inevitable lot. ROBERT OWEN's system, if rightly understood and faithfully carried out, rectifies all these anomalies. It makes man the proprietor of his own wealth, and of the elements of production – it places him in the condition to enjoy the entire fruits of his labour, and surrounds him with circumstances that will make him intelligent, rational, and happy.

There can be little doubt that Hetherington, Lovett and others were

---

[29] *BS*, no. 6 (16 April 1842), 4; *NMW*, 9, no. 2 (9 January 1841), 17; Lovett and Collins, *Chartism. A New Organisation for the People* (2nd edn., 1841), pp. 97–8; *LWLN*, no. 128 (4 May 1845), 5. There is a good discussion of Lovett's and Collins' contribution to Chartist ideas on education in Harold Silver, *English Education and the Radicals* (Routledge and Kegan Paul, 1975), pp. 73–89. John Cleave's opinions after 1835 are harder to trace because so many issues of his periodicals have not yet been relocated. In a review of O'Brien's edition of Buonarroti in 1836, however, Cleave noted that the principles of the book furnished 'the only basis for a healthy state of society' (*CWPG*, 3, no. 32, 6 August 1836, 4).

circumspect, however, about their social views in the early years of the LWMA. Nonetheless it is also clear that they probably helped to shift the language of Chartism at least somewhat in an Owenite direction at this time. In particular, they popularised the dichotomy of 'social vs. political' reform – the most important means of indicating the new social radical views – on many occasions. This contrast was, for example, strikingly evident in the founding statement of the LWMA, which proposed that the aim of an equality of rights was 'not in order to lop off an unjust tax or useless pension, or to get a transfer of wealth, power, or influence for a party; but to be *able to probe our social evils to their source, and to apply effective remedies to prevent, rather than unjust laws to punish'*. Such formulations did not encode an Owenite plan. But they did indicate a way of thinking which was perceptibly different from most forms of traditional radicalism, and which was rhetorically sign-posted by the juxtaposition of 'social' to 'political' reform.[30]

However, while Lovett, Hetherington and their associates played an important role in the making of Chartism, as well as in its subsequent split into moral and physical force camps, they had less to do with its mainstream development. This centred upon the Midlands, O'Connor and the *Northern Star*. We will obviously never know how many amongst the estimated four million people who attended Chartist meetings, mainly in the centre and north of the country, also held Socialist views. Calculating the influence of Owenism among the great body of Chartists is in fact enormously difficult, since the views of most Chartists were recorded only as 'cheers' at appropriate points in their leaders' speeches. It is hard enough even to be sure what people meant exactly in defining themselves as Chartists, Socialists or Owenites. Should we include amongst the latter, for example, the Bath Chartist prisoner brought before the bar, who said – perhaps by way of offering a disingenuous defence – that he agreed with Robert Owen that char-acter was formed by circumstances? Many other Chartists might have confessed to holding such 'Socialist' views. Certainly we must dis-count the possibility of any great degree of precision behind the oft-quoted *Leeds Times'* 1842 statement that 'political Socialism' had become the creed of the great majority of the working classes. 'Social-ism' was here identified with the general belief that some form of

[30] *HM*, no. 21 (19 September 1840), 161–2, where Hetherington wrote that 'the first grand desideratum is a universal abstract standard of virtue, that shall be equally applicable to all men; but, before this can become available as a practical rule in morals, it is necessary that *the conditions of men should become much more equal* than at present, for the conflicting interests and relations of life, arising from class distinctions, would at all times neutralize, and render inoperative, any such abstract moral standard, however excellent it might be in itself'; *NAG*, no. 28 (9 July 1842), 223; no. 24 (11 June 1842), 190–1; *Regenerator*, no. 1 (1 June 1844), 13; *ST*, no. 27 (8 September 1849), 210; *Address and Rules of the Working Men's Association* (1836), p. 3.

economic regulation in favour of the poor was necessary, rather than with more specifically Owenite views of community of goods or the abolition of competition. How then is it possible to ascertain more precisely how much common ground between the two movements was actually perceived by many of their adherents?[31]

In effect it is impossible to offer a very conclusive case because so much of the evidence is inadmissable. Contextualising the history of ideas relies upon our ability to excavate reasonably coherent statements in order to piece together the threads of meaning woven between texts and their background. To construct even the semblance of a 'discourse' demands an adequate number of documents (of which reports of speeches are definitely an inferior variety) reflecting a sufficient range of opinion to identify discursive boundaries and barriers, and to delineate not only shades of thought, but also breaks from previous patterns of thinking. But all that the diffuse, fragmentary and ambiguous accounts of this period often offer us are very brief discussions from which to generalise. We are left with a pastiche of impressions whose collective meaning, while it has important corrective advantages, fails to amount to a coherent picture about which we can make the kind of discursive conclusions that are possible in a discussion of one text or a body of works by a single author. To some extent this is only to argue that the reconstruction of any discourse upon the basis of widely dispersed periodical literature, especially when this literature itself often involves the recreation of oral reports, must be more provisional than other forms of textual treatment. Here we must also rely much more upon interpretations of the social, political and economic context of ideas than does more purely textual exegesis. But this too is rarely easy to provide. The pieces to this particular puzzle presented here thus indicate the variety of contacts which would have to be considered by a more exhaustive social-historical analysis than can be undertaken here. They will be introduced in ascending order of their importance to our understanding of Owenite–Chartist relations, from the relatively insignificant to the opinions and views of Owenite leaders and of the founders of 'Charter Socialism'.

Firstly, then, there are isolated incidences of mutual contact reported in the Chartist and Socialist press: at the Leigh Socialist branch, noted Robert Buchanan in 1839, the Chartist agitation had already drawn away many members; at Birmingham, Holyoake later wrote, George White and his fellow Chartists had aided the Socialists when the latter got into trouble during theological debates; a group of

---

[31] J. B. Leno, *The Aftermath, with Autobiography of the Author* (1892), p. 51; D. Thompson, ed., *The Early Chartists* (Macmillan, 1971), p. 255; *NMW*, 12, no. 7 (13 August 1842), 58.

Norwich Chartists announced that they were only seeking the Charter in order to establish co-operative communities; at a Sunderland Chartist meeting, a man said he favoured Owen's views, but that the Charter should be carried first; at the John Street Institute in London, a Socialist allowed that the Charter would permit grants of land to be made available for home colonisation, and thoughtfully proposed Owen as the first Minister of Education under a Chartist government; another John Street member, Ruffy Ridley, mentioned that he was a Socialist before becoming a Chartist, and asserted that the Charter was necessary to get communities; at Arnold, a discussion between a Chartist and a Socialist Missionary resulted in a vote of 500 for Chartism as the best means of reform, and thirty for Socialism (nationally such a ratio would have yielded some 300,000 Owenites); the Socialist Missionary J. C. Farn said that he supported the Charter, although home colonisation was the only ultimate answer to social distress, and ran for parliament at Glasgow; a prison warder confiscated a Socialist pamphlet (C. J. Haslam's *Letters to the Clergy*) from a visitor to a Chartist prisoner; another Socialist lecturer, George Phillips, advised the Chartists of Stowbridge to proceed 'carefully, but firmly, in their agitation for the Charter'; lecturing in Scotland, Robert Cooper stated that most of the Socialists at Dunfermline were Chartists; at Fallsworth, a discussion between Ellis, Social Missionary, and Leach, Chartist Missionary, resulted in a nearly unanimous vote for the Charter (so reported the *Northern Star*, at least); in London, a member of Owenite branch 32 reported in December 1838 that the Socialists there were divided on the question of the utility of initial political reforms, and noted that 'one half of the Socialists in London are now using their energies in furtherance of radicalism' (perhaps 500 Owenites were active in the metropolis at this time); at a Home Colonisation Society (a fund-raising branch of the Rational Society) meeting held by Owen in London in June 1842, however, a Socialist named Parry proposed that the Charter be first attained, but was defeated by a large majority (scarcely surprising in this locale) on a show of hands; it was announced proudly in the *New Moral World* in May 1840 that in the Midlands a physical force Chartist had exchanged his gun and bayonet for a violin (no doubt a more harmonious instrument of reform) after converting to Socialism.[32]

---

[32] G. J. Holyoake, *Sixty Years*, 1, p. 107; *NMW*, 8, no. 15 (10 October 1840), 236; *NL*, no. 75 (23 March 1839), 2; *NS*, no. 205 (16 October 1841) 7; no. 207 (30 October 1841), 6; no. 214 (18 December 1841), 2; *NMW*, 10, no. 2 (10 July 1841), 15 (Ridley later joined Barmby's London Communist Propaganda Society, see *NMW*, 10, no. 9, 28 August 1841, 71–2); 10, no. 43 (23 April 1842), 341; HO 44/38, see also HO 41/30 for extensive discussions between the Bishop of Exeter, the Home Secretary, and various correspondents on the spread of Socialism in 1840; *NMW*, 5, no. 37 (6 July 1839), 586; 10, no. 41 (8 December 1838), 124; *BS*, no. 13 (5 June 1842), 11, also reported in *NS*, no. 239 (11 June 1842), 8; *NMW*, 7, no. 84 (30 May 1840), 1258.

Then there are the statements given at various times and places by the more important Owenite leaders and lecturers, or by Chartists who leaned heavily in the direction of supporting Owenism. Amongst the latter group, for example, Lawrence Pitkethly was recorded as advocating the Charter in order to gain the advantages of Socialism with political security, and noting that this was the only difference he and many other Chartists had with Owen. At a Sheffield meeting, Isaac Ironside listed some of his 'ulterior views in supporting universal suffrage', such as a national bank, the severance of church from state, and most importantly, giving further facilities for establishing co-operative communities. At Trowbridge, the Chartist lecturer for the West Riding, G. M. Bartlett, prophesied that primogeniture would prevent the Socialists from buying all of the land in the country, and concluded that universal suffrage was thus first necessary, though thereafter a co-operative form of industry such as Owen proposed could be established. At Birmingham, the Chartist John Mason insisted that it was 'the *social despotism*' that destroyed happiness 'as the despotism of law invades our political freedom', and hence that 'the struggle for democratic liberty must triumph in the establishment of social justice'.[33]

Many of the better-known Socialist leaders were occasionally critical of Chartism, but they also lent at least lukewarm support at times. Charles Bray said at Coventry in 1839 that he would accompany the Chartists in extending the suffrage, shortening parliaments, and introducing the ballot and payment of members. The longtime Owenite William Pare chaired a Birmingham meeting to raise funds for the victims of the Welsh uprising of 1839. George Alexander Fleming wrote that the Socialists had no desire to place any obstructions in the way of political reformers, and admitted the utility of their goals at a Sunderland meeting in 1841, while disputing the direct benefits to be expected from them. In 1837, one of Owen's closest associates, John Finch, opposed the continuance of the House of Lords. In the following year, too, he termed himself a 'Radical Reformer' and 'zealous advocate' of annual parliaments, vote by ballot, universal suffrage, and the abolition of monopolies and repeal of unjust laws, though still terming these 'relatively minor objects'. William Hawkes Smith, active in the reform movement in 1819, responded to some of the attacks upon radicalism of the *Morning Chronicle* with a vindication of both Owenism and Chartism. At Northampton in 1840, another Socialist Missionary named Taunton recommended that Owenites support the Charter. John Watts, a former political activist in Leeds and a very popular Manchester Socialist lecturer, actively supported the Charter,

---

[33] *NMW*, 6, no. 61 (21 December 1839), 972; *NS*, no. 46 (29 September 1839), 8; no. 155 (31 October 1840), 2; *ChP*, no. 1 (18 November 1843), 9.

holding in 1839 that although it was only a stepping-stone to community, it was worth contending for as a right of the people if community were not endorsed as the nearest road to happiness. A year later, too, he protested at Burnley that while all Socialists believed the principles of political equality to be just, not all Chartists were Socialists.[34]

The vehement atheist Charles Southwell was also among those who spoke frequently in favour of the Charter while employed as a Social Missionary. Southwell claimed in 1842 that 'those who called Socialism "moral Chartism"' captured the true nature of what Socialism had been before it was 'churched, shorn of its consistency, [and] its preachers bereverended', a reference both to the sectarian qualities of the Rational Society and the temporary requirement of its lecturers to take the title of 'Reverend' in order to hold meetings in some locations. In late 1840 Southwell lectured on the subject of Chartism at the John Street Institute, and in early 1841 was reported as speaking at a Birmingham Chartist soirée in honour of White, Binns, and Vincent, just released from prison. At a London speech in September 1844 attended by the German communist exiles Wilhelm Weitling, Karl Schapper and other foreign socialists, he also called himself a Socialist, Chartist, and a whole-hog republican, a description which probably suited much of this particular audience as well.[35]

The Socialist most concerned with forging theoretical links with Chartism was another Social Missionary and former member of the Central Board of the Rational Society, James Napier Bailey. An erudite speaker, Bailey was also amongst the most prolific (and eclectic) of the Socialist authors of the early 1840s. Besides lecturing and writing on mesmerism, 'phreno-magnetism' and similar popular topics, he

---

[34] *Champion*, no. 43 (3 March 1839), 5; *NS*, no. 159 (28 November 1840), 1. On Pare's sympathy towards Chartism see also R. G. Garnett, *William Pare* (Manchester, Co-operative College, 1973), p. 25. Pare had been a member of the Birmingham Political Union in 1832: see British Library Add. MS. 27793, fol. 189, and Carlos Flick, *The Birmingham Political Union* (Dawson, 1978), pp. 25–6; John Finch, *The Millennium* (Liverpool, 1837), p. 2 (Finch also claimed to have placarded eight hundred copies of this message throughout Liverpool during the previous election); *NMW*, 5, no. 4 (17 November 1838), 56 – see also the comments on this in *WTS*, no. 293, 6 April 1839, 6; *NS*, no. 182 (8 May 1841), 5; *WB*, 2, no. 15 (12 September 1840), 118; *NMW*, 4, no. 190 (16 June 1838), 272; 6, no. 42 (10 August 1839), 670–1; 5, no. 30 (18 May 1839), 475; 8, no. 15 (10 October 1840), 236. On W. H. Smith's radical background see his *Birmingham Inspector* (1819). John Watts had been a member of the Radical Political Union in 1832. See British Library Add. MS. 27791, fol. 348. The Rev. Arthur Wade also moved in both Chartist and Owenite circles, though his interest seems to have been predominantly in factory and poor law reform rather than Owenism. See T. H. Lloyd, 'Dr. Wade and the Working Class', *MHist*, 2 (1973), 61–83.

[35] *OrR*, no. 5 (1842), 33; *MSA*, no. 598 (27 June 1840), 3; *WB*, 2, no. 14 (5 September 1840), 110; *NS*, no. 174 (13 March 1841), 1; no. 359 (28 September 1844), 1.

produced a succession of essays on themes of interest to Owenites, such as the 'Life of Lycurgus', 'The Pleasures and Advantages of Literature and Philosophy' and 'Sketches of Indian Character'. Bailey's significance, however, lay in the realm of political theory. Unlike Owen and some of his more utopian votaries, he embraced a much more traditional view of what good government consisted in: it was to be cheap, effective, disinterested, entirely elective and representative of all classes. As to achieving these goals, he stated in an 1842 essay, it was his firm belief that 'under the present arrangements of society, the *"People's Charter"* is the only means whereby we can obtain a government of this kind'.[36]

These sentiments led Bailey in 1843 to attempt to unify the Chartists and Socialists – both of whom were in considerable difficulties at this point – under the banner of 'Republican Socialism' or 'Charter Socialism'. There is no evidence that he contemplated such a move prior to 1842, although O'Brien had pleaded for unity between the Chartists and Socialists as early as 1840. Two of Bailey's early periodicals, the *Monthly Messenger* (1840) and the *Torch* (1842) contain much literary and philosophical speculation, a smattering of Owenite political economy, and the occasional denunciation of earlier radical plans (he commented on Paine's scheme to remit taxes to the poor, for example, that 'a system which proposes to improve the condition of mankind by the distribution of money, can never be a final good system of reformation'). Sometime in 1842, however, probably primarily as a response to the debate within the Rational Society respecting paternal and democratic forms of government (which we will examine in the next section), Bailey began to propound strongly democratic and Chartist opinions. In January 1843 he commenced a new journal, the *Model Republic*, advertised as the organ of the 'Society for the Encouragement of Socialist and Democratic Literature', which probably consisted of himself and a few friends.[37] In the first issue of the new paper, Bailey defined clearly both the opinions he wished to propagate and the audience to whom he wished to appeal:

[36] Six of Bailey's essays, originally published at Leeds in 1840–41, were reprinted as *The Social Reformers' Cabinet Library* (1848); *Essays on Miscellaneous Subjects* (1842), p. 185. Bailey was a member of the Central Board in 1838–39, and resigned on grounds of ill health. See the *AACAN. Minute Book of the Central Board, 1838–40*, 23 July 1838, 10 January 1839, 8 April 1839.

[37] *SS*, no. 4 (9 February 1840), 4; *MM* (1840), 130–2; *Torch*, no. 4 (1842), 64. It is also possible that the *London Social Reformer* was edited by Bailey (he is mentioned in it several times), in which case his activities in the furtherance of democratic Owenism began in 1840. On the face of other evidence, however, this is probably not the case, unless Bailey preferred to write literary essays for two years before taking this debate up actively again.

Persons holding these views constitute a class of reformers distinct from those Chartists who would employ physical violence in accomplishing their purposes, as well as from those Socialists who would be satisfied with any form of government that would supply them with the necessaries of life and the amusements of community. The possession of political power they regard as the inalienable birthright of the people; nor would they be content with any form of government that would deny the exercise of this right, to its subjects. Paternal forms of government, whether they relate to small societies or nations, they look upon as identical with paternal forms of humbug or paternal forms of despotism. Their motto is not 'war to the knife, and blood to the horse-bridles'; nor is it 'community under any form of government, whether despotism or democracy'; neither do they clamour for 'a fair day's wages for a fair day's work', which has been considered by some to be the highest object of legislatorial policy: but they sigh for a change in the political and social institutions of the world, – a change which shall afford to all equal rights and privileges, abolish mercantile competition and rivalry, and place society upon an equitable basis; in short, the objects they have in view, and for the accomplishment of which they shall not cease to labour, are, the acquirement of political power for the people, and the formation of Home Colonies on the plan originally laid down by the philosopher of Lanark.

The need for unity between the two movements, Chartism and Owenism, was thereafter a theme frequently reiterated in the seven month life of the journal.[38]

Bailey not only promoted this alliance more relentlessly than anyone else. He also expressed more clearly than other Owenites what communitarianism meant to the more politically minded Socialists. The 'model republic' was not merely something which might be established at Harmony. Nor was it an institution which could be embodied only at Westminster. It represented, instead, the political side of communitarianism, which was not as far removed from earlier forms of republicanism as Owen's own conceptions were. Very often the Owenites had deliberately denied themselves the use of a political vocabulary, even while addressing the moral and economic issues assumed to constitute the rational core of radical discourse. In Bailey's formulations, however, it is readily apparent how easily this language could be restored to an overtly political context:

Every community is a republic. Its very basis is the government of the many for the benefit of the many; its principal feature – the equal division of labour, and the products of that labour amongst all; its end and aim, the application of every scientific discovery for the mutual benefit and happiness of all. It supports no idlers who live on the labour of others – none are there pensioned but the sick, the aged, and the helpless – those whom the tender mercies of competitive society too often consign to one of the two bastilles, the prison or the workhouse. It would set a wholesome example to society, and exemplify the benefits to be derived from healthy labour, saying to the idle consumers of the produce of other's labour –

[38] *MR*, no. 1 (1 January 1843), 3.

'Ye idle drones, that rather pilfer than your bread obtain
By honest means like these, look hear and learn
How good and sweet and honourable a thing it is
To live by industry'.

This then is the Model Republic which we seek to establish, the very basis of which is the People's Charter and the rights of man.[39]

Bailey and his friends thus aimed to fuse the identity of Socialism with that of republican democracy. They sought to demonstrate not merely that the substantial social content of 'pure democracy' was realised in community of property, equal labour, and equal rewards, but as specifically, also, to acknowledge the legitimacy of the formal mechanisms of political democracy in a socialist conception of society. They wished therefore to prove that the six points of the People's Charter were 'embodied in the Rational System of Society, so that every true Socialist, wishing well to his country and the world, must be both Radical and Socialist in principle'. If Socialist communities were not 'intended politically to embody the spirit of the People's Charter', Bailey announced, 'then we are not communitarians'. That they were so intended, he believed, could be proven both by reference to Owen's *Development of the Principles and Plans on Which to Establish Self-Supporting Home Colonies* (1841), or equally by questioning 'ten or a dozen Socialists at random, taken from all parts of a public meeting, as to what may be their political creed'. If the ballot was not an issue for the Socialists, Bailey insisted, this was because 'on the principles of the Rational Society, there will be no such evils as bribery and intimidation to remedy'. But this did not imply for the country as a whole that the ballot was not both just and immediately necessary.[40]

If Bailey tended to follow Owen on the question of voting within the Rational Society, he nonetheless lambasted the generally unpolitical character of the Socialists, claiming that 'many, very many of the Chartists' were also Socialists, 'whilst comparatively few of the Socialists are to be found assisting the Chartists'. Instead the Socialists thought

that Communities will work out their own political rights when once established . . . they seem quietly to trust to the natural progress of democracy, and are tame to the fact, that unless we remodel the constitution through Parliament, the same oppressors of themselves and of the Chartists, the same enemies to both systems of innovation must remain at the helm for many a year to come, and the rising spirit of democracy will take a very long time – perhaps half a century, to remove them, unless accompanied by a general and continuous agitation. In fact, they leave the Radicals and the Chartists to work all the intermediate stages for them, between the Old Immoral World and the New Moral World, instead of co-operating with them towards both objects at the

[39] *Ibid.*, no. 6 (1 June 1843), 87. [40] *Ibid.*, no. 3 (1 March 1843), 38–9.

same time; instead of establishing, through Parliament, a rational government as well as rational communities out of doors.

Especially singled out by Bailey for criticism as 'the opponents of the People's Charter, or who remain passive or neutral in that just struggle' were Owen himself, the Sheffield Socialist Isaac Ironside and G. A. Fleming. The latter two of these, however, we have already noted as having spoken favourably of the Charter – but in 1838. Fleming, in particular, was now accused of having 'more than once whipped up to the poll a host of opinions and arguments against the Chartist body', and of unjustly castigating Chartist factionalism, lack of financial support, appeals to physical force, and general lack of progress. These weaknesses Bailey conceded. But he protested that they did not provide sufficient cause for hostility to Chartism, or for simplistic comparisons of its fortunes with those of the Socialists, such as the *New Moral World* under Fleming seemed prone to make:

Are they similarly circumstanced – have they ever been so? Why, the exchequer is low for the very same reason that they have done little in so long a time, that they have appealed to physical force, that they have been imprisoned and transported – and this reason is, that they are intrinsically the People or lower orders of society, while their brother Socialists are, many of them, included in what is termed the Middle Classes. They are the *poor* – and therefore have not money to advance their cause – and are uneducated – and substitute physical for moral force – and are transported and imprisoned and otherwise persecuted – and also quarrel among themselves, like any other party of men placed in similar circumstances. Now, however much it may be so with some people, we will venture to say that in the eyes of Mr. Fleming, poverty is *not* a crime: how then can he reconcile with his sentiments of philanthropy the reiteration of such statements as these when he knows the facts to have originated in the *poverty* of his fellow creatures?

Thus were exposed the practical paradoxes of the doctrine of the formation of character. Violence was an evil circumstance not to be countenanced, for it merely created further violence and ill-will. Blame, however, was illogical since circumstances alone occasioned behaviour. Owenism could justify either reaction to Chartism. In the final analysis it was perhaps only political opinion which dictated the course chosen by individual Socialists in their relations with Chartists.[41]

It is difficult to estimate how much support Bailey attracted in his efforts to unify both movements. Probably little was forthcoming. Thomas Frost gave the 'Charter Socialists' a few sentences in his autobiography. Elsewhere they seemed to have escaped notice. It is possible that a section of the London Socialists supported Bailey for a time, though they were clearly unable to pay the upkeep of the *Model*

[41] *Ibid.*, 38–41.

Republic. The concept of 'Charter Socialism', however, was predictably ignored by the *New Moral World*. Still, Bailey's significance lay not in his hopeless plan for a unified movement led by Fleming and O'Connor, but in his contribution to the growing intra-Owenite struggle over the management of the branches and the Queenwood community, to Owenism's own encounter with democratic radicalism rather than Chartism's meeting with Owenism at the national level. Before examining how this problem finally provoked a terminal breach between the major Socialist factions, however, let us see what can be concluded about the larger question of the relation of Chartism to Owenism.[42]

The evidence we have considered so far has been based upon Chartist–Socialist meetings or relations in which the Owenite component can be relatively confidently distinguished, despite the objections introduced. These, without doubt, composed the majority of contacts which Chartists had with 'socialists' and their ideas. But they do not entirely exhaust the catalogue of Socialist–Chartist connections. There were, of course, other individuals and organisations which any history of the coincidence of socialistic and Chartist ideas would have to consider, but which intermingle with our theme here only tangentially, either because their socialism was not of the Owenite variety, or because too little is known about them.[43] Weighing the impact of Owenism upon Chartism also involves ascertaining the importance of a group whom (to distinguish them from the Owenites) it would be best to call the 'social Chartists', especially O'Brien, Harney and their followers. These were not termed 'socialist' at this time, since this category was reserved primarily for the Owenites, though they inherited the title at a later date. But their own ideas and programmes were compounded of Owenite and other social radical elements. In O'Brien's case, both Owenite and Spencean doctrines co-existed in a programme which was popularised as the chief alternative to O'Connorite Chartism from the early 1840s onwards. O'Brien was without doubt an important Chartist leader, but after quarrelling with O'Connor – merely over his right to express his own views, O'Brien insisted – he was pushed away from the centre of activity. This, with the meagre coverage which the *Northern Star* now gave him, ensured a greatly reduced impact on the Chartist movement for his ideas over the next

---

[42] T. Frost, *Forty Years' Recollections* (1880), pp. 40–1; in September 1842 John Cramp alluded to a discussion between a lecturer and a 'Charter Socialist' (*NMW*, 11, no. 11, 10 September 1842, 90), otherwise there is virtually no mention of Bailey's plans; *MR*, no. 3 (1 March 1843), 43.

[43] O'Brien to Thomas Allsop, Allsop Collection, London School of Economics, Misc. 525/1. On relations between the two leaders, see Asa Briggs, 'Feargus O'Connor and J. Bronterre O'Brien', in J. W. Boyle, ed., *Leaders and Workers* (Dublin, Mercier Press, 1966), pp. 27–36.

ten years. After 1848, however, he was prominent again for a few years.[44]

Harney's views will be treated in greater detail in relation to the Fraternal Democrats and the later development of Chartism in the next chapter. But Owenism clearly influenced his plans much less than O'Brien's. In an excellent biography, A. R. Schoyen has established that what Harney ingested as a youth in the NUWC were not systematic beliefs, but vaguely defined concepts such as the right of labour to its fruits, as well as a general hostility to all forms of 'aristocracy', monied, landed or otherwise. What must additionally be stressed is the obviously Spencean contribution to Harney's social radicalism (and this clearly involves a reversal of previous appraisals of Thomas Spence's impact upon radicalism after 1820). This came about, in particular, through the medium of the early Chartist organisation called the East London Democratic Association, and the activities of the septuagenarian Spencean, Chartist and co-operator Allen Davenport. Harney's comment, in August 1845, that 'His creed was – and Thomas Spence had taught it him – that 'the land is the people's farm', and that it belongs to the entire nation, not to individuals or classes' might be treated in isolation (as Schoyen apparently did) as an incidental reference designed to induce the sacrosanct associations which invocations of established authorities obligingly provide. What makes this connection much more significant, however, is an examination of Harney's views at certain other points. In his first major speech before the East London Democratic Association in June 1837, for example, he clearly preached not only confiscation of the land, but also the management and rental *by each district* of its own lands, which was precisely Spence's plan, and not even the statist version of it partially adopted by O'Brien. The contents of Harney's short-lived *London Democrat* (April–June 1839) merely show how deeply entrenched this essentially agrarian radicalism was amongst Harney's circle of friends. The emphasis in this journal was almost entirely upon the nationalisation of the land, 'the natural source from

---

[44] See for instance *PCA*, no. 3 (March 1842), 48; *CM*, no. 1 (1843), 42, on John Goodwyn Barmby, an active East Anglian Chartist who also served as a national convention delegate, and who sought to ally his own curious hybrid of mystical Saint-Simonism with Chartism. The *Social Pioneer* (no. 4, 3 March 1839, 31) also mentions the obscure 'Society of Democratic Socialists' (S. Mosely, Secretary), which in early 1839 voted to become a branch of the new Manea Fen community. A number of Socialist emigration societies, such as the party Thomas Hunt led to Wisconsin, which published a 'Constitution of Pure Democratic Communism', also had Chartist supporters amongst them. The constitution is preserved in the Owen Collection, Holyoake House, Manchester, item 1323. On the societies see my 'John Adolphus Etzler, Technological Utopianism, and British Socialism: The Tropical Emigration Society and its Venezuelan Mission, 1833–48', *EHR*, 101 (1986), 31–55.

whence the revenues of a country should be derived', as 'C. R.' put it.[45]

The variety of forms of social radicalism circulating in this period nonetheless indicate that we exercise some caution in applying the generic category of 'socialism' to describe them. Once it is clear that social radical views were in fact much more widespread than has previously been suspected, there is nothing to be gained by attempting to define their common characteristics by the indiscriminate application of 'socialism' to all of them. Contemporary usage was more circumspect. In fact, this helps considerably to clarify the precise influence of Owenism on radicalism at this time, for it is likely that the vast majority of references to 'Socialism' by Chartists in fact concerned Owenite Socialism, and not a more general usage, which only began to circulate in and after 1848. When O'Brien called for unity between the Chartists and Socialists in 1840, for example, the Owenites were obviously the 'Socialists' to whom he appealed. Taking these various arguments together, and assembling what evidence is available, we can therefore conclude that Owenism and Chartism took each other considerably more seriously, debating a much broader range of issues, and offering each other considerably more support, at least for a time, than has hitherto been generally assumed. McCabe's statement that Owen's followers 'were not at all indifferent' to but rather 'fraternized with the Chartists everywhere' seems, with certain qualifications, to be substantially true.[46]

However, such a conclusion must remain partially suspended pending the outcome of a sufficient number of autopsies on the fate of local Owenite branches, the careers of their individual members, and the relation of both to local Chartism. In some towns, the Owenites and Chartists met on the same premises, and sometimes shared lecturers, social functions, and even leaders. But we cannot yet be sure how often this was the case. The debate on Socialism in the House of Lords in early 1840 made much of such connections. The conclusions of such proceedings, however, can hardly furnish adequate evidence or guidance for modern historians. In lieu of a more securely grounded conclusion, then, it might be helpful to offer the rudiments of an historical overview of the connections between Chartism and Socialism. This

---

[45] Schoyen, *The Chartist Challenge. A Portrait of George Julian Harney* (Heinemann, 1958), p. 8, which however alters the meaning of the quote by leaving 'him' out. Harney later emphasised that co-operation should be substituted for competition and that labour and rewards should be equal (*ibid.*, pp. 135, 180, 186); *NS*, no. 407 (30 August 1845), 8; *LD*, no. 38 (4 June 1837), 297; *LDem*, no. 3 (27 April 1839), 23; no. 6 (18 May 1839), 41; no. 7 (25 May 1839), 51. There is also a contribution by Allen Davenport on universal suffrage in no. 9 (8 June 1839), 69. For Davenport's version of Spence's plan see his *The Life, Writings, and Principles of Thomas Spence* (1836).
[46] *SS*, no. 4 (9 February 1840), 4.

allows us to see that there was, in fact, a definite pattern of development in the relations between the two movements.[47]

If we enumerate the occasions on which Chartists and Socialists met to debate one another, or compared each other's views and organisations, and especially those where the Owenites praised and sought to accommodate themselves to the goals of the Chartists, it is clear that most of these fall into the 1836–40 period. Writing in 1838, the Bradford Owenite Samuel Bower, distinguishing between 'the friendly section' and the 'anti-Socialist section' amongst the Chartists, proclaimed that it was 'an important fact, that a large section are favourable to, at least, the economic views of the Socialists, and seek political power merely as an effective instrument for removing the competitive principle from society'. Several months later, he also spoke of 'a large number of Socialists who, like myself, have sought political freedom in universal suffrage'. But he then added, without explanation, that their numbers were constantly diminishing. Concurrently, however, O'Brien, though complaining that many radicals repudiated social communities as 'mere phantoms of the brain', while many Socialists saw universal suffrage as an obsolete political change, hazarded the view that 'if I mistake not, all the more intelligent Radicals are becoming Socialists. I find this to be the case in London. I know it to be the case in Birmingham, and from the letters of Mr. FINCH and others in the *Star*, I conclude that the same process of amalgamation is going on in the North'. A year earlier, the *New Moral World* had disparaged 'persons strangely compounded of the Socialist and Politician' who sought to engage themselves on behalf of the Chartists. But by 1840, there were very many more complaints from the Chartists that the Socialists were actively impeding them, and seemed 'to despise' univeral suffrage, as 'Scotus' put it in O'Brien's *Southern Star*.[48]

What accounts for this shift? It seems very likely, as Schoyen suspected some twenty years ago, that the events of 1839 – the spectre of revolution – led the Owenites to withdraw abruptly from politics. Many of the Socialists doubtless shared the views of the Manchester *Herald of the Future*, which declared in December 1839 that:

---

[47] The Lords' proceedings were reprinted as an unpaginated special edition of the *New Moral World* on 15 February 1840. In the case of at least one of its assertions – that at Dudley, the membership of the Chartist and Socialist bodies was nearly identical, either their lordships were in error, or modern historians have found little trace of this overlap. Probably very few of the assertions made on this occasion were entirely accurate.

[48] S. Bower, *The Peopling of Utopia* (Bradford, 1838), p. 3; Bower, *A Sequel to the Peopling of Utopia* (Bradford, 1838), pp. 4, 19; *NS*, no. 32 (23 June 1838), 4; *NMW*, 3, no. 121 (18 February 1837), 129; *SS*, 2, no. 3 (3 May 1840), 4. *Paul Pry's Third Ramble Through the New Moral World* (Doncaster, 1840) also noted that while Chartists and Socialists had formerly mixed freely, men like Fleming were now attacking Chartist 'outrages' (p. 4).

The Chartists during the last year or two have excited the country to a considerable extent, and so long as they adopted the weapons of argument and persuasion, we sympathised with them, and watched their proceedings with much interest; admitting as we did, the abstract justice of the first principles of their political creed, though differing on Social Economy, as well as in the anticipated benefits which were expected to flow from the adoption of the People's Charter. But now that argument has been replaced by threats and denunciations, the power of brute force, the fierce and vindictive ebulition of passion, recommended as the means to work out political regeneration, we most solemnly protest against the suicidal folly of men, so mad as to throw away all chance of gaining their object, by such dangerous and indefensible measures. Change in opinion must precede change in institutions, and the former, once fairly accomplished, will soon work out the latter.

Nor can we ignore the possibility that the Owenites sought actively to help foil violent revolutionary tactics when the opportunity to do so presented itself. Evidence of this is exceedingly scarce. But Lloyd Jones did later recall that the Socialists had generally taken a stand against the Chartists' 'Sacred Month' offensive in 1842 (when a general strike was contemplated), and that he had been chosen to present the Socialist case at a Chartist meeting where thousands were present, and had succeeded in convincing them all of the folly of such proceedings. He was later informed, too, that plainclothes police had been present as the police chief, Sir Charles Shaw, had believed Jones' life to be in danger.[49]

Not all Socialists retreated from the reform agitation, however. As late as October 1840, a Dundee Owenite announced that he was

a friend to political reform, and would do all in my power to promote it . . . My advocacy of Socialism does not prevent my supporting the movement for the Charter. I attend Chartist meetings, vote for Chartist resolutions, sign Chartist petitions, and subscribe to Chartist funds. The Socialists generally do the same; and yet many Chartists suppose that we are opposed to their agitation.

The general Chartist impression did indeed contradict this view. Reflecting in early 1846 on the history of relations between the two movements, the *Northern Star* singled out for thanks John Watts, G. A. Fleming (who as we have seen was attacked by Chartists on other occasions), and George Jacob Holyoake, with 'two or three others'. But it also noted that 'the great body of the "Rationalists" preferred constituting themselves into a "sect", rather than mingle with "the people", which, had they done, they would not only have benefited the people, but would also have strengthened themselves, and more extensively propagated their principles'. There was also a regional dimension to this relationship, moreover. Chartist–Owenite connections were

---

[49] A. Schoyen, *Chartist Challenge*, p. 100; *HF*, no. 3 (7 December 1839), 35 (see also *NMW*, 10, no. 1, 3 July 1841, 7, where a Socialist explains how he has lost faith in political change); *NWC*, no. 5994 (14 June 1879), 3. Jones' role at this meeting is confirmed in 'Chartism and the Trades' Unions', *Our History* Pamphlet no. 31 (1963), p. 4.

probably more frequent in the north, and especially in Scotland, than in the west (except perhaps for Chelmsford), Wales, and the south outside of London (where both movements were weaker anyway). To the extent that we can judge from surviving issues of periodicals, the Welsh Chartist press was generally silent on the question of socialism, or explicitly denied that Chartism sought an equality of social rights. In Scotland, where Owen's achievements at New Lanark were helpfully a matter of regional pride, amicable and firm relations between Chartists and Socialists seem to have lasted from the mid-1830s up to 1850 and beyond.[50]

Other reasons help to account for both the continuing support for Chartism by some Socialists through the mid-1840s, as well as the neglect by many Chartist leaders of the Socialists in the same period. Particularly important, especially after early 1843, was O'Connor's shift in emphasis from the pursuit of the Charter to the establishment of the Land Plan. This stole much of the Socialists' thunder since they were now no longer the sole proponents of large-scale egalitarian home colonisation. The exact reasons for O'Connor's relatively dramatic shift in emphasis towards the Land Plan have been the subject of some debate. But the idea of home colonisation was hardly a complete novelty to most Chartists. Some had always expressed an interest in the land, especially as a result of O'Brien's teachings, but also in connection with the propagandising of men such as Hetherington and Lovett. This interest had been conceived in part, however, in relation to the idea of collective ownership of the land rather than novel forms of settling it. Lesser known radicals such as Thomas Ireland (who had been among the founders of the LWMA) and one 'M. M–n' respectively urged the nationalisation of the land, and the abolition of all individual property, particularly in machinery, in the early 1840s. One short-lived periodical, the *Chartist Pilot*, fully endorsed O'Brien's

---

[50] *TS*, 2, no. 103 (3 October 1840), 4; *NS*, no. 432 (21 February 1846), 3; *WV*, no. 29 (7 September 1839), 3, no. 40 (23 November 1839), 4; *WS*, no. 7 (28 November 1840), 1 (see also miscellaneous copies of the *Trumpet of Wales* and *Advocate and Merthyr Free Press* from 1841 in HO 45/54 and 45/242); *TS*, 1, no. 46 (31 August 1839), 361 which claimed that many radicals agreed with the Socialists on the question of property; in early 1840, however, the editor of this paper denied that the Chartists were associated with the Socialists and accused the enemies of political reform of circulating such rumours (2, no. 79, 18 April 1840, 2). An article later in the year, too, claimed that many Scottish radicals thought that the 'co-operators' wanted to destroy the Chartist agitation (no. 115, 26 December 1840, 4). The Glasgow *Scottish Patriot* also denied that the Chartists sought an equal division of land and other property (1, no. 8, 24 August 1839, 113), but otherwise was quite silent on the question of socialism. The editor did, however, protest when the police interfered with Socialists distributing their leaflets on the Green on Sundays, but denied that his comments meant that he had been influenced by Socialist ideas (3, no. 61, 29 August 1840, 137). This would again suggest that the avoidance of socialistic subjects was a conscious strategic decision.

precepts on land nationalisation, while as early as February 1842, the *National Vindicator* combined an attack upon class legislation with a virtually Socialist account of machinery. The *Chartist Circular*, too, alleged that paper money was no equivalent to labour in exchange, though such (O'Brienite?) allusions to Owenite exchange theory were comparatively rare in Chartist circles. Most importantly, O'Brien himself continued to propound a compromise, pluralistic position on the whole question of socialistic measures, writing in 1843 that the best general plan was for an 'endless variety of social arrangements' ranging from small farms to communities.[51]

Neither O'Brien nor his ideas ever came remotely close to dominating mainstream Chartism in the 1840s, however. The novelty of the Land Plan was that it was Feargus O'Connor, hero to millions, who now demanded the repossession of the land, not any lesser leader or newspaper scribbler. Nor was this the only sign of change in O'Connor's views. In 1842–43, he also began to emphasise more frequently the role of machinery in the creation of social distress, at times seemingly charging it with virtually *all* of the woes faced by the working classes, which had previously been an exclusively Owenite emphasis. What the allotment system would generate, O'Connor now claimed, was morality and respect for the laws, equality and a free market, an increase in the value of the land, and a home surplus 'larger than the false and capricious trade of the whole world'. In addition it would make labour wholly independent of capital, but also give capitalists a good return in the meantime. Retrospectively all of these claims have the same unreal, if curiously familiar, air about them that many of the Owenites' plans sometimes did. This is surely not surprising, since, with slight variations in emphasis, all of them had been employed for some twenty years by socialists.[52]

However else O'Connor's thinking may have altered during these years, he certainly seems to have ingested a strong dose of social logic. Since the beginning of the Chartist movement, he had conceived political power to be the means and social happiness the end of radical reform. But it was one thing to suggest that the land was the only means of effecting the salvation of the working classes. It was quite another to become so obsessed by the idea that, by late 1845, O'Connor

[51] *NAG*, no. 12 (19 March 1842), 90; *ECC*, 1, no. 19 (1841), 75–6; *ChP*, no. 12 (18 November 1843), 9; *NV*, ns no. 14 (12 February 1842), 3; *CC*, no. 37 (7 June 1840), 149; *PMGRF*, no. 8 (1843), 60. On the *Chartist Pilot*, see my note of the same title. Even by 1838, it was clear that some Chartists were more aware of the need to specify economic reforms than the radicals had been in 1831–32. See for example, *WTS*, no. 264 (16 September 1838), 2108.

[52] *ECC*, 2, no. 60 (1843), 29; no. 68 (1843), 61. On the Land Plan see Alice Mary Hadfield, *The Chartist Land Company* (Newton Abbot, David and Charles, 1970).

had completely reversed the causal relationship between political and social power, now asserting that 'the possession of the land by a very small minority will lead to the establishment of the People's Charter, before, under the existing disparity of classes, political agitation will lead to the same result'. O'Connor's shift in strategy – whose significance is too often undervalued – thus had profound consequences both for the concentration of Chartist energies, and for any understanding of the relationship between the 'social' and 'political' factors in Chartist theory. It led him closer to Owen than at any previous point in his career. Indeed, O'Connor even stated that he looked upon 'the experiments made by Mr. Owen for the improvement of the physical condition of all classes of society, but more especially the working classes, as having far exceeded in utility those of any other individual who has ever lived before him', while still preferring the 'co-operative' to the communal system.[53]

Did the Chartists consciously consider allying with the Socialists in this period? The failure of an attempted partnership with the middle classes in 1843 permitted other allies to be considered, and rendered the avoidance of Socialist ideas for the sake of Whig-radical sensibilities less necessary. 'No union with them! let us rather annihilate them as a class', cried the exasperated *London Chartist Monthly Magazine* in disgust with the middle classes, turning instead to the possibility of confederating with the socialists, 'our mutual allies . . . our nearest kin, but once removed'. That this had not occurred so far, the editor admitted, was certainly in part the fault of the Chartists:

The Socialists have defined their ends and aims – they have told us what they mean to do, and how they mean to do it. We have not done this, and consequently they may reasonably entertain some doubt or suspicion of us. All that we have definitively said is, that we want the Charter; but what for, or

---

53 *ES*, no. 43 (12 September 1842), 1; *ECC*, 2, no. 115 (1843), 249; *NS*, no. 270 (14 January 1843), 4; no. 416 (1 November 1845), 1; O'Connor, *The Land and Its Capabilities* (Manchester, 1842), p. 115. For evidence that other Chartists were startled by O'Connor's change of views see, e.g., *NS* no. 293 (24 June 1843), 8. In 1842, O'Connor defined the objects of the Charter to be '*first*, to develop the entire resources of the country, and, *secondly*, to ensure a more *equitable* distribution of the increased productions . . . to be independent of the foreign grower, the wholesale importer, and retail speculator, a large, a very large portion of society must be their own producers, and their own consumers' (O'Connor, *The Land and its Capabilities*, p. 34). This change is acknowledged to some degree in Eric Glasgow and Donald Read's *Feargus O'Connor, Irishman and Chartist* (Edward Arnold, 1961), pp. 111–12, which terms the Land Plan in 1845 'an important shift in emphasis. For the rest of his political career achievement of the Land Plan took precedence in O'Connor's mind over achievement of the Charter'. But these authors only emphasise that O'Connor now believed that the Land Plan 'could be' achieved before the Charter, not that it *had* to be, as it would seem O'Connor did think for at least a time. James Epstein's very useful biography, *The Lion of Freedom. Feargus O'Connor and the Chartist Movement, 1832–1842* (Croom Helm, 1982) does not address this problem, though it de-emphasises the novelty of O'Connor's interest in the land (p. 256).

what we will do with it, we have left to vague conjecture and uncertainty. They have had no friend – we may use it as an enemy. It is time to express ourselves more clearly ... If, after a candid review of their system, we can conscientiously and consistently concur with them, let us do so – let us pledge them our assistance, and in return we may hope for their support.

In 1843, we also find new Chartist praise for both the Socialists' emphasis on the land and their forms of organisation, as well as a new sophistication in the *Northern Star* about the realities of inequality in America (under the editorship of Harney, who supported the American Agrarian League). Even O'Connor now announced that 'America never had a republic', not because it had been subverted by slavery, but because of social inequality. In return, some of the Socialists praised O'Connor's new interest in the land and the growing discussion of economic issues in the *Northern Star*, and congratulated themselves that their own ideas were at last prevailing in Chartist circles. But, instead of preparing the ground for an alliance between the two movements, these manoeuvres probably had the opposite effect: they made one unnecessary. Not that such a merger was ever probable in the first place. As long as Chartism was centred upon O'Connor and Socialism on Owen, it was exceedingly unlikely. Both, as we have seen, may well have contemplated such a union in 1841. But both were also doctrinaire, headstrong and inveterately egotistical, and nothing came of this plan. Instead Owen, at least, had chosen in 1841 to plunge into a new political undertaking entirely of his own design. As he proceeded, it became increasingly evident that he was, once again, not averse to forcing his own will upon his followers to ensure its success. At a time when many socialists had ingested radical precepts, this instigated a revolt which doubtless assisted in the annihilation of the whole Socialist project. But it also resulted in the clearest expression of Owenism's own, internal brand of democratic, social radicalism.[54]

The Rational Society and the revolt over Queenwood

Although Owen's political nostrums only created a major uproar in his own ranks in the early 1840s, his inclinations towards the new Socialist organisation were apparent by 1835. Consequently the

[54] *LCMM*, no. 1 (June 1843), 15–17; *NS*, no. 271 (21 January 1843), 4; on early Chartist praise for the Socialists' organisation, see the *Champion*, no. 184 (22 March 1840), 2, and for evidence that the Chartists liberally copied from it, see William Hill, *The Rejected Letters* (1843), p. 1, and Eileen Yeo, 'Some Practices and Problems of Chartist Democracy', in J. Epstein and D. Thompson, eds., *The Chartist Experience* (Macmillan, 1982), p. 367; *NS*, no. 337 (27 April 1844), 4; no. 338 (4 May 1844), 1; *NMW*, 11, no. 43 (22 April 1844), 345–6; no. 42 (15 April 1843), 336; 9, no. 2 (9 January 1841), 17 (specifically with reference to Lovett and Collins).

suspicions attached to his political reputation were not long in reviving. As early as the AACAN congress of June 1837, a debate about the most suitable government to inaugurate a community 'created more division than any other question submitted to the Congress', Lloyd Jones later recalled. But it ended with the unanimous resolution that the rule of one individual was indispensable for the first two or three years (a proposal, it will be recalled, which had been accepted by William Thompson and his followers some years earlier). The aim of this plan was purportedly only to deter that 'delay, blundering, and endless talk' which those unused to democratic association were prone to under the usual mode of government of such societies, by elected committee.[55] But the expression of such sentiments provoked rumblings from the ranks of the reformers. A letter to the radical *London Dispatch* protested that this decision would result in a despotism, contending that

under a despotism you are to learn the *principles*, and acquire the *practice*, of democratic government. Did ever a mechanic learn his trade without working at it? The absurdity of this position must be apparent to the lowest capacity. How can equal rights and equal laws exist under a despotism? I leave these sages to determine. They say the institutions of society have deteriorated every character, therefore you are incompetent to regulate your own arrangements. Although you create wealth for others, you are destitute of the skill to create wealth for yourselves; although you possess discernment enough to elect a despot, to invest him for two or three years with absolute power, yet your judgement is so weak that you are unfit to govern yourselves. Was there ever such a mass of inconsistencies put together in the resolution and reasoning (if it can be so called) of any public body?

To this Lloyd Jones, defending the congress decision, replied that no despotism was implied, since all members of the community had to be designated by a three-fourths majority, and since the 'despot', after all, could be recalled by congress at any time. The editor of the *Dispatch* replied that an elected despot was no better than any other. Another writer rejoined that it was a democratic arrangement, with the editor again retorting that a paper constitution was no guarantee against despotism in fact. Possibly in response to this exchange, the *New Moral World* insisted a few weeks later that New Harmony during Owen's absence had exhibited a 'severe practical condemnation of the democratical theories' so lauded by many.[56]

The institutional mechanisms of the AACAN remained largely unchanged until the congress of 1841. Originally it had been planned to have the President elected by 'Senior' and 'Junior' councils of twelve

---

[55] Lloyd Jones, *The Life of Robert Owen*, pp. 306–7.
[56] *Manual of the AACAN* (1836), p. 34; *NMW*, 3, no. 149 (2 September 1837), 366; 4, no. 176 (10 March 1838), 153; no. 181 (14 April 1838), 195; 3, no. 137 (10 June 1837), 247–8; *LD*, no. 40 (18 June 1837), 316; no. 42 (5 July 1837), 332; *NMW*, 3, no. 143 (22 July 1837), 314.

members each, but this was apparently soon dispensed with. The rapidly expanding branches instead elected their own officers and delegates to congresses, the congresses and Central Board chose the Social Missionaries and regulated district-level affairs, and the congresses and Board nominated the head of the organisation and his assistants. A number of important aspects of this form of organisation, including the idea of class meetings and leaders, were copied from the Methodists, from whom a number of Socialists (at least at Manchester) had defected. Owen's general leadership was only rarely questioned during the early years. The *New Moral World* normally insisted both that he could be trusted with great power, and that the constitution of his organisation was democratic. Owen's lieutenants, the most important of whom included Lloyd Jones, a former journeyman cotton-spinner, Alexander Campbell, a carpenter and builder, James Rigby, a plumber and glazier, and G. A. Fleming, a house-painter, were generally steadfastly loyal. Nonetheless Owen and the Central Board resolutely stipulated that their own theory of government would have to be applied to the first community to be built, even at the expense of delaying its inception. Two estates, in fact, were offered to them in 1838–39 by devoted disciples, one at Wretten belonging to James Hill, the other the property of William Hodson, near March in Cambridgeshire. In both cases, however, the Central Board, while initially favourable, declined on the grounds that each owner was too concerned to implement his own ideas of socialism. This was especially true in the case of Hodson, who hoisted the tricolour above the Union Jack at his community and craved too much local democracy (some suspected power for himself) for the taste of the Central Board.[57]

After the estate near Tytherly, Hampshire, also known as Queenwood or Harmony, was finally acquired in August 1839, the question of communitarian government again became a matter of practical importance. The causes of the decline of earlier communities were reconsidered, and new forms of government speculated upon. One scheme even proposed that the sectarian character of the Socialist organisation could be perfected with the election of a Patriarch and

[57] *NMW*, 4, no. 205 (29 September 1838), 399; 5, no. 2 (3 November 1838), 22; *WB*, 1, no. 2 (27 July 1839), 9–11; the Board, in fact, had clearly resolved to keep as tight a rein as possible over the development of the movement, refusing to allow a group of about forty members of Branch 12 in Liverpool (who termed themselves 'requisitionists') to secede to form a new branch, and threatening to withdraw their branch charter if they could not settle their differences among themselves. The Board also failed to grant a requested charter to Edinburgh because of the divisions amongst the Owenites, and in August 1841 threatened to suspend all branches which did not fully comply with all its laws and instructions (*Minutes of the Proceedings of the Liverpool Branch of the AACAN*, 1840, 32–3); *AACAN. Minute Book of the Central Board*, 15 October 1838; *National Community Friendly Society. Minute Book of the Board of Directors*, 17 October 1838, 20 October 1838, 18 August 1838.

Bishops, and John Finch thus wrote Owen, addressing him as 'your most sacred highness', to propose himself as the first 'Bishop of the New Moral World'. No doubt he derived some satisfaction, at least, after his failure to see the post created, by assuming the role at an Owenite fancy dress ball. But most reacted rather differently to the problem of authority in the Socialist movement. Fervent democrats like Thomas Hunt typically responded to Owen's suggestion that the working classes were incompetent to direct operations on their own with the warning that Owen sought to establish two classes in the new community: one productive, and the other 'educational'. Moral fitness and not previous experience, he urged instead, should be the sole attribute required of governors.[58]

In the spring of 1840 the Socialist movement was at the height of both its popularity and notoriety. The 1838 Congress had reported thirty-three branches with some 1,700 paying members. Now some sixty branches with approximately 4,000 members were active. Halls of Science were springing up across the country, with perhaps 50,000 attending Sunday lectures. The visiting French socialist Flora Tristan claimed that the Owenites had nearly 500,000 adherents at this time, while the *Journal of the British Empire* put the number at 140,000. The Central Board and branches had distributed as many as two million tracts in the previous year. Clerics across the nation had begun to rise in alarm, and the Lords entertained appropriate measures for containing the Socialist threat to marriage, religion, property and sound morals. At this time, shortly after Chartism had suffered several severe setbacks, the debate on government among the Socialists began to intensify. A variety of discussions about which forms of democracy might be compatible with socialism resulted. Considering a number of proposals on the subject, the *London Social Reformer* warned that 'the trumpet has been sounded to prepare to appoint Patriarchs and Bishops !!! in all the Branches', and affirmed its opposition to priestcraft of every type, 'whether it be an Ecclesiastical, or a Social, priesthood'. The paper further suggested that the entire Owenite organisation be more centralised to increase the efficiency of the Central Board, but that district boards should be chosen by and from the branches in each district. It also proposed that female delegates might make the annual congresses more representative. As for the government of Harmony, its head should be selected democratically, with all adults electing

58 *NMW*, 6, no. 43 (17 August 1839), 681; 7, no. 63 (4 January 1840), 995; 7, no. 80 (2 May 1840), 1278–80; R. B. Rose, 'John Finch', *THSLC*, 59 (1957), 170; *NMW*, 8, no. 17 (24 October 1840), 271; James Murphy, 'Robert Owen in Liverpool', *THSLC*, 112 (1961), 93; *WB*, 1, no. 11 (28 September 1839), 94–7.

the heads of their departments, who would form the council. Half of the latter should then vacate their positions every three months

and be filled up, not by *selection* or *election*, but by equal proportions of the sex, by *rotation*, so that all contests can be by this means avoided ... Experience having shown us that habits of governing beget pride and arrogance of character, incompatible with the well-being of any community; if they come then as a matter of right, the holding of office will no longer be regarded as a reward for superior merit, real or supposed, in the individual.[59]

Contributing to this discussion, William Hodson conceded that elections *were* disruptive in the branches, but presumed this was primarily because it was incumbent upon the branches to elect members to the Tytherly community. Since all of the Socialists were exceedingly anxious to savour the delights of the new moral world, this responsibility had caused 'unpleasant contests of one with another, which men have not yet been trained to bear with philosophical equanimity – and feud, disgust, or jealousy, in those left behind'. Tytherly itself, Hodson felt, should be governed by rules of its own devising and adoption, since no community could possibly be successful which did not elect its own directors. To these persistent criticisms the congress and Central Board had two replies. As Fleming pointed out, Hodson as owner of the land had actually appointed himself as president of the 'Hodsonian community' at Manea Fen for five years, and retained the power of naming two of the six directors of the community. To this Hodson replied that three-quarters of the members and one-half of the directors had the constitutional power to eject him if they pleased. Secondly, the Central Board insisted that the original rules of the association must be followed to ensure that congresses, who represented shareholders in the branches, made laws for any community until such time as the capital had been repaid.[60]

Throughout 1840 the rift between the Central Board and the increasingly militant democratic Owenites in the branches widened. Benjamin Warden wrote to Hodson complaining that 'nothing has been *worse* managed than Tytherly', and urged the Owenites to arouse 'that democratic spirit amongst you, govern yourselves, return to first principles, maintain that glorious principle of equality of right and condition, and we shall be united, and victory will crown our efforts'. Hodson wrote again on this topic to Owen, claiming that the need for three governors at Harmony in less than six months proved that

---

[59] *Proceedings of the Third Congress of the AACAN* (Leeds, 1838), p. 65; Flora Tristan, *Flora Tristan's London Journal* (G. Prior, 1980), p. 241; *WB*, 1, no. 16 (19 September 1840), 125; Robert Ainslie, *An Examination of Socialism* (1840), p. 64; *NMW*, 8, no. 1 (4 July 1840), 2; *LSR*, no. 1 (2 May 1840), 5; no. 2 (9 May 1840), 12–13.

[60] *WB*, 1, no. 46 (30 May 1840), 375; no. 43 (9 May 1840), 350; *NMW*, 7, special issue (30 May 1840), 1270–2; 8, no. 21 (21 November 1840), 323.

The Socialists are the worst of all men to submit to be governed by others, and they themselves be silent. We have found this to be the case here, which induced me to throw the government into the hands of the members. It is in vain to suppose intelligent men will be governed by a Governor appointed by Congress . . . the members must have the power of electing their own Chairman, Board of Directors, and other officers – in fact they must be self-governed.

Owen, meanwhile, increasingly expressed the view that it was the democratic inclinations of the Harmony inhabitants which created such disruption there. But this promoted Samuel Bower, who had spent some time at the community, to respond that he did not remember

that any individuals ever expressed themselves as having the notion that they were to govern themselves. A great deal of theorizing was, no doubt, indulged in, on the subject of government and on many other subjects, but the interest of everyone to act in accordance with the laws of the society, and to yield obedience to the constituted authorities, was always clearly understood. Further, I do not remember any instance where the governor was refused the co-operation of the members, or prevented by them from carrying into operations his plans. The attempt to form a community at Tytherly has not hitherto been successful, certainly, but the primary causes of failure lie elsewhere than in the conduct of the members.[61]

Then came the inauguration of the 'elective paternal' form of government. Its initial introduction at Harmony, with the governor choosing his own assistants, may have been immediately necessary in order to secure Owen's support and facilitate the economic progress of the community. But there is no doubt that attempting to extend the scheme elsewhere was extremely ill-timed. Some discussion of local organisation had occurred at the 1839 Congress, when it was revealed that one branch, for example, had no less than twenty-three officials of various kinds (though some argued that 'Many were gratified with the distinction, and took more interest in the branch in consequence'). The adoption of the new form of management by the branches was first proposed by the Central Board in November 1840 as a prelude to decisions to be made by a congress the following spring. Simultaneously, the district boards were to be deprived of any useful function by placing the branches directly in communication with the Central Board. As we saw above, Owen advertised the new scheme before the sixth annual congress of May 1841 and argued strenuously for its adoption during the congress itself. Especially during the past year, he claimed, the branches had been in a state of continual division, which

[61] *WB*, 2, no. 18 (3 October 1840), 140–1; no. 20 (17 October 1840), 157; no. 21 (24 October 1840), 163.

had arisen from the old principle of individuality obtaining throughout the branches. There had been a contest for office – a contest for power – a contest for almost everything, which was in accordance with the views of the old world. That contest must now cease; and he was of the opinion that until it had ceased, they could never exhibit a successful community.

The branches therefore could elect their own leaders, but the latter should choose their own officers. The congress, which Charles South-well complained was overloaded with 'backbone Owenites' ready to obey Owen's every beck and call, resolved to adopt this plan, and recommended that each branch accept the new principle of government by a majority vote.[62]

Two members of this congress, including Southwell, warned that the branches were likely to regard the new system as an infringement upon their liberties. Not all were to react this way. On an outing into the Surrey countryside a number of members from London spoke in favour of 'the patriarchal system' of governing, inferring that what they took to be the failure of pure democratic socialism perhaps meant that an ideal combination of monarchy, aristocracy and democracy corresponded to similar divisions in human nature. However, most of the branches about which there is adequate information appear to have split sharply on the issue. Owen, it seems, had merely succeeded in giving them a new cause for division instead of a means of achieving unity. From Lambeth it was reported in March 1842 that some members objected that the new principle concentrated too much power in the hands of a single individual, though two years later the system was reported as functioning there. At Branch A1 in London considerable discussion was devoted to the implications of the system, which in April 1842 received a vote of confidence of thirty-five to twenty-five. In October 1842, however, Thomas Hunt was elected as president there, and termed the unity form of government a 'pure democracy'. But it also seems that he had modified the system, since no measure could be adopted without a majority of the members of the council. At Manchester a division on the subject produced no resolution until abstaining members agreed to co-operate, when a

---

[62] *Proceedings of the Fourth Congress of the AACAN* (1839), p. 69; NMW, 8, no. 21 (21 November 1840), 324; 9, no. 22 (29 May 1841), 338; Charles Southwell, *Confessions of a Freethinker* (c. 1845), p. 62. There had also been some variation in past modes of electing branch officers. Initially branches were supposed to be governed by an 'elder brother' and two 'assistant brothers' elected by the members (*ibid.*, 1, no. 19, 7 March 1835, 145). In 1836 it was decided that branches should elect as many managers as they liked (2, no. 84, 4 June 1836, 353), and this loose provision for a 'council' was still in force in 1837 (3, no. 137, 10 June 1837, 2552). Its numbers were restricted to seven in 1839 (*Proceedings of the Fourth Congress of the AACAN*, 1839, p. 69), and in 1840 it was decided that this group should elect its own president (*Supplement to the Laws of the UCSRR*, 1840, p. 2).

successful vote of thirty-two to twenty-nine was recorded in favour of the new form of government. At Sheffield, Isaac Ironside later claimed, the system worked fairly well, because as President he reasoned carefully with all who disagreed with him. By the spring of 1842, twenty-two branches had accepted the new form of government, while nine had rejected it.[63]

By the eighth congress of May 1843, however, it appeared that the scheme generally had collapsed. Where it had succeeded, one delegate claimed, 'they had diverged more or less from it, as laid down in the constitution of the Society; and where it had been strictly carried out, it had failed, and they had been obliged to return to the old democratic system'. At London, for example, where most branch members, it was emphasised, were working men, the President's choice of a council was agreed upon by the other branch members. Stockport intimated that it would return to the old form of government, while Oldham agreed this was advisable because 'they knew that all men were fallible, and that the best men were liable to err'. Holyoake, with Southwell now waging a militant atheistical campaign, also remained one of Owen's loudest critics. Reporting that 'the good sense of the majority of branches' had 'reduced the paternal government to nearly a dead letter', he added that 'if popular support is to be sought, congress must lay its ban upon this prime paralysis of enthusiasm'.[64] But after the middle of 1842, the focus of opposition to Owen's mode of management shifted increasingly away from the branches and towards the congresses, the Central Board, and the government of Harmony. The power of the Central Board had already been the subject of several attacks in the Chartist press at the end of 1841. These were renewed in mid-1843 with an exchange lasting several months between 'Gracchus' (possibly G. J. Harney), who contended that the Owenite system, with the president choosing his own council, was undemocratic, and ought to be replaced by direct democracy, and William Galpin, representing Owen's case for the lack of unity in all such elective councils. At the same time, the Charter Socialists led by James Napier Bailey com-

[63] *NMW*, 9, no. 23 (6 June 1841), 355; 10, no. 8 (21 August 1841), 63; no. 37 (12 March 1842), 291; 13, no. 2 (6 July 1844), 15; 10, no. 44 (30 April 1842), 351, 360; 11, no. 18 (29 October 1842), 146; no. 20 (12 November 1842), 164; *Report of the Proceedings of the Eighth Annual Congress of the Rational Society* (1843), p. 157; *NMW*, 10, no. 47 (21 May 1842), 378.

[64] *Ibid.*, 9, no. 48 (27 May 1843), 386; 11, no. 47 (20 May 1843), 377, 379–80; *Movement*, no. 18 (1843), 139–40. For a discussion of the operations of the paternal form of government in the Whitechapel branch, see the *Rational Society. Minute Book of Directors*, no. 2, 18 October 1844. On Holyoake's opposition to Owen, see Leo Grugel, *George Jacob Holyoake* (Philadelphia, Porcupine Press, 1971), pp. 15–42. He and Southwell may have had a hand in the publication of *The Atheist and Republican* and *The Blasphemer* in 1842.

menced an independent assault on their *'bête noire'* (as Thomas Frost put it), the paternal system of government.[65]

Inside the Rational Society much of the opposition to the powers of the Central Board and Harmony governor derived from Owen's devastatingly inefficient financial management of Harmony after the decisions of the 1841 congress. At this time, Owen stated that a few wealthy supporters were willing to step forward if control over the economic development of the community were retained in his hands. Perhaps as much as £20,000 was forthcoming, some £12,000 of which represented half the personal fortune of a Dublin printers' draughtsman, Frederick Bate, who became wealthy through a windfall inheritance from two spinsters who were his tenants, and who thus contributed a third of the total expenses of the community. But Owen, having spent £30,000 already, now demanded a further £5,000. By the 1842 congress, bankruptcy loomed upon the horizon. At a special congress later that year a resolution was passed against Owen which stated that the feeble financial status of the Society was chiefly due to his over-confidence in capitalists, and in turn to the unbounded faith placed in Owen by the officers of the Society. Thomas Hunt, shortly to emigrate to the US, translated these sentiments into the accusation that the form of government had been one of 'pure despotism'. Some of these views were echoed by the residents of Harmony themselves, who later complained about the power of the Governor to send anyone away, the general lack of co-ordination between the Governor, the heads of the various departments, and the members, the admission of some members who had not first served in any branch of the Society, and favouritism in the allocation of rooms, clothing and food. Later it was asserted that different standards of housing and food or 'class distinctions' were regarded as acceptable provided Owen alone was affected, but were attacked when some of the 'most useless members of the Establishment' were granted the same privileges. To remedy this the members proposed a greater measure of control over their own affairs through the election of a governor and council of six, of whom they would choose three. But this was rejected by the special congress.[66]

Much the same course of events occurred at the next congress in May and early June 1843. The delegate from Harmony insisted that the working classes (the community included harness-makers, bricklayers, sawyers, wheelwrights, agricultural labourers, plumbers,

---

[65] *NS*, no. 207 (30 October 1841), 6; no. 212 (4 December 1841), 5; no. 213 (11 December 1841), 7; no. 288 (20 May 1841), 7; no. 290 (3 June 1843), 3; no. 294 (1 July 1843), 7; T. Frost, *Forty Years' Recollections*, p. 41.

[66] *NMW*, 11, no. 7 (13 August 1842), 51–5; no. 8 (20 August 1842), 62; 13, no. 51 (14 June 1845), 418; 11, no. 48 (27 May 1843), 390–2.

tailors and shoemakers) craved a change in the constitution, and gave details of clashes between the governor and members of the community. The chief problem seems to have been a lack of consultation by the Governor and his assistants with the members. The latter had also become particularly irritated at the Governor and his officers taking supper separately from the rest of the members, and evidently securing special foodstuffs for their table alone. The former practice Owen defended as making 'consultation' easier, though he agreed that meals should be the same for all except when guests were present. But the problem of the system of government generally clearly lay behind these complaints. Alexander Campbell urged the Congress to have a veto power over the President's choice of a Central Board, with the same system to be followed in the branches. Fleming proposed further that the congress choose the Central Board, while Galpin insisted that the President must do so. Owen threatened to resign if the latter system was not retained. Campbell's compromise view was accepted, whereby the congress would confirm the president's nominations, and Owen remained President and also became Governor of Harmony. A further attempt to secure the expulsion of members only by a two-thirds vote of the entire community was also repulsed by Owen. Less than a month later, however, Galpin resigned as President of the Society and Owen resumed the post, once again choosing his own Central Board.[67]

Such was the situation as Owenism's greatest experiment entered its second decade. Branch membership had fallen steadily since 1842; twenty-five members of the Lambeth branch emigrated together to America, as did many of the Bolton branch, who were primarily quilt-makers, while the best of Glasgow's members became discouraged and joined the Etzlerites. Large numbers of Manchester members deserted, it was said, because the prospects for entering community seemed so slender. Funds were not flowing into the Society's coffers rapidly enough to meet expenses. Many leaders were also quitting. Both Galpin and Alexander Campbell, for instance, withdrew to the Ham Common Concordium, whose members considered that the 'love-spirit' could only be manifested, at least to begin with, to a small group of 'Sacred Socialists'. Compared to brighter days, the congress of 1844 was a rather sad affair. Only eighteen branches were represented, and there were some rather petty struggles over relatively minor issues amongst the delegates.[68]

[67] *Report of the Eighth Annual Congress of the Rational Society*, pp. 67, 70, 157–8; NMW, 11, no. 48 (27 May 1843), 386–7, 391–2; no. 49 (3 June 1843), 399–403; no. 50 (10 June 1843), 409; 12, no. 1 (1 July 1843), 3; no. 2 (8 July 1843), 12.

[68] *Ibid.*, 11, no. 48 (27 May 1843), 395; 12, no. 48 (25 May 1844), 377; *Sacred Socialism* (1843).

It was at this bleak moment that, as the *Northern Star* put it, 'The democracy of Socialism . . . rebelled against the aristocratic government of which it had complained, and . . . substituted the rule of democracy in its stead.' Considerable irritation was first expressed at Owen's style of leadership, and in his absence he was accused of always interrupting his opponents and intolerantly overriding his critics among the 'family' at Harmony. Refusing to elect Owen chairman of the Congress, the delegates nominated John Finch instead. Later evidence indicates, however, that a number of delegates planned to overthrow the existing Central Board even prior to the Congress, since a clause in the Society's rules which allowed anyone donating £1 to the community fund to vote at Congress was exploited to disqualify several members and form a new majority in the Congress as a whole. Fearing the imminent collapse of the whole movement, the branches thus moved to take power away from Owen and wield it themselves. At first Owen was re-elected President and nominated his old Central Board, which was approved. Some irritation was evident when the Congress moved that only one form of meal be made available at Harmony. But the break was finally precipitated by a motion, carried by a vote of eight to three, to have the resolutions of the Central Board and Harmony governor sent directly to all delegates on a regular basis. At this Owen baulked and offered his resignation, which was accepted, Frederick Bate and several others resigning from the Central Board at the same time. John Buxton, a thirty year old calico printwork engraver, became President, assisted by a Central Board 'composed of working men *entirely*', as one observer put it, and vowing that Harmony would 'be governed according to working men's ideas'. 'The working men have now taken their own affairs into their own hands', said John Finch, although it was plain for nearly all to see that such affairs as still existed would soon be quickly back in the hands of the aristocracy and middle classes in the bankruptcy court and on the auction block.[69]

Despite the opposition of some of Owen's colleagues, Buxton and his associates nonetheless soldiered on. The new President embarked upon a tour of the branches, after which he concluded that 'the Society must have become *branchless*; and, like a sappling ripped by an unkindly frost [begun] to droop, and perchance to wither and die', had the congress not acted in accordance with the general wishes of the members. Unfortunately he does not seem to have been much of a 'Moral Napoleon' himself. Lloyd Jones, at least, termed him 'a very weak man, and on every ground incompetent', and said that as far as

[69] *NS*, no. 367 (23 November 1844), 4; *NMW*, 12, no. 50 (8 June 1844), 401–2; 13, no. 43 (19 April 1845), 339; 12, no. 51 (15 June 1844), 412–16.

his effect on the organisation was concerned, 'there was never from the moment he took office any hope that he could do anything, but accelerate its ruin'. Nonetheless Harmony was thenceforth governed through much more consultation, to the relief of many of its members, and the Central Board later claimed that the 'entire abolition of the appearance of class distinctions' had taken place in the community. The new régime also had some moral support. Holyoake and his associates at the *Movement*, who had been sniping for several years at the 'united interests' and 'charity' of the 'Socialist Parliament', whose attempts to 'harmonize' they regarded as despotism disguised as 'business', lent what assistance they could. But in reality the Society was already almost branchless, frozen and withering. There were still two further congresses in May and in the summer of 1845, at which recriminations were the chief business of the day. Most of Owen's old guard blamed the pressure towards internal democracy for the financial failure of the Society, while the members of Harmony and the present executive rather more accurately held mismanagement prior to the 1844 congress responsible. Much of the first few days at the May congress was spent deciding who was eligible to be a delegate, a somewhat odd proceeding given the paucity of candidates. But eventually money became the chief topic of interest. The remaining members of Branch A1 (and most London members were reported to be 'working men') devoted a day's wages each to the cause. But elsewhere, Lloyd Jones commented sourly, it seemed that the practical proceedings in many of the branches consisted in 'dancing the Polka, speculative discussions, and the manifestation of eccentricity'. These, alas, were not occupations conducive to raising a large sum of money in a short period of time, though Owenite cultural activities generally were probably fairly lucrative. In these circumstances, too, those who believed that democracy would save the Society at the last moment quickly lost their illusions. Harmony itself suffered from crop failure (the worst in fifty years, it was claimed), infestation by vermin which destroyed what did grow, and petty theft by day labourers who were ill-paid and insufficiently imbued with socialist enthusiasm.[70]

The final accession of a more traditional conception of democracy in the Rational Society was a hollow victory at best. We cannot even be sure that such a goal represented the wishes of the majority of Owenite branch members at the peak of the movement in 1840–41, since these had mostly voted with their feet by 1845. But this is probably the case.

[70] *Movement*, 2, no. 58 (1844), 29; *NMW*, 13, no. 6 (3 August 1844), 44; *NWC*, no. 5994 (14 June 1879), 3; *NMW*, 13, no. 37 (8 March 1845), 292; *Movement*, 1, no. 27 (1843), 209–10; no. 36 (1844), 286; no. 44 (1844), 373–6; *NMW*, 13, no. 48 (24 May 1845), 381–3; no. 50 (7 June 1845), 402; no. 39 (22 March 1845), 312.

There is, however, much greater certainty in the proposition that the final success of the members of the Harmony community (many of whom had been Chartists, according to a report sent to the Home Office in 1840 by the Rev. Henry Lloyd) in achieving a substantial measure of self-government did reflect their aims since virtually the inception of the community. Now the Governor acted according to a majority of his own committee, a 'more liberal' system which seems largely to have mirrored the views of the community as a whole.[71]

But it would be senseless to portray the events of 1844–45 as the teleological resolution of twenty-five years of democratic struggle against paternalistic conceptions of socialism. Owen, after all, was not a total autocrat, and was not seen to be by many Socialists. Most Rational Society members doubtless would have preferred to follow him into community than to sacrifice Queenwood upon the altar of radical democracy. Much of Owen's critique of politics, in fact, was accepted in principle by many of his followers, though they preferred to modify (by rotation, for example) rather than to supersede more traditional democratic institutions. It was mainly when Owen's own failure became widely evident that the virtues of collective control became transformed into necessities for many of those involved. Otherwise many Socialists probably accepted both Owen's leadership and the rationale behind his wish to mitigate the worst of the 'political' effects of such organisations by, for instance, abolishing the ballot. As we have seen, J. N. Bailey also shared this view, while William Hodson prominently advertised his agreement that government by age was the best ultimate form of social management.[72]

Nor is it easy to conclude, if we review the twenty years between the foundation of the London Co-operative Society and the fall of Queenwood, that the meeting of Owenite economic analysis and political radicalism created a socially conscious radical movement which grew slowly in strength. On the socialist side, those who planned to use political power to achieve a society substantially based upon Owen's plans probably had as coherent an ideology and more widespread support in the schemes of the BAPCK in 1829 as the Charter Socialists did in 1843. In the 1840s the ideas of social radicalism, of course, were far more widespread, as well as comprehended as an alternative form of social and political thinking. But credit for this does not rest entirely with Owenism, and must be fairly distributed across the spectrum of social radical propagandists. To those who sought to teach social

71 HO 44/38. Lloyd visisted Harmony and asked a member of the community if there were any Chartists there: 'In answer to the question . . . he admitted with an appearance of cautious reserve, that most of the people at Queenwood have been Chartists, but added that "the Social System has done much to keep down the Chartists!"'
72 *WB*, 2, no. 7 (18 July 1840), 49.

reform to the Chartists rather than political reform to the Owenites, the social radicalism of Harney and O'Brien, taken together, may have been equally as important as Owenism in conveying the experience and theory of early socialism to the second half of the nineteenth century, though O'Brien himself was of course much indebted to Owenism. Nor should his role in the early and mid-1830s be underestimated, though he was relatively isolated after 1840, and was certainly far less successful as a publicist by comparison with the cumulative, collective efforts of organised Socialism.

The larger question of the nature of the evolution of the economic programme of radicalism in this period has not concerned us here, however. Owenite reasoning probably made a substantial contribution to this development, but it is not possible to generalise accurately about this until much more information is available about the intellectual differences between reformers in different regions. Nonetheless, the extent of Socialist connections with the Chartists was clearly much greater than has usually been assumed, and followed an historical trajectory whose direction was largely dictated by the threat of violence by the Chartists. Though no substantial degree of unity was ever effected between the two movements, many Owenite leaders spoke out in favour of the Charter in the late 1830s, with rather fewer supporting it after 1839–40.

Democratic political socialism never achieved much national recognition in the years leading up to 1845. This partially resulted from Owen's own influence on the movement, and from popular association of his views on marriage, religion and private property with the programme of 'socialism' generally. When co-operation rapidly expanded in the late 1820s and again in the late 1840s, it quickly attempted to shed these unsavoury connections. When Socialism became nationally prominent in 1839–42, it was often viewed as a democratic movement by its working class followers in particular, many of whom had earlier probably been involved in some form of political reform activity. But as a movement, it never became committed to the cause of parliamentary reform until 1845. As we saw in the case of Owen, the failure of communitarianism and of privately funded social revolution finally necessitated the increasing recognition of the probable contingency of economic reform upon the possession of political power. In the hands of Bronterre O'Brien and a number of old Owenites, as we will now see, democratic political socialism also at last became enshrined in a nationally recognised programme which was widely understood as irrevocably uniting the causes of social and political progress.

7

The legitimation of political socialism

Although Owen's personal influence was largely eradicated after the Queenwood débâcle, this did not signal the complete demise of Owenism either as a movement or as an intellectual phenomenon. But the main organisations built up painstakingly over a decade dissolved fairly quickly. Unable to survive on cultural events alone, some remaining branches dissolved into secularist, self-help or educational institutions, and, as the communitarian wave passed, attempted to reinterpret the meaning of the ideals to which they had become committed. G. J. Holyoake, for example, set out to give socialism a more individualist foundation in which the ideas of self-formation and personal responsibility could play a greater role. A few Owenite leaders who could afford it retreated into mystical withdrawal. Others slid into bohemianism. Socialism, Lloyd Jones lamented, had become by the mid-1840s 'a receptacle for all moral and intellectual delinquents – empty-headed young men bordering on idiocy, babblers and quibblers, long-haired, bearded and vegetarians, etc'.[1] For at least some of its votaries, Owen's plan had become synonymous with the new eccentric world where individual self-expression signified the beginning of the supersession of irrational social prejudices. At least the threat of uniformity seemed to have passed.

But a number of Owenites did not lose faith in the possibility of collective change, and went on to contribute to the last upsurge in practical socialist reform of this period during and after 1848. Those who participated in these final exertions came to embrace a much more political programme than Socialism had ever officially countenanced before 1845. They also became much more predisposed to entering into an alliance with the radical reformers. Simultaneously, many remain-

---

[1] J. McCabe, *Life and Letters of G. J. Holyoake*, 1, p. 113. What Holyoake termed 'Galpinism', which was a mélange of White Quaker and Greavesite views, also attracted both Alexander Campbell and Samuel Bower (*Reasoner*, 1, 1846, 265–6; *SAPTJ* (1843–4), pt 27, 12–14, pt 31, 60–1. For Holyoake's new views see his *Rationalism* (1845).

ing Chartists adopted a new programme of social reform which owed much to thirty years of socialist agitation. The decade after 1845 thus saw the emergence of a reform plan upon which the majority of both Owenite and Chartist leaders could agree. Hence there was a clear reconciliation, spurred on by the failures of Queenwood, O'Connorville, and Kennington Common, of many of the past divisions between Owenite and Chartist.

This process of accommodation is considered here in terms of the activities and plans of the Owenites from 1845–50, then with respect to Chartist developments in this period. Special attention is given to the highly significant attempt at union between the social and political reformers between 1850 and 1852. Finally, these efforts are analysed in relation to the arguments developed in previous chapters concerning the relationship between socialism, radicalism and democratic theory from 1820 to 1845.

After 1848 the language of British radicalism was ineradicably altered by the entrenchment of the duality of 'social' and 'political'. This transformation was lent tremendous momentum by the European revolutions. But it had also begun many years earlier, and owed much to the apparent verification of many of Owenism's predictions by the events of the 1840s. Nonetheless, social radicalism after 1850 did not carry forward the same set of emphases that had distinguished Owenism. Ultimately the economic rather than the moral dimensions of the socialist critique of the analyses and strategies of political radicalism which were integrated into the language of working class radical reformers after 1848. Elements of the latter strand in socialism, and of the desire to supersede more traditional forms of politics, still continued to circulate after 1845, and indeed have remained central to socialism ever since. But while Owenism and socialism generally – for the two must now begin to be treated separately – did come increasingly to embrace more statist forms of social organisation, these cannot be understood as early forms of 'totalitarian democracy', although some elements which have been associated with that history are present in Britain after 1850.

Owenism radicalised, 1845–50

The failure of Queenwood was a fatal blow to organised Owenism. In addition, though one other community experiment persisted for a number of years (the Pant Glas farm begun by the Leeds Redemption Society) and efforts were begun at Sheffield and elsewhere, the ideal of the communitarian millennium inaugurated by private means also perished with Owen's final and greatest effort.[2] Several uncharacteristically Owenite acts of violence marred the last departures from the Hampshire community, and the tenets of necessity were flung aside as a barrage of recriminations, lawsuits and counter-claims began which was to last nearly twenty years.[3]

'Circumstances' failed to account for so devastating a failure. Personal responsibility had to be assigned and errors admitted if not atoned. For Owen, the Harmony episode induced the final rejection of the idea that private capital could begin the communitarian revolution. Yet this acknowledgement of a lifetime of strategic blunders appeared much less dramatic (though O'Brien recognised its significance) than might have been the case.[4] For in some ways it merely represented the further extension of demands for state intervention and management which first Owen and then his followers had made since 1813. But from this concession many Owenites also deduced that major social reforms could never begin without essential political changes. The social Chartists had, after all, been correct in their strategy. Tory and Whig governments had not supported Owen in thirty years of petitions and letters. To place the entire onus of reform on the state meant that the burden had now shifted to reforming the state itself.

However, the failures of 1848, like those of 1832, also turned many towards the more limited aims of local economic independence and self-government and away from national political reform. Non-political co-operation enjoyed a boom such as it had not seen for twenty years. William King of Brighton, one of the founders of shopkeeping co-operation in the early 1820s, was still alive, in fact, and in the *Christian Socialist* insisted that co-operation had 'never been political, but always founded on self-exertion, Social Co-operation and saving', complaining that the Chartists and Red Republicans had perverted the doctrine.[5] Some Owenites (notably G. A. Fleming) took on leading roles in the trades' union movement, and set up a new propaganda association, the Organization of Labour League, in 1848. 'Social in-

---

[2] On the origins of the Pant Glas estate see *HC*, no. 8 (August 1847), 57–8. The government of this community was to be elective, with the Redemption Society indicating its fundamental principles but the colonists framing their own laws (*SA*, 1, no. 20, 9 December 1848, 313). On the Redemption Society generally see J. F. C. Harrison, *Social Reform in Victorian Leeds* (Leeds, Thoresby Society, 1954). On the founding of an 'industrial farm' by Ironside and others at Sheffield, see the *Leader*, no. 27 (28 September 1850), 626–7.

[3] A lawsuit concerning Queenwood creditors was still in progress in 1861. See the *Co-operator*, 2, no. 17 (October 1861), 79.

[4] *NS*, no. 633 (8 December 1849), 8.

[5] *CS*, 2, no. 50 (11 October 1851), 226–7. On the more moral, individualistic meaning of 'social reform' invoked here, see *LMR*, no. 1 (6 January 1838), 1–2; *EMD*, no. 4 (1 October 1838), 9; *WMFFI*, 2, no. 23 (8 June 1850), 304–5.

variably succeeds political agitation . . . Baffled in one direction, the masses try another, because the evils they complain of remain un-remedied', explained the *Labour League*, organ of the National Associ-ation of the United Trades and its successor organisation, the National Association of Organised Trades, in which a number of former Owe-nites were also active, and which was later to argue that it possessed universal suffrage and annual or more frequent parliaments 'though we do not profess to be politicians'.[6] Those few who still sought settlement on the land returned to more traditional means of gaining this end. The Co-operative League aimed to buy land to let to families on the individual system, though only five acres were to be allowed to any one family.[7] John Minter Morgan found support for a communitarian scheme similar to Owen's, but guided by the prin-ciples and prelates of the Church of England. A variety of other communitarians struggled on into the 1850s, and then disappeared without leaving so much as a ripple on the becalmed waters of mid-Victorian society.[8]

In Christian Socialism one well-known Owenite leader, Lloyd Jones, found both financial support and an amenable vehicle for continuing the propagation of co-operation. Here, however, there was little public effort to mix radicalism with the principles of co-operation and Chris-tianity. Some toryish views, instead, were expressed on occasion (especially by F. D. Maurice), prompting at least one contemporary to write at Owen's death in 1858 that the Christian Socialists had been 'his disciples, politically, though not religiously'.[9] But this was an oversim-plification of both Owen's views and those of Christian Socialism. For amongst the latter, J. M. Ludlow avowed himself a fairly thorough democrat, while Viscount Goderich's 'Duties of the Age' (whose

[6] *LL*, no. 15 (11 November 1848), 113; *PP*, no. 15 (14 August 1852), 3. See *PE*, 3, no. 19 (5 April 1845), 149 for Fleming's role in the foundation of the NAUT. When he was President in 1852, its objects were described in terms of a 'fair day's wages' (*GS*, 3, no. 95, 24 July 1852, 7). On the NAUT and NAOT generally, see John Belchem, 'Chartism and the Trades', *EHR*, 98 (1983), 558–87.

[7] *Plan of the Co-operative League* (1847), p. 9. On the formation and plans of this organis-ation see *PN*, no. 5 (27 June 1847), 4; *Co-operator*, no. 1 (19 December 1846), 6; *PJ*, 2, 'Annals of Industry', 45; *HowJ*, 2 (1847), 31. It should not be confused with the later Co-operative League founded in March 1852, whose officers included William Coning-ham, Thornton Hunt, E. V. Neale and Owen's secretary, James Rigby, but whose aims were entirely propagandistic (*Transactions of the Co-operative League*, 1852, pp. 1, 5). A 'Social Friends Society' was also founded in January 1847 for the purpose of applying Owen's views (*Reasoner*, 2, 1847, 119–20). It does not appear to have been very successful.

[8] On Morgan's Church of England Self-Supporting Village Society, see for example the *Commonweal*, no. 15 (June 1846), 89–90, and W. H. G. Armytage, 'John Minter Mor-gan's Schemes, 1841–55', *IRSH*, 3 (1958), 26–42.

[9] *DN*, no. 3095 (19 November 1858), 5.

publication was suppressed by Maurice but favoured by Ludlow and Kingsley) was a sustained attack upon all varieties of aristocracy.[10] Ludlow also continued to insist that the most desirable form of government, 'the Socialist State', was one where all would be 'well-placed, well-employed, well-educated'.[11] This phrase directly invoked Owen's views, and helps to demonstrate the continuing prevalence of such ideas in the early 1850s. But Owen's secularism, and now also his quaint if less heretical venture into spiritualism, doubtless prevented him from receiving greater acknowledgement from these quarters.

Those Owenites who embraced parliamentary reform after 1845 did not invariably proceed from the assumption that greater democracy within the socialist movement would have saved Queenwood. Their emphasis instead was upon the necessary role of the state in the reform process, rather than its specific political character. Owen's conclusion in 1846 was that the state alone could found co-operative communities, but not that only a democratic state could do so.[12] That the state could be the sole landlord, whether or not individuals lived in communities, was being counselled by G. A. Fleming's *Moral World*, the short-lived successor to the *New Moral World*, as early as September 1845.[13] But Fleming among others also identified the overtly democratic character of the Owenite method of electing delegates to congresses, for example, as one of the causes of the failure of the Harmony community.[14] A lesson more widely drawn was that greater centralisation of effort might have saved Harmony. A correspondent signing himself 'Social Centralist' noted in O'Connor's *Evening Star* as early as 1842 that if the local Owenite branches had not built sixty Halls of Science (each costing £600 to £6,000), far more funds would have been available. The same point can be made about the Rational Society's distribution of millions of tracts. Both strategies had attracted many to the Socialist cause, but had clearly helped to prevent its fulfilment in community.[15]

It required the European revolutions of 1848 finally to instigate a major commitment to political reform from much of the old Owenite

---

[10] Charles Raven, *Christian Socialism, 1848–1854* (Frank Cass, 1920), p. 64, see also Torben Christensen, *Origin and History of Christian Socialism, 1848–54* (Aarhus, Universitetsforlaget, 1962), pp. 298–303. See also Edwin Seligman, 'Owen and the Christian Socialists of 1848', *PSQ*, 1 (1886), 206–49, and John Saville, 'The Christian Socialists of 1848', in Saville, ed., *Democracy and the Labour Movement* (Lawrence and Wishart, 1954), pp. 135–59.

[11] *CS*, 1, no. 26 (26 April 1851), 201.

[12] Owen, *Letter from Mr. Robert Owen to the New York State Convention*, p. 27.

[13] *MW*, no. 4 (20 September 1845), 29.

[14] *NS*, no. 6 (4 October 1845), 41; no. 11 (8 November 1845), 81–2.

[15] *ES*, no. 39 (7 September 1842), 3.

leadership. It was widely expected that the revolutions would aid the cause of socialism in England. *Lloyd's Newspaper*, for example, noted that 'with the doctrines of Robert Owen large masses of the English people have been imbued', and assumed that this clearly made them receptive to the idea that government could guarantee them the fruits of their labour. Even critics of this trend, like one 'Sosthenes', admitted that 'We do not hear so much indeed of the Socialists as a body as we used to; but their opinions are current among the people, and indeed have much to do with Chartism'. At the end of March 1848, as we have seen, Owen's proposed 'Practical Measures' finally conceded that representation should be co-extensive with taxation.[16] After this, Owen left for four months for Paris to convert the French. In July the Owenite rump established a new periodical, the *Spirit of the Age*, which declared amongst its objects the complete revision of the laws on primogeniture, the abolition of capital punishment, an extension of the franchise to the entire male population, and equal electoral districts, as well as the introduction of a 'just and equitable' organisation of labour, with the unemployed being located both in workshops and in home colonies.[17] Within the next few months, a linkage of socialist and democratic political measures was proposed by a number of Owenite leaders in a variety of locations. In October Alexander Campbell and others joined T. S. Duncombe's National Association of the United Trades, and urged 'That as the State may be regarded as the representative power of the people, the land should be placed under its guardianship – not to be sold, but let at such a standard of rental as may be required for revenue purposes, and the general exigencies of the State.'[18] More ambitiously, Owen himself called for the formation of a congress elected by universal suffrage from European peoples, whose goal was to be the division of all Europe into co-operative communities.[19]

This clear commitment to political reform was not, however, pervasive among the old Owenites. Some were suspicious of the trend of European socialism, with the Leeds co-operator James Hole, for instance, arguing that English socialists wanted to level society upwards, and the French, downwards. Still others, such as Alexander Campbell, were first laughed at and then ignored for continuing to propose that 'social emancipation' precede political reform. No political opinions marred the founding statement of the League of Social Progress, created as a propaganda organisation by the majority of former Owen-

---

[16] *LWLN*, no. 277 (12 March 1848), 1; 'Sosthenes', *Tracts for the People. Communism and Chartism* (1848), p. 4; *NS*, no. 544 (25 March 1848), 3.
[17] *SA*, 1, no. 1 (1 July 1848), 203.
[18] *Ibid.*, 1, no. 12 (14 October 1848), 182.
[19] *Ibid.*, 1, no. 13 (21 October 1848), 203.

ite leaders in December 1848.[20] Other socialists continued to regard all political involvement as a delusive and divisive mistake, at least for the time being. The head of the Leeds Redemption Society, David Green, for example, did not doubt that all should have an equal right to vote in community, but remained very hostile to the insinuation of political views into the socialist movement. Thus he argued against the 'ultra-liberal principles' of the *Spirit of the Age* that

It is doubtful whether this union of what must for a long period be party politics, with the cause of commercial association, will prove beneficial or otherwise. It would have been well if, in the present position of society, the two things could have been kept distinct. Long before the state or government can justify or wisely meddle with the organisation of labour, labour must have proved over and over again, by practical illustrations, that it is organisable. But to exemplify these illustrations pecuniary aid is wanted, and unfortunately radical principles and wealth are seldom united in the same persons. At the present stage of progress, there is not any necessary connection between politics and association. When association has demonstrated itself to such an extent as to have become an important element of society, government must take cognizance of it. But that is the task of the future age.

Such objections, however, were not only immediately tactical and practical, but were also based in the older, unpolitical attitude of many socialists. Green, for instance, added that he had

always felt it a very difficult and delicate task to mix up politics with communism . . . Communism is of no party; it knows of no politics. The miserable distinctions of Whig, Tory, or Radical, belong to the old world. They could not exist in a new social state. My own feelings are in accordance with what is termed liberalism; but it is not necessary to advocate this in advocating communism. I esteem politics as but a meretricious ornament to communism. The Redemption Society cannot recognise any faction in the political world, and more especially so as it includes amongst its members men of all grades and politics. To introduce politics, would be to introduce another element of discord.[21]

This complaint was also probably still viewed sympathetically by the Owenite conductors of the *Spirit of the Age* and its successor, the *Spirit of the Times*, throughout 1848–49, despite their initial pronouncements on political reform. For a considerable distance still remained between

---

[20] *Leader*, no. 1 (30 March 1850), 4; W. H. Marwick, *The Life of Alexander Campbell* (Glasgow, Glasgow and District Co-operative Association, n.d.), p. 12. The League included Lloyd Jones, Henry Corss, J. E. Smith, Henry Ivory, Henry Hetherington, G. A. Fleming, G. J. Holyoake, Robert Buchanan, Alexander Campbell and James Rigby, as well as Jacob Dixon and the Chartist Walter Cooper (*Rules of the League of Social Progress*, 1850, p. 4).

[21] David Green, *The Claims of the Redemption Society Considered* (1849), p. 25; *HC*, no 19 (July 1848), 153, 155. Green did, however, apparently support the aims of the People's League, which sought manhood suffrage, vote by ballot, and triennial parliaments. At least he appeared at one of its meetings. See *SF*, 1, no. 5 (5 July 1848), 7.

most Owenites and most Chartists. Commenting on developments in August 1849, the editor of *Spirit of the Times*, Robert Buchanan, described the socialists and communists of France and Germany as having both a social creed and republican principles of political organisation, but noted of Britain that the Chartists sought republicanism, while Owen's followers espoused social equality through the establishment of communities.[22] In late October 1849 Alexander Campbell and about thirty others founded the Social Reform League, which in an early address proclaimed the old Owenite orthodoxy that communism was consistent with any 'tolerable' form of government, and which, at least until the spring of 1850, does not seem to have pursued too vociferously any particular programme of political reform.[23] Now, however, a significant change in strategy was agreed. But to explain more fully the new alliance attempted in this year, we must first consider briefly the evolution of Chartism after 1845.

Chartism socialised, 1845–50

The experience of 1848 had an even more dramatic impact on Chartist thinking than it did upon that of the Owenites.[24] There were three main reasons for this. The Land Plan, which mesmerised much of the movement between 1843–48, now came to be seen as at best a very slow and cumbersome mode of social transformation, if not a hopeless and expensive fiasco which had drained much of the enthusiasm for political reform of the early years of the movement.[25] Secondly, the Kennington Common meeting and subsequent events in 1848–49 were widely regarded as having nullified existing Chartist strategy and disgraced its leadership. In Europe the democratic revolutions appeared initially triumphant. In Britain, despite some outbreaks of violence, it was the public order of special constables which won the

---

[22] *ST*, no. 22 (4 August 1849), 173.

[23] *WT*, 1, no. 5 (3 November 1849), 74; no. 19 (9 February 1850), 295.

[24] On Chartism in the 1845–52 period see Gammage, *History of the Chartist Movement*, pp. 291–402, Slosson, *Decline of the Chartist Movement*, F. Gillespie, *Labor and Politics in England* (Durham, NC, Duke University Press, 1927), pp. 1–109, Schoyen, *Chartist Challenge*, pp. 178–276, D. C. Morris, 'History of the Labour Movement in England, 1825–1852', Ph.D., University of London (1952), pp. 776–830, Prothero, 'London Working Class Movements, 1825–1848', pp. 259–74, and most recently John Belchem, 'Radicalism as a "Platform" Agitation in the Period 1816–1821 and 1848–1851', Ph.D., University of Sussex (1977), pp. 101–468.

[25] This was certainly the opinion of Thomas Almond in a letter to the *Northern Star* (no. 532, 1 January 1848, 7). *The Cause of the People* commented on O'Connor that he 'never seemed to know whether he sought the "Land" or the "Charter"; talked of all sorts of nonsense about the sudden prosperity to follow the attainment of either one or the other' (no. 5, 17 June 1848, 33).

day.[26] O'Connor, it was widely believed, had been bluffing. The Chartists had never sought revolution, and lacked the means of instigating it anyway. Finally, Chartism also ceased to be a narrowly British movement at this time. The European revolutions helped to provoke the large-scale importation of foreign socialist doctrines into British radical circles, especially in London. Harney's Fraternal Democrats had always been inclined towards continental socialism to some degree, both through Harney's own interest in Babouvism and Jacobinism, and via contacts with foreign exiles (especially the Germans) in London.[27] But these early influences were as nothing compared to the enormous publicity given to the national workshop proposals of Louis Blanc and other schemes after early 1848, which were now prominently associated with the phrase, 'the organisation of labour'. Such projects, as the *Leader* later put it, 'established the connection of the great principle of concert, with the actual state of society, and taught the working classes that their redemption was within reach of their own will'. They also directly instigated the proclamation of a variety of quasi-syndicalist plans by British trades' unions. One of these, for example, was put forward in August 1848 by the Committee of Metropolitan Trades, and requested that after the government had introduced a bill to set up self-supporting home colonies, it should also establish a 'Labour Protecting Board' to be elected by the working classes and also entitled to a seat in the Commons, the President being a member of the Cabinet. The Board was to oversee all trades to ensure that no more than a fair day's labour was done in any, with laws being passed to ensure a fair wage for all work.[28]

This combination of circumstances underlay the official Chartist acceptance of a largely socialist programme in 1851. Its accession owed little to Feargus O'Connor, who in 1848 was still fulminating that all *he* meant by the term 'social' was its 'general and extensive meaning' of 'the fitness of things to society', and not 'its sectional, undefined and

---

[26] See W. J. Vernon's comments on this in *NS*, no. 552 (20 May 1848), 7. See however D. Goodway, *London Chartism*, pp. xiv, 77, 221, for a proposed revision of this view, and Henry Weisser, *April 10: Challenge and Response in England in 1848* (New York, University Press of America, 1983), p. 290. John Saville's new study, *1848* (Cambridge, Cambridge University Press, 1987) unfortunately appeared too late for use here.

[27] On the background to the Fraternal Democrats see Mary Davis, 'The Forerunners of the First International: The Fraternal Democrats', *MTy*, 15 (1971), 50–60, and Christine Lattek, 'The Democratic Friends of All Nations', and 'Radikalismus im Ausland. Die Entwicklung des deutschen Frühsozialismus in London 1840–1852', in Claeys and Liselotte Glage, eds., *Radikalismus in Literatur und Gesellschaft des 19. Jahrhunderts* (Basel, Peter Lang, 1987), pp. 39–64. See also Henry Weisser, 'Chartist Internationalism, 1845–48', *HJ*, 14 (1971), 49–66, and for an earlier view, T. Rothstein, 'Aus der Vorgeschichte der Internationale', *Ergänzungshefte zur Neuen Zeit*, 17 (1913), 1–44.

[28] *Leader*, no. 75 (30 April 1851), 822; *TMW*, no. 13 (12 August 1848), 61–2.

limited sense, as applied to the professors of that principle'.[29] But O'Connor nonetheless also assisted demands for 'Something More' than the Charter through his insistence that the Charter alone was insufficient to gain the land for the working classes, and by his continuing argument that after the land was gained the Charter itself would follow.[30]

Even before 1848 there is evidence that more Chartists were moving towards socialism. The *Northern Star* after the mid-1840s carried an increasing number of articles and letters asserting that landlords had no intrinsic right to the soil but only to implements used on and improvements to it.[31] Thomas Frost wrote and lectured in favour of common property in late 1847, and flatly declared himself a communist a year later.[32] The language often used to refer to the Land Plan also became ever less distinguishable from that of Owenite communitarianism. One toast to the Land Company at a London meeting, for instance, was to 'co-operative labour and community of interests'. J. F. C. Harrison has also discovered a few Chartists who from despair decided to emigrate to America, but planned to set up an Owenite colony there when they arrived.[33]

After the revolution began in France, the *Northern Star* (still edited by Harney) hastily reprinted and began discussing those socialist plans which had become available. Particularly important was the national workshop project of Louis Blanc, first introduced in March 1848, soon more widely publicised by Thomas Cooper, and mentioned and debated on many subsequent occasions during the next several years.[34] The Fraternal Democrats now became much more forthcoming in their proposals for the common ownership of land.[35] A surprising number of new periodicals also appeared which advocated a similar course. R. G. Gammage's *Midland Progressionist*, for example, argued that 'as the soil was never created by the hands of man', it ought to be possessed in common, and appropriated by the state (with compensation to heirs) whenever a landowner died.[36] C. G. Harding's *Republican* praised new plans for the organisation of labour.[37] James Leach's

[29] *Labourer*, 3 (1848), 259.
[30] *NS*, no. 384 (22 March 1845), 1; no. 416 (1 November 1845), 1.
[31] *Ibid.*, no. 482 (16 January 1847), 5.
[32] *Ibid.*, no. 523 (30 October 1847), 1; no. 574 (21 October 1848), 2.
[33] *Ibid.*, no. 483 (23 January 1847), 8; J. F. C. Harrison, *Living and Learning 1790–1960* (Routledge and Kegan Paul, 1961), p. 105.
[34] *NS*, no. 543 (18 March 1848), 4. Blanc's plans were printed as *Socialism: the Right to Labour* (1848) and *The Organization of Labour* (1848). See also Thomas Cooper, ed., *The Land for the Labourers* (1848). Blanc's views generally are discussed in Leo Loubère, *Louis Blanc* (Chicago, Northwestern University Press, 1961).
[35] *NS*, no. 553 (27 May 1848), 6; no. 562 (29 July 1848), 1.
[36] *MP* (1848), 59–60, 65–6.
[37] *Republican* (1848), 46–7.

English Patriot and Irish Repealer dropped its Hibernian appeal in favour of a new subtitle, 'Herald of Labour and Co-operation', and adopted the principle of an equal reward for equal labour.[38] The old anti-Socialist lecturer and recent convert to Chartism, Joseph Barker, insisted that since the land had been given as common property to all, no man had 'a right to any portion of land, but in subjection to the national will'.[39] J. B. Leno and G. Massey's *Uxbridge Spirit of Freedom* proclaimed 'all born of humanity co-inheritors of their birthplace and earth', while the 'Chartist Poet', J. E. Duncan, avowed himself in favour of co-operative communities, labour exchange bazaars, and nearly every other radical and socialist reform he could think of.[40] Even in the Tory heartland of Cambridge, a group of artisans announced their acceptance of O'Brien's land nationalisation programme.[41]

The widespread acceptance of socialist ideas among Chartists in 1848 and later was not inspired solely by the French revolution or Harney's propagandistic efforts. It also exhibited, in particular, the results of Bronterre O'Brien's continuous agitation from the late 1830s onwards. This at least was the opinion of the enormously popular radical journalist, G. W. M. Reynolds, who observed that

Some years ago the necessity for social reconstruction was but dimly seen, and the principle but little understood; until the French Revolution of 1848, and its various consequences, opened the eyes of the millions throughout Europe . . . Of the first and foremost teachers of social rights, Mr. Bronterre O'Brien was assuredly pre-eminent in the country; and now he has the satisfaction of beholding the fruits of his long unrewarded labours, in the amount of prosyletism which has at length done homage to his teachings.[42]

In fact, O'Brien himself had been nearly stifled by his peripheral role in Chartism after O'Connor's ascendancy, and later lamented that the O'Connorite faction had driven him 'in disgust and despair out of the movement altogether' after 1840.[43] His position in 1848 was also weakened by the emigration of a number of his followers to America during the previous few years.[44] But O'Brien still enjoyed sufficient support to publish two journals in 1848–49, in which he urged every existing organisation to adopt his own mixture of Owenite social and

---

[38] *EP*, no. 10 (23 September 1848), 74.

[39] *People*, 1, no. 4 (24 June 1848), 29–32; Barker, *The Social Reformer's Almanac for 1848* (Wortley, 1848), p. 251.

[40] *USF*, no. 7 (October 1849), 95; *Divinearian*, no. 3 (December 1849), 1.

[41] *OFP*, no. 4 (December 1849), 45.

[42] *RWN*, 1, no 9 (30 June 1850), 2.

[43] O'Brien, *A Vision of Hell* (1859), p. 104. See further *Mr. O'Brien's Vindication of his Conduct at the Late Birmingham Conference* (Birmingham, 1842), for one of his final counterblasts at O'Connor and the *Northern Star*.

[44] This, at least, was the opinion given in *RPI*, no. 21 (30 March 1850), 161–2.

Chartist political programmes. The Chartists generally, he complained, would 'never make any progress, as long as they adhere to this old clap-trap cry of taxation'. Land and all public enterprises, such as railways and utilities, should be owned and managed by the whole population, although O'Brien insisted that no government had the right to issue currency, which should emanate from the exchangers themselves.[45] The pinnacle of O'Brien's efforts was reached with the formation in October 1849 of the National Reform League. This embodied all of his plans for the land, labour, currency and exchange, and quickly attracted interest and support.[46] It was to become one of the most long-lived British reform organisations of the second half of the nineteenth century, and would help to link early with later forms of socialism in the 1880s.

Another dimension of the socialist influence upon Chartism in this period, though one whose proposals are extremely difficult to judge, concerns the acceptance of moral force arguments by the radicals. How far such sentiments soothed Chartist passions in the early 1840s is unknown. But at least one report assigned them a significant role in dictating the eventual outcome of 1848. This was claimed by the secularist *Freethinker's Magazine*, which wrote in 1850 that

the army of democracy was divided into 'moral force men' and 'physical force men' – one of the most unfortunate causes of division that ever afflicted a party. Thus were the people divided into two sections. The Owenite doctrine, wrote one who has had the best opportunity of knowing, 'Went through the ranks of Chartism and decimated them. It convinced all its thoughtful men. All who had the head to plan insurrection, and who might have made it respectable by their intelligence, and formidable by their courage, withdrew – and Chartism was left bare, boisterous, and impotent'. These are hard words, but they were verified in 1848 and 1849.

A similar conclusion, but concentrating more specifically on the events of April 10, was reached by Douglas Jerrold.[47] For most Chartists, however, the discovery of socialism in 1848 and later raised new questions about the ends, rather than the means, of reform. Now, for the first time (besides Land Plan discussions), Chartists came to concentrate upon the problem of what would come *after* the Charter had been achieved, rather than upon the steps necessary to secure its passage.

---

[45] *PP*, no. 1 (11 November 1848), 10; no. 3 (25 November 1848), 41–3; no. 2 (18 November 1848), 28.
[46] The prospectus and regulations of the National Reform League are given in the *SR*, no. 11 (20 October 1849), 85–7. The League had at least three branches by early 1850 (*NS*, no. 644, 23 February 1850, 2).
[47] *FM*, no. 7 (1 December 1850), 200; *DJWN*, no. 92 (15 April 1848), 483.

Alliance strategies, 1850–52

While the Chartists between 1848 to 1850 increasingly discussed socialist ideas and schemes, the Owenites now openly sided
with the political reformers in greater numbers than at any time since
1838–39. Emboldened by the revolutions, which had proven that
political reforms were widely desired and had popularised interventionist economic ideas, radicals and socialists alike began to see
some sense in co-operating with each other. This trend towards accommodation was evident as early as May 1848, when a sympathetic
lecturer remarked that

Since the French Revolution, Socialism in this country has become political,
has mixed with Chartism in public meetings, and united in propositions for
political change. What is more important, Chartism has become Socialist. At
some of the great open-air meetings, the people have been warned to 'give no
heed to those who would persuade them that it is not in the power of
government to secure to them constant work and fair wages'.[48]

One sign of the new spirit of conciliation was the decline of formal
debates between both camps on the incompatibility of their respective
means and ends. The previous month had witnessed one of the last
such discussions between Owenite and Chartist lecturers, when Alexander Campbell and Philip McGrath met at the John Street Institute to
recite the same undialectical arguments that had made conciliation so
difficult in the past. Complaints were still occasionally voiced about
aspects of Owenite philosophy, such as the doctrine of circumstances,
which one radical described as 'a startling and repulsive announce-
ment to ordinary thinkers'.[49] During the next several years, there were
few if any formal set-tos, and the spirit of antagonism which had
fouled too many official meetings of the two movements was dispelled
in favour of an atmosphere of collective endeavour and mutual
support.

It took some time, however, before the growing warmth and sense
of rapprochement on both sides was actually translated into practical
attempts at combined association. The first important formal effort to
unify the social and political reformers only occurred in the autumn of
1850. The possibility of such a meeting, however, had been impending
throughout the preceding year. In late 1849, for instance, Alexander
Campbell openly approved of all of the principles, both social and
political, of O'Brien's National Reform League. In early 1850, another
former Social Missionary, Robert Buchanan, was reported as attending
a meeting of Harney's Fraternal Democrats. Especially in London,

[48] *PolP*, no. 5 (Supplement for May 1848), 89–91.
[49] *NS*, no. 544 (25 March 1848), 3; *Leader*, 1, no. 25 (14 September 1850), 585.

contacts between Owenites and Chartists were probably extensive and virtually continuous at this time.[50]

Three other factors now facilitated an alliance. Clearly important was the deepening sense of frustration and gloom which pervaded Chartist ranks after 1848. Some twelve years had passed since the first great meetings had commenced the new campaign for political change. Enthusiasm for continental developments aside, it was clear that decades more might now be required before Britain was ripe for reform. 'We are no nearer the attainment of our object than when the People's Charter was first promulgated', grumbled a Cambridge Chartist in the autumn of 1849, echoing an all-too-prevalent sentiment. The failure of political reform as a method was therefore partly responsible for new Chartist sympathy for socialistic property theories. No doubt this was to some degree the result of identifying an intransigent parliament with the existing, grossly unequal system of property ownership. Some part of the Chartist acceptance of socialist ideas can thus be explained in terms of the fulfilment of a prescient warning given a decade earlier by the Cirencester Chartist John Beecham, who wrote that while contemporary Chartists did not want to interfere with private property, 'let the property holders pause – if they will interpose property as a bar to the rights of the people, they challenge its destruction. Socialism, which is now a system of opinion, may become a system of practice . . . Let them put off the revolution ten years, and they may have to yield to a community of Socialists instead of a nation of Radicals'.[51]

European developments also played a specific role in this process, and offered a distinctive moral to would-be political reformers. The progress of events in France had seen the gain of universal suffrage, after all, followed by the loss of revolutionary momentum. Political rights, in this context, now appeared to have a much more transitory value than most Chartists had hitherto assumed would be the case. As the Owenites had long suggested, it was possible, in fact, for the people to possess and wield political power, but with any practical benefits thereof slipping like sand through their clumsy fingers. A National Reform League address of January 1850 thus insisted that '*political* without *social* rights, would be, not only useless, but untenable (for any length of time), by the poorer or dependent classes, – a fact placed beyond dispute by the late events on the Continent'.[52]

---

[50] *NS*, no. 635 (22 December 1849), 8; no. 637 (5 May 1850), 1.

[51] *OFP*, no. 2 (October 1849), 15; *WV*, no. 15 (1 June 1839), 3. The *Freethinkers' Magazine* commented simply that 'Kennington Common and the monster petition exploded Feargus O'Connor. The Charter "pure and simple" weltered a wreck upon public opinion' (no. 7, 1 December 1850, 200).

[52] *NS*, no. 639 (19 January 1850), 7.

Finally, with the abatement of the hysteria of 1848, both socialism and Chartism achieved a more respectable public image. Once it was clear that any genuine threat of revolution had passed, or indeed had never existed, a degree of intellectual curiosity began to be manifested about the goals of the continental revolutionaries, and correspondingly about some aspects of the programmes of domestic reformers. The discussion of even major social reforms by hitherto relatively orthodox liberals – John Stuart Mill is the most famous case in point – now became possible in a way which would have been unthinkable three or four years earlier. The *Spectator*, for example, commented in May 1851 on 'a state of the public feeling considerably altered since 1848. Although standing with practical England in the remote and shadowy region of "isms", neither Chartism nor Socialism is quite the bugbear that it once was: common sense begins to regard each as a rude husk that may contain some kernel of truth, that may be worth analysis'.[53] With the declining influence of both O'Connor and Owen, too, neither movement was conceived as being as extreme as it had once been. Each, rather, could now be seen more in terms of a set of abstract doctrines than the partisan programme of one leader.

Throughout the spring of 1851 socialist measures were discussed increasingly in Chartist circles. Reflecting the new spirit of conciliation, a series of *Chartist Tracts for the Times* declared that Owen's plans might be implemented after the Chartists had attained political power. The *National Instructor*, now one of the more important Chartist papers, unabashedly detailed many socialistic schemes and theories in its pages, even granting the typical Owenite assertion that 'the individual system' had been useful only in 'the infancy of society'. Some Chartists also acknowledged the past importance of socialist agitation. The Chartist leader Rufford was reported, for example, as saying at this time with respect to social reform that 'any good that comes in that direction we shall owe to noble Robert Owen'.[54] A new label was invented to describe the growing trend in the radical reform movement. Especially in the manufacturing districts, reported Harney, Chartists were being transformed into what was now called 'Chartists and much more'. The title stuck, and began to be widely adopted as a means of self-description.[55]

The Owenites now also perceived that the Chartists were much more receptive than they had been to discussions of social ends. Robert Buchanan, for example, praised their improvement over the situation

[53] Quoted in *NS*, no. 704 (3 May 1851), 1.
[54] For example, *NS*, no. 651 (13 April 1850), 1; no. 653 (27 April 1850), 1; no. 655 (11 May 1850), 7; *Chartist Tracts for the Times* (c. 1850), p. 7; *NI*, no. 13 (17 August 1850), 193–5; Henry Solly, *James Woodford*, 2, p. 220.
[55] *NS*, no. 645 (2, March 1850), 1.

'some years ago', when, as he put it, working men were asked what they would do with the Charter, 'the answer generally was a most mysterious shake of the head, accompanied by a low growl, as if his intentions were too horrible to be divulged', adding that 'Fat, alderman-looking men trembled at the ominous shake, others only laughed, as they took the shake to be an unfailing sign of ignorance'. In May a new Owenite organisation, the League of Social Reform, was founded. It included two delegates from the Fraternal Democrats, and moved to establish friendly relations with all parties seeking the political rights of the people. Attempting to avoid some of the leading mistakes the socialists had formerly made, it also abstained from identifying with any particular theological creed, admitting that this tended 'in the existing state of public opinion upon such subjects materially to retard the acceptance of the practical views of Socialism by Society'.[56] Co-operation was now evident in a variety of different locations. From Brighton, Paisley (which with Bradford praised French socialism and discussed various types of social reform), Glasgow and Edinburgh, it was announced that Chartists and socialists were working together in the cause of reform. This task was clearly facilitated by the Social Reform League's avowal that it 'did not accept any "ism", neither that of Fourier, Owen, or any one else, but simply desired a union of all sects and parties of Social Reformers to form in a propaganda of the principles of Social Reform'. In June delegates from all over Scotland, which appears once again to have been particularly unified, also unanimously supported the National Reform League programme.[57]

All of these efforts culminated in a grand 'democratic conference' held in August and reconvened in October. This brought together reformers whose only previous contacts had been informal, or whose political differences, indeed, had precluded them making any earlier attempt to meet. Present were delegates from the Executive Committee of the National Charter Association, the Social Reform League, the National Reform League, the Fraternal Democrats, and the Parliamentary Reform Association. Given the diversity of views represented, there was clearly some danger that old hostilities would quickly mar the atmosphere of collective endeavour. But relations between the groups appear to have been amicable at the first meeting. G. J. Holyoake reported, in any case, that all parties had agreed in principle on the desirability of amalgamating their efforts.[58] In early

[56] *GS*, no. 26 (29 March 1851), 8; 'Minutes of the Congress of Social Reformers, 13–16 May 1850', MS., Bishopsgate Institute, fols. 5, 7.
[57] *NS*, no. 656 (18 May 1850), 1; no. 658 (1 June 1850), 1; *RWN*, no. 4 (26 May 1850), 7; no. 8 (23 June 1850), 7.
[58] *Leader*, 1, no. 22 (24 August 1850), 509; no. 23 (31 August 1850), 537.

October, the conference consented to the formation of the 'National Charter and Social Reform Union', whose goal was to be the establishment of 'a just, wise, and a good Government, and such an equitable distribution of the fruits of industry, as may be conducive to the best interest of all members of the commonwealth'. Tensions were present, however, even when the discussion was kept fairly vague. Some division emerged, for example, on the question of whether the phrase 'by peaceful and legal means' should be included in the statement about the goals of the new organisation. With thirteen votes on each side, Holyoake cast the deciding ballot against its inclusion, declaring that the conference did not want to censure those who rejected a reliance upon these means alone. Evidently the Owenites did not have the upper hand in conducting the proceedings.[59]

Other fissures in the new alliance were soon evident. Walter Cooper provoked some irritation by stating that 'He knew that hundreds, aye, thousands of Socialists, throughout the kingdom, believed that the Chartists were in favour of a physical force revolution. He was aware of the numerical strength of the Chartists, but would they not be benefited by the aid of the advanced minds of the Socialists?' Cooper admitted that the success of socialism was now predicated upon the passage of the Charter, but warned that the conference must clearly support the eventual application of socialist principles. Otherwise adherents of the latter 'would think that the Conference was only a trap to catch silly Socialists, and drag them into the excesses of the past.' This elicited an angry address from the National Charter Association, which deprecated the proposed union on the grounds that the Owenites had never encouraged Chartism in the past, and did not even count democracy amongst their own aims. Cooper's immodest plea for deference to 'advanced minds' was also not appreciated.[60]

Tensions like these could have been anticipated at such a meeting. But more indomitable problems soon arose. Arriving later than the other National Reform League delegates, Bronterre O'Brien quickly became dismayed by the fruitless results achieved so far, and persuaded his colleagues to withdraw from the conference and place the question of union before the country as a whole. Since O'Brien was still a nationally recognised Chartist leader with a considerable following, widely scattered though it might have been, this course of action clearly endangered the entire proceedings. 'Warm words' were exchanged with Harney and others at this point. The National Reformers proved intractable, however. But they also argued that, in the current

---

[59] *Ibid.*, no. 29 (12 October 1850), 681.
[60] *NS*, no. 677 (12 October 1850), 1; no. 678 (19 October 1850), 5. Cooper later embezzled funds from the Christian Socialists.

political climate, no union such as that proposed would serve to bring together the disparate groups of reformers spread across the country. O'Brien did not, therefore, retire because the alliance seemed wrong in principle, but for tactical reasons similar to those of the Fraternal Democrats the previous year, but which the latter now apparently disregarded.[61] The National Reform League delegates' statement on their departure explained that:

> Our withdrawal from the Conference was simply an act of policy or prudence on our part, to prevent disunion in the Chartist ranks, of which the whole of our society forms an integral part. The great majority of the Chartist body are not Communists, nor Socialists, nor National Reformers, nor Trades' Unionists, nor members of any of the bodies said to be represented at the Conference. They are simply Chartists, that is, men desirous of being represented in the Commons House of Parliament according to the principles declared in the *People's Charter*. To preserve the integrity and unanimity of this body ought, we think, to be a prime consideration with every association represented in the Conference, and with every individual out of it holding Chartist principles. On no account should such integrity and unanimity be, for a moment, endangered by obtruding the views or projects of any particular social or political-economical sect upon the body, *as a reform to be worked out in common with the Charter.*

These objections now won over a significant portion of the delegates to the meeting. Opposition on similar grounds was also voiced, for example, by O'Connor, Ernest Jones and W. J. Linton. Centrifugal tendencies had begun to pull the entire project apart.[62]

Nonetheless the conference as a whole rejected these contentions. In mid-November, after further discussions, a programme was issued which comprised the attainment of the Charter, nationalisation of the land, a free press and education, better employment of labour, and a more just distribution of wealth. The prevailing mood of the delegates remained optimistic. Some, like Holyoake, continued to see union of the Chartists and socialists as 'inevitable'. Others were convinced that this programme would ensure that working class Chartists would now be much clearer about their eventual goals. One remaining member of the National Reform League contended, for example, that

> The producers, the workers, are not apathetic as to the progress of the Charter, but . . . are quite convinced that the mere possession of political power would not ensure their extrication from the evils which afflict society, unless accompanied by certain social rights, which ought to be made plain to their apprehension by their leaders.[63]

[61] *Leader*, 1, no. 30 (19 October 1850), 706; no. 31 (26 October 1850), 730; *NS*, no. 679 (26 October 1850), 5; *DR*, 1 (November 1849), 205.

[62] *Leader*, 1, no. 33 (9 November 1850), 772–3; *NS*, no. 680 (2 November 1850), 1; no. 681 (9 November 1850), 1. Jones' views are given in *RWN*, ns no. 27 (16 February 1851), 14.

[63] *Leader*, 1, no. 34 (16 November 1850), 793, 797; 2, no. 43 (18 January 1851), 61; no. 52 (22 March 1851), 277.

This opinion appears to have had some foundation, in fact. For when various local Chartist, working class and reform organisations recorded their opinions about the conference proceedings, most approved the proposed union of programmes. The conference delegates themselves did their best to assuage past fears and promote the spirit of union, insisting in an address that 'at the Conference none gave a more prompt and hearty support to the People's Charter, "name and all", than the representatives of the socialists'. G. A. Fleming, now editor of the *Northern Star*, also claimed that the old grounds of mutual antagonism had now been surpassed. Thus he informed his readers that:

Some years ago, the Political and Social Reformers of this country held aloof from each other, each under the impression, that the mode of action pursued by each of them was of itself sufficient for the objects they had in view. We have been present at, and taken part in, discussion as to the relative merits and the superiority of each of these modes, in which not a little warmth on both sides was exhibited. These foolish divisions have, happily, passed away. The socialists, while still confining their exertions to what they consider their legitimate sphere of action – namely, the diffusion of knowledge as to the nature of the Social institutions best adapted for the harmonious development and healthy gratification of the physical, mental, and moral faculties of man – have, we believe, learned that individuals can do but little for the practicalisation of their views; that, in order to succeed, they must have the support and protection of just and equal general laws; and that, if Political does not precede, it must at least accompany Social reform. The Chartist body, on the other hand, have, we believe, discovered that political changes are valueless in themselves, and only to be struggled for as instruments through the use of which they may achieve Social emancipation and independence.[64]

Such prognoses proved to be overly optimistic, however. The question of union quickly incited further and more open divisions among the Chartists in particular. Then a London Chartist assembly in May 1851 supported a programme which included nationalisation of the land, a Manchester conference in February (at which only eight delegates were present) presided over by O'Connor determined that no further questions should adulterate agitation for the Charter. Then in April O'Connor himself again lambasted both socialism and communism, insisting that the latter entailed the idle sharing the fruits of labour with the industrious. Some other Chartists clearly wanted nothing at all to do with socialism, either, particularly with French socialist reform plans. The Manchester Charter Association was especially vehement about what it termed efforts 'to attach a kind of mongrel Socialism to Chartism . . borrowed from the Parisian school of philosophers'. For this involved a conception of government opposed to what was seen as the entire bent of traditional British radicalism:

[64] *NS*, no. 684 (30 November 1850), 8; no. 685 (7 December 1850), 1; no. 682 (16 November 1850), 4.

In England we are content that government should mind its own business; what we desire is, that we should be allowed to mind ours, interrupted as little as possible by the officiousness of centralised power. We feel how greatly the civilised world is indebted to Gallic genius in many particulars, but we have not observed anything in the social economics of France which we would care to adopt in the practices of this country. Whilst, therefore, we are favourable to 'Social Rights', we disbelieve in the 'right' of government to regulate them; and are wholly opposed to adding plans for the reconstruction of society, to a mere political measure like the Charter.[65]

In fact, such objections proved all too widespread. The net effect of all these discussions was not a formal association of reformers, for as Fleming admitted, 'no tangible union resulted'. After all of these exertions, the results were certainly meagre and widely disappointing. What did transpire, however, could still be seen as possessing some value, at least from the socialist point of view:

These meetings . . . and similar discussions throughout the country, have not been unproductive. Their fruits are to be seen in what may be called the Socialistic tone of the late Conference. To a larger extent than upon any former occasion, the delegates occupied themselves with Social questions; and the Programme, as ultimately adopted, includes most of the fundamental principles advocated by the Social Reformers. In this direction the Chartist movement has undoubtedly extended itself, and if properly directed, may look for a large accession of numbers and influence.

The exact extent of Chartist support for such measures nationally is however quite difficult to gauge, as is the precise nature of socialistic beliefs and 'social' preferences amongst the Chartists generally in this period. This is in part because such a wide variety of 'social' programmes was now available. We know that the Nottingham and Halifax District Chartists, for example, urged their delegates in March 1851 to vote for land nationalisation, while North Lancashire gave instructions to support co-operative societies. Other Chartist groups were less precise in their inclinations. At the April conference one London delegate said that his constituents were tired of 'the mere alphabet of political reform' and wanted a discussion of social rights and labour questions. But the Potteries' delegates demanded that agitation for the Charter be kept distinct from other matters. At Bradford, a group of reformers terming themselves the 'Socialist Democrats' moved to found the Bradford Democratic Association in July. But this appears to have been a relatively isolated development. Other-

[65] *Leader*, 2, no. 54 (5 April 1851), 325–6; *NS*, no. 693 (1 February 1851), 1; *GS*, 2, no. 28 (12 April 1851), 12; *RWN*, no. 97 (20 June 1852), 13; *NS*, no. 696 (8 March 1851), 1. O'Connor himself nonetheless spoke far more favourably of Owen after 1848. See *NS*, no. 595 (17 March 1849), 5, no. 650 (6 April 1850), 1. There is even some evidence of a more positive view as early as 1843. See in particular O'Connor's *Practical Work*, p. 115.

wise, Chartist activity declined steadily throughout the summer of 1851, and fewer reports thus are available from which to conjecture.[66]

By 1852 the surviving active Chartists were being advised by only three leaders, George Julian Harney, Ernest Jones, and Bronterre O'Brien, with some assistance from G. W. M. Reynolds and the various conductors of the *Leader*. The zeal for union of the previous year seems to have dissipated rapidly in the face of disagreements and declining enthusiasm for reform in general. Some socialists now also seem to have taken this as a sign that political reform was not worth seeking for the time being. Fleming continued to insist upon the exigency of pursuing both social and political reform, 'the Siamese twins of progress'. But he nonetheless also declared that 'just now the social effort is the instrument which is most ready to hand, and which the people are most capable of using. They can work for that without any greater legislative power than they at present possess. For that they need not ask the aid of Parliament. To some extent upon that question their fate is in their own hands.' Driving the wedge even further between the reformers, various of the Chartists now renewed their claims concerning the priority of political activity in order to avoid losing even more of their own supporters. Harney disavowed the limited co-operative aims of the engineers' union, claiming that only a few could be helped in this manner. W. J. Linton reached a similar conclusion, as did Ernest Jones, who engaged in a divisive debate with Lloyd Jones on the subject of co-operation versus political reform. To some extent the old battle lines of the 1840s were merely being reoccupied once again. Yet it is clear that co-operators in the 1850s were sometimes as ambitious as the advocates of syndicalism in the GNCTU had been. Some of William Newton's engineers, for example, continued to see co-operation as 'individual Republicanism, the true democracy of production', and to push for the election by the trades of their own managers, and the government of industry by individual trades. This vision of the 'co-operative commonwealth' helped to keep the notion of national producer co-operation alive until the revival of socialism in the 1880s.[67]

Yet this vision of co-operation, so different from the lapse into consumerism which historians have usually found in the period, was not seen as a unifying element in the early 1850s. Nonetheless, some basis for compromise was still evident in 1852. The radicals certainly

[66] *NS*, no. 701 (12 April 1851), 4; no. 699 (29 March 1851), 1; no. 700 (5 April 1851), 7–8; no. 715 (19 July 1851), 1.
[67] *Ibid.*, no. 750 (20 March 1852), 4; no. 755 (1 May 1852), 4; *ER*, 2 (1852), 18; *NP*, 2 (1852), 793–866; *Englishman*, no. 4 (28 January 1854), 58.

widely agreed that social ends at least needed to be discussed more seriously, if not actually appended to the Charter itself. Many Chartists thus probably conceded with the *Weekly Advisor* that parliamentary reform was only desirable in order to introduce social reforms such as co-operation. Of course the new co-operation of the 1850s was usually, though not always, perceived as considerably less revolutionary in its aims than the Owenite variety had been because 'community' was now only rarely among its ends. But this also made co-operation easier for many Chartists to support, particularly when it emphasised the extension of democracy to the realm of production. For similar reasons, many Chartists probably did not support the full programme of land nationalisation, with farms of varying sizes rented out to the public in associations, which Ernest Jones was to promote for the next six years in the *People's Paper*. Nonetheless a degree of accommodation might have been reached which recommended co-operation, political reforms and some commitment to public ownership of land and/or manufactures (for the social Chartists were themselves divided on this question). But, Harney reported in August, there still remained between the social and political reformers 'a want of mutual confidence, a suspicion, and a jealousy producing results almost as disastrous'.[68]

Thus even when the socialists were willing to abandon what the *Christian Social Economist* termed '*scientific* socialism', 'the desire for a perfect state of society', and to embrace political reform and government by universal suffrage, the practical requisites of union were still lacking. Both social Chartists and socialists did substantially agree upon the practicability of collective landownership and administration, though the former were always more sceptical about its communitarian variation. The Chartists, however, were divided on the question of how the cause of co-operation ought to be linked to the Charter, though they knew that political reform had to proceed it. Even after 1848, too, not all of the Owenites were convinced that this was necessary. Many saw much of independent value in the new co-operative efforts, provided their aim was eventually to supersede the competitive system entirely, rather than merely to provide a dividend to selected consumers. Co-operation, therefore, which might have been one of the best meeting grounds for Chartists and Owenites, failed to perform this function. Its goals were limited enough to suit most Chartists, but never sufficiently connected to political reform to gain wider appeal. Its scope was potentially wide enough to suit all socialists, too. But the right mixture of elements had not yet been

[68] *WA*, no. 1 (3 January 1852), 1–2; *PP*, 1, no. 5 (5 June 1852), 4; *StF*, no. 1 (14 August 1852), 10.

achieved, though co-operation would become increasingly political in later decades.[69]

The grand effort at Chartist–socialist union thus collapsed before it could ever seriously be tested. Owen himself, still a noble figure to many observers, continued to herald the millennium for a few more years, though in ever fainter and more fragile tones. He played no important role in the negotiations for political union. Moreover, he succeeded in alienating large numbers of former supporters and attracting a considerable amount of ridicule (which he shrugged off with characteristic abandon) after his conversion to spiritualism at the age of 80. Owen was not the only one who became isolated from the remnants of the reform movement, however. Some of his leading disciples went on to new enterprises in the 1850s and abandoned the forum of social and political debate entirely. Others, such as Isaac Ironside and Robert Buchanan, became deeply involved in local politics. A few abandoned neither the national arena nor the cause of political reform. Lloyd Jones, in particular, remained active in this regard, later becoming secretary to the Labour Representation League on its founding in 1869. O'Connor drifted off into insanity and died soon thereafter. O'Brien became increasingly isolated after 1852, though he continued to seize every available opportunity to publicise his views, becoming what Holyoake termed 'a sort of Perambulatory Dissenter, attending every meeting, and disagreeing with everything and everybody'.[70]

The prospects for meaningful union, whatever they had seemed to be in 1848–51, thus disappeared after 1852. The leaders of the reform movement had lost interest, and so had most of the rank and file. The working classes, Harney moaned, seemed to be 'content as their fathers had been in the "good old days"', and without their enthusiasm neither social nor political reform had much of a future. Only Ernest Jones seriously pushed the united causes of land nationalisation and parliamentary reform through the end of the 1850s. He was not without some success in this regard. The *People's Paper*, which was selling 4,000 copies weekly until Chartism went into steep decline in 1854, united disparate groups of reformers and helped to maintain the semblance of widespread as well as common struggle. Though he apparently had little sympathy with communitarianism, Jones helped

---

[69] CSE, no. 1 (22 November 1851), 5.

[70] PWRM, no. 9 (14 June 1851), 129; G. D. H. Cole, *A Short History of the British Working Class Movement, 1789–1947* (George Allen and Unwin, 1948), p. 211; *Reasoner*, 12 (1852), 258–9. Holyoake added that 'the idea of Mr. O'Brien forming a party reminds one of what Lord John Russell once said to Mr. Roebuck – "if the honourable member formed an administration, it must be of himself"'. O'Brien may also have tried to associate himself with the Christian Socialists in this period, before being roundly rebuffed. See Christensen, *Origin and History of Christian Socialism*, p. 103.

to keep alive late Chartist interest in the land. Most importantly, he regarded its collective ownership and management as the most significant reforms which would have to follow the Charter. In this sense, it was Jones who carried forward the banner of socialist–Chartist union through to a new era of reform agitation. Other social Chartists attempted a revival of the movement in 1858, and praised Owen at his death that year as having contributed greatly to the cause of social amelioration. But their efforts were short-lived.[71]

[71] *PP*, no. 132 (11 November 1854), 4; *Vanguard*, no. 1 (1853), 2; *NU*, no. 8 (4 December 1858), 59. On Jones, see generally John Saville, *Ernest Jones, Chartist* (Lawrence and Wishart, 1952), pp. 13–84.

8

Social radicalism, the state and revolution

The convergence of the social and political reformers after 1845 marked an important if disappointing nexus in the history of British radicalism. Unpolitical socialism, far more ambitious than consumer co-operation but nonetheless uninterested in parliamentary reform, would never again inspire much support. Nor could working class radicalism any longer neglect the delineation of at least some 'social' ends. Thirty years of arduous effort had not attained the ballot for the unpropertied working classes or the 'perfect state of society' for Owenism. Many Chartists were forced therefore to conclude that until the economic power of the landed and commercial aristocracies had been curtailed considerably, significant social and political reform could never be achieved, or would remain of only superficial value. Many socialists also deduced that without state action the prospects for meaningful social reform were extremely limited. Others added to this the belief that in order to generate the mass appeal necessary for political reform, socialism itself would have to reflect the more traditional democratic aspirations of working class radicalism.

Though there was certainly more social radical activity in the 1850s and 1860s than has been hitherto recognised, a detailed examination of this period would probably contribute little to our understanding of the central themes treated here.[1] A new language of politics had been established by the early 1850s which did not alter substantially in the near future, and indeed has retained many of its leading characteristics to the present day. The 'social' critique of liberalism had been firmly established, and the outlines of modern political debate broadly sketched. In turn the model of representative democracy popularised

[1] On this development see Trygve Tholfsen, *Working Class Radicalism in Mid-Victorian England* (Croom Helm, 1976), Gillespie, *Labor and Politics in England*, Chimen Abramsky and Henry Collins, *Karl Marx and the British Labour Movement* (Macmillan, 1965), Royden Harrison, *Before the Socialists* (Routledge and Kegan Paul, 1965), and Neville Kirk, *The Growth of Working Class Reformism in Mid-Victorian England* (Croom Helm, 1985).

by Paine and others in the 1790s had been dealt a severe, though by no means mortal, blow by the demand for a vastly more sophisticated conception of the relationship between economics and politics, by the critique of liberal political economy, and by the aspersions cast upon the ostensible value of mass political participation regarded as an end in itself. 'Social democracy', in turn (though the phrase itself was not yet widely in use), was increasingly recognised as a new and powerful incarnation of modern radicalism. The spectrum of political beliefs between liberalism and socialism was now considerably more complex than it had been a quarter of a century earlier.

Two other forms of social radicalism also grew out of the experience of the 1840s whose relationship to the debates detailed here is both important and hitherto largely unexplored: revolutionary socialism, and a new type of republicanism which attempted to incorporate aspects of socialism without embracing either economic regulation or secularism. Both ideals would be profoundly important for the evolution of radical movements throughout Europe during the rest of the nineteenth century and beyond. Each also represented a response to the failures of both early socialism and early nineteenth century working class radicalism, as well as to attempts to wed the remnants of both movements at the end of the 1840s. After summarising the development of 'political socialism' – the doctrine that a socialist programme should be implemented by means of political reform and essentially managed or directed at the level of the nation-state – this chapter considers how its votaries responded after the mid-1840s to the failure of the Chartist strategy of parliamentary petitions and mass demonstrations by subdividing into more clearly demarcated moral force and revolutionary wings. Seen from the perspective of later forms of socialism, the creation of a revolutionary variety of socialism was a dramatic break from most past strategies. Consequently, it has usually been seen as one of the chief elements in the development of 'scientific' from 'utopian' socialism. Though the new form of socialism had distinctly continental roots, it emerged in part from a debate over the failure of both Owenism and Chartism. Here the role of the political development of the young Friedrich Engels, though apparently unimportant at the time, was to prove of immense significance.

The emergence of a further form of social radicalism broadened the spectrum of mid nineteenth-century British as well as European political thought even more. After the 1848 revolutions had popularised a variety of socialist schemes and widely dispersed criticisms of traditional political reform, radicals and republicans responded in part by accepting elements of the new social language and its implied programmes. In Britain, moreover, a republican revival of sorts took place in the early 1850s which owed much to the successes of some of the great continental revolutionaries of 1848, particularly the Italian Giuseppe Mazzini and the Hungarian Lajos Kossuth. But these leaders, both of whom were exiled in Britain for a time, were not merely immensely popular representatives of the struggle against autocracy and despotism. Mazzini in particular also helped to inspire in England the creation of a new variety of republicanism which accepted some key elements of the socialist programme while strenuously rejecting others. The reconstruction of radicalism in the 1850s, in turn, assisted in provoking further reaction against more centralised forms of state administration, which were associated with some forms of socialism, but now also seen as patterned upon the continental despotisms. A renewed emphasis upon local self-government in British radicalism corresponded with similar strands in both Owenism and Chartism, and helped to hinder the wider acceptance of ideas of a more centrally administered economy. Owenism, nonetheless, remained identified with the notion of reformist intervention in aid of the poor and the creation of a neutral bureaucracy working on behalf of the public good. Its more millennial political goals were thereafter largely disregarded, and later nineteenth-century socialists such as the Fabians became attracted to it for the humanitarian rather than the utopian political implications of its social theory.

Early and modern political socialism

This book has focussed upon three areas of early socialist political thought: the assault upon 'naive' political reformism from the perspective of a more sophisticated conception of commercial society; the moral and perfectionist critique of 'politics' and existing modes of adjudicating conflicts; and the articulation of conceptions of the duties of government and the best form of social, political and economic administration. Each of these aspects constituted a dimension of the new 'social' language which had been broadly diffused by mid-century. Taken together, they created – at least for those socialists close to republicanism – a paradigmatic reconceptualisation within radical political thought, a new and widely accepted if not unchallenged consciousness of the inappropriateness of an older language and its assumptions and objects to the social, political and economic conditions of mid-century. The Machiavellian moment had now largely passed. The Marxist moment was dawning.

What this new language symbolised, especially by the widespread use of the couplet of 'social *and* political', was the level of complexity of economic debate reached within radicalism by 1852. This often entailed not so much the pursuit of a specific new programme as a clarification of the relationship between political and economic reform. Radicals clearly had always intended that economic changes, not to mention the rehabilitation of public virtue, would follow the inception of popular governments. It was a leading verse in the radical catechism that the abolition of primogeniture and other aristocratic legislation would reduce the existing disproportionate ownership of wealth.[2] In the 1830s and 1840s such assumptions were linked to further demands for factory and poor law reform and similar legislation. The political programme of radicalism thus always at least tacitly comprised certain consequent economic changes. 'What else has the Charter ever been regarded as but as the means to social ends?', inquired the O'Connorite Thomas Clark in 1850, opposing amalgamation with the social reformers.[3] To many, the social implications of the Charter were as obvious, if implicit, as the demands of the reformers of 1832 had been. They therefore required no new slogans or programmes which would distract the multitude from political agitation.

But the aims of many Chartists in 1850 were not expressed in the same manner as they had been in 1836. Juxtaposing 'social' to 'political' reform for large numbers not only entailed the admission that certain economic goals were sought with the Charter, but also signified the adoption of a socialistic programme. The tacit moral-economic liberalism of many early Chartist pronouncements had been widespread, but came under increasing attack by the mid-1840s. Now, for many, the identification of a specific 'social' sphere symbolised the belief that poverty could never be alleviated by the normal functioning of the market. Instead it was presumed that more widespread and continuous action by the state was necessary, though elements of self-help were of course also an important part of a 'social' discourse. (However, this lies outside of our concerns here.) One of the most notable casualties in this regard, though it never disappeared completely, was the slogan which symbolised the Chartist economic programme in the late 1830s and early 1840s. Writing in 1850, one Christian Socialist noted that

the Democratic Politician looks now upon political reform, but as a means to an end – that end being Socialism. The watchwords of Chartism in 1839 were 'a full day's wages for a full day's work'. That cry long since gave place to the more defined idea of the 'organisation of labour'. This latter opinion is, I am quite aware, by far too little comprehended by many of those who are loudest in their demands for the Franchise, but it should also be borne in mind that the leaders of the popular party in this country are not so ill-informed thereon.[4]

[2] For example, *CL*, no. 6 (13 October 1819), 89.
[3] *NS*, no. 681 (9 November 1850), 5.
[4] *CS*, 1, no. 7 (14 December 1850), 53. The writer is probably F. D. Maurice.

For socialists or social Chartists this older slogan was now a sign of immaturity. It invoked the habits of a pre-industrial age when master and man were more intimately acquainted and competition had not yet erupted into universal viciousness, before the great extremes of wealth and poverty had made the two nations so sure of their mutual antagonism. It also symbolised a far more traditional attitude towards labour and the organisation of work than that which socialism had popularised since 1815. 'The idea of "a fair day's wages for a fair day's work" is emblematical of serfdom and slavery', declared G. W. M. Reynolds:

It presupposes the existence of a class who work for another class who pay wages for the work done: it admits the division of the community into two sections – one toiling for pay, and the other living upon the produce and profits of that toil. But so long as such distinctions and divisions exist, must the class that is hired be the slaves and the bondsmen of the class that hires.[5]

Of course, not all Chartists now agreed that it was necessary to supersede completely a system of class divisions. The thought probably never occurred to most, despite the popularity of land nationalisation and national workshop proposals in the early 1850s. But simplistic assumptions about the causal effects of political reform upon economic well-being were certainly less common by mid-century. The idea that the mere assumption of political power sufficed to provide the poor with bread and work by reducing the general burden of taxation was passing away. So, too, was the notion that popular participation in politics should be construed as the chief aim of possessing the franchise. To this extent, the notion that the pursuit of collective virtue and the avoidance of 'corruption' was one of the primary goals of the political process had now been displaced partially, and the ends of government more clearly defined in economic terms. 'The idea of obtaining a vote, merely for the sake of voting, is fast becoming obliterated from the public mind, and thousands are already inquiring "what will the vote do for us?" or rather "what will it enable us to do for ourselves, supposing that we are fortunate enough to obtain it?"', observed Gammage in late 1852.[6] Nonetheless the individual moral benefits of universal suffrage and social advantages of participation had not been forgotten. Even communists such as Reynolds voiced such traditional republican concerns.[7] But the perception of the economic aims of democracy was now both more sophisticated and more prevalent, and discussions of the more strictly political virtues of democracy certainly became less common in this period, or more closely tied to economic debates.

---

[5] *RWN*, ns no. 6 (22 September 1850), 1. [6] *PP*, 1, no. 25 (23 October 1852), 6.
[7] *RWN*, ns no. 22 (12 January 1851), 1.

Many radicals at mid-century were also willing to concede that economic development had vindicated much of the socialist analysis. By 1850 the idea that working-class distress was entirely or even largely ascribable to taxation was almost extinct, at least amongst working-class leaders. Nor was it necessary to embrace land nationalisation to condemn the diabolic effects of unbridled *laissez-faire*. Many who shrank from approving more all-encompassing socialist economic programmes still agreed that competition engendered by the avaricious and overly hasty introduction of machinery and abetted by the class legislation of capitalists and landowners was the chief cause of distress. The experience of the 1840s and the compounded effects of the urbanisation of labour, widespread misery in the factory districts and elsewhere, and the continuing cycles of boom and bust despite the repeal of the Corn Laws, made any concentration upon the effects of governmental expenditure alone far less convincing than in the previous two decades. It is to the Owenites' credit that, in the spirit of union, they did not harp on the fact that the economic analysis they had popularised for more than thirty years, if not its programmatic deductions, was relatively commonplace by 1850.

The millennial goals of abolishing all traditional forms of government and politics, the family and private property, in favour of the models of primitive society, Quakerism, or any other quasi-utopian end were, however, much less widely emulated by mid nineteenth-century reformers. Radical scepticism concerning such proposals in the 1820s seemingly had been vindicated by the widespread failure of Owen's lifelong efforts to create an alternative society in microcosm. These aims had been associated with communitarian socialism in particular, and even more with Owen's special blend of primitivism, republicanism and radical Dissent. But they were not identified with the socialist enterprise as a whole. The Owenite contribution to the political ideas of mid-Victorian radicalism can thus be measured primarily in terms of the popularisation of a particular economic analysis, the displacement of the taxation-centred assumptions of earlier reformers, and the diffusion of the idea of the interventionist state. Owen – as well as other writers such as Carlyle – thus failed to convince the radicals that the institutions of representative democracy only mirrored the chaotic individualism of commercial society generally and would have to be supplanted by more enduring and broadly beneficial principles of organisation. A leading premise of Owenite communitarianism had been that only small social units could ensure sufficient social control over the proliferation of vice to obviate the need for lawyers, police, prisons and institutionalised punishment. The only alternative to this which also dispersed such control throughout society generally, and which in this period was articulated chiefly by James Elishama Smith, was mutual supervision via a combination of state and economic institutions. Such ideas, though they did not propose to interfere with the individual family system, never seem to have found much support. Moreover, after 1845 many socialists came to presume that future communities would have the state as landlord exacting 'tribute' from them. This precluded any further elaboration of an anti-political ideal in these terms. The continuing existence of something like parliamentary institutions was therefore probably assumed by most remaining socialists at mid-century.[8]

The principal focus of socialist activity in Britain would never again be the small-scale community despite the later appeal of, for example, some of William Morris's writings. Faith in the virtues of communitarianism was never again strong enough to embrace the utopian assumptions which community life entailed for Owen. Instead, with the unification of ideas of social and political reform after 1845, the notion of a socialist state – reluctantly though it was conceded by many – had begun to come of age, though it would only be much more widely accepted some fifty years later. The divorce of the federalist, semi-autarkic communitarian conception of future government from the active, interventionist and more managerial ideal implied by socialist economic criticisms was no longer feasible, or at least, would never again be widely accepted.

A sense of the permanence of parliamentary institutions did not, however, mean that some reformers did not continue to hope for the advent of a new ideal of political behaviour. Residual echoes of the moralist repugnance for politics emanated from various quarters in the early 1850s. Some of the Christian Socialists, for example, argued that until politics became suffused with religion, no genuine progress was to be anticipated. 'So long as politics are regarded as the conflicts between Whig, and Tory, and Radical; so long as Christianity is regarded as a means of securing selfish ends, they will never be united', reflected F. D. Maurice in early 1848, later insisting that 'Parties are felt to be stale, obsolete, helpless, the men who belong to them are ashamed to confess it . . . The people's Charter is an assertion that Government cannot be carried on for or by parties; all the various forms of Socialism declare that men, whatever ends they propose for themselves, must co-operate for these ends'.[9]

These views, however, represented a habit of mind rather than a

---

[8] *ST*, no. 4 (31 March 1849), 30.
[9] *PolP*, no. 1 (6 May 1848), 1; no. 17 (Supplement for July 1848), 283; see also *PR*, no. 3 (April 1850), 131–2. Attribution for these articles is given in C. Raven, *Christian Socialism*, pp. 372–4.

serious proposal for the renovation of government. Elsewhere hostility to traditional partisanship took other forms. Some radicals moved tentatively towards anarchism in this period. The expatriate O'Brienite John Campbell, for example, published a pamphlet in Philadelphia which cited Godwin extensively and proclaimed that 'There cannot be liberty where there are factions and parties, because each represents that it alone is patriotic . . . Every political organisation is an evil, is a despotism'. These views coalesced easily with the quasi-anarchist schemes of Josiah Warren, Stephen Pearl Andrews and others in America. But such sentiments were certainly uncommon in Britain. Like Owen, O'Brien himself denied that he sought to emulate Proudhon in abolishing government, and the moralist rejection of politics in fact produced little support for European anarchism among British radicals, though philosophical individualism, often patterned upon American writers, waxed luxuriantly during the 1850s and 1860s. In late 1853, for example, a dissident group of O'Brienites broke away from the National Reform League to found a 'London Confederation of Rational Reformers' dedicated to the defence of the 'sovereignty of the individual' (Warren's slogan, later taken up in Mill's *On Liberty*) and the proposition that society progressed through the segregation rather than the aggregation of individuals.[10]

The American model revisited

One of the most important ways by which the socialist critique of radicalism was vindicated by the 1850s concerned the social and economic development of America. The United States constitution and form of government never ceased being an important model for British radicalism well into the mid-Victorian era and later.[11] But from the late 1830s onwards the American ideal was treated with increasingly greater scepticism. Far more commonly, a separation was now made in radical discussions between the wise design of America's form of government and the growing inequalities of her social system. The popularisation of such distinctions can be directly linked to the influence of Owenism. O'Brien's widely read and clearly Owenite-inspired articles in the *Poor Man's Guardian*, which hammered home the social message on every possible occasion, were an important turning point in this process. Entitling a leading article in late 1834 'Another Chapter on America, Explaining the Causes of Social Evil', for example, O'Brien

[10] John Campbell, *A Theory of Equality* (Philadelphia, 1848), p. 15; *JA*, no. 25 (14 June 1852), 195; *Leader*, 4, no. 186 (15 October 1853), 999. On the development of individualism, see especially the writings of William Maccall, who assumed the editorship of *The People* when Joseph Barker embarked for America.

[11] See Henry Pelling, *America and the British Left* (Adam and Charles Black, 1956).

described the various analyses (taxation, absence of free trade, surplus population, paper money, lack of a national bank, and so forth) proposed to account for distress. But he insisted that these shared one essential assumption in common:

Every political quack has his own nostrum, and while no two of them agree as to the remedy, they are all unanimous in tracing the evil to the Government; or, in other words, they all agree, that by adopting their peculiar modes of treatment, the Government might cure the body-politic. Now, the example of America is a poser for all these empirics. There, we find a people in possession of all we are in quest of here, and yet the Americans are not much more prosperous than ourselves. They have rich and poor as we have; fluctuations and bankruptcies as we have; broken hearts and broken heads as we have. The only difference between our condition and theirs is one of degree ... if they have not already converged to the same point, it is only because America is a younger country, and because the democratic form of its government is a drag upon the aristocratic movement of its social combinations. These combinations are favourable to aristocracy, because favourable to accumulation.[12]

A sharper focus upon American difficulties resulted from President Jackson's battle with the banks and the financial panics and failures which surrounded this. Such conflicts did not lie outside the scope of traditional radical analyses, since Paine, Cobbett and others had prophesied the perilous effects of an abuse of paper money upon the political system. But their implications now seemed more serious. Some thought republicanism itself was threatened. In 1834, for example, the *Destructive* observed that 'Under a republican form of Government, the despotism of money has blistered the productive classes in the United States', concluding that 'to the industrious many, one form of government is about as good as another, until this despotism is overthrown; except insofar as one form of government gives the opportunity of overthrowing it which the other does not'. Though some Chartists insisted that 'a fair day's wages' prevailed in America, or that 'we hear of nothing but prosperity from the USA', more critical views were increasingly circulated during the Chartist years. But it was often still assumed that popular sovereignty would remedy any distress. Warning that the American system of paper money was sure to undermine her free institutions, the Chartist *Brighton Patriot* for example commented in 1837 that

the Government of America, really emanating from the people, and the people themselves, have discovered that their independence is a mere phantom, and whatever the public in England may be taught by the generality of the newspaper press, they may depend upon this, that the President, Congress, and people of America are determined upon having a gold and silver currency, and nothing else.

[12] *PMG*, 3, no. 186 (27 December 1834), 369.

A month later, too, the same paper cheered the fact that 'in America the people roused themselves, and, possessing the power, they are at this moment trampling on the monied aristocracy, and deriding the impotent rage of the banks'. Faith in the recuperative powers of the American people was thus often reaffirmed in the Chartist years. For 'democracy' entailed popular participation as much as it did a particular set of institutions or their economic consequences. The United States could not but remain a powerful symbol of collective political activity, therefore. The Chartist G. M. Bartlett, for example, promised in 1842 that 'under the Charter system of Representation, the purity of legislation will depend entirely upon the enlightened will of the majority, and here we have proof of, not only the soundness, but of the utility of this system, for the majority have always an interest in being right. America affords us striking evidence of this'. But other Chartists were markedly less confident. In 1839, for example, the *True Scotsman* reported on a circular warning that a landed aristocracy was fast rising in the United States which eventually would overthrow its constitution. Social Chartists were particularly liable to lament (as Thomas Hunt did in 1840) that 'this much-desired democratic principle is not productive of the great good to the many they so fondly anticipate. Witness the United States of America, whose working population, judging from their complaints, are in a condition little better than our own'. And a year earlier James Elishama Smith had insisted even more harshly that

The time of political allusions (sic) is passed. Of those who fancy that the republican government be the panacea for the cure of all evils, there are but few among the men of sound mind. The government of the United States is no longer the *beau idéal* of political institutions. Every one who has not lost his senses knows that the cheapest government is not the best, that among all species of despotism, that of the lynch law is the worst, and that of all the aristocracies, that of the parvenus and shopocrats claims the most distinction.[13]

Confidence in the ability of republican institutions alone to cure American evils without a dramatic departure from previous economic policies had waned further by the end of the 1840s. Social radical papers such as the *Midland Progressionist* commonly adverted to American extremes of rich and poor. Only comparatively rarely did radicals continue to insist upon America's manifest and inevitably increasing affluence. Many there *were* better off. But by 1848 social Chartists such as the poet J. B. Leno had come to believe that a 'pernicious' system

[13] *DPMC*, no. 63 (12 April 1834), 73; *Charter*, no. 37 (6 October 1839), 577; *MCJ*, no. 19 (7 August 1841), 152; *BP*, no. 122 (20 June 1837), 2; no. 125 (11 July 1837), 2; *TS*, no. 59 (30 November 1839), 3; *NV*, no. 12 (29 January 1842), 3; Thomas Hunt, *Chartism, Trades Unionism and Socialism* (1840), p. 5; *PenS*, no. 119 (27 July 1839), 4.

there also led many to suffer considerable privation, sometimes for long periods, despite universal suffrage. If the land were nationalised, however, Leno expected all to prosper. Others were even critical of the design of the American political system. G. W. M. Reynolds for example maintained that the United States had no need for either a Senate or President, both being in his view modelled on aristocratic institutions.[14] But most concentrated upon articulating some kind of firm distinction between the theoretical advantages of republican government, and the disabilities of the social system which prevailed in America. This permitted American political institutions to be lauded while competitive political economy was denounced. The widely-discussed booklet, *America Compared to England* (1849), for example, alleged that what prosperity the United States could boast of resulted entirely from her form of government, but then severely condemned the evils of American competition. This compromise allowed even diehard communists to enthuse over American republican virtues. Thornton Hunt declared that 'the Americans are the true champions of democracy in the world. Nothing, we believe, will crush, or even check the power of America: she will go on to show what democracy can do, and to show the English people what are the true elements of political power'. Another social Chartist admired the fact that

America has no princesses to bestow upon Prussian princes; consequently her citizens are not taxed to pay their dowries. Neither has she a little tribe of suckling leeches, princes and princesses, – Alfreds, Helenas, Patricks, etc, – all growing up to an age when their hands will be dipped in our pockets. In fine, America, being neither afflicted with a monarchy, accursed by an aristocracy, or saddled with a State Church, is really rich, and truly prosperous.

Even G. J. Harney, one of the most adamant publicisers of American ills in the mid-1840s, while admitting that much misery existed in the US, praised the low cost of government there. G. J. Holyoake, too, assured an audience in 1846 that whatever difficulties America had were 'self-correcting, and its progress permanent'. With the emergence of the anti-centralisation movement in the 1850s, renewed praise for American freedom from governmental interference was also heard from some quarters.[15]

From the mid-1850s onwards British radicals also increasingly condemned one institution as particularly blemishing the reputation of

[14] *MP* (1848), 15–16; *People*, 1 (1848), 58 (Barker nonetheless argued for a substantial measure of state economic activity; *ibid.*, 161); *NS*, no. 661 (22 June 1850), 5; *RWN*, ns no. 33 (30 March 1851), 1.
[15] R. Russell, *America Compared to England* (1849), p. 177; *PolEx*, no. 16 (13 June 1853), 245; *RWN*, no. 332 (21 December 1856), 7; *DR* (1849–50), 30–3; *Reasoner*, 1 (20 August 1846), 190; *Leader*, 9, no. 440 (28 August 1858), 867.

American democracy: slavery. Reformers had never denied the existence of the slave system, usually denouncing it as a remnant of British
aristocratic misrule. The evils of the system, however, were pointed to
more frequently by social Chartists as their right to criticise America
was more widely conceded. The LWMA, for instance, decried 'that
black *reminiscent of kingly dominion* – slavery' in 1838. By mid-century
the issue rose in importance, with one radical paper commenting in
1850 that 'just now the Republic in the West is of small account in the
affairs of Europe, and this is just on account of slavery'. A few years
later, G. W. M. Reynolds even advised that a civil war might be a
blessing in America given its contamination by the inheritance of
slavery from Britain. When war finally came in 1861, too, radicals
dissociated it from the operations of democracy whenever possible.
However, Joseph Barker among others denied that the slave system
was responsible for the conflict, citing instead the differing economic
interests of north and south. Harney, too, insisted that

Democracy has never yet been fully and fairly tried in America . . . Slavery is
the very antipodes of democracy, and the fault of the founders of the American
republic was that they compromised with an evil and tolerated a sin implanted
on the soil of their country under the monarchical rule of England.[16]

By the early 1860s, a much more sophisticated radical conception of
American politics was evident than had existed even thirty years
earlier. In particular a distinction between its social system and political institutions was widely recognised, and Owenism's role in popularising this was often conceded. America, it was now often alleged,
contained 'the elements of all the injustice and inequalities of Europe in
regard to PROPERTY', and thus proved that a republican constitution
alone was not sufficient to bring prosperity to the working classes.[17]
Only new economic arrangements would settle the question of class
inequality once and for all.

Politics and revolution

The popularisation of revolutionary socialist doctrines in Britain after the mid-1840s posed a rather different challenge to working
class radicalism. Most of these new theories originated in continental
socialism and introduced concepts which had virtually never before
been hazarded, much less seriously entertained, in British socialist
circles. No Chartist revolutionary had ever explained at length why

---

16 *CPG*, no. 49 (15 September 1838), 2; *SF*, 3, no. 116 (14 September 1850), 8; *RWN*, no.
    319 (14 September 1856), 9; *LA*, 2, no. 10 (2 January 1861), 4; *BRP* (1861), 378; *JI*, 12, no.
    50 (27 February 1862), 2.
17 Robert Dick, *Autobiography and Poetical Compositions* (1863), p. 15.

violence alone could terminate the existing system. Such a strategy also had virtually no adherents among the British socialists. But the more Jacobin continental socialists, of whom there were many in exile in Britain after about 1850, were not at all averse to discoursing upon the advantages of violent revolution, the desirability of conspiratorial organisations, the utility of terror as a revolutionary tool, and the benefits of revolutionary dictatorship. These doctrines were anathema not only to the Owenites but equally to most social Chartists. Few non-Owenite social radicals shared a taste for the community of perfect righteousness as Owen had described it, or any adaptation of this to the nation-state. In part this was precisely because of the additional intolerance and coerciveness which it was felt such schemes would entail. And if British political socialism was sceptical of these aspects of communitarianism, it placed even less faith in revolution. Doubtless 1848 did occasion the wider dissemination of Blanquist and Babouvist conceptions of violent revolution and conspiratorial insurrection in England. These had been discussed in London emigré circles for at least a decade previously, but were otherwise little known elsewhere despite O'Brien's translation of Babeuf's *Conspiracy* and the cosmopolitan connections of Harney, and were not popular even after 1848.[18]

Virtually alone among the British social radicals in making some effort to legitimise a theory of revolutionary dictatorship, Harney in fact prophesied the failure of the French reformers in July 1848 unless 'a new revolution should give a second BABEUF the authority of another ROBESPIERRE'. Subsequently he also suggested, perhaps for the first time in the native literature of British radicalism, that 'certain circumstances might justify revolt even against a parliament elected by universal suffrage'. This, however, provoked an outraged response from his fellow social Chartist D. C. Collet, who echoed the more common radical view in retorting that:

The doctrine laid down by Mr. Harney . . . seems to me to strike at the root of all democracy. The notion that a higher sanction can be found for government than the consent of the governed is the excuse for all the tyrannies that have ever existed . . . A democrat is one who has faith in democracy – one who believes that a form of government which includes the whole people will best contribute to the welfare of the whole people. The man who raises the force of circumstances above the popular sovereignty may be an honest, intelligent, and justice-loving man, but a democrat he is not. If the fraternal democrats accept Mr. Harney's doctrine, they are not democrats, but something else.[19]

[18] O'Brien's edition of Buonarroti was the first important introduction of the terms 'bourgeoisie' and 'proletariat' in England. These terms are defined at pp. 69n and 139n.

[19] *NS*, no. 558 (1 July 1848), 3; *Reasoner*, 6 (1849), 186–7. See also Ernest Jones' comments on the inadequacy of universal suffrage in the context of the French working classes having elected a middle class government, in *PP*, 1, no. 3 (22 May 1852), 1.

Nor was Harney's prevaricating defence against the charge that he had
counselled private assassination calculated to deny his acceptance of
that doctrine.[20] Elsewhere, too, he printed a piece by Cabet on the need
for temporary revolutionary dictatorship, and castigated such men as
Blanc and Considerant for being too 'tender-hearted' in their view of
governments who ruled only by force. 'By force they must be overthrown', he insisted, 'and by terror brought to a sense of justice.' The
inevitability and value of class antagonism was also stressed by other
socialists. After 1848, Ernest Jones for one frequently drove home the
message that class friendship and fraternisation was impossible, and
that it was 'a NECESSITY that some classes should be enemies' because
of their opposed interests.[21]

The idea of socialism-as-revolution was therefore new to Britain.
Long identified with the complete absence of political enthusiasm,
socialism was now rapidly thrust into the opposite camp. A decade of
painstaking labour was virtually thrown away. No sooner had the
Owenites and others partially succeeded in shedding their association
with infidelity, and in having their aims understood in terms of a series
of at least initially moderate economic reforms, than an unwelcome
family of European relations decamped and threatened anew their
fragile grasp upon respectability. This completely altered the meaning
of the term 'socialism' in the eye of much of the uninformed public.
One of Blanc's associates noted in 1849 of England that:

> The word SOCIALISM is a nightmare to many – that word is no sooner uttered in
> their presence, than their affronted imagination creates the most terrible
> images; they see torrents of blood flowing in the civil strife; they tremble for
> their property, the sanctity of their homes, the peaceful worship of their
> religious belief . . . This is a terrible obstacle, we confess, for, with Englishmen,
> an idea, however wrong it may be, when generally adopted, scarcely yields to
> the most glaring refutation. Public opinion in this country is the most absolute
> tyrant that ever swayed over a society.[22]

Such associations did much to counterbalance the positive publicity
which the revolutions had lent to some forms of socialist experimentation. O'Brien himself felt compelled to deny he was a Babouvist. To
little avail, probably, Lloyd Jones and others repeatedly pointed out
that the British socialists had always deprecated violence and that
socialism itself had 'no more to do with political revolutionists, than
any other phase of economical science'.[23]

[20] *RWN*, ns no. 29 (2 March 1851), 14.
[21] *DR*, 2 (1850), 136–9; 1 (1849), 199; *NP*, 2 (1852), 708. See also the later comments
favouring military dictatorship in England in the *NT*, 2 (1855), 105.
[22] *LBMR*, no. 4 (November 1849), 130.
[23] *NS*, no. 732 (15 November 1851), 3; *Leader*, 1, no. 9 (25 May 1850), 205; 3, no. 129 (11
September 1852), 873.

Communitarianism and Marxism

Part of the transformation of the idea of socialism around 1848 involved forsaking communitarianism and acknowledging the possibility or necessity for statist, or at least centrally funded, socialism. Such a conclusion had been accepted by the majority of Owenite leaders after the collapse of Queenwood. In the same period it was also reached by the young Friedrich Engels, who within a few years rapidly passed through many of the stages of the relationship between socialism and politics the Owenites had evolved through over thirty years. Despite the clear impact of Owenite political economy upon his thinking at this time, the possibility of a British socialist element in Engels' early political thought has not been seriously considered, though the usual point of departure for analysing this is his British writings of the period.[24] Yet it is clear not only that such a dimension existed, but that it had considerable implications for the conception of politics which Marx and Engels would jointly work out between 1845 and 1850.

At the time of his departure from Germany Engels regarded himself as both a revolutionary and a communist. Though historians have acknowledged a variety of alterations in his views during these first years in England, they have not found evidence of changes in these two fundamental beliefs. Most have assumed, therefore, that Engels simply dismissed as archaic the anti-revolutionary stance of the Owenites.[25] Yet important shifts in these basic ideals can be discovered which are clearly derivative of Engels' interest in Owenism at this time.

Soon after reaching Britain in the autumn of 1842, Engels confirmed his desire and expectation that a revolution would shortly take place there. In his first article written from England in November 1842, he concluded that the Chartists would otherwise wait for many a year before achieving the Six Points. Their strategy was thus hopelessly ineffectual, for the middle class would never 'renounce its occupation of the House of Commons by agreeing to universal suffrage, since it would immediately be outvoted by the huge number of the unpropertied'. Several months later, describing the strikes and disturbances of 1842, Engels further asserted that 'a revolution by peaceful means is impossible . . . only a forcible abolition of the existing unnatural con-

---

[24] See further my 'The Political Ideas of the Young Engels, 1842–1845', *HPT*, 6 (1985), 455–78, from which this section is primarily drawn. See also Lewis Feuer, 'The Influence of the American Communist Colonies on Engels and Marx', *WPQ*, 19 (1966), 356–74.

[25] For example, Morton Cowden, 'Early Marxist Views on British Labor, 1837–1917', *WPQ*, 16 (1963), 39.

ditions, a radical overthrow of the nobility and industrial aristocracy, can improve the material position of the proletarians'.[26]

Soon involved in local Socialist activities, Engels in the coming months grew to appreciate much of the Owenite perspective on England's present and future. Naturally he was prone to dismiss radicalism pure and simple. In mid-1843 he heartily applauded the Owenites' propensity to 'laugh at the mere Republicans, because a republic would be just as hypocritical, just as theological, just as unjust in its laws, as a monarchy'. In keeping with his 'triarchy' conception of development adapted from Moses Hess, however, where revolution in England was first to be practical, in France political, and in Germany philosophical, Engels expected British radicalism to follow French rather than domestic socialist strategies, since these were more sophisticated politically. This was doubtless the sort of advice he offered Chartist friends such as James Leach. But Engels did not necessarily embrace a French socialist – and correspondingly revolutionary – political programme himself. Instead he now began to show signs of accepting an anti-revolutionary strategy. One of the objections against French communism, he noted, was that

They intend overthrowing the present government of their country by force, and have shown this by their continual policy of secret associations . . . Even the Icarians, though they declare in their publications that they abhor physical revolutions and secret societies, even they are associated in this manner, and would gladly seize upon any opportunity to seize a republic by force. This will be objected to, I dare say, and rightly, because, at any rate, secret associations are always contrary to common prudence, inasmuch as they make the parties liable to unnecessary legal persecutions. I am not inclined to defend such a line of policy, but it has to be explained, to be accounted for; and it is done fully so by the difference of the French and English national character and government.[27]

This is one of the first indications that Engels had begun to approve a 'British' – which is really an Owenite – perspective on revolution. Such a move was in part instigated by his conclusions about the problem of radical leadership. The predominant self-interest of the British middle classes meant that Chartism in 1842 had 'not yet been able to gain any hold among educated people in England and will remain unable to do so for some time yet'. Amongst the Chartists themselves, moreover, 'the party's educated spokesmen' were 'lost among the masses'. In Germany, however, the stronghold of socialism lay in the middle classes, though Engels added that 'We . . . hope to be in a short time supported by the working classes, who always, and everywhere, must

[26] Karl Marx and Frederick Engels, *Collected Works* (Lawrence and Wishart, 1975–), 2, pp. 368–9, 374.
[27] *Ibid.*, 3, pp. 389, 410.

form the strength and body of the Socialist party'. Nonetheless it is clear that Engels saw such middle class support as valuable, and believed that it was only natural for 'the better and more intelligent among the rich' to 'declare themselves in agreement with the workers and support them'. In the British case, this meant specifically that the intellectual achievements of Owenism and the political will and power of Chartism had to unite. Far more than most Owenites, however, Engels certainly envisioned the future as lying with the proletariat as a *class*, for despite 'all their roughness and for all their moral degra-dation', it was 'from them that England's salvation must come, they still comprise flexible material; they have no education, but no preju-dices either, they still have the strength for a great national deed – they still have a future'. Soon they would therefore be victorious, 'and then the mass of the English workers will have the choice only between starvation and socialism'. In the meantime, however, Engels conceded that while the average Chartist was 'more than a mere republican, his democracy is not simply political', socialism was unfortunately 'very little developed' within Chartism as a whole.[28]

The 'socialism' Engels urged the Chartists to embrace was essen-tially Owenite communitarianism. He was himself very well ac-quainted with its aims. In late 1844 he offered an extensive description of the Harmony community (which some of his friends had visited) to his German readers, assuring them that its inhabitants 'live better with less work, have more leisure for the development of their minds, and . . . are better, more moral people than their neighbours who have retained private property'. On a visit home, at Elberfeld, he com-mended to an audience of burghers Owen's plans for communal organisation, terming these 'the most practical and the most fully worked out'. Engels insisted in a characteristically Owenite fashion, moreover, that it was 'not intended to introduce common ownership overnight and against the will of the nation, but . . . it is only a matter of establishing the *aim* and the *ways* and *means* of advancing towards it'. Even more significantly, he now stressed that the establishment of socialist communities was the only means by which revolution could be *avoided* in England. This, again, was by the late 1830s a fairly common Owenite assertion. The concentration of capital and impover-ishment of the working classes, Engels allowed, would bring England to the brink of social revolution 'unless human nature has changed by that time'. But rather than welcoming revolution, he urged his audi-ence to concern themselves 'above all with the measures by which we can avoid a violent and bloody overthrow of the social conditions'. To this end, however, there was 'only *one* means, namely, the peaceful

[28] *Ibid.*, 2, pp. 368–9; 4, pp. 227–8; 3, pp. 445–6, 467; 4, p. 518.

introduction or at least preparation of communism . . . we must make it our business to contribute our share to humanising the condition of the modern helots'.[29]

This attitude towards revolution lasted for somewhat less than two years. Between the autumn of 1844 and spring of 1845, Engels surrendered this approach to violence in favour of physical-force Chartist views. Probably spurred on by the obviously impending catastrophe of British communitarian socialism, he now sought other and firmer guarantees of the forthcoming renovation of society. Much of what is novel in the political theory of *The Condition of the Working Class in England* in 1844 took the form of a heightened awareness of the inevitability as well as, more importantly, the necessity for class antagonism and hatred. Engels still hoped the Chartists would soon become socialists, but now criticised what he regarded as Owenism's unhistorical and overly negative approach to revolution. His views at this point are worth quoting at length, since they became the basis of so many subsequent judgements of Owenite politics generally:

English Socialism arose with Owen, a manufacturer, and proceeds therefore with great consideration towards the bourgeoisie and great injustice towards the proletariat in its methods, although it culminates in demanding the abolition of the class antagonism between bourgeoisie and proletariat. The Socialists are thoroughly tame and peaceable, accept our existing order, bad as it is, so far as to reject all other methods but that of winning public opinion. Yet they are so dogmatic that success by this method is for them, and for their principles as at present formulated, utterly hopeless. While bemoaning the demoralisation of the lower classes, they are blind to the element of progress in this dissolution of the old social order, and refuse to acknowledge that the corruption wrought by private interests and hypocrisy in the property-owning class is much greater. They acknowledge no historic development, and wish to place the nation in a state of Communism at once, overnight, not by the unavoidable march of its political development up to the point at which this transition becomes both possible and necessary. They understand, it is true, why the working-man is resentful against the bourgeois, but regard as unfruitful this class hatred, which is, after all, the only moral incentive by which the worker can be brought nearer the goal. They preach instead, a philanthropy and universal love far more unfruitful for the present state of England. They acknowledge only a psychological development, a development of man in the abstract, out of all relation to the Past, whereas the whole world rests upon that Past, the individual man included. Hence they are too abstract, too metaphysical, and accomplish little.

Here were outlined many of the elements which would later be elaborated in the distinction between 'utopian' and 'scientific' socialism. In particular, Engels insisted that in order to progress by seizing the historical moment Owenism now had to 'condescend to return for a moment to the Chartist standpoint', or what was the same, to 'recede for a moment to the French standpoint in order to proceed beyond it later'. An acceptance of the role of revolution in the process of transformation was thus crucial to the making of a 'scientific socialism' based upon newly reformulated economic and historical analyses.[30]

Even now, however, though Engels warned that 'the revolution must come; it is already too late to bring about a peaceful solution', he added that 'it can be made more gently than that prophesied in the foregoing pages'. To the degree that socialist ideas were disseminated, irrational violence and bloodshed might be avoided, and a far superior form of revolution develop. Here we can see that Engels clearly accepted some elements of the philosophy of necessity in its application to class conflict, and saw these as a means of avoiding the excesses of previous revolutions:

In proportion, as the proletariat absorbs socialistic and communist elements, will the revolution diminish in bloodshed, revenge, and savagery . . . Communism stands, in principle, above the breach between bourgeoisie and proletariat, recognises only its historic significance for the present, not its justification for the future . . . English socialism, i.e., Communism, rests directly upon the irresponsibility of the individual. Thus the more the English workers absorb communistic ideas, the more superfluous becomes their present bitterness, which, should it continue so violent as at present, could accomplish nothing . . . Meanwhile, I think that before the outbreak of open, declared war of the poor against the rich, there will be enough intelligent comprehension of the social question among the proletariat, to enable the communistic party to conquer the brutal element of the revolution and prevent a 'Ninth Thermidor' . . . And as Communism stands above the strife between bourgeoisie and proletariat, it will be easier for the better elements of the bourgeoisie (which are, however, deplorably few, and can look for recruits only among the rising generation) to unite with it than with purely proletarian Chartism.[31]

By 1845–46, therefore, and particularly as a result of his increasing association with Marx, Engels had renounced most of his adherence to the Owenite conception of revolution. It is no mere coincidence, either, that the articulation of the materialist conception of history, one of the two elements of the new 'scientific socialism' offered by Marx at this time (the other being the theory of surplus value, according to Engels' later account) coincided with the failure of Owenite communitarianism. Queenwood was for Engels the graveyard for virtually all earlier forms of socialism. Given its fate, the inevitability of historical revolution could be embraced with far greater confidence. All of the forms of incremental socialism with which Owenism had experimented for thirty years were now out of the question. Co-operative

---

[30] *Ibid.*, pp. 525–6.   [31] *Ibid.*, pp. 580–2.

enterprises had 'always perished because they were unable to compete with the "contending" private bakers, butchers, etc.', and because the working classes had remained too divided amongst themselves. 'Local Communism' was impossible because the economic achievements of the dominant productive system would always surpass or crush it competitively. Revolution, moreover, could be neither restricted to or contained by national boundaries. Communism was thus only possible as the act of dominant peoples 'all at once', and simultaneously throughout the industrialised countries.[32]

If the existing system could *only* be overthrown by violence, however, Engels hastened to add that there were a variety of positive aspects to this process. Revolution was now required 'not only because the *ruling* class cannot be overthrown in any other way, but also because the class *overthrowing* it can only in a revolution succeed in ridding itself of the muck of ages and become fitted to found society anew'. The strategy of revolution was not therefore only practical. Through it would be remade the human beings who would inhabit the future, more just and moral world, and also cleanse the prejudices of the past in the act of recreating the future. Thus was solved the recurrent Owenite difficulty of re-educating the present generation for life in the new social order. In a sense, however, Marx's and Engels' formulation of this problem was as optimistic as that of earlier socialists, since they expected a substantial alteration of character to take place equally quickly, if perhaps less totally. But if we consider that the failure of Queenwood was also laid at the doorstep of socialist 'character', Marx and Engels' comments clearly reflected their own judgement on this matter. The new character of the future would have to be at least partially remade during the revolutionary process itself, they concluded, to avoid importing too much irrationality from the old world into the new, and forever threatening a resurgence of the old order.[33]

Some traces remained, at least up to 1848, of Engels' earlier Owenite beliefs. In the 'Principles of Communism' (October 1847), the question as to whether private property might be abolished peaceably was answered by the statement that 'It is to be desired that this could happen, and Communists would certainly be the last to resist it'. However, this was directed primarily at the prospect of conspiracies rather than the general issue of the use of violence. In his correspondence, Engels argued as early as October 1846 that the aims of the communists could only be met through 'democratic revolution by force', and informed Marx that he had written to Harney (hardly an Owenite on this question) 'gently attacking the pacific nature of the

[32] *Ibid.*, 5, pp. 461–2, 371–2.   [33] *Ibid.*, p. 53.

Fraternal Democrats'. The *Manifesto of the Communist Party* (1848) stated bluntly, too, that 'The Communists disdain to conceal their views and aims. They openly declare that their ends can be attained only by the forcible overthrow of all existing social conditions.' This view was to be maintained until discussion of some forms of peaceful transition was resurrected thirty years later.[34]

But the new theory of revolutionary communism did not entail a complete break from Engels' earlier communitarian sympathies. The 'Principles of Communism' pandered to Fourierite and Owenite tastes alike by including provisions for 'the erection of large palaces on national estates as common dwellings for communities of citizens engaged in industry as well as agriculture, and combining the advantages of both urban and rural life without the one-sidedness and disadvantages of either'. In the *Manifesto*, however, such plans were reduced to the statement that communism would include the 'combination of agriculture with manufacturing industries; gradual abolition of the distinction between town and country, [and] a more equable distribution of the population over the country'.[35] Despite the continuing importance to Marx and Engels of the need to supersede the existing division of labour, such proposals were not thereafter central to the communist or social democratic movement in most European countries during the remainder of the nineteenth century. They do indicate, however, remnants of the course followed by the young Engels as he moved from revolutionary to Owenite to social Chartist to Marxist positions, a process of development whose Owenite stage obviously had considerable consequences for his political ideas at the time. If Engels' later notion of the abolition of the state in communist society entailed the virtual disappearance of coercion, too, and not merely a reduction in the overall size of the state, communitarian Owenism clearly furnished him with some early inspiration for such a belief. But Engels probably felt that it was unlikely that coercion could be so far exterminated if the locus of socialism was the nation-state rather than the community. This would have been, as we have seen, to commit an error exactly analogous to that of republicans who sought to replicate the ancient virtues in a commercial representative democracy. Instead he likely believed that police functions would be reorganised, democratised, and released from their previous class basis, rather than abolished entirely. In this sense Engels probably did not identify 'the state' *per se* with class rule to the extent that is often presumed, but also conceived that other, similar but more just forms of social organisation could supplant the existing state without requiring the

[34] *Ibid.*, 6, p. 349; 38, pp. 82, 88; 6, p. 519.   [35] *Ibid.*, pp. 351–2, 505.

'abolition' of government or politics generally. This more neutral conception of government may also have been inspired in part by Owenism, though this cannot be asserted with certainty.[36]

Republicanism revived

The transformation of socialism after 1848 and its attempted alliance with Chartism also helped to provoke the redefinition of new forms of British republicanism. In the following decade there correspondingly emerged a new style of anti-communist radicalism which was nonetheless also far more indebted to socialism than radicalism before 1848 had usually been. Renewing its challenge to socialism on a wide variety of issues, republicanism by the 1850s had recaptured considerable support from the working class political reform movement. These gains would not be threatened seriously again by socialist successes for some thirty years.

Much of the early inspiration for this revival emanated from the exiled Italian revolutionary Guiseppe Mazzini, who pursued continental rivalries by attacking Blanc and others of the European socialists, and whose fervent English disciples engaged in a lively propaganda campaign against Italian as well as European despotism generally in the late 1840s.[37] This proved to be an extraordinarily popular cause which helped to unify Whig and working class radicals alike. Mazzini's ideas also exerted a powerful sway. Deeply inspired by his religious and romantic approach to revolution, the Chartist engraver and journalist W. J. Linton almost single-handedly (Holyoake was also helpful) set about constructing a secure individualist philosophical foundation for radical political thought. But this was now also linked to a variety of collectivist enterprises and a strong emphasis upon the social duties of the nation towards the poor and unfortunate.[38] Also supportive of such efforts were the views of the immensely popular Hungarian revolutionary Lajos Kossuth. Many hundreds of thousands – some said millions – poured out to see the republican hero on his arrival and during his tour of Britain in 1849. Fêted by

[36] Cf. Richard Hunt, *The Political Ideas of Marx and Engels*, vol. 2, pp. 212–66.

[37] On Mazzini's influence in Britain see Harry Rudman, *Italian Nationalism and English Letters* (New York, Columbia University Press, 1940). On his hostility to Blanc and others, see the *Leader*, 3, no. 107 (10 April 1852), 340–1. The following section is expanded considerably in my 'Mazzini, Kossuth, and British Radicalism, 1848–54', *JBS*, 28 (1989) 225–61.

[38] On Linton's individualism see for example *CP*, no. 2 (27 May 1848), 9; *Republican* (1848), 185–8; *ER*, 1 (1851), 10–34. On his relations with Mazzini, see W. J. Linton, *European Republicanism* (1893), and on Holyoake's view, *Bygones Worth Remembering* (1905), 1, pp. 202–17. See also generally N. J. Gossman, 'Republicanism in Nineteenth Century England', *IRSH*, 7 (1962), 47–60.

all parties, he doubtless assisted in swaying public opinion further against European despotism. As with Mazzini, his repudiation of socialism also helped to swing British reformers back towards mainstream radicalism.[39]

These efforts illuminate the evolution of mid-Victorian socialism in a variety of ways. Certainly it is revealing that the sources of radical reaction to socialism after 1848 were largely foreign in inspiration, though Linton had some recourse to the romantic heroism of the seventeenth-century commonwealthmen, carrying articles on Milton, Cromwell, Sidney and others in his journal. The need for continental assistance, however, also clearly reflected the ideological weakness of Chartism in face of the O'Connorite débâcle as well as the considerable attachment to socialism of many radicals after 1848. To some extent mainstream Chartism had simply become less appealing as a cause, too. Owenite socialism could evoke considerable moral passion in its adherents, while land nationalisation satisfied those who demanded a thorough change in social relations. By comparison, after 1848 parliamentary petitions and 'simple' political reform were unenthralling. British republicanism had become too empirical to inspire moral fervour, which thus had to be imported from other sources. Neither Chartism nor 'roast beef' really satisfied some of the Chartists after 1850, as the republican W. E. Adams later recalled: 'We had found a programme, but we wanted a religion. It came to us from Italy . . . The Republic, as [we] understood it, was not so much a form of government as a system of morals, a law of life, a creed, a faith, a new and benign gospel.'[40]

This revival sought to remoralise politics without disregarding institutional requirements or reducing politics to ethics. Such goals echoed a variety of themes which Owenism had helped to popularise. To have rights, the Mazzinians thus typically proclaimed, the people should be conscious of duties, and should calibrate their external political goals by their internal moral progress. This was an obvious criticism of the excesses of the Chartist years, which had marred the image of republicanism in the eyes of the middle and upper classes, and which indicated 'that the people have not yet this conscience of Duty: their outcry for the Right is not the conception of Right, but a reaction

---

[39] On Kossuth's impact in Britain generally see Dénes Jánossy, 'Great Britain and Kossuth', *AEC*, 3 (1937), 53–190. Kossuth and Mazzini's programme is given in Kossuth *et al.*, *Manifesto of the Republican Party* (1855). On his opposition to socialism see the *Leader*, 2, no. 87 (22 November 1851), 1112.

[40] *ER* 3 (1854), 1, 106–12, 182–7, 273–81, 288–97; W. E. Adams, *Memoirs of a Social Atom*, 1, pp. 265–6. Adams and others formed a society with 'strict rules' and a catechism which all candidates were required to master.

against Wrong; a cry forced out by long suffering experience of injury, rather than springing from the conscience – the perception – of Duty, the knowledge of the purpose and end of rights'.[41] Clearly repudiated by the Mazzinians were both the newly anti-sectarian, book-keeping forms of socialism and communism and the older, secular and anti-metaphysical Owenite dogmas. But they equally sought to avoid the pitfalls of secular, *laissez-faire* liberalism, and instead erected a new republican religion based upon Mazzini's nationalist romanticism (and doubtless also contributed to the reformulation of British nationalism in this period). Both socialism and liberalism were thus understood as sharing certain essential characteristics. How, therefore, could communism be the opposite of old world individualism, as it claimed to be, observed Linton on the Icarians, when it was 'based on the same false principle of egotism, self-interest, happiness', not principle but policy, not morality but merely Benthamism run amuck:

It is the old error, at the bottom of all government policies, trade-competitions, and political economies – the old atheistical doctrine of CIRCUMSTANCES – the belief in mere material rather than in man. Man (so considered) is no more lord of the creation, lord of his own will, endowed with the spirit of LIFE (which is GOD), moved by that spirit to development, to growth, treading down circumstances under his feet. Man in Icarie is but the creature of circumstances, his very morality at the mercy of any flaw in M. Cabet's arrangements.[42]

This could be equally taken as a criticism of the inadequacies of Owenism, of course. But even those who sought to reconstruct republicanism in the early 1850s found something to learn from socialism. In this sense it was clearly conceded that socialism had proven the limitations of earlier forms of radicalism. Linton for example agreed with the socialists and social Chartists that the land should be common property, with the state collecting rent though not regulating the amount or location of the land rented, and providing credit and education.[43] What government specifically should not do, however – and here we must finally turn to socialist conceptions of the interventionist state at mid-century – was to plan and organise production. For to do so, Linton believed, would eradicate its republican and democratic character:

Socialism is not always republican. To take an instance. The socialism which would make the State (and let it be the government of even a majority, and however great that majority) the director and dictator of labour, with only this change from our present system – that the workman would be under, instead of the tyranny of single or combined capitalists, the stronger tyranny of a corporate majority: such socialism, however well it might feed the workman, would not be republican, for it would violate individual *liberty* by passing

---

[41] *CP*, 1 (20 May 1848), 1.   [42] *Republican* (1848), 43–5.   [43] *ER*, 1 (1851), 18–23.

beyond the mere protection and provision of elements to an interference with personal action.[44]

This was a criticism not only of much European socialism and communism, but also, invoking a long tradition of British hostility to European despotism, of a trend towards centralisation which in Linton's eyes was shared by each form of polity. The problem was thus to avoid both grand schemes of complete social management as well as merely local reforms which extended no promise of long-term benefit. Unpolitical co-operation was thus a delusion but not a threat to democracy, while communism was both:

I believe that as 'great social experiments' these [co-operative] associations mislead men. This unpolitical socialism is like rebuilding a house from the top, patching it with occasional bricks, instead of laying new foundations. Some stormy day, your amended house, old and new together, will come down about your ears. And at best, supposing the piecemeal job to be practicable, you work at all manner of disadvantages, under present 'institutions'. For the rest, in what form of partnership men may *choose* to better their private estate is not a political question, nor one for our consideration here. The political question is when, going beyond co-operation to communism, men assail the right of Family and Property. Co-operation may, or may not, be Republican: Communism is not.[45]

Through Joseph Cowen and similar mid and later Victorian republicans, Linton and others thus sought to define and popularise a new political position between *laissez-faire* radicalism, itself newly incarnated in Cobdenism, and atheistical, overly statist socialism, and drawing upon the great popularity of the exiled continental republicans (and later of Garibaldi as well). In terms of its opposition to continental socialism, one of the most important elements of the new republican critique was its decisive rejection of anything like centralised economic regulation. This evoked considerable radical as well as socialist sympathy in Britain, where, as we have seen, local control had considerable support across the political spectrum. Let us finally examine more closely, then, the treatment of this issue in light of the diffusion of centralist continental proposals at the end of the 1840s.

Intervention and centralisation

A tradition of radical opposition to greater governmental centralisation doubtless helped to hamper the mid nineteenth-century acceptance of both British and European schemes for national economic management. In the first instance, the far greater centralisation of

---

[44] *Ibid.*, 2 (1852–3), 69–70. [45] *Ibid.*, 1 (1851), 179.

most European nations was usually identified with monarchical abso-
lutism. As the British government began to assume new powers in the
early decades of the century, and particularly when these seemingly
implied the imposition of greater 'discipline' upon the working classes,
radicals often warned that the customary liberties which underlay their
own constitutional monarchy were threatened thereby. Particularly in
opposition to the new Poor Law, an 'odious system of Centralization
... imported from the Continent', and the establishment of new police
forces in the 1830s and 1840s, Chartists and Tory radicals alike had
often criticised centralisation *per se*. The *Chartist* commented typically
in 1839 that:

Local governments have been looked upon, from the time of the Romans down
to our day, as the strongholds of liberty, and such they have always proved
themselves. We esteem it to be a positive proof against the practical liberty of a
people, that they are unable to appoint a constable, light an extra lamp, or
mend the paving of a street, except through the intervention of the State. This
is of the very essence of an absolute monarchy; it is carrying the power of the
State into minutiae with which the State has no business to interfere – it is
weaving a net about us which cramps our every movement, and restricts us in
all healthful exercise of our individual will. There is little doubt that these
things would be better done by the State than they are ordinarily done by local
boards; but the difference by no means compensates for the loss of control over
our own immediate affairs. There is little doubt that we should all enjoy better
health if the State obliged us to go to bed every night at 10 o'clock.

Centralisation was also linked to the need to maintain the ancient
constitution and the 'localizing and even individualizing system of our
Saxon ancestors' endorsed by the *English Chartist Circular*, as well as to
the increasing distance between rich and poor. Feargus O'Connor thus
warned in 1845 that 'a government of *centralization* is but the representation of the communism of the wealthy, elected by capitalists,
whether of land or money, for the mere purpose of administering the
labour-wealth of the country to the wants, the whims, and the necessities of the privileged'. It was consequently frequently assumed that the
passage of the Charter would mean that, instead of more centralised
control, 'a full and perfect system of local self-government' would
'speedily follow'.[46]

Exceptions to this opposition nonetheless became more frequent
during the middle and later 1840s. O'Connor, for example, praised the
Belgian railway system, which belonged to the public and was centrally managed by the state.[47] In one of the first attempts to clarify and
vindicate the more useful forms of centralisation, Samuel Kydd, one of

---

[46] *Constitutionalist*, no. 15 (6 October 1839), 2; *ECC*, no. 8 (1841), 36; *Chartist*, no. 12 (21
April 1839), 3; *Charter*, no. 38 (13 October 1838), 593.
[47] *NS*, no. 470 (24 October 1846), 5.

the most socialistic of the later, minor Chartist leaders, argued in 1846 against the renowned Tory radical critic of centralisation, Richard Oastler, that it was only the misdirection and not the principle itself which was wrong, citing the example of a group of northern coal miners who had been 'centralised' and had thereby been able to hire an attorney to defend their rights.[48] This rationale was elsewhere extended to a variety of other phenomena. Respecting sanatory reforms, Harney for example contended in late 1847, 'The principle of local self-government is ... by no means incompatible with an efficient central supervision. On the contrary the one is indispensable, in operations of such magnitude, to the efficiency of the other'. Ernest Jones, too, later designed a new Chartist organisation which included considerable centralisation, which he defended with the argument that 'Conventions and elections are the very source of bickering, disunion, and ruin, and our plan avoids them at least as much as possible'. But he too later ceded considerable ground to the new Anti-Centralization Union, railing against the growth of bureaucracy and 'red tapeism', and strongly applauding the Union's endorsement of the principle of the political division of labour against the 'centralising' health regulations proposed by the Social Science Association.[49]

The considerable revival of anti-centralisation sentiments among radicals during the mid-1850s and later was led by the eldest son of the prominent Birmingham Owenite William Hawkes Smith, Joshua Toulmin Smith. His *Local Self-Government and Centralization* (1851) powerfully asserted the superiority of local government over centralised rule in terms of both administrative efficiency and the creation of public virtue and political liberty. Shortly thereafter was formed the Anti-Centralization Union, whose aim was 'the annihilation of the entire system of government by bureaucracy, and the restoration of the constitutional system of *individual responsibility* in every department of state, and of *municipal action* in all home affairs'. The new organisation engaged in a prolonged agitation, much of which was assisted by ex-Chartists, against the emergent bureaucracies of the metropolis and what was seen as the emulation of a continental style of national government. One of the most important organisers of the movement was the Sheffield Chartist and Owenite Isaac Ironside, whose 'ward-

---

[48] *Ibid.*, no. 470 (24 October 1846), 5. Oastler's comments, which provoked Kydd's immediate response, are in no. 466 (17 October 1846), 6. O'Connor also said as early as 1838 that 'Socialism was a simple contrivance by an incorporation of communities to do that for certain members of the community which the government should do for all without any exception' (British Library Add. MS. 27820, fol. 280), which certainly could have lent itself to a statist interpretation.

[49] *NS*, no. 518 (25 September 1847), 4; *PP*, 4, no. 205 (5 April 1856), 1; 5, no. 278 (29 August 1857), 4; no. 290 (21 November 1857), 5.

mote' local government scheme aimed to recapture power for local activists. This plan, which John Salt has argued in fact verged upon anarchism, was certainly not incompatible with the Owenite component in Ironside's ideas, though it clearly conflicted with the centralising strand in Owenism which had been strengthened after 1845. The Union, which had a number of local branches, was also identified with the European republicanism of Mazzini and others, and, taking its cue from Toulmin Smith's acclamation of co-operation but rejection of 'centralizing' communism, doubtless helped to prevent schemes for the 'organisation of labour' from increasing in popularity. Its efforts also probably helped to relocate radical political debate generally upon a more traditional terrain, where fear of monarchical and state usurpation – rather than the economic relations of classes within civil society – remained the central issue. Thus the *Leader* reflected in mid-1854, for example, that the key problem of political freedom would be solved once both the military and government were 'localized'. So, too, radical papers began to warn that the notion of a 'paternal' government implied widespread intervention because the people had 'abnegated their pretensions to self-government'. Such discussions had been far less prevalent ten years earlier, before the issue of European despotism again assumed a prominent position on the radical agenda.[50]

To the extent that the notion of a centralised, more regulatory state found acceptance amongst both radicals and socialists, it was the events and ideas of 1848 which promoted this trend. But even after 1848 some socialists continued to claim that their plans involved little more governmental interference than existed at present, namely only the parliamentary regulation of communities.[51] Nonetheless the principle of state intervention had also been at least a tacit part (and sometimes much more) of Owenite socialism from its origins. This willingness to counsel intervention, rather than its communitarian concerns, was by mid-century widely recognised as one of the most important elements in the legacy of Owenism to Victorian social and

---

[50] Joshua Toulmin Smith, *Local Self-Government and Centralization* (1851), pp. 11–12, 348–58; *SFP*, 5, no. 214 (3 February 1855), 6; *Leader*, 5, no. 228 (5 August 1854), 732; no. 230 (19 August 1854), 781. Smith was also the author of *The Parish: Its Obligations and Powers: Its Offices and Their Duties* (1854). On him see W. H. Greenleaf, 'Toulmin Smith and the British Political Tradition', *PA*, 53 (1975), 25–44. On Ironside's schemes see especially John Salt, 'Experiments in Anarchism, 1850–1854', *THAS*, 10 (1971), 37–53. The centralisation debate generally is sketched in David Roberts, *Victorian Origins of the British Welfare State* (New Haven, Yale University Press, 1960), pp. 67–104. Also useful are William Lubenow, *The Politics of Government Growth* (Newton Abbot, David and Charles, 1971), and Philip Corrigan and Derek Sayer's penetrating *The Great Arch* (Oxford, Basil Blackwell, 1982), pp. 114–65.

[51] *Leader*, 1, no. 20 (10 August 1850), 466.

political thinking. Owen had originally argued that the state should provide employment only in the event of 'cases of sudden great depression' in the demand for labour. The first stage of his plan of 1817, however, was to pass 'an Act of Parliament to nationalize the poor'.[52] He had often thereafter fulminated against 'politics', but equally as often insisted that 'the real science of government is to form arrangements to produce the greatest amount of improvement in the state, and to secure the highest degree of happiness for the whole population'. Despite the implications of these sentiments, the subsequent thirty years had seen few elaborate inquiries into centralised planning in Owenism. The schemes of Gray and Bray, in particular, did not find widespread popular support. Nonetheless for some socialists every deepening crisis of poverty and unemployment further strengthened the legitimacy of the principle of intervention. As we have seen, the period of trades' union agitation during the mid-1830s, in which Owenite planning ideals and union notions of organisation overlapped, was extremely important in this regard. 'Nothing can be more just, more in consonance with the first principles of society, than that every member of society, able and willing to work, should be provided with employment by the State', the radical *Weekly True Sun* had argued in 1833, in one of the clearest justifications of this type in this period:

When a labourer is in full employment, the State never fails to appropriate a full portion of his earnings: when the means of employment fail him, the labourer has, if justice is to regulate our social economy, an undoubted right to demand from the State employment or means of support. It is but just that the State should provide for the welfare of every man, who when he has the power is liable to be called upon to contribute to the necessities of the State. The whole scheme of society, in its best aspect, is but a plan for the insurance by each other of the various members, and all those who may be called on to contribute when they have the means, to the expense of insurance, are undoubtedly entitled to have the benefit of that insurance, when these means have failed them.[53]

Such sentiments were also echoed directly within the unions at this time. 'Of all great and important public undertakings, government, and government only, as trustee for the nation, ought to be the sole proprietors, that taxation might be superseded by the legitimate profits that ought to attend the employment of national as well as individual wealth' was the view of the *Official Gazette of the Trades' Unions* in 1834. From this perspective, it was the experience of the GNCTU which also brought Owenism closest to the ideal of national agricultural, commercial and industrial management, and furthest away from communi-

---

[52] Owen, *NVS*, pp. 86, 184.   [53] *WTS*, no. 3 (24 February 1833), 2.

tarianism. This moment was most clearly captured in John Francis Bray's *Labour's Wrongs and Labour's Remedy*.[54]

Nonetheless it was a much more piecemeal approach to intervention which gradually gained a degree of public acceptance during the 1830s and 1840s. For some socialists every apparent failure of liberal political economy contributed to its growth. Attacks on the weakness of the wages fund theory were clearly central to the argument favouring greater regulation, as J. S. Mill would later also concede. In late 1838, for example, a Glasgow trades' unionist wrote that while the economists treated labour as a commodity subject to the same natural laws as other commodities, it had been proven that trades' unions were responsible for higher wages.[55] But the case for greater intervention was also applied to many other issues. Of these poor relief and factory reform were the most important, while Owen and his followers also often called for the establishment of a national bank as well as a national system of education.[56] By the collapse of Queenwood, moreover, the expansion of government in other areas gave greater credence to earlier claims. The expropriation of land for railways in the 1840s, for example, provided perhaps the most important precedent for violating private property in the public interest, and was frequently cited by those seeking greater governmental economic activity in the middle years of the century. For many Owenites, however, the natural development of commercial society itself demanded a greater role for the state. The Leeds socialist James Hole, for example, considered that 'the functions of the state have increased with the wants of society, and the wants of society increase with the means of gratifying them'. It was in this sense, then, that what I have elsewhere termed 'economic socialism' – the willingness to legitimise the increasing needs created by a more extensive market society and to expand the scope and volume of production accordingly – corresponded with political socialism, the recognition that centralised, if not parliamentary, institutions would inevitably play an important role in production and distribution rather than the primary role being assigned to communities.[57]

By the early 1850s, socialism more than any other contemporary school of thought was strongly identified with that new form of 'paternal' government or positive state activity on behalf of the common good and interests of the majority which we would today anachronisti-

---

[54] *OGTU*, no. 3 (21 June 1834), 18.   [55] *ML*, no. 3 (August 1838), 37–8.

[56] For example, *NMW*, 3, no. 129 (15 April 1837) 197–8; *PMG*, 4, no. 212 (27 June 1835), 579.

[57] *NS*, no. 651 (13 April 1850), 1; no. 655 (11 May 1850), 1; James Hole, *Social Science and the Organization of Labour* (Leeds, 1851), p. 127. Hole also argued for 'a just union of the local and central principles' which steered between *laissez-faire* and Carlyle's notion of benevolent despotism (p. 133).

cally call the 'welfare state'. Any form of public improvement – common baths, hospitals, free libraries, ragged schools – could be pointed to as evidence that society was 'tending towards Socialism'. All forms of regulation and protection proved that the desire for intervention was widespread, even if, as Thornton Hunt acknowledged, it was usually accompanied by 'a perfect unconsciousness of the doctrine or of the true principle upon which the agitators proceed'. For a few years, at least, such ideas were more widely and favourably discussed than they had been either earlier or the next several decades. Caught up in the spirit of reform, even non-socialist Chartists like Joseph Barker concluded that the duty of government was also to guarantee employment.[58] But it was Owenism, reinforced by the continental emphasis on the 'organisation of labour', which expressed this most clearly at the level of refined theory. The individual principle had merely brought 'anarchy, ignorance, inequality and strife'. It might indeed be true that 'industry may develop itself, riches may increase, and capital accumulate prodigiously' under the existing system. But nonetheless the distribution of the results was never 'in favour of the working bees'. What intervention there was seemed aimed only at perpetuating existing inequalities. Discussing 'the powers of government in relation to communism', one socialist insisted that

The present system is professedly based on non-interference. Yet they do interfere. But with a discrimination worthy of their cause, they abstain from all intervention save that which oppresses the poor and enriches the capitalist. The principle of non-intervention is so absurd, so mischievous, so injurious in its practice, that they seek some means to relieve themselves, and to make the old, rotten machinery of their system work smoother.[59]

The demand for intervention was always, thus, a plea for social justice as well as a call for an end to industrial anarchy. 'The propaganda of association asks for a social government' was how Holyoake summarised this principle in 1849, adding that 'By a Social Government it means a government which shall guarantee the means of subsistence to all *industrious* citizens. Idleness may die – capacity may attain to opulence – but industry should have the means of living, otherwise the state is not the Parent of the People whom it abandons to destitution, and order is menaced and civilisation is contradicted'.

---

[58] *Operative*, no. 50 (13 December 1851), 185–6; *Leader*, 1, no. 30 (19 October 1850), 710; *People*, 3 (1850–51), 36. For general background on this development see D. Roberts, *Paternalism*, pp. 30–61, D. Roberts, *Victorian Origins of the Welfare State*, A. J. Taylor, *Laissez-faire and State Intervention in Nineteenth Century Britain* (Macmillan, 1972), E. Barry, *Nationalisation in British Politics* (Cape, 1965).

[59] *PPe*, no. 13 (27 January 1849), 195–6; *SA*, 1, no. 8 (16 September 1848), 113; 2, no. 26 (20 January 1849), 68.

Against Proudhon, too, one socialist insisted that 'the Government that is to come must be an *Organisation of Industry*, precisely because the social state which we are approaching must be pre-eminently industrial'. Another social radical dismissed the Manchester school and contended that the true function of government was to aid in 'the maintenance and enforcement of justice between man and man – for the protection of the weak and ignorant . . . from the strong, the selfish, the cunning, and the unscrupulous; for the protection of the virtue, the intelligence, the civilization of the human race'. Such comments clearly indicate the emergence of that ideal of positive liberty which would be defended in the more sceptical but nonetheless clearly co-operative socialism of Mill, and more broadly adopted in a variety of forms of radicalism, neo-liberalism and socialism after 1880. That such an ideal had already been established in these quarters, however, was amply demonstrated in an Owenite-inspired *Labour League* editorial of the autumn of 1848, which explained that

Liberty consists not in the *right* but in the *power* given to each individual in the community to develop his faculties. There can therefore be no true or general freedom enjoyed by any individual until society is so constituted as to secure to every one of its members a sound education, without which the human mind cannot be developed; and secondly, the means of labouring profitably for themselves and the community at large, without which human energy is either stifled or perverted into mischief and crime. The State must intervene on higher grounds than are now dreamt of by popular politicians and statesmen . . . This would produce true liberty for all; without such measures all others are but as sounding brass and tinkling symbols.[60]

This interpretation of the meaning of liberty was still honoured in some of the leading radical papers of the 1850s, too. Reviewing Herbert Spencer's individualist tract, *Social Statics*, the popular *Leader* for example acknowledged that if 'his definition of the true function of Government – viz, that it is merely for the protection of the person and property', was accepted, then 'all his arguments respecting state interference are unanswerable'. But it concluded that 'if you think, as we think, the function of Government is larger, and that it is needed to *govern* society as well as to protect it, then you may reasonably dissent'. Government, Gammage also argued in 1853, ought not thus to be understood as 'a mere taxing machine', but instead 'existed for the sole purpose of promoting the welfare of the people'. After this period, however, such sentiments became increasingly rare, doubtless in large measure owing to the relative prosperity of the period.[61]

[60] *Reasoner*, 6 (1849), 227–8; *Leader*, 2, no. 82 (18 October 1851), 997; *RWN*, no. 240 (18 March 1855), 7; *LL*, 1, no. 7 (16 September 1848), 49.
[61] *Leader*, 2, no. 51 (15 March 1851), 249; *PP*, 2, no. 52 (30 April 1853), 5.

Radical discussions about the potential scope of governmental economic and social activity were often remarkably vague, no doubt in part to avoid further strife among the reformers, but also because exploring a middle ground of mixed private and public, state and local institutions was far more complicated than merely defending a single principle. Far too few, certainly, heeded Bronterre O'Brien's advice that it was necessary to steer clear of the 'fatal delusion' that there was no intermediate course between competition and full community of property, between state compulsion and liberal anarchy. In 1848 and after it was the widely discussed state-workshop plans of Louis Blanc which first provoked serious disagreement among social radicals about the justifiable limits of such intervention, for here the government was to employ virtually all labour. The liberal political economists had of course immediately condemned such ideas, and the Christian Socialists soon followed in their wake.[62] But the socialistic *Herald of Co-operation*, too, had its own grounds for dissenting with such proposals:

we object to government being made the supreme regulators of production, at least in the sense of Louis Blanc, and for the simple reason that the central government is totally incompetent to the task. Government may grant power to local bodies to carry out 'the details, to regulate the hierarchy of each man's functions', and so on; but government itself cannot, without a machinery far too costly, too cumbersome for successful working, and dangerous to liberty from the difficulty of controlling it, undertake to be the supreme regulator of production.[63]

In some respects it is surprising that more Chartists and socialists did not voice such views. For a belief in the great importance of local government was deeply rooted among the radicals and socialists alike, and is in some respects the characteristic British contribution to European radicalism generally in this period. By the 1850s most social radicals had tried to work out a reasonable compromise on this issue. Thus the *Leader*, in reviewing Toulmin Smith's principles, agreed that while 'in theory Centralization is the culminating point of national perfection', local self-government could prove very valuable if it were genuinely democratic and not 'the vicious, peddling, jobbing, parochial forms which it assumes in England'.[64] Some were certainly willing to push their federalist or anti-centralist views to great extremes. In the most important test case for this principle, not only

---

[62] *PPe*, no. 13 (27 January 1849), 195–6. For a radical liberal opinion, see for example, *VP*, no. 1 (22 April 1848), 9–11. This journal was associated with Charles Knight, an important populariser of classical political economy. For the Christian Socialist view, see *JA*, no. 2 (10 January 1851), 14.

[63] *HC*, no. 18 (June 1848), 145–6.

[64] *Leader*, 2, no. 56 (19 April 1851), 370–1.

Proudhon but also J. F. Bray, among others, supported the Confederacy during the American civil war despite their hatred of slavery.[65] And we should recall that William Thompson had opposed the Saint-Simonian interpretation of the sphere of governmental action many years earlier, pointing out that while the French wanted to put all under the direction of government, the British preferred communities aided by those improved laws which a reformed parliament would pass. This contention, and the republican preference for federated, local control – but without the abolition of central institutions which underlay it – was probably far more widely shared than has been hitherto evident. Certainly it represents an important contribution to a tradition of socialist political thought which has too often and too uncritically stressed the benefits of centralisation without considering the alternatives.[66]

Conclusion: the state and the origins of social radicalism

No long-term detailed, technical debate about the intricacies of administration, the relation between political and economic elements, or of local and central powers emerged from the experience of early British socialism. Owenism did make a substantial contribution to the debate on the nature and scope of government in early nineteenth-century Britain. But it is virtually impossible to point to a single 'classic' text which might be said to be representative of its approach to this question, or a specific programme which presented a characteristically Owenite solution to the problem or outlined the boundaries of the discourse to be used in discussing it. There were a variety of reasons for this. Clearly the possession of political power remained too remote. Unlike the French, British socialists were never actually called upon to institute a major experiment for the employment of labour, and would of course have had a much smaller bureaucracy to call upon had they done so. But Owenism also never recovered sufficiently from its older anti-political as well as communitarian biases to aid in the construction of a form of socialism appropriate to the new climate and conditions of 1848. Nor did the socialists wish to antagonise the radicals further by arousing their prejudices against centralisation. 'Government' was also too often still entrapped in the same amorphously moral concept of parental care with which Owen had begun half a century earlier at New Lanark. The language of 1849 had not evolved far beyond that of 1820 in the description of a new socialist journal which proposed that

---

65 See Royden Harrison, 'British Labour and the Confederacy', *IRSH*, 2 (1957), 78–105.
66 *MRBH*, no. 8 (11 June 1831).

'The soil, capital, intelligence, and labour of a nation ought to be combined and directed as to promote the interests and well-being of all the children of the State'. Such sentiments were well intentioned. But they often lacked any sense of the complexities of administration, of the development of different regions, industries and trades, or of conflicts between the component parts of the state. In large part this was because Owenism had concentrated upon communitarianism so much during the 1840s. Despite the plans of John Gray and John Francis Bray, political planning at the level of the nation-state, which was the point of departure for most forms of socialism after 1848, had not been seriously considered by most socialists during the previous decade. Owenism had thus thought in terms of communities too long, and also knew too well, perhaps, that a nation could never fulfil the stringent moral requirements of community life. Perhaps it also simply suspected, what Richard Carlile once hinted the socialists had not yet realised, that it was 'one thing to manage a sect, another to rule a nation'.[67]

Nonetheless some tentative socialist plans embracing the nation were occasionally discussed in the late 1840s. *Reynolds' Political Instructor* published a short article describing 'the general establishment of co-operative associations; the state being composed of congeries of such associations, with a central government'.[68] This vague ideal was probably similar to that entertained by most Owenites at this time. Communities and local co-operative associations would be retained, and with them a substantial measure of self-government and administration. This would not, therefore, require much expansion of the powers or size of central government. The future state in this sense was probably envisioned by most socialists in much the same terms as those described in 1840 by G. A. Fleming, who agreed with Bronterre O'Brien that it was necessary to

'Make your *deliberative* and *elective* power as large as possible; make your *administrative* and *executive* power as small as possible: I care not how few hands you entrust these functions to, so that they be popularly elected and subject to revision and removal by the body which appoints them'. This expresses pretty accurately our theory of government, and is *essentially* a democracy, in which the people govern as a whole through the medium of the wisest officers they can select.[69]

One important consequence of this bias in favour of decentralised administration was that by the 1880s, and after the revival of British socialism and the maturation of continental social democracy, Owenism gained a reputation for contrasting strongly to the more statist

[67] *SA*, 2, no. 26 (20 January 1849), 72; *CPR*,; no. 3 (2 November 1839), 35.
[68] *RPI*, no. 19 (16 March 1850), 151.   [69] *NMW*, 7, no. 80 (2 May 1840), 1282.

varieties of late nineteenth-century socialism. This contrast rested partly on the ostensibly voluntary character of communitarianism by comparison with the compulsory collectivism of the continental socialists. Nonetheless Bronterre O'Brien rightly insisted that Owen implied that all would have to enter co-operative communities, since he included no provision for living elsewhere. But subsequent attempts to categorise Owenism in relation to other forms of socialism have also been misleading. One important account argues, for instance, that O'Brien 'believed in state intervention in the processes of production and distribution, so as to ensure a just share of wealth for the working class', which 'points towards the nationalization of industries', while 'Robert Owen, on the contrary, had not the slightest faith in political action'. This confuses the relationship between means and ends as well as the terminology appropriate to such a discussion. Owen did not oppose public ownership of industries, but would probably not have seen such intervention as 'political action'. His emphasis against O'Brien (who was more flexible in any case) on this point concerned the question of the decentralisation of industries in communities, and on the mixture of public and private ownership. A further comparison of types of socialism argues that the Owenites differed fundamentally from later socialists because they did not advocate state action, but voluntary association in communities.[70] But we have seen that the conception of the state in Owenism shifted considerably after about 1845, and that of course a very considerable amount of intervention was recommended prior to this. A more useful focus here is upon the degree of centralisation involved, as we have seen, rather than the question of 'intervention' *per se*. Another fruitful means of distinguishing between many forms of earlier and later socialism, too, is that which the Owenites themselves typically used in indicating their own reliance on reason and argumentation as means of social change against those who counselled violence. In fact, given Owenism's use of stadial theories of history and its articulation of a relatively sophisticated theory of the removal of the product of labour from the labourer, the choice of a revolutionary means of social reform is the most important distinguishing feature dividing 'utopian' from 'scientific' socialism – terms which should now best be dispensed with in favour of a simple and less absolute separation into early and later socialism.

Nonetheless the Owenite contribution to British radicalism lay more in the diffusion of a 'social' language and set of arguments than it did in the propagation of a specific programme. Much of our own political

[70] A. Plummer, *Bronterre*, p. 40; J. McCabe, *Life and Letters of G. J. Holyoake*, 1, p. 43; E. T. Craig, *Memoir and In Memoriam of Henry Travis* (c. 1885), p. 11n.

language is in fact derived from the alterations in the political, social and economic ideas during the period studied here. The gradual fashioning of a new 'social' conception of democratic theory dates from the birth of socialism in the decade after 1815. This form of democracy was 'social' in three primary senses. It took cognizance of the central importance of the economy to politics, and made this an explicit rather than merely tacit element in political debate. It recognised the value of democratic participation in extra-parliamentary institutions, extending this notion into the 'social' sphere of co-operatives, trades' unions, communities and the family in an effort to give the labouring population greater control over their lives than they had ever possessed previously. Finally, it advised a higher moral purpose than mere partisanship offered, and sought to refashion the ideas of public, national and international interest to ensure greater peace, justice and well-being for all. Correspondingly it demanded the education and moral improvement of all those who were to assist in the building of the new society, and thus the renewed pursuit of public virtue, and of 'the knowledge of right and wrong, of true and false modes of action, and the culture of good habits', as the means of 'the social mode of improvement' were described in 1856. Centrally, therefore, 'social reform' meant the desire to improve the conditions of the entire population, especially with regard to basic needs. Such a change could not be effected merely by electing new governmental officials, no matter how wide the franchise. Nor could its results ever be guaranteed without the creation of a superior morality which was applied to the public and private realms alike. In this sense to be a 'social reformer' also meant to seek 'political reform through an improvement in our domestic relations, habits, and feelings', and 'to believe in the potency of virtue as an element of progress and guarantee of civilization', as the Amalgamated Engineers' journal put it in early 1851. Republican virtue was thus to be wedded to a more intimate sociability.[71]

These ideals, however, took many forms even within Owenism. The emergence of other types of social radicalism during the first half of the nineteenth century also served to widen as well as to complicate the range of meanings of key terms in the reformers' political vocabulary. By 1850 the language of republicanism and radicalism was thus highly fragmented compared to its relative homogeneity early in the century. Most of the key terms of radical politics now had a much greater range of connotations attached to them. To take only one, though very important, example, the term 'democracy' had a wide and often con-

---

[71] *Leader*, 7, no. 343 (18 October 1856), 1000; *Operative*, no. 9 (1 March 1851), 130.

fusing variety of resonances attached to it by the 1850s.[72] To be a 'democrat', observed Ernest Jones in 1852, might now 'mean anything or nothing'. For working class leaders in particular, many of whom were also acquainted with at least the outlines of French and German radical theories, much of the ambiguity attached to such terms after 1848 resulted from the popularisation of continental terminology, which sometimes varied significantly in meaning from its British equivalent. One of the exiled German revolutionaries explained, for example, how new connotations of this term had been thrown up by the events of 1848 and later:

In Germany and France the term, 'Democracy or Socialism', signifying a compromise between the small middle class, which is far more numerous in those countries than it is in England, and the working class have of late become odious, and with good reason, to the proletarian; the former having given ample proofs of their determination to leave the position of the working man unaltered, by maintaining the system of profits and wages. The proletarians, therefore, have raised their proper standard, the standard of 'Communism'.[73]

Other socialists refrained from invoking 'democracy' because of its ambiguity as well as its association with the existing political process. The communitarian emigrationist followers of J. A. Etzler, who included many former Owenites as well as Chartists in their ranks, commented for example that:

The name 'Democracy' comfortably adjusts itself to whatever stage the mass of mind has advanced; most elastically stretching itself at the will of those who are at once its masters and its slaves. We see, in this country, men, from the Tory to the extreme Radical alike vaunting themselves the friends of Democracy. Each is a defender of the mass of mind possessed by his sect; and each maintains that aught other than this is the converse of liberty, no matter whether it be behind or in advance of him. At last, so clearly has it been perceived how small is even the largest size of the mass which the name Democracy covers that many of the Associationists sickened at the poverty-stricken use that has been made of the old covering, have flung it on one side – have repudiated the name. These, therefore, are termed aristocratical by fanatics who are offended at the non-worship of their god.[74]

Further contributing to cloud the meaning of 'democracy' was a sociological conception of 'the democracy' as the largest class and opposite of 'the aristocracy', about whose definition Holyoake commented that

---

[72] On 'democracy' in early socialism see Jens Christophersen, *The Meanings of 'Democracy' as Used in European Ideologies from the French to the Russian Revolutions* (Oslo, Universitetsforlaget, 1966), pp. 111–30.

[73] *NP*, 2 (1851), 895; 1, (1851), 433. The latter article was probably written by J. G. Eccarius.

[74] *MS*, no. 35 (6 September 1845), 277.

As the practical struggle of politics in England is between aristocracy and the unaristocratic classes, the English use of the word democrat is intended solely as the antithesis of aristocracy; and those who so name themselves probably mean to say, that they would desire to do for England what Kossuth says the laws of March, 1848, did for Hungary – viz. substitute a democratic monarchy for an aristocratic monarchy.[75]

Further, the phrases 'Social Democracy', 'Socialist Democrat', 'Republican Socialist' and 'Democratic Socialist' also circulated increasingly after 1848, as well as the new continental class language of 'proletariat', 'bourgeoisie' and 'bourgeois republic'.[76] These were also linked to the notion of a 'social revolution', as when a lecturer described the French revolution of 1848 as 'a social, not a political revolution. It was labour aiming to become better to do in the world'. Still in service in the early 1850s, too, was 'true democracy', not only in Owen's writings but also those of socialists like Reynolds, who wrote that 'The dissolution of inequalities is the aim of true democracy; for no state of society will ever become virtuous, contented and happy till every man shall possess his just proportion of distinction in that society and his fair share of the produce of the earth'.[77] This was perhaps closest to the meaning with which Owenism had begun to invest the term twenty-five or so years earlier, when 'democracy', without any 'social' additions, was more easily definable than at mid-century.

Though it had certainly played an essential role in undermining older forms of radical discourse, Owenism never seriously succeeded in dealing a significant blow to the notion that short-term popular representation ought to remain a leading radical goal. Nor, as we have seen, did most of its leaders, despite Owen's own ideas, wish to set aside such an assumption. The intervening years, many later Chartists conceded, had vindicated Owenism's criticisms of many radical arguments, and witnessed the steady integration of many aspects of the social critique into the language of working class radicalism. Few radicals, however, were ever willing to dispense with traditional democratic ideas to such an extent as to embrace, for example, either government by age or the necessity for even a temporary despotism. In this sense the fervent, unalloyed devotion to the common good for

---

[75] For use of 'the democracy' in this sense, see the *Prompter*, no. 1 (13 November 1830), 2; *Reasoner* 15 (1853), 197.

[76] Two of the first uses of 'social democracy' are in *NS*, no. 609 (23 June 1849), 5, and *ST*, no. 17 (30 June 1849), 131. For 'Socialist Democrat' see *NS*, no. 648 (23 March 1850), 1, and for 'Republican Socialist', *NS*, no. 654 (4 May 1850), 1. Harney uses 'bourgeois republic' in *NS*, no. 570 (23 September 1848), 5.

[77] *DJWN*, no. 91 (8 April 1848), 472; *RWN*, ns no. 335 (13 April 1851), 8. For an example of the use of 'democracy' in association with a range of 'social' meanings, but not in a socialist manner (e.g. that the law should not give preference to labour over capital) see John Langford, *English Democracy* (1853), pp. 71–7.

which Owen had called, and the ideal of a single, undifferentiated common interest upon which the most enthusiastic forms of communitarianism were based, were never widely accepted. Too many remained sceptical of the extreme claims about potential virtue upon which Owen's notions of communitarian government seemed to rely. Most found the prospect of abolishing the traditional family wholly unpalatable. Too many desired at least to establish their political rights as citizens first, before testing their moral capabilities as saints. And among these rights, without doubt, many perceived an ideal of individual development which seemed somehow at odds with some of Owen's leading ideas, or at least his own expression of them. Owen's radical critics would thus largely have concurred with the *Leader*'s comment, on his death in 1858, that 'it appeared that the docility, the orderliness, the "like mind and like wants", engendered by his system, were results incompatible with the free development of the free man, making of him a mental and moral mechanism, or, in other words, what to Robert Owen was abhorrent, a slave, or the ready victim of a tyrant, if not a tyrant himself'.[78]

For most social radicals at mid-century it was therefore the economic rather than the moral dimension of 'society' which was essential to the new social understanding of radical politics. Most would have concurred with the Chartist George White's 1855 conclusion that

As regards the *name* of a government, it matters little; the great point at issue is this: Shall the mass of mankind be in a continual misery for the benefit of a few? ... To tell a starving and half-naked man, who is willing to be a useful member of society, that he lives under a government, whether Constitutional or otherwise, is adding mockery to insult and injury.

Despite its own ambiguity on this matter, therefore, what Owenism had helped to supersede was a bias shared by both Painite radicalism and classical political economy in favour of a rigid separation between 'society' and 'government', which culminated in a wish to circumscribe the activity of politics. Whether centrally or locally, many social radicals now believed that government could divest itself of what was, from the working class point of view, its overwhelmingly punitive character. By providing for the wants of the majority, government could prove that it did not function only to curtail the wickedness of mankind, or to permit the avarice and profusion of some while suppressing the legitimate needs of others. Hence Thomas Cooper reflected that if Paine were alive in 1849

I think he would have come to the conclusion that, although Society and Government were different in their *origin*, they ought *now* to be intermarried:

[78] *Leader*, 8, no. 452 (20 November 1858), 1244.

that the Government should *now* be the Executive of the Great Society, into which all our lesser Societies should merge their selfish interests. If Government comes to be popularly viewed in this light, it will then have to bend its attention to the laws of Association, or Co-operation, into which all lesser societies will begin to be considered as merged. It will discover how immediately the resources of the human family can be augmented by the *economy* resulting from Association: it will discover a new universe of blessing of which the *political economists* never dreamed.[79]

Though it exerted great energies over thirty years in attempting to defeat many of the central propositions of radicalism, Owenite socialism was for most of its adherents, and ultimately even for Owen himself, also a variety of radicalism. James Elishama Smith was correct in several senses when, ruminating in the early 1850s upon the development and demise of Owenism, he concluded of it that 'Socialism is the last form of theoretical republicanism'.[80] Having never achieved its utopia, Owenism remained republican even in its most ambitious moments, when it threatened to, but never did, lose sight of traditional forms of politics. But Owenism also transformed existing ideals of public virtue and collective participation to suit its own concerns with sociability, economic justice, and the extension of democracy into other forms of civil association. Moreover, if republicanism as it had been understood prior to the late eighteenth century had required direct participation in small-scale societies, then the rise of Owenism can also be understood in part as a final attempt to revive classical republicanism. Correspondingly, the decline of Owenism also signified the virtual demise of a concept of socialism based upon the ideal of the small republic. By 1850 this was rapidly being replaced by the notion that socialism and the nation-state were not incompatible, and the conclusion that the small community could no longer serve as the locus of socialist discussion. Thus it was that socialism came to embrace the modern nation-state, as republicanism, through the theory of representative government, had after 1776.

Though its ideas persisted through the Fabians and others to wield some influence even in the first decades of the twentieth century, Owenism perished almost incidentally amidst the verification of many of its prophecies.[81] Contemporaries did not doubt that its most enduring legacy to Victorian England was not the ideal of 'community', but that of paternal care for the labouring classes, and, with the notion of the 'social state', of the duty to provide a subsistence for the poor. Later forms of socialism still retained something of

---

[79] *DLA*, no. 3 (17 November 1855), 9; *PIS*, no. 13 (14 April 1849), 100.
[80] *FH*, 12 (1853–54), 827.
[81] Useful on the later influence of Owenism is Edward Royle's 'The Owenite Legacy to Social Reform', *SHP*, 1 (1980), 56–74.

Owenism's confidence in the moral perfectibility of mankind, but rarely accorded this any central role in the process of future social transformation. Nonetheless gerontocracy was to emerge, with the same purpose of avoiding conflict during transfers of power, as a widespread form of practical rule in many later nominally socialist societies. But a preference for this type of government has never predominated within socialist political theory. Indeed, demands for the wider extension of more traditional forms of democracy throughout socialist societies are once again resurgent in Europe, Asia and elsewhere. Whatever their outcome, this is evidence enough that the debates begun in Owenism are yet far from having run their course.

Bibliography

(Place of publication is London unless otherwise noted.)

1 MANUSCRIPT AND TYPESCRIPT SOURCES

Allsop Papers, London School of Economics
Barnsby, G. 'The Dudley Working Class Movement, 1832–60', Typescript Series no. 8, Central Library, Dudley
Bray Collection, British Library of Political and Economic Science
British Library, Additional MSS
Brougham Papers, University College, London
Hamilton Papers, Motherwell Public Library
Holyoake Collection, Co-operative Union Library, Manchester
Home Office Papers, Kew: HO 41/30, 44/38, 45/54, 54/242, 64/18
Internationaal Instituut voor Sociale Geschiedenis, Amsterdam, Minute Books:
   Association of All Classes of All Nations, Minute Book of the Central Board, 1838–40
   Minutes of the Proceedings of the Liverpool Branch of the Association of All Classes of All Nations
   National Community Friendly Society, Minute Book of the Board of Directors, 1838–43
   Rational Society, Minute Book of Directors, no. 2 (1843–45)
Lovett Collection, Birmingham Central Reference Library
Maclure MSS, The Workingmen's Institute, New Harmony, Indiana
Minutes of the Congress of Social Reformers, 13–16 May 1850, Bishopsgate Institute
National Library of Scotland, MS. Letters
National Library of Wales, Owen MSS
Owen Collection, Co-operative Union Library, Manchester
Pare Papers, Goldsmiths' Library, University of London
Place, Francis. *Proceedings and Papers Relating to the National Union of the Working Classes, 26 October 1830–11 January 1834*, Goldsmiths' Library, University of London
Sever, John. *James Morrison of the 'Pioneer'. Notes on his Life and Background* (Typescript, 1963), Cambridge University Library

2 UNPUBLISHED THESES AND DISSERTATIONS

Belchem, John. 'Radicalism as a "Platform" Agitation in the Period 1816–1821

327

and 1848–1851: with Special Reference to the Leadership of Henry Hunt and Feargus O'Connor', Ph.D., University of Sussex (1977)

Carr, H. J. 'A Critical Exposition of the Social and Economic Ideas of John Francis Bray; and an Estimate of his Influence upon Karl Marx', Ph.D., University of London (1943)

Cole, W. A. 'The Quakers and Politics, 1652–1660', Ph.D., University of Cambridge (1955)

Cook, D. R. 'Reverend James Elishama Smith: Socialist Prophet of the Millennium: a Study of Socio-religious Radicalism in the British Working Class Movement of the 1830s', M.A., University of Iowa (1961)

Grant, Alistair C. 'George Combe and his Circle: with Particular Reference to his Relations with the United States of America', Ph.D., University of Edinburgh (1960)

Janes, Eileen. 'The Quest for the New Moral World: Changing Patterns of Owenite Thought, 1817–1870', M.A., University of Wisconsin (1963)

Kemnitz, T. M. 'Chartism in Brighton', Ph.D., University of Sussex (1969)

Knipe, J. 'Owenite Ideas and Institutions, 1828–1834', M.A., University of Wisconsin (1967)

Montgomery, F. A. 'Glasgow Radicalism, 1830–1848', Ph.D., University of Glasgow (1974)

Morris, D. C. 'The History of the Labour Movement in England, 1825–1852: the Problem of Leadership and the Articulation of Demands', Ph.D., University of London (1952)

Oliver, W. H. 'Organisations and Ideas Behind the Efforts to Achieve a General Union of the Working Classes in England in the Early 1830s', D.Phil., University of Oxford (1954)

Parsinnen, Terry M. 'Thomas Spence and the Spenceans: a Study of Revolutionary Utopianism in the England of George III', Ph.D., Brandeis University (1968)

Prothero, Iorwerth. 'London Working Class Movements, 1825–1848', Ph.D., University of Cambridge (1966)

Rosen, Frederick. 'Progress and Democracy: William Godwin's Contribution to Political Philosophy', Ph.D., University of London (1965)

Storch, Robert. 'Owenite Communitarianism in Britain', M.A., University of Wisconsin (1964)

Wolfe, S. F. 'The Political Rhetoric of English Radicalism, 1780–1830', Ph.D., University of York (1976)

Yeo, Eileen. 'Social Science and Social Change: a Social History of Aspects of Social Science and Social Investigation in Britain 1830–1890', Ph.D., University of Sussex (1972)

3 PERIODICALS

(An asterisk indicates that only single or occasional numbers have been consulted.)

Advice to Labourers, 1829
Advocate and Merthyr Free Press, 1841*
Advocate of the Working Classes, 1826–27
Age of Civilization, 1816–18
Agitator and Political Anatomist, 1833*
Anti-Socialist Gazette, and Christian Advocate, 1841–42
Associate, 1829–30

Barker's Review of Politics, 1861–63
Beacon, 1844
Birmingham Co-operative Herald, 1829–30
Birmingham Inspector, 1817
Birmingham Labour Exchange Gazette, 1833
Black Dwarf, 1817–24
Brazen Head, 1836*
Brazen Trumpet, 1798
Brighton Patriot, 1836–39
British Co-operator, 1830
British Statesman, 1842–43
Briton, 1819
Bronterre's National Reformer, 1837
Cap of Liberty, 1819–20
Carlile's Political Register, 1839
Carpenter's Monthly Political Magazine, 1831–32
Carpenter's Political Letters and Pamphlets, 1830–31
Cause of the People, 1848
Champion, 1814–22
Champion and Weekly Herald, 1836–40
Champion of What is True and Right, 1850–51
Charter, 1839–40
Chartist, 1839
Chartist Circular, 1839–42
Chartist Pilot, 1843–44
Christian Social Economist, 1851
Christian Socialist, 1851–52
Cleave's Penny Gazette, 1837–44
Cleave's Weekly Police Gazette, 1835–36*
Cobbett's Twopenny Trash, 1830–31
Cobbett's Weekly Political Register, 1802–36
Common Sense, 1830
Commonweal, 1845–46
Communist Miscellany, 1843
Communitist, 1844–46
Constitutionalist, 1839–40
Co-operator, 1846
Co-operator, 1860–71
Cosmopolite, 1832
Crisis, 1832–34
Daily National Intelligencer, 1825*
Daily News, 1858*
Daily Union, 1846*
Deist, 1842–43
Demagogue, 1834*
Democrat and Labour Advocate, 1855
Democratic Review, 1849–50
Destructive and Poor Man's Conservative, 1833–34
Divinearian, 1849*
Douglas Jerrold's Weekly Newspaper, 1846–51
Economist, 1821–22
Edinburgh Monthly Democrat, 1838*

Educational Circular and Communist Apostle, 1841–42
English Chartist Circular, 1841–44
Englishman, 1854
English Patriot and Irish Repealer, 1848
English Republic, 1851–55
Evening Star, 1842–43
Family Herald, 1843–54
Fleet Papers, 1841–44
Free Enquirer, 1829–35
Freethinker's Magazine, 1850–51
Gauntlet, 1833–34
Gazette of the Exchange Bazaars, 1832
Glasgow Sentinel, 1850–58
Gorgon, 1818–19
Halfpenny Magazine, 1840–41
Herald of Co-operation, 1847–48
Herald of the Future, 1839–40
Herald of the Rights of Industry, 1834
Herald to the Trades' Advocate, 1830–31
Hetherington's Twopenny Dispatch, 1836*
Howitt's Journal, 1847
Independent Whig, 1806–21
Isis, 1832
Jersey Independent, 1855–62
Journal of Association, 1852
Labourer, 1847–48
Labour League, or Journal of the National Association of United Industry, 1848
Leader, 1850–60
Lion, 1828–29
Livesey's Moral Reformer, 1838–39
Lloyd's Weekly London Newspaper, 1842–52
London American, 1860–63
London Chartist Monthly Magazine, 1843*
London Co-operative Magazine, 1826–30
London Democrat, 1839
London Dispatch, 1836–39
London Mercury, 1836–37
London News, 1858
London Social Reformer, 1840
Louis Blanc's Monthly Magazine, 1849
McDouall's Chartist Journal, 1841
Magazine of Useful Knowledge, and Co-operative Miscellany, 1830
Man, 1833
Manchester and Salford Advertiser, 1836–42
Manchester Herald, 1792–93
Manchester Observer, 1818–23
Midland Counties Illuminator, 1841
Midland Progressionist, 1848
Midland Representative and Birmingham Herald, 1831–32
Mirror of Truth, 1817
Model Republic, 1843
Monthly Liberator, 1838*

Monthly Messenger, 1840
Monthly Repository, 1806–38
Moral World, 1845
Morning Star, or Herald of Progression, 1844–47
National Association Gazette, 1842
National Instructor, 1851
National Reformer, 1846–47*
National Union, 1858
National Vindicator, and Liberator of the West and Wales, 1841–42*
Newcastle Weekly Chronicle, 1879*
New Harmony Gazette, 1826–29
New Moral World, 1834–45
Niles' Weekly Register, 1825*
Nonconformist, 1841–52
Northern Liberator, 1837–40
Northern Star, 1836–52
Northern Tribune, 1854–55
Notes to the People, 1851–52
Odd Fellow, 1839–42
Official Gazette of the Trades' Union, 1834
Operative, 1838–39
Operative, 1851–52
Operatives' Free Press, 1849–50
Oracle of Reason, 1842
Patriot, 1792
Penny Papers for the People, 1830–31
Penny Satirist, 1837–46
People, 1817
People, 1848–52
People's Journal, 1846–49
People's Magazine, 1841*
People's Newspaper, 1847
People's Paper, 1852–58
People's Press, 1847–48
People's Review of Literature and Politics, 1850
Phrenological Journal, 1823–24*
Pioneer, 1833–34
Pioneer and Weekly Record of Movements, 1851
Plain Speaker, 1849
Political Economist and Universal Philanthropist, 1823
Political Examiner, 1853
Political Soldier, 1833
Politics for the People, 1848
Politics for the Rich and Poor, 1836
Poor Man's Advocate, 1832–33
Poor Man's Guardian, 1831–35
Poor Man's Guardian, and Repealer's Friend, 1843
Potters' Examiner and Workman's Advocate, 1843–45
Power of the Pence, 1848–49
Promethean, or Communitarian Apostle, 1842
Prompter, 1830–31
Quarterly Review, 1817*

Radical, 1836
Radical Reformer, 1832
Reasoner, 1846–63
Reformists' Register, 1811–12
Reformists' Register and Weekly Commentary, 1817
Regenerator, 1844
Register for the First Society of Adherents to Divine Revelation at Orbiston, 1825–27
Republican, 1819–26
Republican, 1848
Republican, or Voice of the People, 1831–32
Reynolds's Political Instructor, 1849–50
Reynolds's Weekly Newspaper, 1850–60
Robert Owen's Journal, 1850–52
Robert Owen's Millennial Gazette, 1856–58
Robert Owen's Weekly Letters to the Human Race, 1850
Scottish Patriot, 1839–41
Scottish Trades' Union Gazette, 1833
Sheffield Free Press, 1851–57
Shepherd, 1834–38
Sherwin's Political Register, 1817–19
Social Pioneer, 1839
Social Reformer, 1849
Some Account of the Progress of the Truth As It is in Jesus, 1843–44
Southern Star, 1840
Spirit of the Age, 1848–49
Spirit of the Times, 1849
Standard of Freedom, 1848*
Star in the East, 1836–40
Star of Freedom, 1852
Stephens's Monthly Magazine, 1840*
Stepping-Stone, 1862–63
Sun, 1821–24
Torch, 1842
Trades' Free Press, and Mechanics' Weekly Gazette (Weekly Free Press), 1825–31
Trades' Messenger Weekly, 1848
Transactions of the Co-operative League, 1852
True Scotsman, 1839–41
Trumpet of Wales (Udgorn Cymru), 1841*
Union, 1831–32
Union, 1842–43
Uxbridge Spirit of Freedom, 1849*
Vanguard, 1853
Voice of the People, 1848
Ware Patriot, 1833–34
Weekly Advisor, 1852
Weekly Herald, 1836
Weekly Tribune, 1849–50
Weekly True Sun, 1833–39
Western Star, 1840
Western Vindicator, 1839*
Westminster Review, 1839*
White Hat, 1819

Wooler's British Gazette, 1819–23
Working Bee, 1839–41
Working Man's Advocate, 1836
Working Man's Association Gazette, 1839*
Working Man's Friend and Family Instructor, 1850–52
Working Man's Friend and Political Magazine, 1832–33

4 BOOKS AND PAMPHLETS

Adams, W. E. *Memoirs of a Social Atom* (2 vols., Hutchinson, 1903)
Address and Rules of the Working Men's Association (1836)
An Address from the Working Men's Association to the Working Classes, on the Subject of Education (1838)
An Address to the Members of Trades' Societies, and to the Working Classes Generally . . . by a Journeyman Bootmaker (1833)
Ainslie, Robert. *An Examination of Socialism* (1840)
Articles of Agreement Drawn up and Recommended by the London Co-operative Society for the Formation of a Community on Principles of Mutual Co-operation (1825)
Augustine. *The City of God* (Dent, 1942)
Bailey, James Napier. *Essays on Miscellaneous Subjects* (Leeds, 1842)
  The Social Reformer's Cabinet Library (Leeds, 1841)
Bailey, Samuel. *Essays on the Formation and Publication of Opinions* (1821)
Bamford, Samuel. *Passages in the Life of a Radical* (1844)
Barclay, Robert. *A Catechism and Confession of Faith* (1673; 13th edn., 1803)
Barker, Joseph. *The Social Reformer's Almanac for 1848* (Wortley, 1848)
Bellers, John. 'Proposals for Raising a College of Industry', in A. Ruth Fry, ed., *John Bellers 1654–1725* (Cassell, 1925)
Bernard, James. *A Theory of the Constitution* (1834)
Blanc, Louis. *The Organization of Labour* (1848)
  Socialism: the Right to Labour (1848)
Bolingbroke, Henry St. John, Viscount. *Works* (5 vols., 1754)
Bower, Samuel. *The Peopling of Utopia* (Bradford, 1838)
  A Sequel to the Peopling of Utopia (Bradford, 1838)
Bray, Charles. *An Essay Upon the Union of Agriculture and Manufactures and Upon the Organisation of Industry* (1844)
  Phases of Opinion and Experience During a Long Life (1879)
  The Philosophy of Necessity (2 vols., 1841)
Bray, John Francis. *Labour's Wrongs and Labour's Remedy* (Leeds, 1839)
Brown, Paul. *Twelve Months at New Harmony* (Cincinnati, 1827)
Buchanan, Robert. *An Exposure of the Falsehoods, Calumnies and Misrepresentations of a Pamphlet Entitled 'The Abominations of Socialism Exposed'* (Manchester, 1840)
Buonarroti's History of Babeuf's Conspiracy for Equality, ed. James Bronterre O'Brien (1836)
Burgh, James. *Political Disquisitions* (3 vols., 1774)
Burton, Robert. 'An Utopia of Mine Own', in Glenn Negley and J. Max Patrick, eds., *The Quest for Utopia* (College Park, McGrath Publishing Co., 1971)
Campbell, Alexander. *Address on the Progress of the Co-operative System* (Glasgow, 1831)
Campbell, John. *A Theory of Equality; or, the Way to Make Every Man Act Honestly* (Philadelphia, 1848)
Carlyle, Thomas. *Critical and Miscellaneous Essays* (5 vols., 1899)

Chartist Tracts for the Times (n.p., n.d.; c. 1850)

Clarkson, Thomas. *A Portraiture of Quakerism* (3 vols., 1806)

Collins, Anthony. *A Philosophical Inquiry Concerning Human Liberty* (4th edn., Glasgow, 1749)

[Combe, Abram]. *The New Court. No. 1* (n.p., n.d.)

Combe, Abram. *An Address to the Conductors of the Periodical Press* (Edinburgh, 1823)

   Metaphorical Sketches of the Old and New Systems (Edinburgh, 1823)

   Observations on the Old and New Views (Edinburgh, 1823)

   The Religious Creed of the New System (Edinburgh, 1825)

   The Sphere for Joint-Stock Companies (Edinburgh, 1825)

Combe, George. 'Phrenological Analysis of Mr. Owen's New Views of Society', *Phrenological Journal*, 1 (1823–24), 218–37

Constitution and Laws of the Universal Community Society of Rational Religionists (1839)

Cooper, Thomas. *The Life of Thomas Cooper* (4th edn., 1883)

   ed., *The Land for the Labourers, and the Fraternity of Nations* (1848)

Craig, E. T. *An Irish Commune. The Experiment at Ralahine, Co. Clare, 1831–1833* (1920; rpt. Dublin, Irish Academic Press, 1983)

   Memoir and in Memoriam of Henry Travis (c. 1885)

Cumberland, Richard. *A Treatise of the Laws of Nature* (1727)

Dalrymple, John. *An Essay Towards a General History of Feudal Property in Great Britain* (1758)

Davenport, Allen. *The Life, Writings, and Principles of Thomas Spence* (1836)

Derisley, John. *An Address to the National Union of the Working Classes* (1832)

Dick, Robert. *Autobiography and Poetical Compositions* (1863)

Dunbar, James. *Essays on the History of Mankind in Rude and Cultivated Ages* (2nd edn., 1781)

Dunning, Thomas. 'Reminiscences of Thomas Dunning', in D. Vincent, ed., *Testaments of Radicalism: Memoirs of Working Class Politicians 1790–1850* (Europa, 1977)

Edwards, Jonathan. *A Careful and Strict Enquiry into the Modern Prevailing Notions of That Freedom of the Will* (1754; rpt. New Haven, Yale University Press, 1957)

Engels, Friedrich. *Socialism, Utopian and Scientific* (New York, International Publishers, 1972)

An Essay in Answer to the Question, Whether does the Principle of Competition . . . or the Principle of United Exertions . . . Form the Most Secure Basis for the Formation of Society? (1834)

Ferguson, Adam. *An Essay on the History of Civil Society* (1767), ed. Duncan Forbes (Edinburgh, Edinburgh University Press, 1966)

   Principles of Moral and Political Science (2 vols., Edinburgh, 1792)

Finch, John. *The Millennium. The Wisdom of Jesus and the Foolery of Sectarianism* (Liverpool, 1837)

Fletcher, Andrew. *Andrew Fletcher of Saltoun. Selected Political Writings and Speeches*, ed. David Daiches (Edinburgh, Scottish Academic Press, 1979)

Fox, George. *An Epistle to All Professors* (1673)

   The Journal of George Fox (Dent, 1948)

Frost, Thomas. *Forty Years' Recollections* (1880)

A Full Account of the Farewell Festival Given to Robert Owen on His Departure for America (1844)

The General Council of the First International 1864–1866. Minutes (Moscow, Foreign Languages Publishing House, n.d.)

Gerrald, Joseph. *A Convention the Only Means of Saving Us From Ruin* (3rd edn., 1794)

Godwin, Francis. 'The Man in the Moone', ed. Grant McColley, in *Smith College Studies in Modern Languages* (Northampton, 1937–38)

Godwin, William. *Enquiry Concerning Political Justice*, ed. Isaac Kramnick (1793; rpt. of 1798 edn., Harmondsworth, Penguin Books, 1976)

Gray, John. *An Efficient Remedy for the Distress of Nations* (Edinburgh, 1842)

A Lecture on Human Happiness (1825)

The Social System: A Treatise on the Principle of Exchange (Edinburgh, 1831)

Green, David. *The Claims of the Redemption Society Considered: or, the Principles of Home Colonization* (1849)

Grotius, Hugo. *De Jure Belli ac Pacis* (1625; rpt. Oxford, Clarendon Press, 1925)

Hall, Charles. *The Effects of Civilization on the People in European States* (1805)

[Hamilton, A. J.] *Prospectus of a Plan for Establishing an Institution on Mr. Owen's System in the Middle Ward of the County of Lanark* (n.p., 1822)

Harrington, James. *The Political Works of James Harrington*, ed. J. G. A. Pocock (Cambridge, Cambridge University Press, 1977)

Hartley, David. *Observations on Man* (2 vols., 1749)

Haslam, C. J. *A Defence of the Social Principles* (1837)

Letters 1 to 12 to the Clergy of All Denominations (1839)

Hazlitt, William. *The Spirit of the Age* (1825; rpt. Oxford, Oxford University Press, 1966)

Hebert, William. *A Visit to the Colony of Harmony in Indiana* (1825)

Heckewelder, John. 'An Account of the History, Manners, and Customs of the Indian Nations, Who Once Inhabited Pennsylvania and the Neighbouring States', *Transactions of the Historical and Literary Committee of the American Philosophical Society* (Philadelphia, 1819)

Hennell, Mary. *An Outline of the Various Social Systems and Communities Which have been Founded on the Principle of Co-operation* (1844)

Herzen, Alexander. *My Past and Thoughts* (1924; rpt. 3 vols., New York, Alfred Knopf, 1968)

Higginson, Edward. *Human Equality* (Hull, 1840)

Hill, William. *The Rejected Letters . . . Refused Insertion in the Northern Star . . . September 23 and October 14, 1843* (1843)

Hints Addressed to the Radical Reformers (Glasgow, 1819)

Hobbes, Thomas. *A Letter about Liberty and Necessity* (1677)

Hodgskin, Thomas. *Labour Defended Against the Claims of Capital* (1825)

Hole, James. *Social Science and the Organization of Labour* (Leeds, 1851)

Holyoake, George Jacob. *Bygones Worth Remembering* (2 vols., T. Fisher Unwin, 1905)

Rationalism. A Treatise for the Times (1845)

Sixty Years of an Agitator's Life (2 vols., T. Fisher Unwin, 3rd edn., 1893)

ed. 'Unpublished Correspondence of the Robert Owen Family', *Co-operative News*, 35 (1904), 437–8, 465–6, 493–4, 549–50, 589–90, 705–6, 733–4, 769–70, 825–6, 853–4

Howell, George. *A History of the Working Men's Association from 1836 to 1850* (Newcastle upon Tyne, Frank Graham, 1973)

Hume, David. *Enquiries concerning Human Understanding and concerning the Principles of Morals* (Oxford, Clarendon Press, 1975)

Essays Moral, Political and Literary (Grant Richards, 1903)

Hunt, Thomas. *Chartism, Trades Unionism, and Socialism* (1840)

'K' [William King]. *The Useful Working Population* (1831)

Knight, Henry. *A Lecture on Irresponsibility* (Hulme, 1838)

Kossuth, Louis, Ledru-Rollin, Alexandre and Mazzini, Joseph. *Manifesto of the Republican Party* (1855)

Langford, John. *English Democracy: Its History and Principles* (1853)

Lee, R. E. *Victimization, or Benbowism Exposed* (1832)

Lee, Richard. *The Rights of Man* (1795)

Leno, J. B. *The Aftermath: with Autobiography of the Author* (1892)

Linton, W. J. *European Republicanism. Recollections of Mazzini and His Friends* (1893)

   James Watson: a Memoir (1879; rpt. Clifton, Augustus M. Kelley, 1969)

   Memoirs (1895)

Locke, John. *Two Treatises of Government*, ed. Peter Laslett (1690; rpt. Cambridge, Cambridge University Press, 1970)

Loskiel, George Henry. *History of the Mission of the United Brethren among the Indians in North America* (1794)

Lovett, William. *Life and Struggles of William Lovett in his Pursuit of Bread, Knowledge and Freedom* (1876; rept. McKibbon and Kee, 1967)

Lovett, William and John Collins. *Chartism. A New Organisation for the People* (2nd edn., 1841)

Lowery, Robert. *Address to the Fathers and Mothers, Sons and Daughters, of the Working Classes, on the System of Exclusive Dealing* (Newcastle upon Tyne, 1839)

Macdonald, Donald. 'The Diaries of Donald Macdonald, 1824–1826', *PIHS*, 14 (1942)

Macintosh, T. S. *An Inquiry into the Nature of Responsibility* (Birmingham, 1840)

Maclure, William. *Opinions on Various Subjects* (2 vols., New Harmony, 1831)

Manual of the Association of All Classes of All Nations (1836)

Marriott, Joseph. *Community. A Drama* (Manchester, 1838)

Marx, Karl, and Engels, Frederick. *Collected Works* (Lawrence and Wishart, 1975–)

Masheder, Richard. *Dissent and Democracy* (1864)

Masquerier, Lewis. *Sociology; or the Reconstruction of Society, Government and Property* (New York, 1877)

Mather, J. *Socialism Exposed; or, the Book of the New Moral World Examined* (1839)

Memoirs of the Life and Writings of Michael Thomas Sadler (1842)

Mill, John Stuart. *A System of Logic* (Longmans, Green and Co., 1906)

More, Thomas. 'Utopia', in Henry Morley, ed. *Ideal Commonwealths* (1888)

Morgan, John Minter. *Hampden in the Nineteenth Century* (2 vols., 1834)

   The Revolt of the Bees (1826)

   Tracts (2nd edn., 1849)

Murray, Hugh. *Enquiries Historical and Moral, Respecting the Character of Nations and the Progress of Society* (Edinburgh, 1808)

Neville, Henry. 'Plato Redivivus; or, a Dialogue Concerning Government', in Caroline Robbins, ed., *Two English Republican Tracts* (Cambridge, Cambridge University Press, 1969)

O'Brien, James Bronterre. *The Life and Character of Maximilian Robespierre* (1838)

   Mr. O'Brien's Vindication of His Conduct at the Late Birmingham Conference (Birmingham, 1842)

   State Socialism! Propositions of the National Reform League (1885)

   A Vision of Hell; or, Peep into the Realms Below, alias Lord Overgrown's Dream (1859)

O'Connor, Feargus. *The Land and its Capabilities* (Manchester, 1842)

A Practical Work on the Management of Small Farms (2nd edn., Manchester, 1845)

Ogilvie, William. *An Essay on the Right of Property in Land* (1781)

[Owen, Robert]. *Institution of the Intelligent and Well-disposed of the Industrious Classes* (n.p., n.d., c. 1800)

Owen, Robert. *Address of Robert Owen. Delivered at the Great Public Meeting Held at the National Equitable Labour Exchange* (1833)

An Address to the Socialists (1841)

The Book of the New Moral World (7 pts, 1836–44)

The Catechism of the New Moral World (Leeds, 1838)

The Coming Millennium (1855)

A Development of the Principles and Plans on which to Establish Self-Supporting Home Colonies (1841)

Dialogue entre la France, le Monde, et Robert Owen (Paris, 1848)

Dialogue entre les Membres de la Commission Executive, les Ambassadeurs d'Angleterre, de Russie, d'Autriche, de Prusse, de Hollande, des Etats-Unis, et Robert Owen (Paris, 1848)

A Dialogue in Three Parts Between the Founder of the Association of All Classes of All Nations and a Stranger (1838)

A Discourse on a New System of Society (1825) ('First Discourse'), in O. C. Johnson, ed., *Robert Owen in the United States* (New York, Humanities Press, 1972)

The Future of the Human Race (1853)

Lectures on an Entire New State of Society (1830)

Lectures on the Rational System of Society (1841)

Letter from Mr. Robert Owen to the President and Members of the New York State Convention (Washington DC, 1846)

The Life of Robert Owen (2 vols., 1857–58)

Manifesto of Robert Owen (Washington DC, 1844)

The Marriage System of the New Moral World (Leeds, 1838)

The Millennium in Practice (1855)

Mr. Owen's Second Discourse on a New System of Society ('Second Discourse'), in O. C. Johnson, ed., *Robert Owen in the United States* (New York, Humanities Press, 1972)

The New Existence of Man upon the Earth (1854–55)

The New Religion (1830)

A New View of Society and Other Writings, ed. John Butt (Dent, 1977)

Permanent Relief for the British Agricultural and Manufacturing Labourers and the Irish Peasantry (n.d., c. 1822)

Practical Measures Required to Prevent Greater Political Changes in Great Britain and Ireland (1848)

Public Discussion between Robert Owen and the Rev. J. H. Roebuck (1837)

Report of the Proceedings at the Several Public Meetings Held in Dublin (Dublin, 1823)

The Revolution in the Mind and Practice of the Human Race (1849)

Robert Owen's Address, Delivered at the Meeting in St. Martin's Hall (1855)

Robert Owen's Address to the Ministers of all Religions (Philadelphia, 1845)

Robert Owen's Opening Speech, and His Reply to the Rev. Alexander Campbell (Cincinnati, 1829)

Robert Owen's Reply to the Question, 'What Would You Do If You Were Prime Minister?' (1832)

Six Lectures Delivered at Manchester (Manchester, 1839)

Socialism Misrepresented and Truly Represented (1848)

A Statement Regarding the New Lanark Establishment (Glasgow, 1812)

Owen, Robert Dale. *To Holland and New Harmony and Back. Robert Dale Owen's Travel Journal 1825–1826*, ed. Josephine M. Elliott (Indianapolis, Indiana State Historical Society, 1969)

Owen, William. *Diary of William Owen, from Nov. 10, 1824 to April 20, 1825*, ed. Joel Hiatt (Clifton, Augustus M. Kelley, 1973)

Paine, Thomas. *The Complete Writings of Thomas Paine*, ed. Philip Foner (2 vols., New York, Citadel Press, 1945)

Paley, William. *Principles of Moral and Political Philosophy* (7th edn., 1790)

[Pare, William]. *An Address Delivered at the Opening of the Birmingham Co-operative Society* (Birmingham, 1829)

Paul Pry's Third Ramble Through the 'New Moral World' (Doncaster, 1840)

Pelham, William. 'Letters of William Pelham', in Harlow Lindley, ed., *Indiana as Seen by Early Travellers* (Indianapolis, Indiana Historical Commission, 1916), pp. 369–417

Penn, William. *The Peace of Europe, the Fruits of Solitude, and Other Writings* (Dent, n.d.)

Preamble and Constitution of the Friendly Association for Mutual Interests (Philadelphia, 1826)

Preliminary Charter of the Rational System (1843)

Price, Richard. *Additional Observations on the Nature and Value of Civil Liberty and the War with America* (1777)

   A Discourse on the Love of our Country (3rd edn., 1790)

   The Evidence for a Future State of Improvement in the State of Mankind (1787)

   'Observations on the Expectations of Lives, the Increase of Mankind, the Influence of Great Towns on Population, and Particularly the State of London, with Respect to Healthfulness and Numbers of Inhabitants', *Royal Society, Philosophical Transactions*, 59 (1769), 89–125

   Observations on Reversionary Payments (2nd edn., 1772)

   A Sermon Delivered at a Congregation of Protestant Dissenters at Hackney (1779)

Priestley, Joseph. *The Doctrine of Philosophical Necessity Illustrated* (1777)

   An Essay on the First Principles of Government (2nd edn., 1771)

   'Lectures on History and General Policy', in *The Theological and Miscellaneous Works of Joseph Priestley*, vol. 24 (1803), pp. 7–463.

Proceedings of the First General Meeting of the British and Foreign Philanthropic Society (1822)

Proceedings of the Fourth Congress of the Association of All Classes of All Nations (Leeds, 1839)

Proceedings of the Second Co-operative Congress (n.d.)

Proceedings of the Third Congress of the Association of All Classes of All Nations (Leeds, 1838)

Proceedings of the Third Co-operative Congress (1832)

Pufendorf, Samuel. *De Jure Naturae et Gentium* (1672; rpt. Oxford, Clarendon Press, 1934)

   The Whole Duty of Man According to the Law of Nature (5th edn., 1725)

Randall, Joseph. *A Brief Account of the Rise, Principles, and Discipline of the People Called Quakers* (Dublin, 1786)

Remarks on the Rational System of Society (1832)

Report of the Committee Appointed at a Meeting of Journeymen (2nd edn., 1821)

Report of a Discussion Which Took Place at Huddersfield . . . between the Rev. T. Dalton and Mr. Lloyd Jones (Manchester, 1838)

Report of the Discussion between Robert Owen and the Rev. William Legge (1839)

Report of the Discussion on Socialism between Messrs. Lloyd Jones and C. Leckie (Glasgow, 1839)

Report of the Proceedings at the Fourth Quarterly Meeting of the British Association for the Promotion of Co-operative Knowledge (1830)

Report of the Proceedings at the Eighth Annual Congress of the Rational Society (1843)

Report of the Proceedings at the Second Quarterly Meeting of the Society for Promoting Co-operative Knowledge (1829)

Report of the Proceedings at the Third Quarterly Meeting of the British Association for the Promotion of Co-operative Knowledge (1830)

'Roger Radical'. *Why Are We Poor?* (1820)

Rules and Regulations of the Equitable Labour Exchange (1832)

Rules of the League of Social Progress (1850)

Russell, R. *America Compared to England* (1849)

Sacred Socialism (1843)

Shaftesbury, Anthony Ashley Cooper, Third Earl. *Characteristics of Men, Manners, Opinions, Times* (1711)

Smith, Adam. *Theory of Moral Sentiments* (1759; rpt. Oxford, Oxford University Press, 1976)

Smith, James Elishama. *Lecture on a Christian Community* (1833)
   The Little Book; or, Momentous Crisis of 1840 (1840)

Smith, Joshua Toulmin. *Local Self-Government and Centralization* (1851)
   The Parish: its Obligations and Powers, Its Offices and their Duties (1854)

Social Hymns (Leeds, 1838)

Solly, Henry. *James Woodford, Carpenter and Chartist* (2 vols., 1881)

Somerville, Alexander. *The Autobiography of a Working Man* (1848)

'Sosthenes'. *Tracts for the People. Communism and Chartism* (1848)

Southwell, Charles. *Confessions of a Freethinker* (c. 1845)

Statement Submitted to the Most Honourable the Marquis of Normandy . . . Relative to the Principles and Objects of the Universal Community Society of Rational Religionists (1840)

Stewart, Dugald. *Collected Works*, ed. W. Hamilton (10 vols., Edinburgh, 1855)
   Outlines of Moral Philosophy (Edinburgh, 1793)

Stuart, Gilbert. *A View of Society in Europe, in its Progress from Rudeness to Refinement* (2nd edn., Edinburgh, 1792)

Supplement to the Laws of the Universal Community Society of Rational Religionists (1840)

Thimbleby, John. *Monadelphia* (1832)

Thompson, William. *An Appeal of One-Half the Human Race, Women, Against the Pretensions of the Other Half, Men* (1825)
   An Inquiry into the Principles of the Distribution of Wealth (1824)
   Labor Rewarded (1827)
   Practical Directions for the Speedy and Economical Establishment of Communities (1830)

Thomson, C. *The Autobiography of an Artisan* (1847)

Toplady, A. *The Scheme of Christian and Philosophical Necessity Asserted* (1775)

To the Operative Classes (1828)

Trenchard, John, and Gordon, Thomas. *The English Libertarian Heritage*, ed. David L. Jacobson (Indianapolis, Bobbs-Merrill, 1965)

Tristan, Flora. *Flora Tristan's London Journal. A Survey of London Life in the 1830s* (G. Prior, 1980)

Tucker, Josiah. *Josiah Tucker. A Selection from His Economic and Political Writings,* ed. Robert Livingston Schulyer (New York, Columbia University Press, 1931)

Vattel, Emmerich de. *The Law of Nations or the Principles of Natural Law* (1758; rpt. Washington DC, Carnegie Institute, 1916)

Wakefield, E. G. *Householders in Danger from the Populace* (1831)

Wallace, Robert. *Various Prospects of Mankind, Nature and Providence* (1761)

Watts, John. *The Facts and Fictions of Political Economists* (Manchester, 1842)

Wilson, B. 'The Struggles of an Old Chartist', in D. Vincent, ed., *Testaments of Radicalism* (Europa, 1977), pp. 193–242

Winstanley, Gerrard. *The Works of Gerrard Winstanley*, ed. George Sabine (New York, Russell and Russell, 1965)

5 SECONDARY LITERATURE

BOOKS

Abramsky, Chimen and Henry Collins. *Karl Marx and the British Labour Movement* (Macmillan, 1965)

Andrews, Edward Denning. *The People Called Shakers* (New York, Dover Books, 1963)

Armytage, W. H. G. *Heavens Below. Utopian Experiments in England 1560–1960* (Routledge and Kegan Paul, 1961)

Backstrom, Philip N. *Christian Socialism and Co-operation in Victorian England* (Croom Helm, 1974)

Barbour, Hugh. *The Quakers in Puritan England* (New Haven, Yale University Press, 1964)

Barlow, Richard. *Citizenship and Conscience: a Study in the Theory and Practice of Religious Toleration in England during the Eighteenth Century* (Philadelphia, University of Pennsylvania Press, 1962)

Barnsby, George. *Robert Owen and the First Socialists in the Black Country* (Wolverhampton, Integrated Publishing Services, 1984)

Barry, E. Eldon. *Nationalization in British Politics: the Historical Background* (Cape, 1965)

Beales, H. L. *The Early English Socialists* (Hamish Hamilton, 1933)

Beecher, Jonathan. *Charles Fourier. The Visionary and His World* (Berkeley, University of California Press, 1986)

Beer, Max. *A History of British Socialism* (2 vols., G. Bell, 1929)

Belchem, John. *'Orator' Hunt. Henry Hunt and English Working Class Radicalism* (Oxford, Clarendon Press, 1985)

Berg, Maxine. *The Machinery Question and the Making of Political Economy 1815–1848* (Cambridge, Cambridge University Press, 1980)

Bestor, A. E. *Backwoods Utopias: the Sectarian and Owenite Phases of Communitarian Socialism in America, 1663–1829* (Philadelphia, University of Pennsylvania Press, 1950)

Bestor, A. E., ed. *Education and Reform at New Harmony* (Clifton, Kelley, 1973)

Black, Antony. *Guilds and Civil Society in European Political Thought from the Twelfth Century to the Present* (Methuen, 1984)

Bonwick, Colin. *English Radicals and the American Revolution* (Chapel Hill, University of North Carolina Press, 1977)

Boston, Ray. *British Chartists in America, 1839–1900* (Manchester, Manchester University Press, 1971)

Boulton, James T. *The Language of Politics in the Age of Wilkes and Burke* (Routledge and Kegan Paul, 1963)

Braithwaite, W. C. *The Second Period of Quakerism* (2nd edn., Cambridge, Cambridge University Press, 1961)

Brewer, John. *Party Ideology and Popular Politics at the Accession of George III* (Cambridge, Cambridge University Press, 1976)

Briggs, Asa, ed. *Chartist Studies* (Macmillan, 1962)

Brinton, Crane. *The Political Ideas of the English Romantics* (Ann Arbor, University of Michigan Press, 1966)

Brown, A. F. B. *Chartism in Essex and Suffolk* (Essex Record Office, 1982)

Buck, Philip. *The Politics of Mercantilism* (New York, Henry Holt, 1942)

Bunzel, John. *Anti-Politics in America. Reflections on the Anti-Political Temper and Its Distortion of the Democratic Process* (New York, Alfred Knopf, 1967)

Calhoun, Craig. *The Question of Class Struggle. Social Foundations of Popular Radicalism during the Industrial Revolution* (Oxford, Basil Blackwell, 1982)

Campbell, Tom. *The Left and Rights. A Conceptual Analysis of the Idea of Socialist Rights* (Routledge and Kegan Paul, 1983)

Chard, Leslie. *Dissenting Republican: Wordsworth's Early Life and Thought in their Political Context* (The Hague, Mouton, 1972)

Christensen, Torben. *Origin and History of Christian Socialism, 1848–54* (Aarhus, Universitetsforlaget, 1962)

Christophersen, Jens A. *The Meanings of 'Democracy' as Used in European Ideologies from the French to the Russian Revolution* (Oslo, Universitetsforlaget, 1966)

Claeys, Gregory. *Machinery, Money and the Millennium: From Moral Economy to Socialism, 1815–1860* (Princeton, Princeton University Press, 1987)

  Thomas Paine: Social and Political Thought (Unwin Hyman, 1989)

Clark, D. M. *British Opinion and the American Revolution* (New Haven, Yale University Press, 1930)

Clastres, Pierre. *Society against the State. The Leader as Servant and the Humane Use of Power among the Indians of North America* (New York, Urizen Books, 1977)

Cohn, Norman. *The Pursuit of the Millennium* (2nd edn., Paladin Books, 1970)

Cole, G. D. H. *Attempts at General Union. A Study in British Trade Union History, 1818–1834* (Macmillan, 1953)

  Chartist Portraits (Macmillan, 1941)

  The Life of Robert Owen (3rd edn., Frank Cass, 1965)

  A Short History of the British Working Class Movement, 1789–1947 (George Allen and Unwin, 1948)

Cole, G. D. H. and A. W. Filson eds. *British Working Class Movements: Select Documents 1789–1875* (Macmillan, 1951)

Colley, Linda. *In Defiance of Oligarchy. The Tory Party 1714–60* (Cambridge, Cambridge University Press, 1982)

Corrigan, Philip, and Sayer, Derek. *The Great Arch. English State Formation as Cultural Revolution* (Oxford, Basil Blackwell, 1982)

Cowherd, Raymond. *The Politics of English Dissent* (Epworth Press, 1959)

Crook, D. P. *American Democracy in English Politics, 1815–50* (Oxford, Clarendon Press, 1965)

Cullen, Alexander. *Adventures in Socialism* (Glasgow, John Smith, 1910)

Deane, Herbert. *The Political and Social Ideas of St. Augustine* (New York, Columbia University Press, 1963)

Desroche, Henri. *The American Shakers. From Neo-Christianity to Presocialism* (Amherst, University of Massachusetts Press, 1971)

Dickinson, H. T. *Liberty and Property: Political Ideology in Eighteenth Century Britain* (Methuen, 1977)

Draper, Hal. *Karl Marx's Theory of Revolution* (2 vols., New York, Monthly Review Press, 1977)

Driver, Cecil. *Tory Radical: The Life of Richard Oastler* (Oxford, Oxford University Press, 1946)

Dunn, John. *Political Obligations in their Historical Context* (Cambridge, Cambridge University Press, 1980)

   The Political Thought of John Locke (Cambridge, Cambridge University Press, 1969)

   The Politics of Socialism (Cambridge, Cambridge University Press, 1984)

   Rethinking Modern Political Theory. Essays 1979–1985 (Cambridge, Cambridge University Press, 1985)

Epstein, James A. *The Lion of Freedom: Feargus O'Connor and the Chartist Movement 1832–42* (Croom Helm, 1982)

Fairchild, Hoxie N. *The Noble Savage. A Study in Romantic Naturalism* (New York, Columbia University Press, 1928)

Faulkner, H. *Chartism and the Churches* (New York, Columbia University Press, 1916)

Fink, Zera S. *The Classical Republicans: an Essay in the Recovery of a Pattern of Thought in Seventeenth Century England* (Evanston, Northwestern University Press, 1945)

Flick, Carlos. *The Birmingham Political Union and the Movements for Social Reform in Britain* (Dawson, 1978)

Foster, John. *Class Struggle and the Industrial Revolution: Early Industrial Capitalism in Three English Towns* (Methuen, 1974)

Fruchtman, Jack, Jr. *The Apocalyptic Politics of Richard Price and Joseph Priestley. A Study in Late Eighteenth Century English Republican Millennialism* (Philadelphia, American Philosophical Society, 1983)

Gammage, R. G. *History of the Chartist Movement 1837–54* (1854; 2nd edn., Merlin Press, 1969)

Garnett, R. G. *Co-operation and the Owenite Socialist Communities in Britain, 1825–45* (Manchester, Manchester University Press, 1972)

   William Pare (Manchester, Co-operative College Papers No. 16, 1973)

Geoghegan, Vincent. *Utopianism and Marxism* (Methuen, 1987)

Gill, J. C. *The Ten Hours' Parson: Christian Social Action in the 1830s* (SPCK, 1954)

Gillespie, Frances E. *Labor and Politics in England, 1850–1867* (Durham, North Carolina, Duke University Press, 1927)

Glasgow, Eric, and Donald Read. *Feargus O'Connor, Irishman and Chartist* (Edward Arnold, 1961)

Goodway, David. *London Chartism 1838–1848* (Cambridge, Cambridge University Press, 1982)

Goodwin, Barbara. *Social Science and Utopia: Nineteenth Century Models of Social Harmony* (Brighton, Harvester Press, 1978)

Gosden, P. H. J. H. *The Friendly Societies in England 1815–1875* (Manchester, Manchester University Press, 1961)

Grave, S. A. *The Scottish Philosophy of Common Sense* (Oxford, Clarendon Press, 1960)

Groves, Reg. *But We Shall Rise Again. A Narrative History of Chartism* (Secker and Warburg, 1938)

Grugel, Leo E. *George Jacob Holyoake. A Study in the Evolution of a Victorian Radical* (Philadelphia, Porcupine Press, 1971)

Hadfield, Alice M. *The Chartist Land Company* (Newton Abbot, David and Charles, 1970)

Harding, Neil. *Lenin's Political Thought* (2 vols., Macmillan, 1983)

Harrison, J. F. C. *Living and Learning 1790–1960* (Routledge and Kegan Paul, 1961)

    Robert Owen and the Owenites in Britain and America (Routledge and Kegan Paul, 1969)

    The Second Coming: Popular Millennarianism 1780–1850 (Routledge and Kegan Paul, 1979)

    Social Reform in Victorian Leeds: the Work of James Hole 1820–1895 (Leeds, Thoresby Society, 1954)

Harrison, Royden. *Before the Socialists* (Routledge and Kegan Paul, 1965)

Harvey, R. H. *Robert Owen: Social Idealist* (Berkeley, University of California Press, 1949)

Henriques, Ursula. *Religious Toleration in England, 1787–1833* (Routledge and Kegan Paul, 1961)

Hexter, J. H. *On Historians* (Cambridge, MA, Harvard University Press, 1979)

Hill, Christopher. *Change and Continuity in Seventeenth Century England* (Weidenfeld and Nicolson, 1974)

Hill, R. L. *Toryism and the People, 1832–46* (Constable, 1929)

Hirschman, Albert O. *The Passions and the Interests. Political Arguments for Capitalism before Its Triumph* (Princeton, Princeton University Press, 1977)

Hollis, Patricia. *The Pauper Press: a Study in Working-Class Radicalism of the 1830s* (Oxford, Oxford University Press, 1970)

Holstun, James. *A Rational Millennium. Puritan Utopias of Seventeenth-Century England and America* (Oxford, Oxford University Press, 1987)

Holyoake, George Jacob. *The History of Co-operation* (2 vols., T. Fisher Unwin, 1906)

    Life of Joseph Rayner Stephens (1881)

Hopkins, James K. *A Woman to Deliver Her People. Joanna Southcott and English Millennarianism in an Era of Revolution* (Austin, University of Texas Press, 1982)

Hovell, Mark. *The Chartist Movement* (3rd edn., Manchester, Manchester University Press, 1966)

Hunt, Richard N. *The Political Ideas of Marx and Engels*, Vol. 1: *1818–1850* (Macmillan, 1975); Vol. 2: *Classical Marxism, 1850–1895* (Macmillan, 1984)

Iggers, George. *The Cult of Authority: the Political Philosophy of the Saint-Simonians. A Chapter in the Intellectual History of Totalitarianism* (The Hague, Martinus Nijhoff, 1958)

Ionescu, Gita, ed. *The Political Thought of Saint-Simon* (Oxford, Oxford University Press, 1976)

Isichei, Elizabeth. *Victorian Quakers* (Oxford, Oxford University Press, 1970)

Jacob, Margaret. *The Radical Enlightenment: Pantheists, Freemasons and Republicans* (George Allen and Unwin, 1981)

Jacob, Margaret and James Jacob, eds. *The Origins of Anglo-American Radicalism* (George Allen and Unwin, 1984)

Johnson, Christopher H. *Utopian Communism in France. Cabet and the Icarians, 1839–1851* (Ithaca, Cornell University Press, 1974)

Jones, David. *Chartism and the Chartists* (Allen Lane, 1975)

Jones, Lloyd. *The Life, Times, and Labours of Robert Owen* (2nd edn., George Allen and Unwin, 1895)

Jones, Rufus M. *The Later Periods of Quakerism* (2 vols., Macmillan, 1921)

Mysticism and Democracy in the English Commonwealth (Cambridge, MA, Harvard University Press, 1932)

Kirby, R. G., and A. E. Musson. *The Voice of the People: John Doherty, 1798–1854: Trade Unionist, Radical and Factory Reformer* (Manchester, Manchester University Press, 1975)

Kirk, Neville. *The Growth of Working Class Reformism in Mid-Victorian England* (Croom Helm, 1985)

Knights, Ben. *The Idea of the Clerisy in the Nineteenth Century* (Cambridge, Cambridge University Press, 1978)

Kramnick, Isaac. *Bolingbroke and His Circle* (Cambridge, MA, Harvard University Press, 1986)

Laures, John. *The Political Economy of Juan de Mariana* (New York, Fordham University Press, 1928)

Levine, Andrew. *The End of the State* (Verso Books, 1987)

Lichtheim, George. *The Origins of Socialism* (New York, Praeger Books, 1969)

Lillibridge, G. *Beacon of Freedom: the Impact of American Democracy upon Great Britain, 1830–70* (Philadelphia, University of Pennsylvania Press, 1954)

Lincoln, Anthony. *Some Political and Social Ideas of English Dissent* (Cambridge, Cambridge University Press, 1938)

Lippincott, Benjamin. *Victorian Critics of Democracy* (Minneapolis, University of Minnesota Press, 1938)

Lockwood, George. *The New Harmony Communities* (Marion, Chronicle Co., 1920)

Loubère, Leo A. *Louis Blanc. His Life and His Contribution to the Rise of French Jacobin Socialism* (Chicago, Northwestern University Press, 1961)

Lubenow, William C. *The Politics of Government Growth. Early Victorian Attitudes towards State Intervention 1833–1848* (Newton Abbot, David and Charles, 1971)

McCabe, Joseph. *The Life and Letters of George Jacob Holyoake* (2 vols., Watts and Co., 1908)

Maccoby, Simon. *English Radicalism 1762–1832* (2 vols., George Allen and Unwin, 1955)

MacLeod, William. *The Origins and History of Politics* (John Wiley, 1931)

Markus, R. A. *Saeculum. History and Society in the Theology of St. Augustine* (Cambridge, Cambridge University Press, 1970)

Marlow, J. *The Tolpuddle Martyrs* (Panther, 1974)

Marwick, Alexander. *The Life of Alexander Campbell* (Glasgow, Glasgow and District Co-operative Association, n.d.)

Mendilow, Jonathan. *The Romantic Tradition in British Political Thought* (Croom Helm, 1986)

Menger, Anton. *The Right to the Whole Produce of Labour* (Macmillan, 1899)

Müller, Hans. *Ursprung und Geschichte des Wortes Sozialismus und seiner Verwandten* (Hannover, Verlag J. H. W. Dietz, 1967)

Myrdal, Gunnar. *The Political Element in the Development of Economic Theory* (Routledge and Kegan Paul, 1953)

Oliver, W. H. *Prophets and Millennialists: The Uses of Biblical Prophecy in England from the 1790s to the 1840s* (Oxford, Oxford University Press, 1978)

Pankhurst, Richard. *William Thompson* (Watts and Co., 1954)

Pankoke, Eckart. *Sociale Bewegung – Sociale Frage – Sociale Politik. Grundfagen der deutschen 'Socialwissenschaften' im 19. Jahrhundert* (Stuttgart, Ernst Klett Verlag, 1970)

Parker, Harold T. *The Cult of Antiquity and the French Revolutionaries* (Chicago, Chicago University Press, 1937)

Peacock, A. J. *Bradford Chartism, 1838–40* (York, St. Anthony's Press, 1969)

Pears, T. C., ed. *New Harmony. An Adventure in Happiness. Papers of Thomas and Sarah Pears* (Clifton, Kelley, 1973)

Pelling, Henry. *America and the British Left* (Adam and Charles Black, 1956)

Pierson, Christopher. *Marxist Theory and Democratic Politics* (Cambridge, Polity Press, 1987)

Plamenatz, John. *Man and Society* (2 vols., Longmans, 1976)

Plummer, Alfred. *Bronterre: a Political Biography of Bronterre O'Brien* (Toronto, University of Toronto Press, 1971)

Pocock, J. G. A. *The Machiavellian Moment: Florentine Political Thought and the Atlantic Republican Tradition* (Princeton, Princeton University Press, 1975)
Politics, Language and Time (New York, Atherton, 1971)
Virtue, Commerce and History: Essays on Political Thought and History Chiefly in the Eighteenth Century (Cambridge, Cambridge University Press, 1985)

Podmore, Frank. *Robert Owen* (2nd edn., George Allen and Unwin, 1923)

Polan, A. J. *Lenin and the End of Politics* (Methuen, 1984)

Postgate, Raymond. *The Builders' History* (Labour Publishing Co., 1923)
Out of the Past: Some Revolutionary Sketches (New York, Vanguard Press, 1926)

Prothero, Iorwerth. *Artisans and Politics in Early Nineteenth Century London: John Gast and His Times* (Dawson, 1979)

Raistrick, Arthur. *Quakers in Science and Industry* (New York, Philosophical Library, 1950)

Raphael, D. D. *The Moral Sense* (Oxford, Oxford University Press, 1947)

Rattansi, Ali. *Marx and the Division of Labour* (Macmillan, 1982)

Raven, Charles. *Christian Socialism, 1848–1854* (Frank Cass, 1920)

Rawson, Elizabeth. *The Spartan Tradition in European Thought* (Oxford, Clarendon Press, 1969)

Reay, Barry. *The Quakers and the English Revolution* (Temple Smith, 1985)

Reeve, Andrew. *Property* (Macmillan, 1986)

Robbins, Caroline. *The Eighteenth Century Commonwealthmen* (Cambridge, MA, Harvard University Press, 1959)

Roberts, David. *Paternalism in Early Victorian England* (Croom Helm, 1979)
The Victorian Origins of the British Welfare State (New Haven, Yale University Press, 1960)

Rosenblatt, Frank. *The Chartist Movement in its Social and Economic Aspects* (New York, Columbia University Press, 1916)

Rothstein, Theodore. *From Chartism to Labourism* (Martin Lawrence, 1929)

Royle, Edward. *Victorian Infidels and the Origins of the British Secularist Movement* (Manchester, Manchester University Press, 1974)

Rudman, Harry W. *Italian Nationalism and English Letters* (New York, Columbia University Press, 1940)

Runciman, W. G. *Social Science and Political Theory* (Cambridge, Cambridge University Press, 1965)

Ryan, Alan. *Property and Political Theory* (Oxford, Basil Blackwell, 1984).

Sargant, William. *Robert Owen and his Social Philosophy* (1860)

Saville, John. *1848* (Cambridge, Cambridge University Press, 1987)
Ernest Jones, Chartist (Lawrence and Wishart, 1952)

Schochet, Gordon J. *Patriarchalism in Political Thought* (Oxford, Basil Blackwell, 1975)

Schoyen, A. R. *The Chartist Challenge: a Portrait of George Julian Harney* (Heinemann, 1958)

Searby, Peter. *Coventry Politics in the Age of the Chartists* (Historical Association, 1965)

Seneca. *Letters from a Stoic* (Harmondsworth, Penguin Books, 1969)

Sewell, William. *Work and Revolution in France. The Language of Labor from the Old Regime to 1848* (Cambridge, Cambridge University Press, 1980)

Shadwell, Arthur. *The Socialist Movement 1824–1924* (Phillip Allan, 1925)

Shklar, Judith. *After Utopia: The Decline of Political Faith* (Princeton, Princeton University Press, 1957)

Silver, Harold. *English Education and the Radicals 1780–1850* (Routledge and Kegan Paul, 1975)

Skinner, Quentin. *The Foundations of Modern Political Thought* (2 vols., Cambridge, Cambridge University Press, 1978)

Slosson, Preston. *The Decline of the Chartist Movement* (New York, Columbia University Press, 1916)

Smith, Kenneth. *The Malthusian Controversy* (Routledge and Kegan Paul, 1951)

Smith, W. A. *'Shepherd' Smith the Universalist* (Sampson Low and Co., 1892)

Soloway, Richard A. *Prelates and People: Ecclesiastical Social Thought in England, 1783–1852* (Routledge and Kegan Paul, 1962)

Stafford, William. *Socialism, Radicalism, and Nostalgia. Social Criticism in Britain, 1775–1830* (Cambridge, Cambridge University Press, 1987)

Stedman Jones, Gareth. *Languages of Class. Studies in English Working Class History 1832–1982* (Cambridge, Cambridge University Press, 1983)

Stein, Peter. *Legal Evolution* (Cambridge, Cambridge University Press, 1980)

Sternberger, Dolf. *Drei Wurzeln der Politik* (Frankfurt, Insel Verlag, 1978)

Stromberg, Roland N. *Religious Liberalism in Eighteenth Century England* (Oxford, Oxford University Press, 1954)

Talmon, Jacob L. *The Origins of Totalitarian Democracy* (New York, Praeger Books, 1960)
    Political Messianism: The Romantic Phase (Secker and Warburg, 1960)

Tarschys, Daniel. *Beyond the State: The Future Polity in Classical and Soviet Marxism* (Stockholm, Läromedelsförigen, 1971)

Taylor, A. J. *Laissez-faire and State Intervention in Nineteenth Century Britain* (Macmillan, 1972)

Taylor, Barbara. *Eve and the New Jerusalem – Socialism and Feminism in the Nineteenth Century* (Virago, 1983)

Taylor, Keith. *The Political Ideas of the Utopian Socialists* (Frank Cass, 1982)

Thistlethwaite, Frank. *The Anglo-American Connection in the Early Nineteenth Century* (Philadelphia, University of Pennsylvania Press, 1959)

Tholfsen, Trygve R. *Working Class Radicalism in Mid-Victorian England* (Croom Helm, 1976)

Thompson, Dorothy. *The Chartists* (Temple Smith, 1984)
    ed., *The Early Chartists* (Macmillan, 1971)

Thompson, E. P. *The Making of the English Working Class* (Harmondsworth, Penguin Books, 1977)

Thornton, A. P. *The Habit of Authority: Paternalism in British History* (George Allen and Unwin, 1966)

Tolles, Frederick. *Quakers and the Atlantic Culture* (Macmillan, 1960)

Tuck, Richard. *Natural Rights Theories* (Cambridge, Cambridge University Press, 1979)

Viner, Jacob. *The Role of Providence in the Social Order* (Philadelphia, American Philosophical Society, 1972)

Voegelin, Eric. *The New Science of Politics* (Chicago, University of Chicago Press, 1966)

Wakefield, C. M. *Life of Thomas Attwood* (1885)

Ward, J. T. *Chartism* (Batsford, 1973)

Waszek, Norbert. *Man's Social Nature* (Bern, Peter Lang, 1986)

Watts, Michael. *The Dissenters* (Oxford, Clarendon Press, 1978)

Weaver, Stewart Angus. *John Fielden and the Politics of Popular Radicalism 1832–1847* (Oxford, Clarendon Press, 1987)

Webb, R. K. *The British Working Class Reader 1789–1848. Literacy and Social Tension* (George Allen and Unwin, 1955)

Weisser, Henry. *April 10: Challenge and Response in England in 1848* (New York, University Press of America, 1983)

   British Working Class Movements and Europe 1815–48 (Manchester, Manchester University Press, 1975)

West, Julius. *A History of the Chartist Movement* (Constable, 1920)

Williams, George Hurston. *The Radical Reformation* (Philadelphia, Westminster Press, 1962)

Wilson, A. *The Chartist Movement in Scotland* (Manchester, Manchester University Press, 1970)

Winch, Donald. *Adam Smith's Politics* (Cambridge, Cambridge University Press, 1978)

Wolin, Sheldon. *Politics and Vision: Continuity and Innovation in Western Democratic Thought* (Boston, Little, Brown and Co., 1961)

Wright, L. C. *Scottish Chartism* (Edinburgh, Oliver and Boyd, 1953)

ARTICLES AND ESSAYS

Aarsleff, Hans. 'The State of Nature and the Nature of Man in Locke', in John W. Yolton, ed., *John Locke: Problems and Perspectives* (Cambridge, Cambridge University Press, 1969), pp. 99–136

Adamiak, Richard. 'State and Society in Early Socialist Thought', *Survey*, 26 (1982), 1–28

Agulhon, Maurice. 'Working Class and Sociability in France before 1848', in Pat Thane, Geoffrey Crossick and Roderick Floud, eds., *The Power of the Past. Essays for Eric Hobsbawm* (Cambridge, Cambridge University Press, 1984), pp. 37–66

Armytage, W. H. G. 'John Minter Morgan's Schemes, 1841–1855', *International Review of Social History*, 3 (1958), 26–42

   'Manea Fen: An Experiment in Agrarian Communitarianism, 1838–1841', *Bulletin of the John Rylands Library*, 38 (1956), 288–310

Bayertz, Kurt. 'From Utopia to Science? The Development of Socialist Theory between Utopia and Science', in Everett Mendelsohn and Helga Nowotny, eds., *Nineteen Eighty-Four: Science between Utopia and Dystopia* (Dordrecht, D. Reidel, 1984), pp. 93–110

Belchem, John. 'Chartism and the Trades, 1848–1850', *English Historical Review*, 98 (1983), 558–87

   'Republicanism, Popular Constitutionalism, and the Radical Platform in Early Nineteenth Century England', *Social History*, 6 (1981), 1–32

Berlin, Isaiah. 'Does Political Theory Still Exist?', in Peter Laslett and W. G. Runciman, eds., *Politics, Philosophy and Society*, 2nd series (Oxford, Basil Blackwell, 1972), pp. 1–33

Bottomore, Tom. 'Socialism and the Division of Labour', in Bhikhu Parekh, ed., *The Concept of Socialism* (New York, Holmes and Meier, 1975), pp. 154–61

Bradley, James E. 'Whigs and Nonconformists. Slumbering Radicalism in English Politics, 1739–1789', *Eighteenth Century Studies*, 9 (1975), 1–27

Brewer, John. 'English Radicalism in the Age of George III', in J. G. A. Pocock, ed., *Three British Revolutions: 1641, 1688, 1776* (Princeton, Princeton University Press, 1980), pp. 323–67

Briggs, Asa. 'Feargus O'Connor and J. Bronterre O'Brien', in J. W. Boyle, ed., *Leaders and Workers* (Dublin, Mercier Press, 1966), pp. 27–36

'National Bearings', in A. Briggs, ed., *Chartist Studies* (Macmillan, 1962), pp. 288–303

Butt, John. 'Robert Owen of New Lanark: His Critique of British Society', in J. Butt and J. F. Clarke, eds., *The Victorians and Social Protest* (Newton Abbot, David and Charles, 1973), pp. 13–32

Carr, H. J. 'John Francis Bray', *Economica*, 7 (1940), 397–415

'Chartism and the Trades' Unions', *Our History* pamphlet no. 31 (1963)

Claeys, Gregory. 'The *Chartist Pilot*: Feminist and Socialist Chartism in Leicester, 1843–4', *Bulletin of the Society for the Study of Labour History*, 45 (1982), 18

'From "Politeness" to Rational Character: the Critique of Culture in Owenite Socialism, 1800–1850', in Lex Heerma van Voss and Frits van Holthoon, eds., *Working Class and Popular Culture* (Amsterdam, Stichting Beheer IISG, 1988), pp. 19–32

'John Adolphus Etzler, Technological Utopianism, and British Socialism: the Tropical Emigration Society and Its Venezuelan Mission, 1833–1848', *English Historical Review*, 101 (1986), 31–55

'Language, Class, and Historical Consciousness in Nineteenth Century Britain', *Economy and Society*, 15 (1985), 239–63

'Lewis Masquerier and the Later Development of American Owenism, 1835–45', *Labor History*, 49 (1988), 230–40

'The Political Ideas of the Young Engels, 1842–1845: Owenism, Chartism, and the Question of Violence in the Transition from "Utopian" to "Scientific" Socialism', *History of Political Thought*, 6 (1985), 455–78

'Reciprocal Dependence, Virtue and Progress: Some Sources of Early Socialist Cosmopolitanism and Internationalism in Britain, 1790–1860', in F. L. van Holthoon and Marcel van der Linden, eds., *Internationalism in the Labour Movement 1830–1940* (Leiden, E. J. Brill, 1988), 1, pp. 235–58

'The Triumph of Class Conscious Reformism in British Radicalism, 1790–1860', *Historical Journal*, 26 (1983), 969–85

'A Utopian Tory Revolutionary at Cambridge: the Political Ideas and Schemes of James B. Bernard, 1834–39', *Historical Journal*, 25 (1982), 583–603

'"Individualism", "Socialism" and "Social Science": Further Notes on a Process of Conceptual Formation, 1800–1850', *Journal of the History of Ideas*, 47 (1986), 81–93

'William Godwin's Critique of Democracy and Republicanism and Its Sources', *History of European Ideas*, 7 (1986), 253–69

'Mazzini, Kossuth, and British Radicalism, 1848–54', *Journal of British Studies*, 28 (1989) 225–61

'Virtuous Commerce and Free Theology: Political Economy and the Dissenting Academies in Britain, 1740–1800', in Istvan Hont and Keith Tribe, eds., *Trade, Politics and Letters: the Art of Political Economy in British University Culture, 1750–1910* (Routledge, forthcoming)

Colley, Linda. 'Eighteenth Century English Radicalism before Wilkes', *Transactions of the Royal Historical Society*, 31 (1981), 1–19

Collini, Stefan. 'The Idea of "Character" in Victorian Political Thought', *Transactions of the Royal Historical Society*, 35 (1985), 29–50

'Political Theory and the "Science of Society" in Victorian Britain', *Historical Journal*, 23 (1980), 203–31

Cowden, Morten. 'Early Marxist Views on British Labor, 1837–1917', *Western Political Quarterly*, 16 (1963), 34–52

Davis, Mary. 'The Forerunners of the First International: the Fraternal Democrats', *Marxism Today*, 15 (1971), 50–60

Diamond, Stanley. 'The Rule of Law and the Order of Custom', *Social Research*, 51 (1984), 387–418

Dunn, John. 'The Identity of the History of Ideas', in Peter Laslett, W. G. Runciman and Quentin Skinner, eds., *Philosophy, Politics and Society* 4th series (Oxford, Basil Blackwell, 1972), pp. 158–74

'The Politics of Locke in England and America in the Eighteenth Century', in *Political Obligations in Their Historical Context* (Cambridge, Cambridge University Press, 1980), pp. 53–77

Feuer, Lewis S. 'The Influence of the American Communist Colonies on Engels and Marx', *Western Political Quarterly*, 19 (1966), 356–74

Fox, Wendall. 'The Kendal Community', *Ohio Archaeological and Historical Quarterly*, 20 (1911), 176–219

Fruchtman, Jack, Jr. 'Politics and the Apocalypse: the Republic and the Millennium in Late Eighteenth Century English Political Thought', *Studies in Eighteenth Century Culture*, 10 (1981), 153–64

'The Revolutionary Millennialism of Thomas Paine', *Studies in Eighteenth Century Culture*, 13 (1984), 65–77

Garnett, R. G. 'E. T. Craig: Communitarian, Educator, Phrenologist', *Vocational Aspect of Secondary and Further Education*, 15 (1963), 135–50

Gatrell, V. A.C. 'Introduction' to Robert Owen, *Report to the County of Lanark. A New View of Society* (Harmondsworth, Penguin Books, 1969), pp. 7–81

Goldie, Mark. 'The Origins of True Whiggism', *History of Political Thought*, 1 (1980), 195–234

Gossman, N. J. 'Republicanism in Nineteenth Century England', *International Review of Social History*, 7 (1962), 47–60

Grant, A. C. 'New Light on an Old View', *Journal of the History of Ideas*, 29 (1968), 293–301

Greenleaf, W. H. 'Toulmin Smith and the British Political Tradition', *Public Administration*, 53 (1975), 25–44

Hampsher-Monk, Iain. 'Political Languages in Time: the Work of J. G. A. Pocock', *British Journal of Political Science*, 14 (1984), 89–116

Harrison, J. F. C. 'Chartism in Leeds', in A. Briggs, ed., *Chartist Studies* (Macmillan, 1962), pp. 65–98

'Chartism in Leicester', in A. Briggs, ed., *Chartist Studies* (Macmillan, 1962), pp. 99–146

Harrison, Royden. 'British Labour and the Confederacy', *International Review of Social History*, 2 (1957), 78–105

Haynes, M. J. 'Class and Class Conflict in the Early Nineteenth Century:

Northampton Shoemakers and the Grand National Consolidated Trades' Union', *Literature and History*, 5 (1977), 73–94

Hillerbrand, Hans. 'The Anabaptist View of the State', *Mennonite Historical Quarterly*, 32 (1958), 83–110

Hont, Istvan. 'From Pufendorf to Adam Smith: Sociability, Commercial Society and the Four Stages Theory', in Anthony Pagden, ed., *The Languages of Political Theory in Early-Modern Europe* (Cambridge, Cambridge University Press, 1987), pp. 253–76

Jánossy, Dénes A. 'Great Britain and Kossuth', *Archivum Europae Centro-Orientalis*, 3 (1937), 53–190

Jolliffe, M. F. 'John Francis Bray', *International Review of Social History*, 4 (1939), 1–36

Kelsey, Rayner. 'American Indians and the Inner Light', *Bulletin of the Friends' Historical Society*, 8 (1918), 54–6

Kramnick, Isaac. 'Republican Revisionism Revisited', *American Political Science Review* 87 (1982), 629–64

Krygier, Martin. 'Saint-Simon, Marx and the Non-Governed Society', in Eugene Kamenka and Martin Krygier, eds., *Bureaucracy* (New York, St. Martin's Press, 1979), pp. 34–60

Lattek, Christine. 'The Beginnings of Socialist Internationalism in the 1840s: The Democratic Friends of All Nations', in F. L. van Holthoon and Marcel van der Linden, eds., *Internationalism in the Labour Movement 1830 to 1940* (Leiden, E. J. Brill, 1988), 1, pp. 259–82

'Radikalismus im Ausland. Die Entwicklung des deutschen Frühsozialismus in London 1840–1852', in Gregory Claeys and Liselotte Glage, eds., *Radikalismus in Literatur und Gesellschaft des 19. Jahrhunderts* (Basel, Peter Lang, 1987), pp. 39–64

Lloyd, T. H. 'Dr. Wade and the Working Class', *Midland History*, 2 (1973), 61–83

Macbride, William. 'Noncoercive Society: Some Doubts, Leninist and Contemporary', in J. R. Pennock and J. W. Chapman, eds., *Coercion* (New York, Atherton Press, 1982), pp. 3–26

Macpherson, C. B. 'The Economic Penetration of Political Theory', *Journal of the History of Ideas*, 39 (1978), 101–18

Miliband, Ralph. 'The Politics of Robert Owen', *Journal of the History of Ideas*, 15 (1954), 233–45

Murphy, James. 'Robert Owen in Liverpool', *Transactions of the Historical Society of Lancashire and Cheshire*, 112 (1961), 79–103

Ogden, H. V. S. 'The State of Nature and the Decline of Lockean Political Theory in England, 1760–1800', *American Historical Review*, 46 (1940–41), 21–44

Oliver, W. H. 'The Consolidated Trades' Union of 1834', *Economic History Review*, 2nd series, 17 (1965), 77–95

'The Labour Exchange Phase of the Co-operative Movement', *Oxford Economic Papers*, ns 10 (1958), 355–66

'Robert Owen and the English Working Class Movement', *History Today*, 8 (1958), 787–96

Palmer, R. R. 'The Fading Dream: How European Revolutionaries have seen the American Revolution', in Stanley Palmer *et al.*, eds., *Essays on Modern European Revolutionary History* (Austin, University of Texas Press, 1977), pp. 89–104

'Notes on the Use of the Word "Democracy" 1789–1799', *Political Science Quarterly*, 68 (1953), 203–26

Parsinnen, T. M. 'Association, Convention and Anti-Parliament in British Radical Politics, 1771–1848', *English Historical Review*, 88 (1973), 504–33

Pocock, J. G. A. 'The History of Political Thought: A Methodological Enquiry', in Peter Laslett and W. G. Runciman, eds., *Philosophy, Politics and Society*, 2nd series (Oxford, Basil Blackwell, 1962), pp. 183–202

'The *Machiavellian Moment* Revisited: A Study in History and Ideology', *Journal of Modern History*, 53 (1981), 49–72

'The Myth of John Locke and the Obsession with Liberalism', in *John Locke* (Los Angeles, William Andrews Clark Library, 1980), pp. 1–24

'Radical Criticisms of the Whig Order in the Age of Revolutions', in Margaret Jacob and James Jacob, eds., *The Origins of Anglo-American Radicalism* (George Allen and Unwin, 1984), pp. 33–53

Prothero, Iorwerth. 'Chartism in London', *Past and Present*, 44 (1969), 76–105

'The London Working Men's Association and the People's Charter', *Past and Present*, 38 (1967), 169–73

Rose, R. B. 'John Finch, 1784–1857: A Liverpool Disciple of Robert Owen', *Transactions of the Historical Society of Lancashire and Cheshire*, 59 (1957), 159–84

Rothstein, Theodore. 'Aus der Vorgeschichte der Internationale', *Ergänzungshefte zur Neuen Zeit*, 17 (1913), 1–44

Rowe, D. J. 'The Failure of London Chartism', *Historical Journal*, 11 (1968), 472–87

'The London Working Men's Association and the People's Charter', *Past and Present*, 36 (1967), 73–86

Royle, Edward. 'The Owenite Legacy to Social Reform, 1845–1900', *Studies in History and Politics*, 1 (1980), 56–74

Rubel, Maximilien. 'Robert Owen à Paris en 1848', *Actualités de l'Histoire*, 30 (1960), 1–12

Salt, John. 'Experiments in Anarchism, 1850–1854', *Transactions of the Hunter Archaeological Society*, 10 (1971), 37–53

Salvemini, Gaetano. 'The Concepts of Democracy and Liberty in the Eighteenth Century', in Conyers Read, ed., *The Constitution Reconsidered* (New York, Columbia University Press, 1958), pp. 105–19

Sartori, Giovanni. 'What is Politics?', *Political Theory*, 1 (1973), 5–26

Saville, John. 'The Christian Socialists of 1848', in Saville, ed., *Democracy and the Labour Movement* (Lawrence and Wishart, 1954), pp. 133–59

'J. E. Smith and the Owenite Movement, 1833–4', in Sidney Pollard and John Salt, eds., *Robert Owen: Prophet of the Poor* (Macmillan, 1971), pp. 115–44

'Robert Owen on the Family and Marriage System of the New Moral World', in M. Cornforth, ed., *Rebels and their Causes* (Lawrence and Wishart, 1978), pp. 107–21

Seed, John. 'Gentlemen Dissenters: the Social and Political Meanings of Rational Dissent in the 1770s and 1780s', *Historical Journal*, 28 (1985), 299–325

Seligman, Edwin. 'Owen and the Christian Socialists of 1848', *Political Science Quarterly*, 1 (1886), 206–49

Sewall, Richard. 'Rousseau's Second Discourse in England from 1755 to 1762', *Philological Quarterly*, 17 (1938), 97–114

Sheps, Arthur. 'The Edinburgh Reform Convention of 1793 and the American Revolution', *Scottish Tradition*, 5 (1975), 23–37

Shklar, Judith. 'The Political Theory of Utopia: From Melancholy to Nostalgia' in Frank Manuel, ed., *Utopias and Utopian Thought* (Boston, Beacon Press, 1967), pp. 101–15

Simons, Richard. 'A Utopian Failure', *Indiana Historical Bulletin*, 18 (1941), 98–115

Stedman Jones, Gareth. 'Rethinking Chartism', in G. Stedman Jones, *Languages of Class: Studies in English Working Class History 1832–1982* (Cambridge, Cambridge University Press, 1983), pp. 90–178

Thomas, D. O. 'Neither Republican nor Democrat', *Price-Priestley Newsletter*, 1 (1977), 49–60

Tillett, A. S. 'Some Saint-Simonian Criticism of the United States before 1835', *Romantic Review*, 52 (1961), 3–16

Tolles, Frederick. 'Nonviolent Contact: the Quakers and the Indians', *Proceedings of the American Philosophical Society*, 107 (1964), 93–101

Treble, James. 'The Social and Economic Thought of Robert Owen', in John Butt, ed., *Robert Owen: Prince of the Cotton Spinners* (Newton Abbot, David and Charles, 1971), pp. 20–51.

Tsuzuki, C. 'Robert Owen and Revolutionary Politics', in Sidney Pollard and John Salt, eds., *Robert Owen: Prophet of the Poor* (Macmillan, 1971), pp. 13–38

Vartanian, Aram. 'Necessity or Freedom? The Politics of an Eighteenth Century Metaphysical Debate', *Studies in Eighteenth Century Culture*, 7 (1978), 153–74

Weiner, Robert. 'Karl Marx's Vision of America: A Biographical and Bibliographical Sketch', *Review of Politics*, 42 (1980), 465–503

Weisser, Henry. 'Chartist Internationalism, 1845–48', *Historical Journal*, 14 (1971), 49–66

Wilson, A. 'Chartism', in J. T. Ward, ed. *Popular Movements, c. 1830–1850* (Macmillan, 1972)

Worden, Blair. 'The Commonwealth Kidney of Algernon Sidney', *Journal of British Studies*, 24 (1985), 1–40

Yeo, Eileen. 'Christianity in Chartist Struggle, 1838–42', *Past and Present*, 91 (1981), 109–39

'Robert Owen and Radical Culture', in Sidney Pollard and John Salt, eds., *Robert Owen: Prophet of the Poor* (Macmillan, 1971), pp. 84–114

'Some Practices and Problems of Chartist Democracy', in James Epstein and Dorothy Thompson, eds., *The Chartist Experience: Studies in Working Class Radicalism and Culture* (Macmillan, 1982), pp. 345–80

Index